D0460960

A CENTURY OF CARING
The Upjohn Story

by Robert D.B. Carlisle

BENJAMIN

The following are current or former trademarks of The Upjohn Company: Accessorone,
Albadry, Albamix, Albamycin, Anora, Caripeptic, Cerelexin, Cer-O-Cillin, Cheracol,
Cheracol D, Citrocarbonate, Cleocin, Cleocin Phosphate, Cleocin T, Clocream, Cortaid,
Current concepts, Cytosar, Depo-Provera, Digitora, ECP, E-Mycin E, Gelfoam,
Gonadogen, Halcion, Haltran, Kaopectate, Lincocin, Lincomix, Loniten, Medrol,
Mercresin, Micronase, Missuky, Monase, Motrin, Myeladol, Orinase, Orthoxicol, O's
Gold, *The Overflow*, Palmo-Dionin, Panalba, Panmycin, Phenolax, Prostin VR Pediatric,
Provera, *Scope*, Solu-B, Solu-Medrol, Super D, Tolinase, Trobicin, TUCO, Unakalm,
Unicap, *Upjohn Intercom*, *Upjohn News*, Urestrin, *Veterinary Scope*, Xanax, Zanosar,
Zymacap

Library of Congress Catalog Card Number: 86-70731
ISBN: 0-87502-191-3

Published and produced by The Benjamin Company, Inc.
                              One Westchester Plaza
                              Elmsford, NY   10523

First printing: February 1987

Foreword

When Dr. W. E. Upjohn developed his friable pill one hundred years ago and thus began the history of The Upjohn Company, he had in mind a number of things, not the least of which was that he wanted to build something that would last.

Last it did, and the story of its growth and contributions to science and society is well documented in the pages that follow.

Yet it would be a mistake to think the whole story is here. The Upjohn Company is a human enterprise, and its story is filled with individual achievements and the intangibles of the human spirit, such as courage, loyalty, and dedication, which are impossible to portray fully on the printed page of history.

But the essence of Upjohn is here—the abiding concern for people, the insistence on quality products and the highest business principles. These and the contributions of Upjohn people have indeed made our first hundred years a century of caring.

R.T. Parfet Jr.

R.T. PARFET, JR.
Chairman of the Board
   and Chief Executive Officer
The Upjohn Company

Preface

The differences between pharmaceutical research and development (PR & D) and writing a centennial history of a drug manufacturer are not as huge as one might think. Each demands a heavy amount of time. Each calls for its own brand of painstaking research and for spreading the load among a variety of skilled individuals.

Before either drug or text sees the light of day, each must survive the trip through a gantlet of exacting analyses and tests. The individuals concentrating on one process or the other are equally concerned about winning an eventual blue ribbon. And if there is more pure science along the road of PR & D, creation of a volume such as *A Century of Caring* is no less challenging.

Of crucial importance to either project are the *precedents*. This document has several ancestors. First and foremost, it drew actively on the voluminous, thoughtful, history-capturing memos written over a number of years by the corporation's second chief executive, Dr. L. N. Upjohn, and his associates. In 1951 the company commissioned Robert Burlingham to write *The Odyssey of Modern Drug Research*; this was followed a decade later by Leonard Engel's *Medicine Makers of Kalamazoo*. Both volumes proved informative.

Like PR & D, writing a century's worth of a corporation's history requires something widely visible at The Upjohn Company, something of which the firm is properly proud: teamwork. *A Century of Caring* benefited from that every step of the way. Charles T. Mangee, corporate vice president for public relations, boosted the project along at critical intervals. From start to finish, Robert D. LaRue, manager of corporate editorial services

and long experienced as both writer and editor, served as "managing editor," making the final decisions on where and what to change. Recommendations on layout and picture selections came from Katrina S. Schuur, art director for professional communications. For the book's publisher, The Benjamin Company of Elmsford, New York, Virginia Schomp, vice president and editorial director, analyzed each line for comprehensibility and style.

Day to day, a Kalamazoo-based team gave the process an extraordinary level of support — dredging through reams of old publications, probing earlier interviews for insights, dissecting for new information. Jeff Palmer and James W. Armstrong III, aided by Jane Parikh, built and sustained this lifeline of activity. Their tireless efforts were managed by Upjohn's centennial coordinator, Philip R. Sheldon, who guided the venture through two summers and two winters with admirable poise, effective problem-solving, and transfusions of timely humor.

What follows on these pages reflects the kind of intense time and toil that PR & D's professionals understand. Here you will find a happy dependence not only on Dr. L. N. Upjohn's historical accounts and the company's earliest files but also on fragments of well over 150 interviews in Kalamazoo, Boston, Raleigh-Durham, Puerto Rico, North Haven, and Brussels, Belgium. This wealth of information has been transformed into a centennial history only because a strong, compatible team shared the project's laboratory bench for so many intense months. *A Century of Caring* resulted because that small team did care.

ROBERT D. B. CARLISLE

Contents

CHAPTER ONE

A NEW DAY, A NEW CENTURY

Dawn has just broken over the Kalamazoo plain. It is April 1986, and the surge of spring in southwestern Michigan is near. At The Upjohn Company, a new workweek is beginning.

At Building 156, next to the huge manufacturing facility Building 41, Pharmaceutical Manufacturing Supervisor Brad Meisling slides out of his car after the 30-mile drive from his lakeside cottage. The time is 6:30 A.M. Entering 156, he dons his uniform and walks out to check the Penicillin Processing line where at 7:05 his work force of 18 will resume labeling bottles, stamping them with lot numbers, filling cases, and preloading syringes with Albadry for the veterinary market. Jackie Talbert, an Upjohn employee for 26 years, also arrives at 156 at 6:30 with the other line personnel. Uniformed, they cluster in the cafeteria for coffee.

At 7:00 A.M. Kalamazoo time, it's only 5:00 A.M. in Phoenix, Arizona, but Warren J. Plants is already stirring there. As Asgrow vegetable seed sales rep for Arizona and New Mexico, he's getting ready for a six o'clock breakfast with one of the 100 farmers on his route.

7:00 A.M. on Kalamazoo's Portage Road. Electrician Don Jewett, hard hat on, heads for the eight sites in and around "Tin City," the Fine Chemicals manufacturing area that he has to check every Monday morning. His first stop is the incoming switch gear, the main fuse box for the entire Portage complex. Any breakdown there and the whole site could be out of business.

By 7:30, attorney Sid Williams of Patent Law is studying a sheaf of papers in his Building 32 office. At 8:00, he'll meet with the managing patent counsel, the patent counsel, and their office manager. They'll review the status of a pending case, then talk over new policies affecting their personnel.

In Puerto Rico, Group Manager Luis Acevedo scans his Monday schedule at the modern Upjohn manufacturing facility west of San Juan, where his operators turn out Upjohn's nonsteroidal anti-inflammatory drugs. He slips on a hair cover and a new *cubra barba*, the gauzy mask for his moustache, and swings off on a tour of the brightly lighted facility with its state-of-the-art production equipment.

Ward Bost, executive director, pharmaceutical business strategy, walks into Building 88, corporate headquarters, in Kalamazoo at 7:45 after a 20-mile trip from Gull Lake, east of town. Usually he listens to his car radio on the way to work, but today he used the time to sort out late thoughts for the twin meetings he coordinates every Monday: the Pharmaceutical Operating Committee at 8:15, and the Pharmaceutical Steering Committee at 10:00. Those sessions shape Upjohn's planning for discovering, making, and marketing new drugs.

By 8:00, activity has shifted into high gear throughout the company's Kalamazoo operations. Sales Representative Carol Smith has pulled up to a building downtown shared by two internists. She finds one in early and gets a few minutes with him. "Doctor, I wonder if you've seen this new clinical study of anxiety in cardiovascular patients," she begins.

The key men in the Office of the Chairman are convening informally at 8:00 this April Monday. Chairman and Chief Executive Officer Ted Parfet, Vice Chairman Dr. Ted Cooper, and President Larry Hoff need to talk over some special items on the agenda for the 10:00 A.M. Pharmaceutical Steering Committee session. They'll also cycle through topics for their regular Monday noon meeting.

In Public Relations, Administrative Secretary Mary Vilardo has just had time to log on to her Xerox Star computer and check the morning harvest of mail when her phone wakes up. This first call has no surprises. Someone wants to know about topical minoxidil solution, Upjohn's compound for treatment of male pattern baldness. When is the Food and Drug Administration going to approve it? Will it work for women? How can you sign up to be part of a field study? Mary listens, then rolls a two-minute tape to give the caller answers to the most frequent questions about the drug.

In the Lovell Street lobby of Pharmaceutical Research and Development (PR & D), Ann Berger, Ph.D., shows her I.D. to Security. She's left her two children at a day-care center and now she's going to her lab on the seventh floor to resume observing T-cells she's been cultivating for the Biotechnology unit.

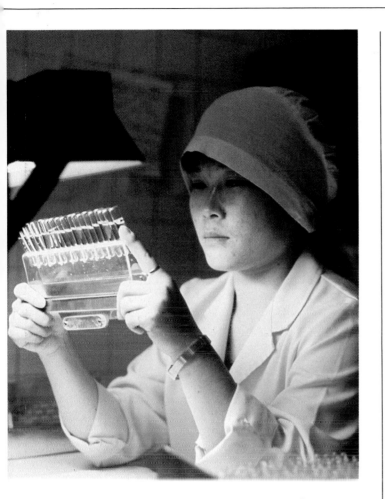

Meanwhile, Compensation Representative Sheri G. Hudachek has parked at Building 88 after the 28-mile drive from her Battle Creek home. Among her tasks this Monday will be talking to colleagues in Employee Relations about the job experiences of new hires and internal transfers, then working up a salary recommendation for each individual.

By 8:15, the 38 professionals in the molecular biology section headed by Leonard Post, Ph.D., are grouped in a conference room. One or another of the scientists will take the floor in a few moments to update the others on research progress.

Meanwhile, in Puurs, Belgium, the afternoon sun is sloping behind the big Upjohn manufacturing plant. Sales Trainer Pierre Perne is lecturing three new sales representatives about the company's product line for treatment of central nervous system disorders. At 2:30, Pierre and the marketing recruits go for coffee and a chat about the material they've covered.

(left) An Asgrow Seed Company employee unloads O's Gold No. 682 hybrid seed corn at the production facility in Parkersburg, Iowa. Asgrow, part of the Upjohn Agricultural Division, maintains production facilities for its vegetable and agronomic seeds in seven countries.

(izquierda) Un empleado de la Compañía Asgrow Seed descarga semilla de maíz híbrida O's Gold No. 682 en la instalación para producción en Parkersburg, Iowa. Asgrow forma parte de la División Agrícola de la casa Upjohn y mantiene instalaciones para la producción de sus semillas vegetales y agrícolas en siete países.

(à gauche) Un employé de la société Asgrow Seed décharge un lot de semences de maïs hybride du type O-Gold No. 682, au centre de production de Parkersburg, dans l'Etat de l'Iowa. La société Asgrow, qui fait partie de la division agricole d'Upjohn, possède des centres régionaux de production de semences de légumes et de semences agronomiques dans sept pays.

（左）アイオワ州パーカーズバーグの生産施設で「オーズゴールド№.682」トウモロコシ交配種子をおろすアズグロー種子会社の従業員。アップジョン農業部門の一部であるアズグローは各種野菜の種子生産施設を7ケ国で運営している。

(right) A production worker inspects a vial of sterile solutions at Korea Upjohn Ltd., The Upjohn Company's subsidiary in Wa Woo Ri, South Korea, one of 18 pharmaceutical manufacturing plants throughout the world. All told, the Upjohn label appears on 250 products, marketed in over 150 nations.

(derecha) Un operario de Producción inspecciona soluciones estériles en la subsidiaria de Upjohn, en Wa Woo Ri, Corea del Sur, que es una de sus 18 plantas manufactureras farmacéuticas en el mundo. En conjunto, la etiqueta Upjohn aparece en 250 Productos, a la venta en más de 150 países.

(à droite) Un ouvrier à la production vérifie un flacon de solutions stériles à l'usine principale de la société Upjohn de Corée. La filiale d'Upjohn à Wa Woo Ri, en Corée du Sud, est l'un des dix-huit centres de fabrication de produits pharmaceutiques de cette société à l'étranger: L'étiquette Upjohn figure sur 250 produits commercialisés dans plus de 150 pays.

（右）韓国ワルリにある子会社、韓国アップジョン社で滅菌溶剤のびんを検査する従業員。韓国の施設は世界中に展開している医薬品製造工場18のうちのひとつ。アップジョンは250種の製品を150ケ国以上で販売している。

As coffee break concludes in Belgium, Hospital Sales Representative John Hall is working his way through the halls of the Duke University Medical Center in Durham, North Carolina. This has been part of his assignment for 14 years, and he exchanges a friendly word or two with almost everyone he passes. He spots a resident he's wanted to see and offers him a pamphlet about a recent medical study. Six states to the north, Medical Science Liaison Bob Thompson is beating a similar path through the offices of Boston's Massachusetts General Hospital. He has a date to see the hospital's chief of psychopharmacology about fresh findings in an extensive clinical study, underwritten by Upjohn, on the use of the company's Xanax in the treatment of panic disorders.

It is now 9:00 A.M. (EST). Ruth Lauer, R.N., a supervisor in the Upjohn HealthCare Services office in Rocky River, Ohio, is visiting the home of two octogenarian clients. One needs a change of dressing, the other is recovering from a stroke and pneumonia. Ruth will tend to their needs until a nurse's aide reports for duty.

By the time Ruth Lauer completes her call, Jackson B. Hester, Jr., Ph.D., a senior scientist at PR & D in Kalamazoo, is settling down for a day of supervising other researchers and sifting through data on tests of possible agents for treating cardiovascular diseases. He also wants to do some thinking about reshaping molecules to make effective drugs. He'll be among the last to leave the building at day's end.

At 10:00 A.M. in Kalamazoo, it is only 7:00 A.M. at Upjohn's agricultural experimental station in San Juan Bautista, California. Research Plant Scientist III, Wayne Fowler, Ph.D., has already driven onto the grounds. This April Monday, he's going to survey his eight-week-old tomato plants now rising a good four inches above the earth and still wet from overnight irrigation.

These are some of the people of Upjohn. They represent nearly 21,000 men and women who conduct the company's business in 600 buildings at 100-odd sites in at least 50 nations. The products they create, manufacture, and market reach consumers in 160 countries. This year of 1986 is the 100th anniversary of their company.

These individuals and their enterprise have covered quite a distance since Dr. William E. Upjohn first set out to sell his innovative "friable" pills a century ago. And what a mix of tasks today's employees handle! Around the world, executives, scientists, tradesmen, accountants, secretaries, sales representatives, production line workers, and thousands more do the daily work that makes up The Upjohn Company.

From the Office of the Chairman on down, these people operate in teams that harness their diverse skills and increase their effectiveness. At any one time, there'll be as many as six New Product Project Teams in session, each coordinating the efforts to steer a new compound to the market. Meanwhile, other people will be clustered in perhaps 20 New Indication and Formulation Systems committees. And then there are whole laboratories and production lines that are teams unto themselves.

But whether they work in groups or alone, Upjohn's 21,000 employees invest their skills and their days in finding ways to improve the health and well-being of mankind. Their dedication and loyalty are the envy of the competition. Because of them, Upjohn ranks among the top 15 drug firms in the world, with sales of more than $2 billion. Because of them and their predecessors, a small southwestern Michigan experiment weathered the challenges of a remarkable century and grew to be a dynamic corporation known and respected throughout the world.

(left) Two Fine Chemicals Division employees overlook a chemical storage tank in the steroid processing area in Portage, Michigan. The Chemical Division makes products ranging from bulk steroids and antibiotics to photochemicals, pigments, dyes, and ag/vet chemicals.

(izquierda) Dos empleados de la División de Productos Químicos Refinados inspeccionan un tanque con substancias químicas almacenadas en el área de procesamiento de esteroides en Portage, Michigan. La División Química hace productos que van desde esteroides y antibióticos en grandes volúmenes, tintes y productos químicos útiles en el Sector Agropecuario.

(à gauche) Deux employés de la division chimie fine d'Upjohn observent un réservoir de stockage de liquides chimiques au centre de traitement et de fabrication des stéroïdes à Portage, dans le Michigan. La division chimique d'Upjohn fabrique divers types de produits, allant des stéroïdes en vrac aux antibiotiques, des photochimiques aux pigments, colorants, et produits chimiques agricoles et vétérinaires.

（左）ミシガン州ポーテージのファインケミカル部門のステロイド処理工場で化学製品のタンクを見る作業員。ファインケミカル部門では、ステロイド、抗生物質、光化学製品、顔料、染料、農薬など広分野にわたる製品を生産している。

(right) An Upjohn HealthCare Services (UHCS) registered nurse in Cleveland, Ohio, attends to an elderly patient at his home. More than 60,000 full- and part-time UHCS "caregivers" in the U.S. and Canada serve the in-home and institutional health care needs of people of all ages.

(derecha) Una enfermera titulada de los Servicios de Salud Upjohn (UHCS) en Cleveland, Ohio, atiende a un paciente de edad avanzada en su hogar. Más de 60,000 "cuidadoras" empleadas de tiempo completo o de media jornada en todos los Estados Unidos y Canadá prestan servicios de enfermería en hogares e instituciones al cuidado de la salud.

(à droite) Une infirmière diplômée des Services de santé Upjohn à Cleveland, dans l'Ohio, s'occupe d'un patient âgé dans son foyer. Plus de 60.000 assistants médicaux à plein temps et à temps partiel de ce service, tant aux Etats-Unis qu'au Canada, donnent des soins aux enfants comme aux personnes âgées.

（右）オハイオ州クリーブランドで老人患者に自宅で付きそうアップジョン・ヘルスケア・サービスの登録看護婦。パートタイムを含めて6万人以上のアップジョン・ヘルスケア・サービス従業員が米国カナダで自宅又は施設で療養するあらゆる年齢の人々の看護をしている。

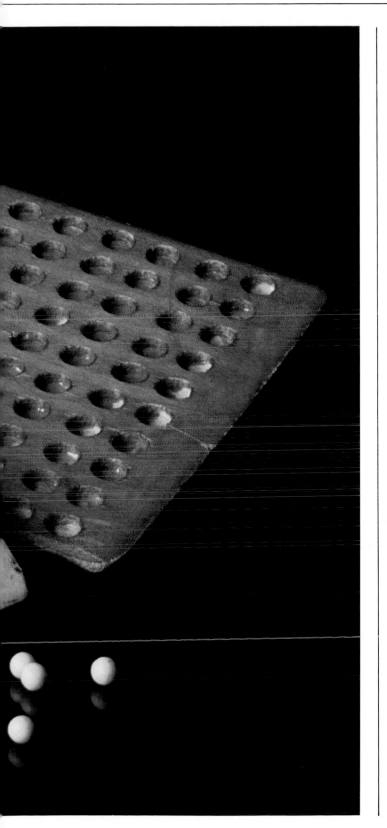

CHAPTER TWO

THE FOUNDER'S FOOTPRINTS

Dr. W. E. Upjohn, a short, stocky figure of a man, stood beside the still pond at Brook Lodge, the country refuge he had cherished for three decades. He had visitors that afternoon in 1932 — a cluster of new salesmen recruited by Sales Director Malcolm Galbraith to market The Upjohn Company's growing catalog of products in the 1930s, 1940s, and beyond.

Through bright blue eyes, "Dr. W. E." scanned the newcomers. He could have told them about his 45 years at the helm of the company and its growth, its moments of trial, its successes. That was not his way. He could have given these new salesmen a torrent of business advice, but that wasn't like him either. Instead, being of a practical, matter-of-fact character, he decided to level with them on a question of concern to many in the company: what would happen to it after he was gone?

"Gentlemen," he said, "it will make no difference when I go." To emphasize his point, he threw a pebble into the pond; the rings spread across the surface, and then the water was quiet once more. "All the ripples will dissipate," he observed. "There will be no changes."

W. E. could not have foreseen how Upjohn's dimensions might grow with time — from 1,186 employees in 1932 to nearly 21,000 today; from a small layout of 22 buildings then to more than 600 worldwide now; from net sales of $8,550,000 to more than $2 billion in 1985.

But Dr. Upjohn's observation was inaccurate in a more subtle sense. The ripples he made in his lifetime, unlike the ones he pointed to that afternoon at the lodge, did not dissipate. They have continued to play against the foundations of the international enterprise that is The Upjohn Company today.

Uriah Upjohn, M.D. (1808-1896), used this pass (insert) to attend medical school lectures in New York City in 1832. Three years later this English immigrant settled in the frontier village of Richland, in the Michigan Territory. His four sons later founded The Upjohn Pill and Granule Co.

Uriah Upjohn, médico (1808-1896), usaba este pase (inserto) en 1832 para asistir a las conferencias de la escuela de medicina en la ciudad de Nueva York. Tres años más tarde este inmigrante inglés se estableció en la aldea fronteriza de Richland, en el Territorio de Michigan. Sus cuatro hijos fundaron más tarde la Upjohn Pill and Granule Co.

Lorsqu'il était étudiant en médecine, Uriah Upjohn (1808-1896) se servait de ce laisser-passer pour assister aux cours de la Faculté de Médecine à New York, en 1832. Trois ans plus tard, cet immigrant anglais s'établit dans le village frontière de Richland, dans le Michigan. Ses quatre fils plus tard fondèrent la société Upjohn Pill and Granule.

ユリア・アップジョン医博(1808〜1896)は、1832年ニューヨーク市の医大に通っていた頃、この学生証を使用した。3年後、このイギリスからの移民の家族はミシガン州のリッチランド村に落ち着き、のちに、四人の子息がアップジョン錠剤・顆粒製造会社を設立した。

W. E. enjoyed using maxims when the occasion was right. One of them was, "There are no supermen." Ironically, he came as close to being one in his company and his community as an individual could. And his influence remains tangible. A senior executive with 25 years of experience at many levels of the company says today, "I feel the founder's presence."

A FAMILY OF BUILDERS

It took energy and enterprise for W. E. Upjohn and his brothers to assemble their Upjohn Pill and Granule Company a century ago. Considering their heritage, however, that achievement should not seem surprising. The men who made and marketed the new pill that would crumble under one's thumb were not the first in their bloodline to dream big and follow through.

The roots of those four brothers were probably in Wales, where early records show the family name was Apjon. Later, presumably in the fifteenth century, after some of the family migrated to England, the name became Upjohn. Four centuries later, in the 1830s, members of the Upjohn line began voyaging to America. They were builders — architects and civil engineers. But one of them had two sons who broke the mold by deciding to become physicians. William and Uriah Upjohn studied medicine at the College of Physicians and Surgeons in New York City. On their graduation in 1834, a professor told them there was an urgent need for doctors on the frontier.

Already witness to the westward tide of settlers flowing along the Erie Canal, William and Uriah hit the trail themselves in the spring of 1835. They headed for the Michigan Territory, where the government land office was offering land at two dollars an acre and where, in the next five years, the population of more than 87,000 would double.

In addition to the broken bones and baby deliveries a doctor could expect anywhere, the region had its full share of disease-breeding swamps and marshes. The all-too-common ague, a malaria-like fever, could be treated with quinine, *if* a doctor had it. A lack of fresh fruit and vegetables made the "Michigan rash," a scurvy-like ailment, a further hazard. In short, young physicians could keep very busy on the grand prairies west of Detroit.

In June 1835, William and Uriah arrived in Kalamazoo County at the settlement named Bronson after its first white resident, Titus Bronson of Connecticut, who had put down his roots there in 1829. His little outpost was set within an oxbow curve of the Kalamazoo River, which years later would give the little town a new name.

The Upjohn brothers decided against staying in Bronson. Instead, they purchased land and pitched their tent some ten miles to the east in the northwest corner of section 31 of Kalamazoo County, near the tiny community of Richland. It was rich land — Warsaw silt loam, with underground root systems so perverse that pioneer-farmers hired ox-drawn "breaking plows" to subdue the soil. There the two young doctors took their bearings in a silence wakened now and then by the eerie howls of brush wolves or the booming of prairie chickens.

Finding these surroundings to their liking, the Upjohns put up a log cabin and set about earning a living. When Michigan joined the Union in 1837, Uriah received his license to practice medicine. William first tried farming, but the need for physicians on that frontier drew him also to medicine. While Uriah settled in Richland, William moved in 1841 to Hastings, 30 miles to the northeast, where he would settle for the rest of his days. A third brother, Erastus, moved to the area in the late 1840s to practice medicine, but after a short time his wife died and he moved west to Nebraska.

preoccupied, although always courteous. If one consulted him professionally, he would talk freely and give advice. Young Dr. Upjohn, as he was then called here, was a thinker."

Uncle William, who turned 70 in 1877 and had no male heirs, may have hoped that W. E. would succeed him. But that was not to be. In 1878, W. E. married Rachel Babcock, daughter of a Kalamazoo pharmacist, and two years later he was practicing independently.

His interests also ranged beyond medicine. When Fred Sweet of Hastings applied in 1879 for a patent on an electrical clock driven by an electromagnet, a half interest was assigned to Dr. W. E., his first venture in business. Although it failed as a commercial venture, the imposing clock still stands on the stair landing behind the front lobby of Building 24 in Upjohn's research complex in downtown Kalamazoo. To this day, it keeps perfect time.

The summer of 1881, Dr. W. E. was tending to the sick and injured in and around Hastings. He had turned 28 that June and was now a father (Rachel Winifred had been born on January 21 the year before). As he made his house calls with his bulky physician's case, people knew him from a distance: young Dr. Upjohn was the only doctor in the area who drove a team.

MEDICINE IN THE EARLY DAYS

In the newspapers of early July 1881, one saddening story stood out: President James Garfield, about to entrain for his reunion at Williams College, had been shot twice by a frustrated office seeker. One bullet grazed the president's arm; the other buried in his back, and doctors could not find it.

Very little could be done. They probed the wound with their fingers, without success. Alexander Graham Bell sounded for the bullet with an electrical device; he failed, too. X-ray technology was still 14 years away, and no adequate antiseptics existed. By July 5, the wound was inflamed. Peritonitis set in, physicians watched and waited helplessly, and on September 19 the 50-year-old president died.

The fact is that a century ago, from the frontier all the way to the White House, doctors practiced medicine in ways very primitive by today's standards. As far back as 1796, Edward Jenner's vaccine had worked against smallpox; by the middle of the nineteenth century, Louis Pasteur had shown that controlled heat could kill microbes in wine. But sophisticated patient treatment lay decades off.

A young boy's toothache illustrates the point. Charles Little and his brother William, future Upjohn employees, lived in Richland in the late 1800s and were the grandnephews of Dr. Uriah Upjohn. Charles, suffering from a bad tooth, was taken by his mother to Dr. Uriah. Will Little went along, and five decades later he recalled the procedure: "Dr. Upjohn took out his jackknife, sharpened the edge of the blade on his boot top and cut around the base of the tooth. He then wrenched it out with an old-fashioned turnkey."

(left) By 1884, W.E.'s friable pill-making experiments had outgrown the attic workshop of his Hastings, Michigan, home. In search of more space, and a steam turbine to power his revolving pans, he set up shop in this nearby abandoned grain mill.

(izquierda) Para 1884 ya era insuficiente el taller montado por W.E. en el desván de su hogar en Hastings, Michigan, para sus experimentos de fabricación de píldoras desintegrables. En busca de mayor espacio para una turbina a vapor que accionara sus cubos giratorios, organizó su taller en este abandonado molino para granos cerca de allí.

(à gauche) En 1884, l'atelier de fabrication de pilules friables de William Erastus Upjohn déborde du cadre trop étriqué du grenier de sa maison de Hastings (Michigan). Pour avoir plus d'espace et utiliser une turbine à vapeur pour actionner ses bacs tournants il installe son atelier dans un vieux moulin abandonné.

（左）1884年には、W．E．アップジョンの「崩れる丸薬」の製造実験は、ミシガン州ヘイスチングにあった自宅の屋根裏部屋の実験室では、納まらない規模になっていた。回転皿用の蒸気タービンを設置する、より広いスペースを求めて、W．E．アップジョンは近くの、使われていない穀物精製所を新しい作業場とした。

(right) Rachel Babcock Upjohn (1856-1905), W.E.'s first wife and mother of his four children, Winifred, William Harold, Dorothy, and Genevieve. Rachel and W.E. met as teenagers in her father's downtown Kalamazoo pharmacy, where W.E. worked as a clerk.

(derecha) Rachel Babcock Upjohn (1856-1905), primera esposa de W. E. y madre de sus cuatro hijos, Winifred, William Harold, Dorothy y Genevieve. Rachel y W.E. se conocieron como adolescentes en la farmacia del padre de ella, en el centro de la ciudad de Kalamazoo, donde William Erastus trabajaba como empleado.

(à droite) Rachel Babcock Upjohn (1856-1905). Première femme de William Upjohn et mère de ses quatre enfants : Winifred, William Harold, Dorothy, et Geneviève. William et Rachel se sont connus très jeunes à la pharmacie du centre-ville à Kalamazoo où travaillait William comme employé.

（右）レイチェル・バブコック・アップジョン（1856〜1905）。W．E．アップジョンの最初の妻で、ウイルフレッド、ウイリアムJr.、ドロシー、ジェネビーブ の四人の子供を産んだ。レイチェルとW．E．アップジョンは、二人が10代の頃、カラマズーの市街地にあった彼女の父親の薬局でW．E．アップジョンが店員をしていたとき知り合った。

(top) This bound catalog (actual size, 2 3/8 x 5 3/8 inches) was first issued in 1886. Its 20 pages listed 191 different friable pill and granule formulas "employing new processes," as the cover pointed out, "which yield products greatly superior and permanently soluble."

(arriba) Este catálogo encuadernado (tamaño actual 2³⁄₈ x 5³⁄₈ pulgadas) se publicó por primera vez en 1886. En sus 20 páginas se ennumeran 191 diferentes fórmulas de píldoras desintegrables y gránulos, "usando nuevos procesos", según se señala en la portada, "de los que se deriva un producto notablemente superior y permanentemente soluble".

(en haut) Catalogue relié, de dimension 6 cm par 13,7 cm environ, dont la première édition a paru en 1886. Dans ses vingt pages, on trouve 191 formules différentes de pilules et granulés friables, avec "de nouveaux procédés de fabrication"-comme l'indique sa couverture-"pour avoir des produits de qualité supérieure et hautement solubles".

（上）1886年に初めて出版されたカタログ（実物寸法は 6 cm×13.7 cm）。表紙に記されているような、「新しい 製法による、高品質で長期間保存後も融解する製品」191 種の錠剤や顆粒が20頁にわたって掲載されている。

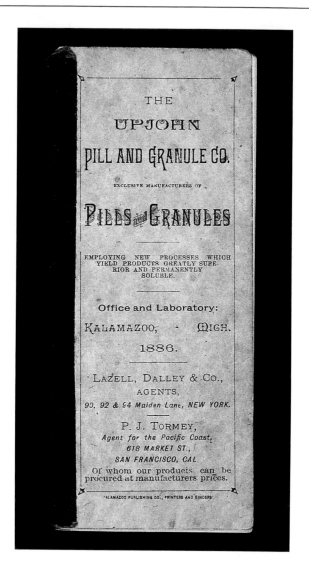

(bottom) This diagram was found on United States Patent 312,041, issued February 10, 1885, to Dr. William E. Upjohn for the "Process of Making Pills."

(abajo) Este diagrama se encontró en la Patente de Estados Unidos 312,041, expedida el 10 de febrero de 1885 al Dr. William E. Upjohn para el "Proceso de Fabricación de Píldoras".

(en bas) Ce schéma a été prélevé d'un brevet américain au No. 312 041 délivré le 10 février 1885 au Dr. William E. Upjohn, l'autorisant à procéder à la "fabrication de pilules".

（下）1885年2月10日発行のアメリカ合衆国特許312041 号に載っている図。W．E．アップジョン博士の「医薬 品の製法」に対して与えられた特許である。

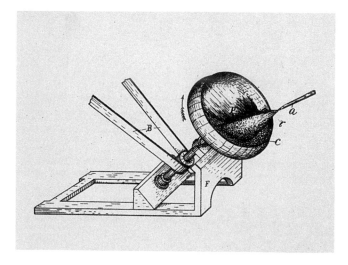

So much for dental surgery. Medicine was scarcely more sophisticated. An elderly Hastings citizen recalled how a nineteenth-century physician provided medicine for his patient. He carried various powders with him in bottles. Once he decided on a treatment, he pulled out the right containers, poured the powders on some paper, mixed them with his pocketknife, and wrapped each dose in a small piece of paper. The contents of his case probably included quinine, alcohol, mercury, strychnine, arsenic, and opium, a popular medicinal of the era. In 1872, some 416,000 pounds of opium were imported into the U.S. for use in the treatment of sore throats, inflammations, diarrhea, sprains, coughs, and sundry other disabilities.

Big-city medicine had few advantages over rural practice. When the famed William Osler served as clinical professor of medicine at the University of Pennsylvania in the 1880s, he used his own microscope; they had none for him. At New York's Roosevelt Hospital, Dr. Howard C. Taylor described the 1891 operating room as a place where there were "no rubber gloves, no face masks and no doctor's caps." At that time, he wrote, "Nurses' caps were for decoration and not for covering the hair. The operating gowns, which were not sterilized, were put on over street clothes."

Along with such crude conditions, the distinction between physician, druggist, and drug-maker was often blurred. Until the mid-eighteenth century, the doctor usually did it all. Even the most advanced physician made medicinal compounds in his own dispensary, after buying raw materials from a wholesale druggist, who also stocked paints, chemicals, and cosmetics. Following the American Revolution, the druggist's emporium gradually gained stature, with apprentices bending over mixing bowls to concoct compounds. But quality control was up to the individual druggist, and no federal standards existed — nor would they for more than a century.

Meanwhile, *patent medicines* — actually secret formulas for which the Crown in colonial days issued "letters patent" — gave the apothecary who invented them the title of "proprietor," hence "proprietary" medicine. (The fact was that few patent medicines ever had a true patent.) They were sold directly to the public, usually with flagrant, unwarranted therapeutic claims. If one couldn't buy his favorite at a drugstore, he would find it at the general store. Newspapers of the early nineteenth century thrived on ads for medicines, and no one openly questioned their makers' claims.

What a selection there was! If a citizen felt poorly, he had mystifying choices, everything from Carter's Smart Weed and Belladona Backache Plasters and Extract of Wahoo to Drake's Plantation Bitters (base: 36.25 percent alcohol), Merchant's Celebrated Gargling Oil for Man and Beast, and Parker's Vegetable Renovating Panacea.

It took the Civil War to hasten improvements. Surgeons needed more medicines than pharmacists could supply, so the manufacture of pharmaceuticals was scaled up. At about that time, pill machines were devised, improved methods of making powdered and fluid extracts were discovered, and the first compressed tablet machine began stamping out products. A new age was beginning.

But did pills of the day work? F. L. Upjohn indicted them in a late-nineteenth century pamphlet. The "mass pills" of earlier years, he wrote, "eventually assume a horny hardness, due to loss of moisture, that is practically impenetrable by the digestive juices." Bullet-hard, the pill would pass through the entire body, its beneficial components unused.

Dr. W. E. Upjohn of Hastings thought there had to be a better way. It may be that the idea came to him after watching small pellets of grain tumble from between the massive grinding stones of a flour mill. Or perhaps he had heard about the Eureka Sugar Coating Pill Machine of 1872, which worked by spinning pills in a pan. No one is quite sure. At any rate, the young physician started experimenting with a revolving pan, powdered formulas, and a spray device in search of a more effective pill.

Those were busy times for W. E. In the morning he'd work away at his pan in the attic of his home, then go downstairs for the rest of the day to try to catch up with the practice of medicine. When he began to get encouraging results in his pill-making, he set up shop in an abandoned Hastings mill where he could tap steam power. And then, as his nephew L. N. wrote years later, the minute a new pill looked promising, W. E. "lost no time in describing it to his friends and colleagues," undoubtedly with zeal. "He wasn't a gabber," L. N. said. "Trifling conversation didn't interest him. But if he had something in mind that he wanted to do, he'd talk about it without stopping."

Day after day, the pans revolved in the old Hastings mill. Little kernels grew into pills, "friable" pills that would disintegrate readily to speed the release of medication in the body. As those pills took shape, so did a concept that was eventually to turn into The Upjohn Company of today.

THE PILL-MAKER'S PROGRESS

Very probably it was the most important letter that young Dr. Upjohn had written in years. Dated March 6, 1884, it was composed in his Hastings home, where his wife Rachel was recovering nicely from the delivery six weeks earlier of their son William Harold. The letter was going to W. E.'s "Brother Henry," Dr. Henry Uriah Upjohn, in Kalamazoo. W. E. wanted his brother's advice, and his chief agenda item, he wrote, "of course is pills." This was hardly a new topic of conversation between them. W. E. noted that "some parties" were urging him to manufacture pills by his new process. Two men had already said they would put up $500 apiece to get the project going. In turn, he had prepared a list of pills as a starter, with prices below those of competitors.

The young doctor faced a clear dilemma. "I have got to make my choice," he wrote, "between making pills in quantities much larger than I have been doing (and to do this I shall have to use someone else's money) or stop making pills entirely as it is too much trouble to carry it on."

The demand for friable pills was growing among physicians in the area without any effort on W. E.'s part. Thus, he added, "I am on top of the fence and don't know which way to jump." He ended by asking Henry not to say anything about the matter to the family as he did "not want to hear it discussed until [he] decided what to do."

Of course, W. E. was already bringing the subject to his older brother. Doing so made a lot of sense because Henry Uriah had the best mechanical skills of the brothers. He also had saved some money from his practice, patented several farm machines, and done well through real estate ventures in Kalamazoo.

Dr. W. E. merely suggested that his brother advise him by letter. But the two met soon afterward, and on the way home from their meeting W. E. stopped in Richland to talk with his younger brother Frederick Lawrence. "F. L."

may not have been a doctor, but he had the family knack with machines. Later, he would invent a way of sugarcoating and polishing pills, as well as a device for counting them.

The next significant step came on October 14, 1884: Dr. W. E. applied for a patent on his pill-making process. It was granted February 10, 1885, and given the number 312,041. Of necessity, the application had to say something about how W. E.'s method worked. The process consisted of "placing in a revoluble [sic] pan nuclei of any suitable material, setting the pan in motion, moistening the rolling nuclei with liquid spray or vapor; sifting into the moistened nuclei powdered ingredient . . . applying to the growing pills spray or vapor . . . and so alternately moistening and powdering until the pills have grown to the desired size."

Dr. W. E. had to say that much, but he did not have to reveal what his "starters" were in the pan, or his formula for the moistening agents, or the makeup of the powders that built up the pills. Those secrets eluded the curious. Once the operation got under way, employees in pill production pledged secrecy to protect W. E.'s technique. Over 20 years, only two employees thought they could make the method work for a competitor, but they found they could not duplicate it.

As the year 1885 cycled forward, young Dr. Upjohn gave the finishing touches to his plan and acted: he moved his family to Kalamazoo, where they settled in a two-room apartment in the "Upjohn Block," a 65-room building that Henry Upjohn had erected on South Burdick Street. W. E. had already spent $3,000 on perfecting his process, and he owed money to a Hastings hardware merchant. For all practical purposes, he was broke. In Kalamazoo, he could get the help he obviously needed from his brother Henry and from other family members.

(left) One of the longest-lived friable pill formulas was Blaud pills, an iron supplement. In the 1886 product catalog it sold for 20 cents per bottle of 100 black-colored pills. In 1956, its last year in the catalog, Blaud pills came in black, pink, chocolate, white, or red.

(izquierda) Una de las fórmulas de Píldoras desintegrables que más perduró fue la de píldoras Blaud, un suplemento de hierro. Según el catálogo de productos de 1886 se vendía a 20 centavos el frasco de 100 píldoras de color negro. En 1956, último año que aparecieron en el catálogo, las píldoras Blaud eran negras, rosadas, cafés, blancas o rojas.

(à gauche) Les pilules Blaud, un supplément de vitamines riche en fer, sont parmi les plus anciennes formes de pilules friables. Dans le catalogue de production pour l'année 1886, ces pilules se vendaient à 20 centimes or le flacon de 100 pilules. En 1956, la dernière année où elles figuraient au catalogue, les pilules Blaud se vendaient sous les couleurs rose, noire, chocolat, blanche et rouge.

（左）崩れる丸薬の中で最も長いライフサイクルを記録したのは、鉄剤のブラウド丸薬であった。1886年の製品カタログによると、この黒色丸薬百粒で1瓶20セントとなっている。ブラウド丸薬が最後にカタログに掲載された1956年には、黒、ピンク、チョコレート色、白、赤の各色があった。

(right) Frederick Lawrence "F.L." Upjohn (1857-1917) was the only one of the four Upjohn brothers who was not a physician. Throughout his 23 years with the company, however, he invented pill production equipment, served as treasurer and vice president, and managed the New York sales office.

(derecha) Frederick Lawrence "F.L." Upjohn (1857-1917) fue el único de los cuatro hermanos Upjohn que no era médico. Sin embargo, durante sus 23 años con la compañía inventó el equipo de producción de píldoras, actuó como tesorero y vicepresidente y administró la oficina de ventas de Nueva York.

(à droite) Frederick Lawrence "F.L." Upjohn (1857-1917), fut le seul des quatre frères Upjohn à ne pas être médecin. Cependant, au cours de ses 23 années au service de la société, il inventa l'équipement de production de pilules, fut trésorier et vice-président, et directeur général de la succursale de ventes de New York.

（右）フレデリック・ローレンス・アップジョン（1857～1917）は、4人のアップジョン兄弟の中で医師にならなかった唯一の人。しかし在職中の23年間に、錠剤製造設備を考案し、財務担当重役、副社長を歴任、ニューヨーク販売部門を統轄した。

The Backdrop for Enterprise

With its 1884 population of 14,000, Kalamazoo was the seventh-largest town in Michigan. That year, the citizens voted to classify it a city, leaving behind its claim of being the nation's largest village.

The sky above this new city by the twisting river was stained with smoke from hundreds of wood and coal stoves and from the factories that had sprouted so quickly — the wagon-makers, the iron foundries, the planing mill. Kalamazoo called itself the "windmill capital of the world" and world leader in buggy manufacture, fashioning 47,000 vehicles in 1887.

But the city had reason to be just as proud of its food products. It had led the state in the 1870s in flour-milling, and a recent infusion of Dutch settlers spread the planting of celery fields. In many ways, this was still a quaint village. Yet it was expanding in spite of itself. Four railroads hauled in and out as many as 42 passenger trains a day. A 22-car trolley system had just started rolling, streets had been gaslit since 1857, and the enterprising had made use of the local phone system since 1881.

For W. E. Upjohn, Kalamazoo was the place where he would turn his dream into reality. There, in the fall of 1885, The Upjohn Pill and Granule Company became an official partnership, owned by Dr. W. E.; his brother Henry; Henry's wife, Dr. Millie Kirby Upjohn; and W. E.'s wife Rachel. However, because the earliest date in company records falls in the following year — a handwritten notation on the first price list — 1886 is considered the firm's date of birth.

Dr. Henry Uriah brought to the enterprise his years as a physician, real mechanical skills, and capital; Dr. W. E. had a decade's experience as a rural doctor and was fascinated by gadgets; F. L., who joined the partnership in 1886, offered an inventive streak; and James T., who became a partner soon after F. L., brought with him a brand-new diploma from the University of Michigan Medical School. Alone or together, these four could think up and build pill-making machines, sorters, sizers, counters, and packagers.

But except for inventor-realtor Dr. Henry, these Upjohns were not businessmen. That meant learning by trial and error. Fortunately for the enterprise, W. E. had many talents applicable to the pharmaceutical trade, and he had character, which helped him raise capital when needed. He could also take advantage of opportunity, and he could benefit from the teachings of experience. With his patented friable pill, W. E., along with his brothers, most certainly had a big jump on the competition.

1886: The First Year

The Upjohn Pill and Granule Company set out to do on a larger scale what the dispensing physician already did: buy ingredients in bulk, blend them into compounds, and then make different dosages from the mixture. But the Kalamazoo partners had a unique "specialty" going for them, the friable pill. In their first full year of business, 1886, the Upjohns applied their special pill-making method to traditional compounding. Physicians welcomed the innovation as long overdue.

James T. Upjohn

(left) In May 1886, the Upjohn brothers and their twelve employees moved into this two-and-one-half story, 36-foot by 36-foot brick structure on Farmer's Alley, in downtown Kalamazoo — the first building erected by the young company.

(izquierda) En mayo de 1886 los hermanos Upjohn y sus doce empleados se trasladaron a este edificio de ladrillos de dos pisos y medio, de 36 por 36 pies, en Farmer's Alley, en el centro de la ciudad de Kalamazoo, el primer edificio construido por la recién creada compañía.

(à gauche) En mai 1886, les frères Upjohn et leurs douze employés vont s'installer dans un immeuble de Farmer's Alley au centre-ville de Kalamazoo. C'était le premier immeuble construit par cette jeune entreprise.

（左）1886年5月、アップジョン兄弟は、12人の社員とともに、カラマズーのファーマーズ通りの二階建て、11㎡のレンガ造りの建物に移った。創立まもないアップジョン社が建てた最初の建物であった。

(right) James Townley "J.T." Upjohn (1858-1936), the youngest of the four Upjohn brothers, upon his 1886 graduation from the University of Michigan School of Medicine. Before he left the company in 1909 he served as head of production, vice president, and treasurer.

(derecha) James Townley "J.T." Upjohn (1858-1936), el más joven de los cuatro hermanos Upjohn, en su graduación, en 1886, en la Escuela de Medicina de la Universidad de Michigan. Antes de separarse de la compañía en 1909, actuó como jefe de producción, Vicepresidente y Tesorero.

(à droite) James Townley Upjohn (1858-1936). Le plus jeune des quatre frères Upjohn, encore appelé familièrement de ses initiales "J.T.", reçoit son diplôme de la Faculté de Médecine de l'Université du Michigan. Avant de quitter la société Upjohn, en 1909, il était directeur de production, puis vice-président et trésorier.

（右）ジェイムス・タウンリー・アップジョン（1858〜1936）は、4人のアップジョン兄弟の末弟。1886年ミシガン大学医学部卒業時の写真。1909年退社するまで、製造担当責任者、副社長、財務担当重役を歴任。

(left) W.E. Upjohn, Christmas 1888. Two years after founding his company, the 5'6", blue-eyed Dr. Upjohn had erected his first building on Lovell Street, hired his first East Coast salesman, added hypodermic tablets to the product catalog, and watched annual sales rise to near $90,000.

(izquierda) W. E. Upjohn, Navidad de 1888. Dos años después de fundada su compañia, el Dr. Upjohn (5' 6" de estatura, ojos azules) había levantado su primer edificio en la calle Lovell, una vez contratado su primer vendedor en la Costa Este, incorporó las tabletas hipodérmicas al catálogo de productos y presenció el aumento de las ventas anuales a cerca de $90.000.

(à gauche) W.E. Upjohn, Noël 1888. Deux ans après la création de sa société, il fait construire le premier bâtiment de la compagnie à Lovell Street, recrute son premier agent de ventes pour la côte Est des Etats-Unis, ajoute des tablettes hypodermiques au catalogue de production, et contribue à la hausse des ventes qui atteignent un chiffre annuel de près de 90.000 dollars.

（左）1888年、クリスマスの**W．E．**アップジョン。身長1メーター70、青い眠のアップジョン博士は、会社創立後2年目にロベル通りに最初のビルを建て、イースト・コーストを担当するセールスマンを採用し、商品カタログに注射器用製剤を加えた。年商が9万ドルに達する頃であった。

(right) Buildings 4, at right, erected in 1888, and 5, erected in 1891, were Upjohn's first on Lovell Street in Kalamazoo. Known to local citizens as "the pill factory," these buildings were razed in 1953. Research building 126 now stands in their place.

(derecha) El edificio número 4, a la derecha, erigido en 1888, y el número 5, erigido en 1891, fueron los primeros de Upjohn en la Calle Lovell, en Kalamazoo. Conocidos en la localidad como "la fábrica de píldoras", estos edificios fueron demolidos en 1953. En su lugar está ahora el edificio 126, para investigaciones.

(à droite) Le bâtiment No. 4 (à droite), construit en 1888, et le bâtiment No. 5, construit en 1891, sont les premiers de la société Upjohn à Lovell Street, Kalamazoo. Appelé "l'usine à pilules" par les habitants du village, cet ensemble de bâtiments a été détruit en 1953. Le bâtiment de recherches, au numéro 126, l'a remplacé.

（右）1888年に建てられた右側の4号館と、1891年に建てられた5号館は、カラマズー・ロベル通りの、アップジョン社最初の建物であった。カラマズー市民から「丸薬工場」と呼ばれたこの二つのビルは、1953年にとり壊され、現在は研究棟である126号館がこの地に建っている。

The Upjohns' first price list that spring showed 186 pill formulas. They were prepared from 56 different drugs — 30 botanicals, 20 chemicals, five alkaloids, and one glucoside. Competitors probably sold many of the same products. There were quinine pills, used for headaches and muscular aches as well as fevers and malaria; a tonic in the form of Blaud iron pills; an anticonstipation pill; and so on. All in all, these were little more than palliatives — they helped reduce the symptoms and effects of disease. Except for the possible therapeutic effect of quinine in malaria, they did not cure.

Where the Upjohn catalog varied from others, in addition to the friable pill, was in the price column. Upjohn products were going for about one-half the prices of the old-style mass-made pills, a situation that generated bitter hostility from competitors. Ignoring their clamor, Dr. W. E., the company's first sales representative, took to the road with the attractively priced catalog, and Upjohn products sold briskly. In no time, the plant assembled in the basement of the Upjohn Block on

Burdick Street was at capacity. The company's chief backer, Henry Uriah, solved that problem by building a two-and-a-half-story, 36-foot by 36-foot structure on Farmer's Alley, behind the Upjohn Block, and linked it and the Upjohn Block with a 30-foot-long bridge at the second story. Ground was broken in late February 1886, and by May the pans were revolving in this new space.

In this setting, F. L. Upjohn made the products, aided by Charles and Gertrude Tillitson. Homer Blakeslee coated the pills, Fanny Church handled the packaging, Fred Hyde shipped out the product, and Mary S. Kirby, sister of Millie Kirby Upjohn, Henry's wife, kept the books. The average wage was $3.50 to $4.00 a week. A foreman in those early times could earn $15.00 a week.

Meanwhile, the partners organized themselves to meet their new business responsibilities. W. E. was named president; Dr. J. T. Upjohn took on the vice presidency; the treasurer's post went to F. L. Upjohn; and a local dry goods merchant from next door on Burdick Street, John M. Gilmore, was made secretary. W. E. sold the pills and F. L. initially ran manufacturing. Dr. Henry Uriah, while maintaining his medical practice, came up with advice, capital, and ideas for production devices. Commercially produced equipment for pharmaceutical manufacturing

was rare, hence such devices usually had to be designed and handmade. Employees found W. E. readily supportive of that effort. He always expressed keen interest and pleasure whenever they developed a new machine or gadget.

For their first year of 1886, the partners had gross sales of $50,000. The boom was yet to come.

That first year had barely ended when the Upjohns were confronted with a most painful, unexpected loss. On January 2, 1887, Dr. Henry Uriah Upjohn died of typhoid fever (ways of preventing it — through public sanitation and vaccination — would not become widespread for decades). Just 43 at his death, Henry Uriah had been pivotal as the senior partner and main financial backer of the company.

It took almost two months to sort out the allocation of his two-fifths interest in the concern. Part of the delay may have been the result of a disagreement. Mrs. Millie Kirby Upjohn had inherited Henry's share. That meant, in the words of Henry's son Lawrence Northcote, "a necessity for buying her out and then that brought in Mother's father, Grandfather Kirby, and he and W. E. had a terrible row."

In late February, Millie Upjohn agreed to accept $8,000 for signing over her husband's interest, mainly to Dr. J. T. and F. L., with smaller increments going to four others. W. E. was not among them. At the same time, the remaining principals formed a new partnership giving W. E. the largest share, with F. L. and J. T. accepting equal, smaller segments. The three brothers accepted employment by the partnership at salaries, respectively, of $1,200, $900, and $600 a year. The final step in this reorganization came the following November when the key individuals signed over their partnership rights to a new corporation, The Upjohn Pill and Granule Company.

Slowly the company's horizons widened. In September 1887, F. L. went to Washington, D. C., to arrange the company's first major exhibit of pills at a meeting of the International Medical Association. W. E. never cared to travel much, but he and Rachel decided to go along. The Upjohns of Kalamazoo had concluded that their friable pill should meet a wider audience, too.

The 1886 product catalog listed two wholesale agents for Upjohn goods. One year later it listed seven. By decade's end the list had grown to 29. But the Upjohns still had to master a tough lesson of their chosen business. The pharmaceutical manufacturer must keep looking for new markets, new uses, and particularly for innovative new products, regardless of how well the current product line might be selling. This is a maxim of the industry, as true today as it was in the 1890s.

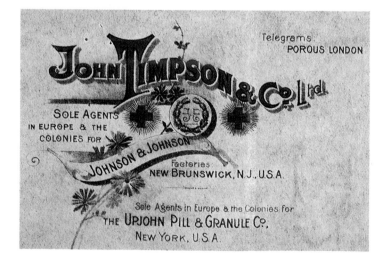

GEARING FOR THE NINETIES

Richland native Charlie Little went to work for Upjohn in 1889 at three dollars a week, rising eventually to plant superintendent. He was first hired to assist the man who had taken over manufacturing, Dr. J. T. Upjohn.

When he reported for work, Little saw that the company was actually turning out "a very limited line." That began to change in the early 1890s. Until then, the firm had purchased powdered extracts in New York and Chicago, but in 1892 Upjohn bought out a New York firm and started making its own extracts. This technology would later allow the company to greatly expand its product line. As of 1892, the company was producing 500 items.

Dr. W. E. wanted dispensing physicians and druggists to know about these products, so when the lavish World's Columbian Exposition opened in 1893 in Chicago, The Upjohn Pill and Granule Company was among the exhibitors. As visitors approached his booth, Dr. Upjohn offered them company stickpins decorated with a miniature bottle of pills and a label showing the Upjohn trademark — Dr. Upjohn's thumb crushing a pill.

To reach a vital marketplace, the company had already opened a New York City sales office on October 15, 1890, in downtown Manhattan. Three salesmen staffed it: Charles A. Prickitt, Archibald M. Stone, and Will Sutliffe. The man in charge, transplanted from Kalamazoo headquarters, was F. L. Upjohn.

F. L.'s domain had its share of growing pains. Kalamazoo-based salesmen were managing to reach dispensing physicians, and they were also selling Upjohn's services as a producer of "buyer's-label" goods, with a retail druggist's name on the package rather than Upjohn's. Unable at first to connect with dispensing doctors, New York sales representatives concentrated on the buyer's-label business and on the "special-formula" business, which consisted of manufacturing another company's specialty products for a set fee. Consequently, the Upjohn label almost dropped from sight for a while in that area. Sales of the special-order items ran up, but their profit margins were slim. In the long run, Upjohn would have to make it by projecting its own image, not someone else's.

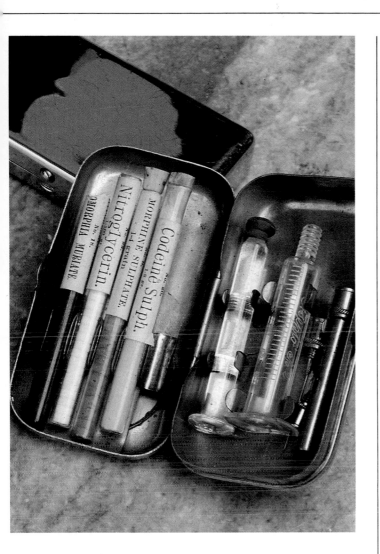

(left) In 1890, Upjohn signed London-based John Timpson & Co.,Ltd., to be its sole sales agent in "Europe & the Colonies." Timpson and his successors marketed Upjohn products in the United Kingdom from then until as late as 1939.

(izquierda) En 1890 Upjohn autorizó a John Timpson & Co, con sede en Londres, como único agente de ventas en "Europa y las colonias". Timpson y sus sucesores distribuyeron los productos Upjohn en el Reino Unido desde entonces hasta 1939.

(à gauche) En 1890, la société Upjohn engage par contrat la firme John Timpson and Co comme son agent exclusif pour "l'Europe et les Colonies". Timpson et ses successeurs ont commercialisé les produits Upjohn au Royaume-Uni, depuis lors jusqu'à fin 1939.

（左）1890年、アップジョン社は、ロンドンを本拠地とするジョン・ティンプソン社と契約を結び、ヨーロッパとその植民地における総代理店とした。以来1939年までイギリス連邦ではティンプソンとその後継者たちが、アップジョン社の製品を販売し続けた。

(right) In 1888, Upjohn began manufacturing hypodermic tablets for physicians to dissolve into a solution for injection into the patient. By 1893 it also offered this syringe and pill case. Compressed tablets debuted in 1899, followed by the formation of a Tablet Department in 1900.

(derecha) En 1888 Upjohn comenzó a fabricar tabletas hipodérmicas para los médicos, que se disolvían en una solución para inyectar al paciente. Para 1893 también ofrecía este estuche para jeringa y píldoras. Las tabletas comprimidas aparecieron en 1899, seguidas de la formación de un Departamento de Tabletas en 1900.

(à droite) En 1888, la société Upjohn se lança dans la fabrication de tablettes hypodermiques, que les médecins pouvaient dissoudre dans une solution pour injection chez un patient. En 1893, elle offrait cette seringue et cette boîte de pilules. Les comprimés sont apparus sur le marché en 1899, suivis de la création d'un service des comprimés, en 1900.

（右）1888年、アップジョン社は皮下注射用錠剤の製造を開始した。医師が溶解して患者に注射するものである。1893年までには、この注射器と錠剤をセットにしたケースも発売している。1899年には圧縮錠を市場化し、1900年に錠剤部門が設立された。

Toward the end of the century, a tragic fire in Kalamazoo had the unexpected outcome of bringing to Upjohn one of its outstanding salesmen of the early years, Frederick Childs, as well as several other experienced people. Board-certified as a drugstore clerk, Childs was working for Hall Brothers, a small Kalamazoo chemical firm, when fire struck it on February 26, 1898. Ten people died, and Hall Brothers went out of business. Childs, who was married to the daughter of W. E.'s sister Mary, Alice Sidnam, then came to work for Upjohn. Born an extrovert, he had a flair for sales. With his agreeable ways and persuasive talk, he could reach physicians, and he had enough drugstore know-how to be a one-man innovator in product development. Childs made his presence felt at Upjohn. Its line was soon broadened to include fluid and powdered extracts.

W. E. also had his own ideas about salesmanship. In the early years, he traveled to England to explore the sale of pills. Company legend has it that his mission suffered because he wore a bowler hat instead of the top hat then typical of British businessmen. In any event, nothing much came from the trip, but in 1890 an Englishman in top hat and frock coat called on F. L. Upjohn in the New York sales office. The visitor, John Timpson, wondered if his firm might represent Upjohn in England. The Upjohns agreed, and Timpson and his successors marketed Upjohn products in the United Kingdom from then until as late as 1939.

In the 1890s, the W. E. Upjohns were becoming established and respected in their new hometown. W. E. ran for Kalamazoo city alderman in 1892 and was elected. Two more children joined Winifred and Harold (as the oldest two were called) — Dorothy, born in 1890, and Genevieve, in 1894. The family had long since outgrown the two-room apartment on South Burdick Street and was now living at the corner of Park and Vine.

Those years saw Dr. Upjohn make his first investment, in 1895, in what he later said "often saved my life." For $1,000 he bought 40 acres of a farm near Augusta, Michigan, owned by his widowed mother-in-law. Foresting had stripped that area of trees in the mid-nineteenth century, and the land was rocky and reluctant. But for W. E., the inveterate builder and tinkerer, it had charm and distinct potential.

At first, he thought he'd run a creamery, using water power produced by damming a brook that ran through the property. That scheme faltered, so he shelved it. But as one option dwindled, W. E. usually set out in a different direction — and so it came about that his summer home, Brook Lodge, eventually stood beside the dammed-up pond. At intervals, W. E. added to the acreage, and he hired a youthful Dutchman, John DeYoung, to farm it for him. Later, in times of stress, nothing delighted the owner more than to reach for his hat, leave the office, and head for his new retreat. There he could forget everything. Rachel and he shared a love of flowers, so he decided to grow various species — irises, lilacs, poppies. When for one reason or another they failed, his interest shifted to peonies. Over time, he planted more than 650 varieties of peonies on 40 acres. They blossomed into an abundant annual display with few rivals anywhere.

INTO THE 1900s

The twentieth century dawned with promise and an intense, restless optimism throughout the United States. A June 1900 photograph of Dr. W. E. Upjohn symbolizes the era ahead: poised at the helm of a Locomobile, he looks eager to set out on the open road. The vehicle's prior owner, a local merchant, had gotten cold feet over piloting it out of his yard, but W. E. was not that timid. Driving off as new owner of the Locomobile, he became the first Kalamazooan to buy a used car.

The 1900 Upjohn catalog offered, among its more than 2,000 products, a commodity almost as unique for the company as the Locomobile was for the city. Upjohn had started producing compressed *tablets*, using a metal dye to stamp them from medicinal powders. This was a quicker, more efficient way to manufacture a form of medicine than building up the friable pill layer by layer. Also, the compressed tablet dissolved as readily in the patient as the friable pill and, purportedly, was easier to swallow. Finally, the compressed tablet was gaining favor among physicians, a fact Upjohn could not ignore.

True, the catalog's introduction praised at length the friable pill's features, but apparently competition from the more popular and more economically produced tablets had squeezed the Kalamazoo partners into adding that form to their line. Actually, Upjohn had been trying to master tablet-making since 1888, when hypodermic tablets debuted in the catalog. Development was slow and frustrating, but by 1900 a Tablet Department had been formed. The Upjohns had seen the future.

(left) The Upjohn display at the 1893 Chicago World's Fair showed the "characteristic push and energy of that progressive house," wrote one observer. Inside the glass and mahogany case were some 3,500,000 multi-colored friable pills. W.E. personally handed out miniature pill-bottle stick pins (insert) to passersby.

(izquierda) Esta exhibición de Upjohn en la Feria Mundial de Chicago en 1893 muestra el "empuje y energía, características de esta progresista empresa", como escribió un observador. Dentro del gabinete de cristal y caoba había cerca de 3.500.000 píldoras desintegrables de diversos colores. W.E. personalmente distribuía estos fístoles en forma de frasco de píldoras en miniatura (véase inserción) entre los transeúntes.

(à gauche) La présentation de la société Upjohn Pill and Granule à l'Exposition internationale de Chicago, en 1893, "constitue la preuve tangible du dynamisme et de la vitalité de cette entreprise progressiste", écrivait à ce propos un observateur. Sous la vitrine de verre et d'acajou, il y avait 3.500.000 pilules friables multicolores. W.E. distribuait personnellement ces épingles ornées d'un flacon de pilules miniature aux visiteurs.

（左）1893年、シカゴ世界博覧会に出品したアップジョン錠剤・顆粒製造会社の展示は「エネルギッシュに躍進するアップジコン社の特長をよく現わしている」と論評された。ガラスと、マホガニーで作られたケースの中には、種々の色のついた崩れる丸薬 350万個が納められていた。この博覧会では、W. E. アップジョン自からが、見学者に薬瓶を型どった衿どめを配った。

(right) This early 1890s Upjohn Pill and Granule Co. ink blotter gave prospective customers all the pertinent information, including the company logo, officers, and addresses of sales offices in New York, under Frederick L. Upjohn, and London, under agent John Timpson.

(derecha) Este papel secante de la Upjohn Pill and Granule Co., ofrecía a los posibles clientes toda la información pertinente, incluyendo el logotipo de la compañía, funcionarios y direcciones de las oficinas de ventas en Nueva York, a cargo de Frederick L. Upjohn, y en Londres, a cargo del agente John Timpson.

(à droite) Buvard datant de 1890, de la société Upjohn Pill and Granule, donnant aux clients toutes sortes d'informations utiles : emblème de la compagnie, dessin de marque, employés et adresses des bureaux de vente à New York, avec Frederick Upjohn, et à Londres, avec pour agent John Timpson.

（右）アップジョン錠剤・顆粒製造会社の、1890年代初期のインク吸取り紙には、社章や役員名、また、フレデリックL. アップジョンの傘下にあったニューヨーク支社の住所や、ロンドンにあったジョン・ティンプソン販売代理店の住所など、見込み客に提供するアップジョン関係の情報のすべてが記載されていた。

Early in 1905, a likable young wholesale druggist, Waters H. Sellman, became an agent for the line. As Sellman recalled, W. E. told him that "if I developed the Upjohn business, he might establish a branch and the managership would be given to me."

Waters Sellman was just getting going when the 1906 San Francisco earthquake wiped him out. Three days after the quake, a cabled message brought $500 from Dr. W. E. to help him get back on his feet, and once a new inventory arrived, Sellman started walking. As L. N. recorded, "He sold his stock out practically by peddling, carrying in a pack on his back as much as he could start out with in the morning, and going up and down the hills . . . until he sold out to the druggists." It was a big challenge, but Sellman had all the talent it took. It did not faze him to ask several physicians to help him detail some new Upjohn products. They agreed and wrote out helpful product justifications, which Sellman blithely used with great impact on 150 other doctors.

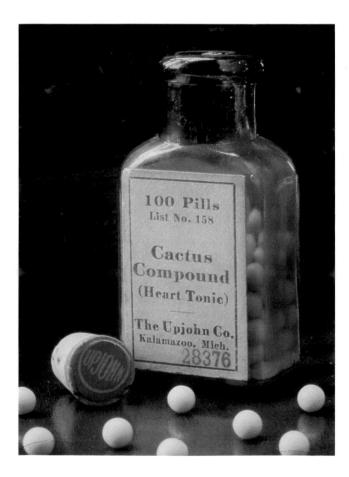

As the area grew and the business burgeoned, W. E. decided that Sellman and Company should become part of The Upjohn Company. Waters Sellman drove a hard bargain. He'd agree only if the founder guaranteed he would run the San Francisco office as long as he lived. Sellman also wanted cash for his $50,000 worth of inventory. In a compromise, W. E. gave him half the amount in cash, half in company stock. Those shares would play a key role decades later when Upjohn became a publicly held corporation.

With the San Francisco office converted into an Upjohn branch in 1911, Waters Sellman concentrated on pushing the company's products far and wide, even overseas. Before turning over the branch managership to his son Richard, Sellman had Upjohn products traveling to the Philippines, China, and India.

One item that Sellman had to detail was Caripeptic Liquid, perhaps the greatest of Fred Childs's contributions to Upjohn. Knowing that the company had to have new specialties to survive, Childs decided to do some mixing and sampling on his own. One lead stemmed from a journal article on the Carica papaya and how its juice was used to soften raw meat. Childs and an associate mixed malt extract, dried papaya juice, 16 percent alcohol (as a preservative), and a secret flavoring. Then Childs worked up a slogan: "A vegetable digestant active under all conditions, acid, alkaline, and neutral." The product, Caripeptic Liquid, came out in 1902, getting a hearty sales push, along with Palmo-Dionin (a sweet yellow cough syrup — Upjohn's first) and Pill Methylene Blue Compound (called "the urinary antiseptic" in ad copy). Caripeptic led Upjohn sales for the next six years. As an active aid to digestion, it continued to find a market through World War II, reaching a sales peak of $304,656 in 1945.

Fred Childs had other ideas. One was his "$5 for $1" campaign, built on quarter-page ads in the *Journal of the American Medical Association* and other magazines. The illustration — a Pill Methylene Blue Compound bottle, or a pint of Caripeptic Liquid, or both — shared space with copy offering the two products for $1. List prices and shipping costs were estimated to total $5 — hence, the "$5 for $1" lure. W. E. eventually balked, condemning the campaign as "cheap advertising reaching a cheap class of buyers."

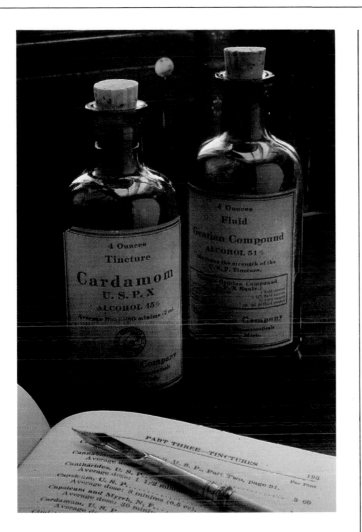

CREATING A DISTINCTIVE SALES FORCE

Those were years when an Upjohn salesman had to be resourceful to make up for all-too-thin specialty lists. George C. McClelland, who took over as sales manager on December 1, 1906, decided his salespeople should have a badge of distinction. So he designed a cabin-style sample bag from alligator skin. (Today, the "alligator" bags, though made of textured cowhide, still mark Upjohn's field sales force, and are carried by many others in the company.)

Soon after, McClelland hired 22-year-old Leo B. Austin from west of Kalamazoo, handed him an alligator bag heavy with samples, gave him $100 in expense money, and sent him off to cover a territory reaching to

(left) By 1900, the Council on Pharmacy and Chemistry of the American Medical Association was chastising the company for selling Cactus Compound, an alleged heart tonic with little therapeutic value. Upjohn dropped the product from its catalog, but unsolicited sales continued until 1947.

(izquierda) Para 1900 el Consejo de Farmacia y Química de la Asociación Médica Norteamericana censuraba severamente a la compañia por vender Compuesto de Cactus (Cactus Compound), un supuesto tónico para el corazón con poco valor terapéutico. Upjohn retiró el producto de su catálogo, pero las ventas no solicitadas del mismo continuaron hasta 1947.

(à gauche) En 1900, le Conseil de pharmacologie et de chimie de l'Association médicale américaine harcelait la société parce qu'elle vendait des produits à base de cactus, un tonique pour le coeur sans grande valeur thérapeutique. La société Upjohn enleva le produit de son catalogue, mais les ventes n'en baissèrent pas pour autant et continuèrent jusqu'en 1947.

（左）1900年にアメリカ医師会の薬事部会は、カクタス製剤を、強心剤として効果が低いとし、製品カタログからはずすよう勧告した。アップジョン社はこの勧告に従ったが、求めに応じて販売するという形で、この製品は1947年まで売られた。

(right) By 1900 the more than 2,000 Upjohn products included compressed tablets, powders, and a variety of fluid products, such as cordials, wines, tinctures, elixirs, and syrups. To reflect this growth in the product line the company adopted a new name, The Upjohn Company, in 1902.

(derecha) Para 1900 los más de 2000 productos Upjohn incluían tabletas comprimidas, polvos y una variedad de productos fluidos tales como cordiales, vinos, tinturas, elixires y jarabes. Para reflejar este crecimiento en la linea de productos la compañia adoptó un nuevo nombre — The Upjohn Company — en 1902.

(à droite) En 1900, plus de 2.000 produits Upjohn (comprimés, poudres, et toute une gamme de produits liquides, tels que liqueurs, vins, teintures, élixirs et sirops) étaient vendus sur le marché. Pour corroborer cette croissance de la gamme des produits, la compagnie changea de nom et s'appela : la société Upjohn, en 1902.

（右）1900年には、アップジョン社の製品は 2,000種以上にのぼり、その中には圧縮錠や粉末のほか、強壮剤、ワイン、チンキ、エリキシル剤、シロップ等の液剤が加わった。広げられたプロダクトラインにふさわしく、1902年に社名を「The Upjohn Company」と変更した。

the Mississippi River. Austin had studied a bit of pharmacy, but he had to live largely by his wits as he called on dispensing physicians. He made a practice of standing when he spoke to a doctor. His rationale was simple. "As long as he was sitting down," Austin explained, "I had control of him. But if he stood up, I lost control of him, because that way we were on the same level."

Austin had another tactic. When a nurse would ask him who was here to see the doctor, he had a set reply: "Just say Upjohn." For many years Austin was known far and wide as "Upjohn." Later, he shared in the task of recruiting and building Upjohn's sales force. If he saw a young man doing a good job as a store clerk, he would interview him. If Austin liked what he heard, he'd hire the man on the spot.

Training of sales personnel was just as impromptu. L. N. described the approach used before 1905: "[It] was a rather simple, unorganized undertaking . . . and after meeting the various people the salesman should know at the office, plus a little last-minute coaching from the sales manager, and perhaps a benediction from W. E. U., the salesman was considered to be a finished product, all ready for business."

Abbreviated, informal techniques like that could backfire. One sales candidate introduced himself with slick talk and by making his calling card disappear up his sleeve. He was immediately hired, briefed on the friable pill, and shipped out to Illinois. Soon, 1,000-lot orders were coming in for Upjohn's Pill Iron, Quinine and Strychnine (I.Q. & S.). Then the man vanished, and complaints from Illinois physicians poured in. It seemed he had told them of a dandy way to save money: They could buy 1,000 I.Q. & S. pills, pour them into a gallon bottle, and then fill it with water. That, he declared, would produce a gallon of Elixir I.Q. & S. at a lower cost than the actual elixir. Of course, the efficacy of the watered-down product was also considerably reduced.

Sales department procedures were bound to change, notably in special-formula and buyer's-label products. These items reached a sales peak in the early 1900s.

Typical of the former, Upjohn made a small laxative pill for The Sydney Ross Company, a venture started independently in New York City in 1891 by F. L. Upjohn and Clarence Riker, a traveling shoe salesman. (The firm's name was borrowed from a doctor's name on a tombstone the two men spotted in a Brooklyn cemetery while on a Sunday outing.) Riker was sure the laxative would sell big in Latin America. Sydney Ross sales did take off, climbing to 15 million pills a month. One special touch: the figure of the Madonna was worked into the Sydney Ross label to help propel sales in the largely Roman Catholic countries of Latin America. This type of contract added what the company considered "good fillers," something for the production department to work on in slack periods.

At the same time, Upjohn had for a while an alternative label: The Lawrence-Townley Company. This label was used in cases where a druggist wished to purchase small lots of buyer's-label style products. Since it was not cost-effective to print the druggist's own label on such small orders, Upjohn used the Lawrence-Townley label, which it had printed inexpensively in large quantities. Its name combined the middle names of F. L. and J. T. Upjohn.

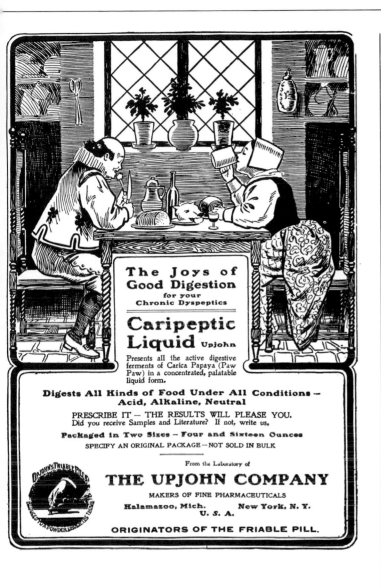

The Joys of Good Digestion for your Chronic Dyspeptics

Caripeptic Liquid Upjohn

Presents all the active digestive ferments of Carica Papaya (Paw Paw) in a concentrated, palatable liquid form.

Digests All Kinds of Food Under All Conditions — Acid, Alkaline, Neutral

PRESCRIBE IT — THE RESULTS WILL PLEASE YOU.
Did you receive Samples and Literature? If not, write us,

Packaged in Two Sizes — Four and Sixteen Ounces
SPECIFY AN ORIGINAL PACKAGE—NOT SOLD IN BULK

From the Laboratory of

THE UPJOHN COMPANY
MAKERS OF FINE PHARMACEUTICALS
Kalamazoo, Mich.   New York, N. Y.
U. S. A.

ORIGINATORS OF THE FRIABLE PILL.

(left) When a local businessman became too frightened to drive it, W.E. purchased this 1899 Locomobile, the first automobile in Kalamazoo. Here, W.E. has just returned in his steam-powered car from a business trip to Warsaw, Indiana, nearly 100 miles south of Kalamazoo.

(izquierda) Cuando un comerciante local llegó a sentirse muy atemorizado de manejar este Locomobile de 1899, W.E. lo compró, siendo el primer automóvil en Kalamazoo. En esta foto W. E., acaba de regresar en su carro accionado a vapor de un viaje de negocios a Warsaw, Indiana, casi a 100 millas al sur de Kalamazoo.

(à gauche) W.E. Upjohn acheta cette "locomobile" de 1899, la première automobile de Kalamazoo, lorsque son propriétaire, un homme d'affaires de la ville, fut pris de panique et eut peur de la conduire. Sur cette photo, W.E. Upjohn vient de rentrer d'un voyage d'affaires à Warsaw (Indiana), à près de 160 km de Kalamazoo, dans sa voiture à vapeur.

（左）土地の実業家がこわがって運転できなかった、1899年型ロコモビールをW．E．アップジョンは購入した。カラマズーで最初の自動車であった。　この蒸気自動車を駆って、カラマズーの約160km南、インディアナ州ワールソー市まで、商用で出かけ、戻ってきた時の写真。

(right) This 1903 medical journal ad implored physicians to prescribe Caripeptic Liquid for "The Joys of Good Digestion." Enjoying good sales throughout its lifespan (1902-1981), Caripeptic Liquid eventually was used more as a vehicle for other types of digestive aids than by itself.

(derecha) Este anuncio en una revista médica de 1903 pedía a los médicos que recetaran Líquido Caripéptico para "El placer de una buena digestión". El Líquido Caripéptico tuvo gran aceptación durante todo el período de su producción (1902-1981), y finalmente se usó más como un vehículo para otros tipos de ayuda digestiva que por sus propios efectos.

(à droite) Pour "les joies de la bonne digestion", prescrivez le liquide Caripeptique. Tel est le message que le journal médical de 1903 adressait aux médecins de l'époque. Battant tous les records de vente (de 1902 à 1981), le liquide Caripeptique, qui a cessé d'exister, servait davantage de véhicule pour d'autres adjuvants digestifs que comme médicament en soi.

（右）1903年の医学雑誌に載った広告。カリペプティック液を「優れた消化作用を得る喜び」というキャッチフレーズで宣伝している。製品のライフサイクル（1902〜1981）を通じて、いつも高い販売量を誇ったカリペプティック液は、単独で投与されるより、他の消化薬との併用剤として用いられることが多かった。

In time, the company saw disadvantages in these services. Buyers nagged to get special treatment. The plant had to cope with a lot of small, special orders. The business was very competitive, and, when challenged with W. E.'s "Is there a profit in it?" the answer was often no. But these sales helped tide the company over until 1908, when a highly successful new Upjohn product, Phenolax, made it possible to drop special-formula, buyer's-label, and dummy-label output.

(left) At the turn of the century, bottling of fluid extracts such as tinctures, cordials, wines, and syrups required a gravity-fed hose from the floor above. As late as the 1930s employees still grappled with this messy method.

(izquierda) A la vuelta del siglo, el embotellado de extractos líquidos como tinturas, cordiales, vinos y jarabes requería el uso de una manguera alimentada por gravedad desde el piso superior. Aún en los años 30 los empleados utilizaban este método desmañado.

(à gauche) Au début du siècle, la mise en bouteille des extraits de liquides tels que teintures, liqueurs, vins, et sirops réclamait l'utilisation d'un siphon pour transvaser les liquides d'un niveau à un autre plus bas. Jusqu'à la fin des années 30, les employés utilisaient encore cette méthode encombrante et peu commode.

（左）19世紀末、チンク剤、強心剤、ワインやシロップといった液体エキスをビンに詰める時は、タンクを高い位置に置き、ホースをつないで作業を行なった。1930年代にいたるまで、社員たちは、この繁雑な方式に苦戦していた。

(right) J.T. Upjohn (lower left) and W.E. Upjohn (top left) pose on the steps of Building 4 with some of the 97 employees of 1904.

(derecha) J. T. Upjohn (abajo, a la izquierda) y W.E. Upjohn (arriba, a la izquierda) posan en los escalones del Edificio 4 con algunos de los 97 empleados de la compañia en 1904.

(à droite) Photo-souvenir de J.T. Upjohn (à gauche, au premier plan) et W.E. Upjohn (à gauche, au second plan), entourés de quelques-uns des 97 employés de la société, en 1904, devant le bâtiment No. 4.

（右）1904年当時、アップジョン社には97名の社員が在籍していた。そのうちの何人かと4号館の前で。前列左がJ．T．アップジョン、後列左がW．E．アップジョン。

ARRIVALS AND DEPARTURES

In 1904, Henry Uriah Upjohn's oldest child, Lawrence Northcote, joined the firm at the age of 31, beginning an association as an employee that would last almost half a century.

After high school and clerking at the Kalamazoo Savings Bank, L. N. had gone to the University of Michigan Medical School, graduating in 1900. He then went west — to the University of Oklahoma, where he taught anatomy and pathology, helped start the medical school, served as school physician, and coached basketball. When L. N. returned to Kalamazoo in 1904 because of the serious illness of his first child, Dr. W. E. invited him to work temporarily for Upjohn. Accepting the offer, L. N. learned his way around the head office, collected tips from Fred Childs about salesmanship, and on December 1, 1906, moved to New York City to take over that sales office. There, he settled into the post that his Uncle Frederick Lawrence had occupied. Born in 1857, F. L. had declared that he would retire on reaching 50. He made good on that promise, stepping down in late 1906, then embarked on a world tour. He would, however, return from his trip not fully finished with Upjohn business.

L. N. Upjohn, the new man in New York, had few illusions about his talents. "I never sold anything to a doctor in my life," he recalled, "and didn't consider myself a salesman. But I taught the salesmen what they were to say." Whenever a new product came in, L. N. would summon the salesmen and teach them all about it from a physician's point of view. Gradually the conference training method came into being.

Meanwhile, the head office in Michigan had a new presence — the founder's only son, William Harold, born in 1884 and known to everyone as Harold. He started with the firm in 1907, several years after attending Kalamazoo College, where he took a number of mathematics courses but was not interested in completing the four-year curriculum. W. E. very much wanted Harold in the company. There was another factor in Harold's decision to join the firm, as his youngest sister, Genevieve, recalled. "He wanted to get married," she said. "In those days they either had a job before they married, or they didn't get married." So Harold Upjohn took the job and was married to Grace Bray on February 20, 1909.

Harold had wanted to be an architect. But once he signed on with the company, he gave it his all. He completed his formal education at the University of Michigan, receiving an A.B. degree in Bacteriology in 1915. As time went by, he became increasingly valuable at many posts in the company. He took an interest in his father's new accounting method for figuring costs separately in sales and production, and, aided by his assistant, Sumner B. Upham, he put his statistical know-how to work for the sales force.

Harold had another dimension of value: a cheerful disposition. His sister Winifred later said, "Whatever we did with Harold, it was always fun."

In a career of 21 years with the company, Harold grew to become the obvious successor to W. E., only to have his life and career cut short by a postsurgical embolism at the age of 44.

Another 1907 newcomer in the head office, a man destined to become Harold's brother-in-law, was Dr. S. Rudolph Light. After graduating from the University of Michigan Medical School in 1904 and interning in psychiatry for a year, Light joined the staff of the Kalamazoo State Hospital (now known as Kalamazoo Regional Psychiatric Hospital) as a resident physician. In 1908, he married Winifred Upjohn. His major contributions to the company came during his many years as production manager, vice president, and member of the board of directors.

Meanwhile, the founder and his family had moved in early 1905 to the former William Wood estate at 530 West South Street, little more than half a mile from the company's expanding complex of buildings in downtown Kalamazoo. Only a few months later, on July 4, Rachel Babcock Upjohn died after a lingering illness. She was 49. Her marriage of 27 years to Dr. W. E. had spanned the birth and early struggles of The Upjohn Company.

THE PHENOLAX PHENOMENON

In this first decade of the new century, Upjohn desperately needed a bell-ringer of a product to succeed the outmoded friable pill. Phenolax was that item. And W. E. himself proposed the touch that converted what had been a losing product elsewhere to a winner so big that it was selling at the rate of 27 million tablets a year four decades after its introduction.

Who first led Upjohn into developing the drug? That depends on whose recollection one prefers. S. R. Light wrote that a "small independent chemical broker" brought the active ingredient to the attention of Harold Upjohn. L. N. Upjohn asserted that Fred Childs came to him with a substance and said, "Here's something new, a *tasteless* laxative. See if you can find out what it is." J. T. Upjohn claimed credit for the discovery in a letter he wrote to the company board in March 1909.

W.E.'s fountain pen and leather briefcase lie upon company stationery as it appeared in 1908.

La pluma fuente y el portafolio de W.E. aparecen sobre papel membretado de la compañía, tal como aparecía en 1908.

La plume et le porte-documents de cuir de William Upjohn sur le papier à en-tête de la compagnie, en 1908.

1908年から使われた社名入り便箋とW．E．アッ プジヨン愛用の万年筆、皮のブリーフ・ケース。

Although there is no way today to choose between these accounts, development seems to have begun when some material was delivered to Upjohn's assay lab in 1907. The substance was a familiar chemical agent, phenolphthalein. Someone in Europe had found accidentally that the material acted as a laxative. Lehn & Fink of New York had used the chemical to make a laxative called Purgen, with little commercial success. Another firm tried, with no better results.

Undismayed, the men of Upjohn brought the substance to Dr. J. T., in charge of manufacturing. He took some of the chemical, blended it with another laxative compound, and made a batch of taste-free pills; he even came up with the name Phenolax. It was almost ready for marketing when W. E. was told about it. His reaction was negative. "We have no business making the same mistake the other companies made before us," he said. Then he turned creative. "Why make a pill?" he asked. "Why not produce a *flavored tablet* to give people the pleasant-tasting cathartic they are waiting for?"

With that, the process shifted to the Tablet Department. There, Charlie and Will Little did some experimenting and soon had a new product to show: a rectangular, pink, mint-flavored wafer, scored in the middle so it could be broken in half. Dr. W. E. approved, and Phenolax went on sale May 1, 1908. The product was billed as a "palatable cathartic." To support the product's introduction, J. T. had a small booklet printed that featured an illustration of the little pink wafers on the cover and a description of phenolphthalein's action inside. The booklet was mailed to every physician in the country along with a sample card containing 10 Phenolax wafers under a parchment cover.

The market results were extraordinary: 19,774,000 tablets the first year; 45,340,000 in 1909; and more than 100,000,000 in 1914. The Tablet Department had to scale up quickly. Will Little devised a machine with two punches and dies on the compressing head. Several of the machines were brought on line, and Upjohn accelerated into 24-hour, three-shift production.

The product was on the march, and Upjohn's fortunes moved forward with it. The company's renewed prosperity was especially timely because it was occurring at a point when the ties between the three Upjohn brothers were being badly — and publicly — strained.

AN ISSUE OF CONTROL

The June 10, 1909, headline in the *Grand Rapids Press* summed up a controversy that had been simmering for several years among the key Upjohns: "Upjohn Brothers Fight For Control." The text asserted that F. L. Upjohn, once again interested in the business after his short-lived retirement in 1906, and J. T. had tried to buy enough stock to take control of the company. Their opponent, W. E., "took steps" to gain control himself by purchasing shares from the Upjohn treasury. Under a court injunction, stock transactions were frozen for 30 days.

This was scarcely a friendly disagreement. The newspaper reported, "The brothers have not been on speaking terms except on most important points in business for months." And people outside were well aware of the squabble. Said L. N. Upjohn, "It was some row . . . and they made it public. There was no secrecy about it. J. T. went around town writing against W. E."

After 20 years together in the firm, the three brothers had developed different styles. To F. L., retirement at 50 had seemed to sum it up. W. E. had quite another outlook. L. N. noted many years later that he could almost hear his uncle, the president, saying, " 'I will make the decisions.' " As for J. T., Dr. Light had this view: "The difficulties seemed to arise from J. T. U.'s jealous resentment of many of the actions of W. E. U. in manufacturing and sales activities." Soon enough, F. L. and J. T. learned they were up against a "diabolically resourceful fighter," as L. N. wrote, a man determined to gain full control of the company "in order to preserve it from threatened stagnation."

The brothers' actions were being viewed critically from many directions. F. L. felt obliged in 1907 to write stockholders to explain that his "private interests," such as The Sydney Ross Company, actually helped in "creating opportunities" for Upjohn. He maintained that information from Sydney Ross salesmen in Latin America could bolster Upjohn marketing in that region.

In June 1908, J. T. wrote to the board on another issue. Since about 1904, he said, W. E. had been "to a considerable extent using the Company's money for his own purposes. . ." J. T. had asked the bookkeeper for an accounting; it showed that as of that June 1, W. E. owed the firm $12,574.82, money used mainly "for house construction and other purely personal matters. . ." J. T. deplored what he saw as "a growing tendency to arbitrary management. . ." A board-designated committee looked into the overdraft, found that W. E. did not question it, and reported that he would begin paying it off, putting up $29,830 of his own stock as security.

Soon, J. T. was protesting again. W. E. had started buying shares from various stockholders, he charged, "without referring the matter . . . to the Board of Directors. . ." It was part of a pattern of what he called "arbitrary dictatorial and possibly clandestine methods. . ." W. E. laid out a countercharge in a letter to the board. His efforts to install a checking system to protect against errors in manufacture and shipment, he stated, had been "thwarted" by the "officer in charge" of manufacturing, his brother J. T.

The frictions intensified in early 1909. By this time, F. L. and J. T. had hired a lawyer; negotiations with W. E. had stalemated. F. L., more moderate than J. T., proposed that the three brothers meet for lunch at the staid Park Club on South Street, and W. E. concurred. There they quickly got to the point.

"Well, what do you think we should do?" F. L. asked an unsmiling W. E.

"I think you had better get some other attorney," the company president replied. He suspected that their counsel wanted to take the entire matter into court.

F. L. and J. T. accepted, and Harry C. Howard was retained to chart a settlement. Finally an agreement materialized: W. E. would buy out his brothers for $208,523 ($50,000 in cash, $54,523 in notes, and $104,000 in bonds). Dr. W. E. did not have the money, so he went to the local banks — chiefly to his friend E. J. Phelps of Kalamazoo National Bank. The papers were signed, notes and bonds were exchanged, and on August 9, 1909, a new company emerged. Its officers: W. E., president; Dr. S. Rudolph Light, vice president; J. S. McColl, treasurer; and Dr. H. B. Osborn, a prominent local physician, secretary. These four made up a new board, along with Harold Upjohn and Dr. Osborn's brother, lawyer J. W. Osborn.

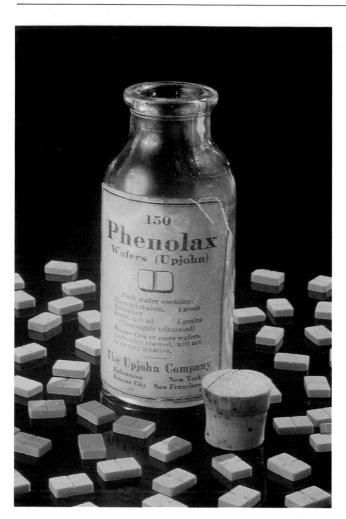

The dust had not fully settled, but W. E. had faith in the promise of Phenolax for the company's security. It turned out that Phenolax profits would pay off the bondholders five years early.

In a bizarre way, the success of Phenolax almost destroyed Upjohn in March 1911. The fourth floor of the building where Phenolax was made was in a constant flux. New, more efficient machinery continually altered the flow of work across the department. Each machine had to be bolted to the floor, and when one was moved or replaced, that often left previous bolt holes open. Early one evening, drying-room heat from the third floor ignited a fire, and flames were sucked through the ceiling by the draft created by the open bolt holes on the fourth floor. By the time firemen got the upper hand, the building interior had been gutted and two other buildings had been damaged.

W. E. was out of town on business. Summoned back, he huddled with Charlie Little, who was in charge of the plant. Calling in an expert witness, the company demonstrated how much stock and equipment had been ruined. Persuaded, the insurance company awarded Upjohn $80,000. W. E. even convinced the insurance company to allow Upjohn Company employees to do the clean-up and salvage work, rather than having it done by outsiders. The result was that no Upjohn employee was laid off while the facility was down. Most of the insurance money, Dr. Light wrote, went to putting the plant into "better condition" than before; W. E. applied the remainder to his debt from the reorganization.

With the work of restoration ended, a happy sequel took place. W. E. called in Charlie Little. "You did a wonderful job," the president told him. "Here is a check for $1,000, and here is some stationery with your name on it as superintendent of plants."

1913: YEAR OF PROMISE

In spite of Phenolax, in spite of the organizational serenity brought about by the brothers' settlement, Upjohn faced a tough fiscal situation at the threshold of World War I. "There were times," Treasurer John McColl remembered, "when we wondered whether we would be able to meet all the obligations as they fell due, and many bank loans had to be renewed over and over again."

As if that dilemma weren't painful enough, Upjohn had the ill fortune at that same time to stumble into what L. N. labeled a "disaster": Kazoo Mints. In 1912, two company salesmen got the idea of producing mint-flavored lozenges. W. E. liked the scheme because it could keep the plant's costly machines busy. So Upjohn pushed ahead. But then New York State lawyers stepped in and blocked the whole project. It seemed that the starch being used as a lubricant on the punch die, while perfectly legal for pharmaceutical manufacture, was classified as an adulterant in the manufacture of food under food and drug legislation. Unwilling to invest further in what was beginning to appear to be at best a sideline, Upjohn paid a $50 fine and surrendered its whole output of Kazoo Mints to federal authorities, who dumped the candies into New York Harbor. Harold Upjohn's postmortem: "It is strange that we should go out of our way to make trouble for ourselves."

The next year, 1913, surely had to be a better one, and in many ways it was. Among 1913's positive events was the opening of a new company headquarters that suggested both elegance and quality. Called the "White Office," it had been designed by that former candidate for an architect's drawing board, Harold Upjohn, and his capable friend Lew Crockett, whom Harold had hired away from a local architectural firm in 1911. Crockett directed Upjohn's wide-ranging building program.

The classical White Office, fronted by four Doric columns, stood on a lawn east of Henrietta Street, flanked on the south by giant elms. The founder's desk was positioned behind five ceiling-high plate glass windows in the front. In back of the desk, two steps up, Harold had created a solarium; there, W. E. could putter around in a pleasing tangle of ferns, palms, and seasonal plants. Nearby stood a three-foot-high Chinese temple gong (still used as a theatrical prop in Kalamazoo's Civic Auditorium), and underfoot, a Persian rug. In the basement, the crew had built a feature requested by W. E.: a 10 x 12 x 4-foot swimming pool. When it was filled, W. E. invited Lew Crockett to join him for an inaugural plunge. No one recalls that the pool was ever used again — except to hold coal for the president's fireplace upstairs. The White Office remained a handsome ornament of the firm until 1934, when it had to be sacrificed to make room for new structures.

(left) The pink, scored Phenolax wafer became the first pleasant-tasting laxative marketed in the U.S. Introduced in 1908, its overwhelming sales success picked up the company's sagging earnings and helped finance the birth of Upjohn's research and development program.

(izquierda) La oblea Phenolax, de color rosado, llegó a ser el primer laxante de sabor agradable que se vendió en los Estados Unidos. Introducida en el mercado en 1908, su abrumador éxito comercial compensó la disminución de ganancias de la compañia y ayudó a financiar el inicio del programa de investigación y desarrollo de Upjohn.

(à gauche) La tablette rose, Phenolax, au goût délicieux, est devenue le premier laxatif commercialisé aux Etats-Unis. Introduit sur le marché en 1908, il a battu tous les records de ventes, aidant ainsi à accroître les revenus de la compagnie. Ses ventes record ont aussi aidé au financement d'un programme de recherches qui débutait à la société Upjohn.

（左）ピンクのフェノラックス・ウェハースは、アメリカで初めて市場化された味のよい緩下剤であった。1908年の発売以来、圧倒的な人気で、アップジョン社の収益を上げるのに大いに貢献し、研究開発部門が誕生する財政的な基盤となった。

(right) Ink blotters, postcards, pamphlets, samples, special prices — even drugstore displays drawn by a popular cartoonist of the day — helped advertise Phenolax to the druggist and the lay public. And all helped Phenolax become part of the zany folklore of the early 1900s.

(derecha) Secantes, postales, folletos, muestras, precios especiales — inclusive anuncios de boticas dibujados por un popular caricaturista de esa época — contribuyeron a anunciar Phenolax a los boticarios y al público no profesional. Y todo ello ayudó a Phenolax a formar parte del absurdo folklore de los primeros años de 1900.

(à droite) Cartes postales, buvards, brochures, échantillons, annonces de soldes, et même des caricatures populaires de l'époque montrant des étalages de pharmacies, ont contribué à la campagne publicitaire pour Phenolax. Et Phenolax est devenu partie intégrante du décor des années 1900.

（右）葉書、パンフレット、試供品、特別価格などが、フェノラックスの宣伝に使われた。また、当時の人気まんが家による薬局の店頭ディスプレーも、フェノラックスを薬剤師や、一般の人たちに宣伝するのに役立った。こうしてフェノラックスは、1900年代初頭の風俗を伝えるものの一つとして数えられるようになった。

(left) W.E. Upjohn (1910). One year after assuming full control of the company from his two surviving brothers, W.E. presided over a company with a workforce numbering nearly 200, annual sales surpassing $900,000, and one of the nation's number one specialty pharmaceuticals — Phenolax.

(izquierda) W.E. Upjohn (1910). Un año después de asumir el total control de la compañía de mano de sus dos hermanos vivos aún, W.E. presidió una compañía con una fuerza laboral de cerca de 200 personas, ventas anuales que sobrepasaban los $900.000 y uno de los principales productos farmacéuticos de la nación: el Phenolax.

(à gauche) W.E. Upjohn (1910). Un an après avoir pris la direction de la société Upjohn, succédant ainsi à ses deux autres frères, William Upjohn présidait une entreprise qui employait 200 personnes. Le chiffre d'affaires de la compagnie dépassait 900.000 dollars par an, et le produit pharmaceutique numéro un, battant tous les records de vente sur le marché, était le Phenolax.

（左）**W．E．**アップジョン（1910年）。存命中の二人の弟から会社の経営の全権を引き継いだ一年後、**W．E．**アップジョンは、アップジョン社を社員数およそ200人、年商90万ドルを越える会社にした。アメリカでトップ製品となった新薬、フェノラックスを持つ会社の社長であった。

(right) Tablet Department workers circa 1910 used this cylindrical file to calculate the thickness of coating for different-sized compressed tablet formulas.

(derecha) Los operarios del Departamento de Tabletas, alrededor de 1910, usaban este registro cilíndrico para calcular el grosor de las capas para las fórmulas de tabletas comprimidas de diferentes tamaños.

(à droite) Les employés de la section des comprimés (vers 1910) se servaient de cet instrument cylindrique pour calculer l'épaisseur de la couche de poudre des différents comprimés.

（右）1910年ごろアップジョン社の錠剤部門の社員は、この円柱型やすりを用いて、いろいろな大きさの錠剤のコーティングの厚さを測定した。

Unquestionably one of the first guests to visit that eye-catching office was W. E.'s second wife, Carrie Sherwood Gilmore Upjohn, the widow of dry-goods merchant James F. Gilmore. W. E. and she were married October 25, 1913; she brought into the marriage three sons, Stanley, Irving, and 18-year-old Donald, who would eventually become chairman of Upjohn's board.

Other events carried out 1913's promise as a year of good fortune, as The Upjohn Company added to its complement of 214 employees two men who would make important contributions to the company's development during long years of service.

Franklin G. Varney was invited to join the firm after seven years in the ministry. His first assignment was to assist the head of manufacturing, but soon, at W. E.'s request, the former minister was calling on employees having money troubles or other forms of distress and giving them counsel. It was an easy next step for him to add duties more typical of employee relations, and in due course the Personnel Department was born, with Varney as its head.

©Michigan Historical Collections, The University of Michigan

The hiring of another key employee in 1913 stemmed from the passage of the Pure Food and Drug Act of 1906 and the passage of Upjohn from a mere compounder of drugs to a research-driven pharmaceutical manufacturer. The former required the company to comply with new federal standards for product quality; the latter required that the company's science evolve with the times and with the opportunities at hand. The employee, Dr. Frederick W. Heyl, was to become known as the father of Upjohn research.

THE DAWN OF RESEARCH

For The Upjohn Company, evolution into a research-based pharmaceutical firm began during an era of sharp concern in Washington over the patent medicines that Americans were buying. There was no standard of control over what was in a drug, how much of any ingredient a drug contained, or whether it contained dirt or other contaminants. For years, the chief chemist of the U. S. Department of Agriculture, Dr. Harvey W. Wiley, had argued for a pure food and drugs act; muckraking journalists joined in. One of them, writer Samuel Hopkins Adams, hit at patent nostrums in a series of *Collier's Weekly* articles in which he charged that their makers offered false or exaggerated claims about supposed health cures.

This campaign led to passage of the Pure Food and Drug Act of 1906, also known as the "Wiley Act." Some patent medicine merchants cried foul, but the new law of the land took steps to eliminate phony cures, witches' brews, and snake oil remedies.

The Wiley Act's protections actually turned out to be less than complete, but the legislation put pharmaceutical firms squarely on notice. Inspectors would now be backing up the law with visits to their premises, and products would be checked.

Of course, responsible drug-makers had long been concerned about quality control. Bad drugs were bad business. Even before the Wiley Act, Upjohn had installed a practice of weighing out specific amounts of drugs, then mixing them into a stated dosage and appropriately labeling the package. However, these methods did not always meet the new tolerances laid down by the Wiley Act. Hence, as L. N. Upjohn wrote, "samples of various products from time to time were picked up and we were charged with misbranding. This applied to all houses, and involved no question of malicious or fraudulent intent."

Part of early Upjohn "research" had to do with precise measurements and assays, activity more aptly termed "control." This work was supervised by Arthur L. Crooks,

a colleague of Fred Childs at the former Hall Brothers. Crooks also aided Childs and others in coming up with new compounds. When L. N. entered the company in 1904, he was understudy to Crooks in the Assay Lab.

Gradually the need for trained researchers widened. Production Manager S. R. Light found in 1908 that a new surgical antiseptic ought to be tested along bacteriologic lines before Upjohn put it on the market. That called for preparing culture media, an incubator, and a qualified person to run the tests. W. E., in accord with his penchant for developing his own equipment, ordered the incubator built on site. He also approved the hiring of Dr. David Levy, a local physician skilled in bacteriology, to spend a few hours each day assisting in the lab tests.

(left) Art Crooks (left), Roy Terpening (center), and Fred Staley (right) manned the company's Assay Lab in 1911. Here they tested the weight, color and ingredients of Upjohn products and determined the ingredients of competitors' products.

(izquierda) Art Crooks (izquierda), Roy Terpening (centro) y Fred Staley (derecha) manejaron el Laboratorio de Análisis de la compañía en 1911. Aquí hacían pruebas sobre el peso, color e ingredientes de los productos Upjohn y determinaban los ingredientes de los productos de sus competidores.

(à gauche) En 1911, Art Crooks (à gauche), Roy Terpening (au centre), et Fred Staley (à droite) dirigeaient le laboratoire de contrôle de la firme Upjohn. Ils y vérifiaient le poids, la couleur et les ingrédients des produits Upjohn, et déterminaient ceux des produits concurrents.

（左）アート・クルックス（左）、ロイ・ターペニング（中央）、フレッド・メテーリー（右）は、1911年当時アップジョン社の分析研究所の研究員であった。分析研究所では、研究員がアップジョン社の製品の重さ、色、成分の試験をし、また競争会社の製品の成分チェックも行なっていた。

(right) Frederick W. Heyl, age 28, in 1913, the year he was hired as the company's first Ph.D. chemist. Though hired to establish a more scientific approach to product quality control, Heyl would come to be known as the "Father of Upjohn Research."

(derecha) Frederick W. Heyl, a los 28 años, en 1913, el año que fue contratado como el primer doctor en química de la compañía. Si bien se le contrató para establecer un enfoque más científico, para el control de la calidad del producto, Heyl llegaría a ser conocido como el "Padre de la investigación en Upjohn".

(à droite) Frederick Heyl, 28 ans, en 1913, année où il fut employé comme premier chimiste de la société Upjohn, détenant un doctorat en chimie. Sa tâche consistait à établir, d'une manière scientifique, la qualité des produits, mais sa réputation était celle du "Père de la recherche", comme on l'appelait souvent.

（右）1913年、会社で最初の化学専攻の薬理学博士として入社した、28才のフレデリックW.・ヘイル。ヘイルは品質管理を科学的に行なう方法を確立するために採用されたのであったが、後に〝アップジョン研究部門の父〟として知られるようになった。

By 1912, bacterial vaccines were coming into vogue and Upjohn had decided to enter into this line. But once again the company found itself without experienced personnel. W. E. then authorized Dr. Light, now vice president, to obtain the services of Will Perkins, a well-trained bacteriologist. Perkins was brought in from Ann Arbor and instructed to set up a bacteriologic lab and a small-animal room. It wasn't long before he was producing vaccines. Before the year was out, the new bacteriologist was involving Upjohn in work that came perilously close to another area of science in which the company had little experience — chemistry. "This directed our attention," wrote Light, "to find a capable chemist and engage him."

He soon found himself on the trail of a young chemistry professor at the University of Wyoming, Dr. Frederick W. Heyl, who had formerly been employed at the Federal Food and Drug Laboratories in Chicago. The two men got together, and Heyl agreed to sign on at a salary of $15 for a 50-hour week. He was the first Ph.D. to be employed by the company.

Reporting on August 1, 1913, Dr. Heyl set up shop in the White Office basement. Harold Upjohn and Lew Crockett had the woodpile and coal bin cleared out, brought in a rolltop desk, and put together a 40 x 40-foot work space — Upjohn's first formal chemical control laboratory, which gradually matured into the company's widely respected Research Division. There, in his basement lab, Heyl and his colleagues began the work that would give added dimension to a saying of the founder's: "Mystery is the fabric from which science has been torn."

Observing the flow of new equipment descending into the basement of his new office, and a corresponding pile of receipts on his desk, the founder was somewhat ambivalent about this new business of research. "This is going to cost me $50,000 before it brings any results," he said, "and I don't know where the money is coming from."

Dr. Heyl's Work Begins

Fred Heyl quickly found a lot to do. Initially, he was charged with finding a way to standardize doses of nitroglycerin; Upjohn preparations wound up being too strong or too weak, a problem shared by many

pharmaceutical houses. By May 1914, Dr. Heyl and his assistant, Fred Staley of the Assay Department, had put their solution into an article entitled "Notes on Estimation of Nitroglycerin," the first research paper published by Upjohn personnel.

Later that same year, a first assistant chemist, Dr. Merrill C. Hart, was hired. Before he joined Upjohn, Heyl's research pursuits had centered on extracting the active principle from plants. Now, Drs. Heyl and Hart investigated the basic principles of the ovaries, work which initiated Upjohn's interest in endocrinology.

At most, 14 men and one woman staffed what was called the Research Department until 1933. Working under crowded conditions, they tried to mesh their studies with the needs of physicians. The first product to emerge directly from their efforts was Digitora, an oral digitalis tablet marketed in 1919, five years after investigations in the lab began. The problem had been how to compensate for the varying potency of digitalis, a long-valued agent for treating heart failure. Heyl's team found that tincture of digitalis, shelved for a year, lost 60 percent of its effectiveness. Part of the loss of efficacy, they determined, was the result of the drug being exposed to light. They designed a protective package, and then

dated the tablets as a guide to whether the drug was still potent enough to be of value.

At about the same time, Upjohn field representatives reported another lead for the new research team: a widespread interest among physicians in systemic alkalizers. The company already had a point of departure in its production of granular effervescing sodium phosphate and artificial mineral waters with an effervescent quality.

Researchers went to work and came up with Citrocarbonate, an alkalizer with a pleasant taste. It was introduced in 1921. At the start, output of Citrocarbonate was modest — 125 pounds a day. Five years later, the plant was making 3,600 pounds daily, and sales for that year of 1926 went over $1 million, the first time any Upjohn product had passed that mark. By 1941, a million and a half pounds a year were being turned out, and Citrocarbonate is still being sold.

(left) The first sales conferences were held at the New York Branch Office in 1909 and soon afterwards at the home office and other branches. These salesmen from New York pose on the steps of the White Office for a conference with senior management in August 1914.

(izquierda) Las primeras conferencias sobre ventas se celebraron en la oficina de la sucursal de Nuevo York en 1909 y poco después en la oficina central y en otras sucursales. Estos vendedores de Nueva York posan en los peldaños de la Oficina Blanca para una conferencia con el gerente principal en Agosto de 1914.

(à gauche) A l'annexe de New York ont eu lieu en 1909 les premières réunions des agents de vente, mais par la suite elles se sont tenues à la maison mère et dans d'autres succursales. Ces agents de New York sont photographiés devant le "White Office", lors d'une conférence des cadres de direction, en août 1914.

（左）初めての販売会議は1909年にニューヨーク支社で開かれ、次いですぐ本社や他の支社でも開かれるようになった。上級管理職者との会議に出席するため、ニューヨークから来た営業担当者たちが"白いオフィス"の階段に並んでいる。1914年8月。

(right) W.E.'s private "White Office," built in 1913, was razed in 1934 to make way for Building 25. The upstairs housed a number of large plants (from Brook Lodge) and his collection of oriental souvenirs, including a Chinese temple gong. In the basement was Fred Heyl's fledgling lab.

(derecha) "Oficina blanca" privada de W.E., construida en 1913, fue demolida en 1934 para construir el Edificio 25. El piso superior alojaba varias grandes plantas (de Brook Lodge) y su colección de recuerdos orientales, inclusive un gong de un templo chino. En el sótano estaba el reciente laboratorio de Fred Heyl.

(à droite) Construit en 1913, le "White Office", bureau privé de William Upjohn, fut démoli en 1934 et remplacé par le bâtiment No. 25. L'étage abritait de vastes plantes (de Brook Lodge), et sa collection de souvenirs orientaux, dont un gong de temple chinois. Au sous-sol, le laboratoire de Fred Heyl.

（右）1913年に建てられたW．E．アップジョン専用の"白いオフィス"は、1934年にとり壊され、25号館の建築用地となる。白いオフィスの上の階には、ブルックロッジから運び込まれた数々の植木が並べられ、中国寺院のどらなど、中国土産のコレクションが飾られていた。地下には、フレッド・ヘイルの新しい研究室があった。

(left) W.E. and Carrie Gilmore Upjohn, in the greenhouse at Brook Lodge (1916). The mother of future Upjohn president and chairman Donald Gilmore, Carrie Gilmore married W.E. eight years after the death of his first wife, Rachel Babcock Upjohn.

(izquierda) W.E. y Carrie Gilmore Upjohn en el invernadero Brook Lodge (1916). Carrie Gilmore, madre del futuro presidente y director de Upjohn, Donald Gilmore, se casó con W.E. ocho años después de que éste perdiera a su primera esposa Rachel Babcock Upjohn.

(à gauche) W.E. et Carrie Gilmore Upjohn, à la serre de Brook Lodge (1916). Carrie Gilmore, mère du futur président d'Upjohn, Donald Gilmore, a épousé William Upjohn huit ans après la mort de sa première femme, Rachel Babcock Upjohn.

（左）ブルックロッジの温室でW．E．アップジョンとキャリー・ギルモア・アップジョン（1916）。のちにアップジョン社の社長、ついで会長となるドナルド・ギルモアの母、キャリー・ギルモアは、W．E．アップジョンが最初の妻レイチエルを亡くした8年後に結婚した。

(right) The company's second branch office opened in Kansas City, Missouri, in 1909 with Malcolm Galbraith as manager. In 1918 the office was moved into this former wholesale liquor house which had been put up for sale because of the advent of prohibition.

(derecha) La segunda oficina de la sucursal de la Compañia abrió en Kansas City, Missouri, en 1909 con Malcolm Galbraith como gerente. En 1918 la oficina se trasladó a este antiguo establecimiento para venta de licores al por mayor, que se había puesto a la venta debido a la reciente prohibición de venta de estos productos en los Estados Unidos.

(à droite) En 1909, la seconde succursale de la société Upjohn s'ouvre à Kansas City (Missouri), et Malcolm Galbraith en est le directeur. En 1918, le siège de cette succursale est transféré dans cet ancien débit d'alcool qui avait été mis en vente à l'époque de la prohibition.

（右）1909年、二番目の支社が、ミズリー州カンサス市に開設され、マルコム・ガルブレイスが支社長に任命された。1918年、禁酒法の施行後、売りに出されていた酒類卸売り業者の建物に、支社は移転した。

At least part of the item's early success can be credited to Fred Heyl's coaching of the sales force. When he was a boy, he had worked in his uncle's drugstore, and he had an idea about what druggists and doctors wanted to know about products. He elected to go into the field to explain to Upjohn salesmen the properties of Citrocarbonate and its chemical action in the body. The sales force became so fired up that the factory had to add a night shift to handle the cascade of orders. Salesmen also found that this tutoring brought them a new level of respect from physicians, who saw that they had done their homework on therapeutics. This outcome "marked the advent of The Upjohn Company as a first-division pharmaceutical house," said the *Overflow* in May 1949. (The *Overflow* was Upjohn's original internal publication, started in December 1909 by George McClelland for sales personnel. Later, Harold Upjohn edited it for a time. The *Overflow* was joined in 1946 by *Upjohn News*; both were replaced in 1962 by the monthly Upjohn *Intercom*.)

New Products from Research

Fred Heyl's researchers followed their success with Citrocarbonate by developing Cheracol, as an improvement on the older cough syrup Palmo-Dionin. The new medication had a cherry color and flavor, and it came in two formulas, one mixed with morphine, the other with codeine. Sales grew rapidly, especially in the morphine-based form. "Some druggists tell me that Cheracol is running five-to-one favorite over all cough syrups," a salesman wrote in 1929.

Then came a far less desirable report: a black market had sprung up for Cheracol with Morphine. Upjohn felt it had no choice but to discontinue that form of Cheracol in May 1930; it would still offer Cheracol with Codeine. The product has been marketed ever since in both prescription and proprietary forms.

Fred Heyl discovered soon enough that he could not run his department passively from a lab bench. To make things happen, he had to be an advocate. In no situation was that more the case than with Upjohn's development of vitamins. Interest in these food supplements was stimulated by a 1922 finding at Johns Hopkins University that rickets, a crippling childhood disease, stemmed not from overcrowding, as earlier science held, but from lack of a certain food element. This was vitamin D, readily available in cod liver oil.

Heyl's associates decided to build this finding into a marketable substance. In 1927, they introduced a flavored cod liver oil. But both Upjohn's and competitors' versions lacked consistency of potency. To cure that, Dr. Heyl formed a small nutrition lab, with Edwin C. Wise in charge. There, animal tests were designed to assure vitamin potency. In 1928, technicians produced a sequel, Super D Cod Liver Oil, the first standardized combination of vitamins A and D to appear on the U.S. market.

Not everyone was convinced. Skeptics scoffed, holding that there was no evidence that cod liver oil was better for you than any other easily digested food. The comic peak of this spate of negativism came when the company found it could not sell the first 50 of 1,000 barrels of cod liver oil Heyl had ordered. It was summer, and the barrels sat in a driveway, smelling to high heaven. "Heyl's Folly," some gibed. However, Dr. Heyl had a potent ally,

Malcolm Galbraith. He had come to the home office in 1923 to be sales manager for Kalamazoo and Kansas City (and then, in October 1929, director of sales). Galbraith believed in Heyl, and they reinforced each other, with Galbraith urging Heyl to create more products and Heyl needling Galbraith to sell more.

The long and short of it was that the odorous inventory was eventually sold and Upjohn reached such heights with its vitamins, including Super D Cod Liver Oil, that by 1945 they accounted for half of the company's sales of $40 million.

A MAN OF MANY PARTS

Dr. W. E. Upjohn had ample reason to feel satisfied as the company he had built moved through the 1920s. The market for the new nutritional products seemed to hold great promise. Meanwhile, his son, Harold, was largely running the company for him. This gave W. E. time, the kind of time he had not known as a young physician or as a pharmaceutical entrepreneur. He now had more hours to devote to his love of nature, to the welfare of his employees, and to the surrounding community.

Under his watchful eye, Brook Lodge had been transformed into a neatly trimmed country estate. The glorious carpet of peonies gave W. E. the greatest of pleasure, but he also turned them into a vigorous business. Approaching them with all the discipline of a scientist, he experimented, made notes, and even wrote a treatise on their care and feeding. Then, in season, coolers were situated in the fields, and three weeks before the flowers were to bloom, some would be cut, stored, specially packed, and shipped to market in California.

Brook Lodge could command as much as $150 for a taproot from someone wanting to start a peony plantation. Dr. Upjohn's peonies also offered one of the finest natural spectacles in the area. People traveled from miles around to the lodge in June to enjoy the riotous floral colors. Not content to stare from a distance, the visitors would enter the grounds, saunter up to the lodge's porch, and even unpack a picnic. Eventually W. E. had to reroute the entrance road to restore peace and quiet.

The tranquility of his flowered grounds meant everything to the founder. He was to be well reminded of that when he and his wife set sail in late 1923 on a grand tour of a dozen countries in Europe, North Africa, and the Near East. They planned to be gone until the latter part of the following summer, quite a commitment for a man not much given to extensive traveling. As their voyaging carried them from winter into spring, W. E. felt a stronger and stronger yearning for home. They cut their trip short, and by spring they were strolling once again across the grounds of Brook Lodge. More than anything else, he wanted to see his fields of peonies.

An Enduring Concern for Others

Dr. Upjohn's abiding concern for his fellow man was an outlook that he took to work with him every day of the week, through all his years of service as physician, community citizen, and business entrepreneur.

Over the years, the founder saw to it that his workers received more than just a week's pay for a week's work. He introduced benefit programs — paid vacations, Christmas bonuses, shortened workweeks — that were highly innovative for the era. At his insistence, Upjohn marched at the forefront in looking out for the well-being of its employees.

Beyond this commitment, the founder carried his concern for others into the surrounding community. He was guided by something he once wrote. God, he said, "has taken man into the scheme of creation and permitted him to become a co-worker." Thus motivated, Dr. Upjohn ran successfully for city alderman seven years after moving to Kalamazoo and served until 1893. Twenty years later, he again entered city politics when the Chamber of Commerce asked him to chair a committee to study alternative forms of city administration.

Photo by Blank-Stoller

Residents approved a city commission form of government, and in the spring of 1918, Dr. Upjohn was elected mayor on the new commission. Actions followed — revising civil codes and ordinances, hiring Kalamazoo's first two policewomen, setting up a purchasing bureau, revamping the accounting system, even a study of milk deliveries. But city politics and contention with his adversaries did not sit well with W. E., and in 1921, at the age of 68, he stepped down.

Philanthropist as well as social innovator and builder, this citizen of Kalamazoo addressed himself to other needs of his fellow residents. As early as 1903, he threw himself into the community effort to erect what is now Bronson Methodist Hospital. At the hospital's December 1905 dedication, contributor W. E. Upjohn shared in the proceedings in his capacity as president of the Kalamazoo Hospital Association.

(left) William Harold Upjohn (1884-1928), W.E.'s only son, joined the company in 1907. During his career he was credited with initiating many of the early employee benefits programs, cost accounting methods, and sales and distribution policies. He died unexpectedly in 1928 at age 44.

(izquierda) William Harold Upjohn (1884-1928), único hijo de W.E., se le reconoce la iniciación de muchos de los primeros programas de beneficios para el empleado, métodos de contabilidad de costos y política de ventas y distribución. Murió inesperadamente en 1928 a la edad de 44 años.

(à gauche) William Harold Upjohn (1884-1928). Fils unique de William Upjohn père, il entre à la société en 1907. Il y fait carrière, et c'est à lui que revient le mérite de plusieurs initiatives, dont l'adoption de programmes d'avantages sociaux en faveur des employés, des méthodes de comptabilité et d'analyses de coût, et des plans de vente et de distribution. Il est mort subitement en 1928, à l'âge de 44 ans.

（左）W. E. アップジョンの一人息子、ウィリアム・ハロルド・アップジョン（1884～1928）は、1907年に入社した。在職中にさまざまな業績を上げたが、他社に先きがけて実施した社員の福利厚生政策、原価計算方式、販売流通政策の導入などが高く評価されている。ハロルド・アップジョンは、1928年、44才の若さで亡くなった。

(right) Lawrence Northcote "L.N." Upjohn, M.D. (1873-1967). The son of co-founder Henry Upjohn, L.N. began his company career in 1904. He later served as New York Branch Office manager (1906-1930), company president (1930-1944), and chairman (1944-1953).

(derecha) Lawrence Northcote "L.N." Upjohn, médico (1873-1967). L.N. era hijo del co-fundador Henry Upjohn, y comenzó su carrera en 1904. Posteriormente desempeñó el cargo de gerente de la oficina de la sucursal de Nueva York (1906-1930), presidente de la compañía (1930-1944) y administrador (1944-1953).

(à droite) Lawrence Northcote Upjohn, médecin (1873-1967). Fils du co-fondateur Henry Upjohn, il a débuté sa carrière en 1904. Il a occupé le poste de directeur régional de la succursale d'Upjohn à New York (1906-1930). Il a été ensuite président de la société (1930-1944), et président-directeur général (1944-1953).

（右）ローレンス・ノースコート・アップジョン医博（1873～1967）。アップジョン社の共同創立者ヘンリー・アップジョンの息子で、1904年入社。後に、ニューヨーク支社長（1906～1930）、社長（1930～1944）、会長（1944～1953）を歴任。

W. E. had a vision of a day when his employees and all of Kalamazoo's citizens would have more leisure time, thanks to a shorter workweek. When that occurred, he projected, Kalamazoo ought to have better recreational facilities to offer them. He decided to do what he could to transform 17 acres south of East Vine Street into what would later be named Upjohn Park. At another point, the founder gave funds to help lay out a Municipal Golf Course at Milham Park. His daughter Winifred had mastered the sport of golf, and he played now and again (in 1927, at the age of 74, he managed a 102 for 18 holes).

Recognizing the key role of the arts as the intellectual and creative center of a community, W. E. took an interest in developing suitable facilities in town. The Kalamazoo Institute of Arts — the "Art Center" — began in 1928 when he joined with the city's board of education to buy a Rose Street home which opened in

1929 as the "Art House." During that same year, he bought an old structure at South and Park streets for a group of actors called the Players, of which his daughter, Dorothy, was a member. Seeing that something better was needed, he announced a plan to build a Civic Auditorium on the same property; it was dedicated October 12, 1931.

To the religious heart of the community, too, Dr. Upjohn welcomed his responsibilities. In a letter to the minister of his church, First Congregational, he said, "If there is any human need which demands our best efforts, it is for a structure designed for worship. Everywhere and always, men have given their best in the designing and building of such structures." When his church and two others were scorched by suspicious fires, W. E. stepped forward to help pay for their reconstruction. And late in life, he gave the funds to design and install the glorious stained-glass South Memorial Window in First Congregational.

(left) An old roll-up telephone directory, W.E.'s pencil, a cost/inventory book, and a bottle of Podophyllin 1/8 grain (used as a caustic), lie on a marble desktop (circa 1920).

(izquierda) Un viejo directorio telefónico enrollado, un lápiz de W.E., un libro sobre costos e inventario y un frasco de Podolfilina de 1/8 de grano (usada como cáustico) aparecen sobre una mesa de mármol (cerca 1920).

(à gauche) Un vieil annuaire du téléphone, un crayon de William Upjohn, un registre d'inventaire, et un flacon de podophylline en granulés que l'on employait comme caustique, reposent sur un marbre (vers 1920).

（左）大理石のデスクの上の古い巻き上げ式電話帳、W. E. アップジョンの鉛筆、原価・在庫帳簿、ポドフィリン1/8（焼灼剤として使われた）の入った瓶（1920年頃）。

(right) Citrocarbonate, the pleasant-tasting antacid, debuted in 1921 at the peak of Phenolax's success. When Phenolax sales started to decline a few years later, Citrocarbonate became the company's number one seller. Both products are sold today.

(derecha) Citrocarbonato, el antiácido de agradable sabor, apareció en 1921 en el apogeo del éxito de Phenolax. Cuando la venta de Phenolax comenzó a decaer unos cuantos años después, el Citrocarbonato se convirtió en el producto de mayor venta de la compañía. Ambos productos se venden actualmente.

(à droite) Le Citrocarbonate, un antiacide au goût plaisant, a été lancé sur le marché en 1921, année des grosses ventes de Phenolax. Mais lorsque les ventes de Phenolax commencèrent à décliner quelques années plus tard, le Citrocarbonate devint le produit le plus vendu de la société. Ces deux produits sont en vente aujourd'hui sur le marché.

（右）フェノラックスの販売が、ピークに達していた1921年、味のよい制酸剤シトロカーボネートが発売された。数年後、フェノラックスの販売が下降し始めたころ、シトロカーボネートが、最有力商品となった。現在でもこの二つの製品は販売されている。

Aiding existing institutions and helping to establish others for which there was a need required funding. How could they all be supported financially on a regular basis? W. E. worked up an answer by forming in 1926 the W. E. Upjohn Civic Trust. By 1942, more than $173,000 of its income had been spent locally — $80,000 to expand parks and playgrounds, $49,000 for the Civic Auditorium, $6,000 for the Municipal Golf Association. Then the trust put more than $24,000 into the Kalamazoo Foundation, an institution Dr. Upjohn had been promoting since 1924 to "receive and administer bequests for the general welfare of citizens of Kalamazoo County." The foundation was launched officially on August 24, 1925. One of its later grants was the sum of $500,000 in 1959 as endowment for a new arts center. In 1986, the Kalamazoo Foundation is the nation's tenth-largest community foundation.

Managers' Conference (1926): back row (l-r) — Waters Sellman, San Francisco Sales; Malcolm Galbraith, Kalamazoo and Kansas City Sales; Fred Heyl, Research; front row — Harold Upjohn, General Manager; John McColl, Treasurer; W.E. Upjohn; S.R. Light, VP, Production; L.N. Upjohn, VP and New York Sales.

Conferencia de gerentes (1926): aparecen al fondo (de derecha a izquierda) — Waters Sellman, encargado de ventas en San Francisco; Malcolm Galbraith, encargado de ventas en Kalamazoo y Kansas City; Fred Heyl, encargado de investigaciones; al frente — Harold Upjohn, Gerente General; John McColl, Tesorero; W. E. Upjohn; S. R. Light, Vicepresidente encargado de la producción; L. N. Upjohn, Vicepresidente y encargado de Ventas en Nueva York.

Conférence des cadres (1926): de gauche à droite, à l'arrière-plan-Waters Sellman, directeur des ventes à San Francisco; Malcolm Galbraith, directeur des ventes à Kalamazoo et Kansas City; Fred Heyl, chargé de la recherche; au premier plan, Harold Upjohn, directeur général; John McColl, trésorier; W.E. Upjohn; S. R. Light, vice-président chargé de la production; L.N. Upjohn, vice-président et responsable des ventes à New York.

部長会議（1926年）：後列左から右へ―――サンフランシスコ販売部門のウォーターズ・ゼルマン。カラマズー及びカンサス市販売部門のマルコム・ガルブレイス。研究部門のフレッド・ハイル。前列左から―――総支配人ハロルド・アップジョン、財務担当重役ジョン・マッコール、社長W. E. アップジョン。生産担当副社長S. R. ライト。そして副社長兼ニューヨーク販売部長のL. N. アップジョン。

Concern for people stimulated the last of Dr. Upjohn's charitable deeds — what he hoped would be "the most important thing I ever did." He came up with a plan for helping local workers hit by a national depression so severe that by 1932 some 12 million Americans were unemployed.

The headline in the *Kalamazoo Gazette* of December 6, 1931, summed up the founder's idea: "Dr. W. E. Upjohn Buys 1,200-Acre Site To Work Out Unemployment Problem Solution." Those acres, mostly in Richland Township, were to be turned into individual farm plots for the jobless people of Kalamazoo, who would be bused from town to work the soil. In parallel, an ongoing farm was to be created to raise crops, chickens, and sheep, and to operate a creamery.

Cultivation of the land and the dream began on a 90-acre potato field in 1932. Unemployed men broke the soil, planted, weeded, and harvested in the fall. They kept some of the crop, while 400 bushels were trucked to town for distribution through the Kalamazoo welfare department. W. E. gave this venture his closest attention, often visiting the site twice a week. He must have been deeply gratified to see as many as 100 jobless people working away in the fields.

Was it logical to expect that factory men could shift easily into farm work? Perhaps not. But W. E. was proceeding with the strongest of convictions. The unemployed could have been put on the dole. However, as L. N. Upjohn remembered, Dr. Upjohn believed that "charity of the dole type was largely wasted." He was convinced that "the best kind of help to be given to the poor was to furnish employment or in some form an opportunity to work and produce something in order that the dollar might not be uselessly consumed."

The founder made another move against the recurring scourge of joblessness. Early in 1932, he put together the W. E. Upjohn Unemployment Trustee Corporation. Some of his personal funds were siphoned into this institution "to study and investigate the feasibility and methods of insuring against unemployment and devise ways and means of preventing and alleviating the distress and hardship caused by unemployment..." The corporation's assets were Richland Farms and 10,000 shares of Upjohn stock. Known today as the W. E. Upjohn Institute for Employment Research, it is a highly respected authority in its field.

Thus Dr. Upjohn launched twin attacks on joblessness. He would do what he could for the unemployed he saw daily on the streets of Kalamazoo. And he would put experienced people to work at devising solutions that might help the entire nation.

Why did this man, considered Kalamazoo's "first citizen," give so freely to community activities? It could be that he in part was swayed by the practice of other industrial leaders, who gave because it was "good for business." But there were other, more important reasons. The daughter of W. E.'s pastor, who lived behind the Upjohns, recalled that "the thing he stressed about himself was that he had been given his vast wealth as a stewardship. It was not given to him to use for himself.

He truly believed that God had given him a great, great deal of this world's wealth to use to help other people."

ARRANGING THE SUCCESSION

Working out programs to benefit his fellow citizens, talking to Malcolm Galbraith about sales goals or to Fred Heyl about the new vitamin research, visiting the production lines, refining the buildings and grounds at Brook Lodge — all this kept W. E. Upjohn amply busy during the mid-1920s. That was the kind of variety he liked. He was better off, he thought, in not letting his one occupation in the company "completely control my mental activities."

As he approached his 70th birthday, in 1923, W. E. was certainly better off for knowing that his son, Harold, had assumed his company responsibilities so well. Harold's growth led him to be named general manager in 1925 and a vice president in 1926. By then, he was largely running the firm, while W. E. had gone into semiretirement.

Then, in October 1928, Harold underwent surgery for a hernia. In recovery, an embolism developed and the doctors could do nothing. On October 15, Harold Upjohn died.

His death was a sudden and sorrowful tragedy for his wife and three children. It was a blow every bit as savage for his father. Likable, cheerful, creative, and disciplined, Harold had many strengths. He was, in L. N.'s words, "an able man of affairs [who] possessed genuine executive ability. He was careful and thorough, [and] exhibited excellent judgment in business matters..." Now Harold was gone. His death, said L. N., "knocked W. E. all out. He had everything planned, and so . . . he had to start all over again."

The founder had some stalwarts nearby — John McColl, Dr. Light, Malcolm Galbraith, Fred Heyl, Lew Crockett. And he was not above slipping into harness himself, although his health troubled him now and then. Late in his life, diabetes was diagnosed, and W. E. tried to be a reasonable patient. Dr. E. Gifford Upjohn, L. N.'s son and W. E.'s grandnephew, took care of him between 1930 and 1932. "I don't think that anything I knew about him," recalls Dr. Upjohn, "indicated he was a weakling, but he always thought of himself as being somebody who had to be careful of his health." In that period, W. E. wrote, "I am . . . eating with care. I have purposely lost some weight and feel better for it. I am sugar free." He also had a chronic problem with bronchitis, irritated by the raw Michigan winters. In search of a warmer climate, he had earlier bought a home in Altadena, California, and later one in Pasadena. There he'd retreat in wintertime, play a little golf, and recuperate.

Who then would mind the store, now that he could no longer look to Harold? W. E. took time to solve that. As an interim measure, he formed an executive committee, chaired by John McColl, to manage affairs during his winters away.

Four days after that committee's formation, in October 1929, Wall Street went on the rocks, and the nation's economy soon foundered, too. Upjohn's president was braced for the onslaught of depression. "Do not cultivate fears," he'd remind his people. "Cultivate hopes!"

The company's strength was more than a matter of attitude. At long last its financial underpinnings were solid. W. E. usually handled matters of financing — he had the connections among the bankers and an astute knowledge of the credit markets. By the late 1920s, Treasurer McColl wrote, "We had for many years followed the principle of getting out and then keeping out of debt, so that when the general stress came we were in a position where no creditor could embarrass us." Once the 1909 indebtedness had been eliminated, management had set up a reserve fund against a rainy day. Part of its dollars had gone into municipal bonds. Although they shrank in value during the depression, they kept most of their worth.

(top) In 1926, Citrocarbonate became the first Upjohn product to surpass $1 million in annual sales. These employees on the Citrocarbonate bottling line had another reason to celebrate, too — theirs was the first department in the company to be air-conditioned.

(arriba) En 1926 el Citrocarbonato llegó a ser el primer producto de Upjohn que sobrepasó $1.000.000 en ventas anuales. Estos empleados de la línea de embotellado de Citrocarbonato tenían otro motivo para festejar: su departamento era el primero de la compañía que iba a tener aire acondicionado.

(en haut) En 1926, le Citrocarbonate est devenu le premier produit Upjohn à surpasser un chiffre de vente d'un million de dollars par an. Ces employés de la section de mise en bouteille du Citrocarbonate ont une autre raison d'avoir le coeur en fête : leur section était la première à être climatisée.

（上）1926年、シトロカーボネートは、アップジョン社で初めて年商 100万ドルを越える商品となった。シトロカーボネートの瓶詰作業を担当していた社員たちにとって、もう一つの祝福すべきことは、ここが全社で初めて空調が入った部門だったことである。

(bottom) Though the company did little journal advertising in the first three decades of this century, every physician and druggist could count on direct mail advertising from Upjohn. These two specialty mailing employees are seen with their labeling machine in 1926.

(abajo) Si bien la compañía se anunció poco en los periódicos en las primeras tres décadas de este siglo, todos los médicos y boticarios podían contar con anuncios que Upjohn les enviaba por correo. Estos dos empleados encargados especialmente del correo aparecen con su máquina rotuladora en 1926.

(en bas) Malgré le peu de publicité dans les journaux pendant les trente premières années de ce siècle, médecins et pharmaciens recevaient régulièrement par courrier les documents Upjohn. Ces deux employés du service postal d'Upjohn sont photographiés près de leur machine à étiqueter, en 1926.

（下）20世紀の、はじめの30年間、アップジョン社はほとんど医学雑誌に広告を行なわなかったが、医師、薬剤師たちは、ダイレクト・メールで送られてくる宣伝物によってアップジョン社製品についての情報を得た。写真は二人の発送専門係と、1926年当時使っていた宛名印刷機。

Finding a Successor

While Upjohn was well fortified against the depression, W. E. still needed to find a successor. Preparing to leave for Pasadena before Christmas 1929, he sent a directive asking key individuals to send carbon copies of all their correspondence to him. In California, he would read the letters, see how the managers dealt with problems, and, as he liked to say, "mull it over."

Who were the men being scrutinized in this way? John McColl, for one, and various sales branch managers — Waters Sellman in San Francisco and L. N. Upjohn in New York — among others. Then, Dr. S. R. Light was to send his letters, too. As W. E.'s son-in-law and an Upjohn employee since 1907, Dr. Light rather expected that he would rank as the prime candidate after Harold's death. He had good reason to anticipate that a family member would be picked to take charge. Upjohn had been a family concern from the start. Relatives including Harold Upjohn; the founder's nephews L. N., Kirby, and Archie Campbell; Genevieve Babcock, sister of W. E.'s first wife, Rachel; Fred Childs, husband of W. E.'s niece Alice Sidnam; the Little brothers, Charles and William — these and other Upjohn relatives had worked for the company, some from the earliest years. So the tradition was strong. But the assignment was not to go to Dr. Light.

Dr. Upjohn pored over sheaves of executive mail all that winter of 1929-30, then made his decision. His successor would be his nephew, Dr. L. N. Upjohn, a company employee since 1904 and New York branch manager since late 1906. This step posed a dilemma for the 56-year-old L. N. He had lived in the New York City area for 25 years; he was reluctant to make the move. But W. E. could be a most persuasive man, and in May 1930, L. N. was named president. He elected to stay in the East for a period, then settled permanently in Kalamazoo in October 1931.

The changing of the guard triggered S. R.'s resignation as vice president and director. But he found many alternative interests. A highly active citizen of Kalamazoo, he was once described as being "president of half the things in town and vice president of the other half." He returned to the Upjohn board in 1937.

Dr. Upjohn's choice of L. N. to succeed him was not the founder's only move to align Upjohn management for the future. W. E. heated up his campaign to persuade his stepson, 35-year-old Donald Gilmore, who had married his daughter Genevieve in 1916, to come into the firm.

W. E. had already prevailed on Gilmore to go on the Upjohn board in 1929. But Donald had been quite content with working for the Gilmore family's dry-goods store. Dr. Upjohn thought that a career with his pharmaceutical company had more to offer; he invited his son-in-law to join him in that enterprise. Gilmore carefully studied the offer but finally advised W. E. that he had "decided to stay in the store." Donald was up against a heavyweight, however. Dr. Upjohn would not accept a turndown, and he kept working on his son-in-law. Finally his arguments paid off. On September 8, 1930, Donald Gilmore went to work for Upjohn, taking a sizable pay cut in the process.

At the same time, W. E. had persuaded L. N.'s son, E. Gifford Upjohn, M.D., to join the company. Gifford Upjohn was yet another Upjohn who had received his M.D. from the University of Michigan. He recalls: "I didn't know how they were going to use me. W. E. didn't know either. He just said that we've got a company here. We've got to make it go. If you can find some way to fit in there and help make the company grow, you make your own job."

(left) Employees of the Statistical Department, Building 18 (January 1926). Notice the overhead fire sprinklers, standard equipment in all Upjohn buildings since the disastrous fire in 1911.

(izquierda) Empleados del Departamento de Estadísticas, Edificio 18 (enero de 1926). Nótese los rociadores de agua contra incendios, arriba, equipo indispensable en todos los edificios Upjohn desde el desastroso incendio de 1911.

(à gauche) Employés de la section des statistiques, bâtiment No. 18 (janvier 1926). A noter, en haut, le système d'extinction en cas d'incendie, équipement standard dans tous les édifices Upjohn, depuis le grave incendie de 1911.

（左）18号館で統計課の社員たち（1926年1月）。大損害を出した1911年の火災事故以来、アップジョン社のすべての建物の標準設備となったスプリンクラーが頭上に写っている。

(right) Company trucks parked in the courtyard of the Lovell Street factory complex are ready to roll with crates of finished goods (1926).

(derecha) Camiones de la compañía estacionados en el patio del conjunto de edificios de la fábrica de la calle Lovell, listos para rodar con cajas de productos terminados (1926).

(à droite) Camions de l'entreprise Upjohn, stationnés dans la cour de l'usine à Lovell Street, fin prêts à transporter les caisses de produits finis (1926).

（右）ロベル通りにある工場群の中庭に駐車した会社のトラック。商品が梱包された木枠を積んで、出発準備が完了したところ（1926）。

(top) After a visit to Upjohn Richland Farms, W.E. came down with a chest cold. Within two days he developed pneumonia. One day later — October 18, 1932 — he died. City workers left their jobs, flags flew at half-staff, and all mourned the loss of Kalamazoo's "First Citizen."

(arriba) Después de una visita a la Hacienda Upjohn en Richland, W.E. regresó con enfriamiento en el pecho. A los dos días contrajo neumonia. Un día después — el 18 de octubre de 1932 — falleció. Los trabajadores de la ciudad suspendieron sus labores, las banderas se izaron a media asta y todos hicieron duelo por la pérdida del "Primer Ciudadano" de Kalamazoo.

(en haut) Revenant d'un séjour à la ferme Upjohn de Richland, William Upjohn attrapa une grippe. Et deux jours plus tard, la grippe se transforma en pneumonie. Le 18 octobre 1932, il rendait le dernier soupir. Drapeaux en berne, les employés de la municipalité quittèrent leurs lieux de travail pour pleurer la mort du "premier citoyen" de la ville de Kalamazoo.

（上）アップジョン社のリッチランド農場への旅行のあと、Ｗ．Ｅ．アップジョンはひどい風邪をひいた。2日後に肺炎を起こし、その翌日、1932年10月18日に死亡した。カラマズー市行政は、その日休みとなり、半旗が掲げられ、市民はカラマズーの「ファースト・シチズン」の死を悼んだ。

(bottom) Dr. W.E.'s portrait (circa 1928) adorned by his glasses, office door title plate, and one of his favorite oriental souvenirs — a Chinese physician's antique pocket scale, used for measuring powdered medicines.

(abajo) Retrato del Dr. W.E. (cerca 1928) adornado por sus anteojos, la placa con su título en la puerta de su oficina y uno de sus favoritos recuerdos orientales — una balanza china de bolsillo antigua, que usaban los médicos para pesar medicinas en polvo.

(en bas) Portrait du Dr. W.E. Upjohn (vers 1928), flanqué de ses lunettes, de sa plaque d'identification qu'il accrochait à l'entrée de son bureau, et un de ses souvenirs d'Orient : une balance de poche, dont se servent les médecins chinois pour mesurer les poudres médicinales.

（下）眼鏡をかけたＷ．Ｅ．アップジョンの肖像画（1928年ごろ）。社長室のドアにかけられた名礼。Ｗ．Ｅ．アップジョンのお気に入りだった中国土産、中国の医師が粉薬を計量するのに用いた携帯計量器の骨董品。

At last, W. E. had orchestrated his succession the way he wanted. From then on he could concentrate on adding the grace notes. Meanwhile, Upjohn's business continued to reflect subtle, yet inevitable change. A sales letter of November 20, 1930, revealed the shift. The company was announcing the "first limited offerings" of hard-filled capsules. Time and competition had moved the company a long way from the friable pill.

A FINAL ACT

One blustery afternoon in mid-October 1932, Dr. Upjohn visited his friends the Reverend and Mrs. J. Twyson Jones. The Reverend Mr. Jones had been the pastor of the First Congregational Church, which W. E. attended, from 1917 to 1923, and the Joneses had lived behind the Upjohns' home on South Street. W. E. was fond of the Joneses and their children. When hard times hit during the Great Depression, W. E. had arranged to install the pastor and his wife at Brook Lodge, where they would find it easier to live on a minister's pension. Mrs. Upjohn had made it possible for the Jones's daughter to attend college. Over the years, the two men had enjoyed many wide-ranging conversations in which they explored their cures for the world's ills.

On this October day, W. E. wanted the Reverend Mr. Jones to go with him on an excursion. Dr. Upjohn thought it was time to take another look at the unemployment project at Richland Farms, but Jones declined.

"No, Rastus," Jones said. "This is a pneumonia-producing day. I don't think we should go out on a day like this and walk."

Dr. Upjohn went on his way and visited the farm on his own, then returned to Brook Lodge. The next day — it happened to be the fourth anniversary of Harold's death — W. E. was taken ill. He quickly weakened, and on Tuesday, October 18, he died in his second-floor bedroom overlooking the pond, with its border of bright fall colors.

The funeral was set for October 20. Local businesses were asked to close, The Upjohn Company shut down, and flags were lowered to half-mast all over the city. In his eulogy at the First Congregational Church, the Reverend Torrance Phelps praised Dr. Upjohn as "a beloved friend, our foremost citizen, and Kalamazoo's greatest philanthropist."

He was that and more to his community and fellow citizens. To his company, he was the founder, a determined, intensely human man for whom every product must be "true to label"; who wanted "Upjohn" to mean for pharmaceuticals what "sterling" did for silver; who insisted that Upjohn people think of themselves as "We," not as individuals working alone. He had demonstrated a lifetime of concern for his employees and his fellow men. But he would not tolerate mediocrity from anyone, holding that "the good is often the enemy of the best."

Many Kalamazooans in October 1932 thought that the "best" had lived among them and now was gone.

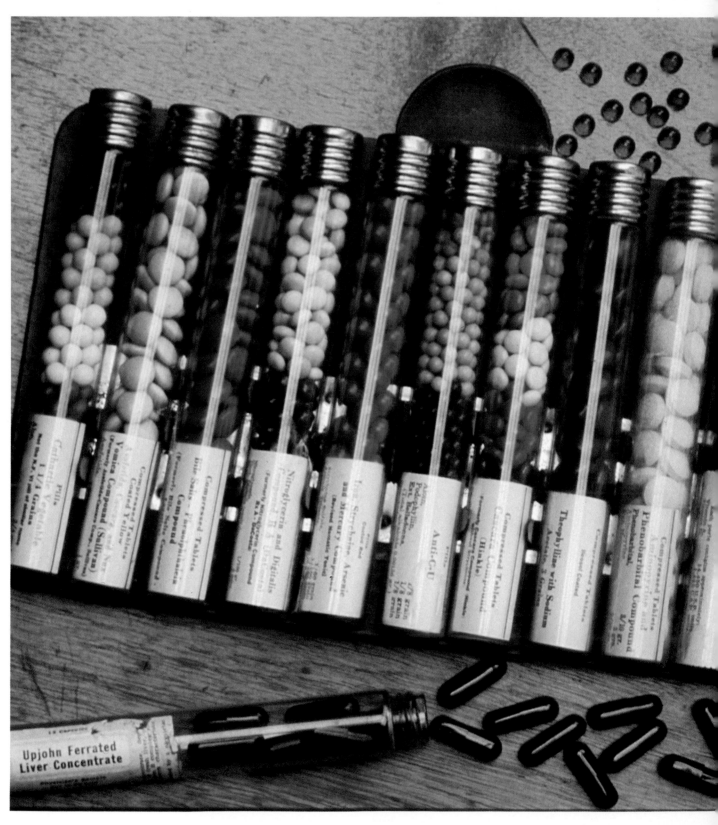

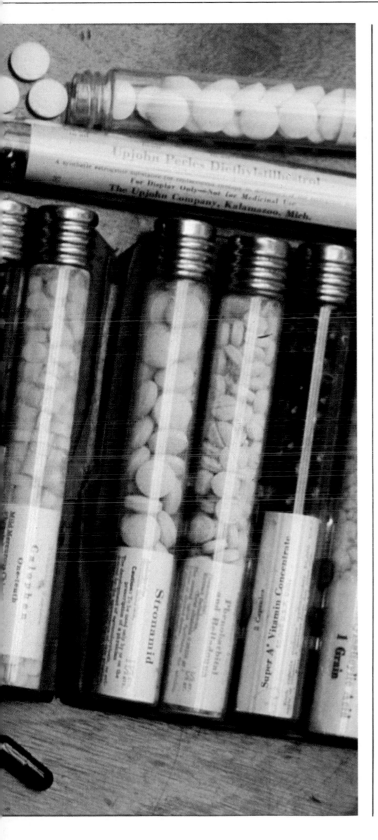

CHAPTER THREE

AFTERMATH AND TRANSITION

The company that W. E. Upjohn left to his successors in 1932 was healthy enough, but misery afflicted the world on every side, and it was spreading.

America's depression preyed on people far and wide. By 1933, at least 15 million American jobless walked the streets — one out of three who had been employed in 1929. In many lands, turmoil flared. Italian dictator Benito Mussolini shouted that the Mediterranean must once again be Italy's sea. Five million Ukrainians starved to death, and in Germany, hundreds of thousands intoned an ominous creed: "Adolf Hitler is Germany and Germany is Adolf Hitler." In the Orient, Japanese militarists thrust their bayonets deeper into China.

For the time being, America worried about itself. A new president assured the citizens on March 4, 1933, that the nation would endure and that "the only thing we have to fear is fear itself." The next day he declared a four-day holiday of all banks to protect their assets. Already beleaguered, the Bank of Kalamazoo shut its doors with the others; it never reopened as the same institution.

The economic tornado was sweeping through the town. By 1932, more than $237,000 had been spent on relief for the poor. In 1933, the federal government stepped in, putting 2,500 people to work. Taxes were cut, but one-third of the citizens still could not pay them on time. Filling some of the vacuum, public works projects paved and widened streets, built Milham Park Golf Course (on land donated earlier by W. E.), put up a juvenile detention shelter and Douglas Community Center, and completed a new park.

Kalamazoo managed better than many places. The paper mills kept busy and Kalamazoo Stove turned out 100,000 units a year, while Upjohn's sales climbed steadily from $6,917,000 in 1929 to $19,376,000 in 1941. After studying 310 American cities in 1937, sociologist Dr. Edward L. Thorndike concluded that Kalamazoo ranked among the top 10 in its quality of life.

Yet, even though the "laboratory," as townsfolk called Upjohn, had been depression-proof, the company and its peers faced more than enough trials in the next decade. Change was already being formulated on sophisticated lab benches. A decade earlier, Frederick G. Banting, Charles H. Best, and John J. R. Macleod had discovered how one scourge of mankind, diabetes, could be controlled with insulin. Not long after, Alexander Fleming came upon the germ-killing mold that was to be purified later into penicillin. The civilized world stood on the threshold of medicine's golden age. For pharmaceutical firms, survival of the fittest demanded that they find cures, not just over-the-counter palliatives. That pursuit sharpened

during the 1930s. Then the industry braced for all-out, three-shift operation after the war-makers fired the diplomats and fielded their dive-bombers and tanks.

The founder, a natural builder, would have relished the challenge of the dozen difficult years ahead.

THE MEN HE LEFT BEHIND

Facing new ordeals, The Upjohn Company needed experienced, muscular hands to guide it. Fortunately, the executive ranks had widened in the last few years of W. E.'s life. His successors combined continuity — some could describe the doldrum days before Phenolax — and the tireless energies of youth.

The team comprised three Upjohn family members buttressed by men not related to the founder: L. N., president; Donald Gilmore, vice president; and L. N.'s son, Dr. E. Gifford Upjohn, new to the company and, by his own request, in training. The balance of the executive load fell on old-timers J. S. McColl, vice president and treasurer; Fred Heyl, director of research; Clarence Chandler, corporate secretary; Will Little, production expert; Lew Crockett, construction man; Malcolm Galbraith, director of sales; and Frank Varney, in charge of personnel. Dr. Harold S. Adams, who had joined the company in 1926, became superintendent of production on S. R. Light's departure in 1930.

Who were these men facing the hard world of the thirties? President L. N. Upjohn marked his 59th birthday the December after W. E.'s death. He had logged 28 years with the corporation, 25 of them as head of the New York branch office. A physician by training but a scholar and teacher at heart, L. N. made substantial contributions to the sales operation in training his field force and sharpening his skills as a sales forecaster. It was said that L. N. was "built with all the dignity that a man needed."

Vice President Donald Sherwood Gilmore, 37 when W. E. died, had a knack for doing the right thing at the right time. Much like his father-in-law, Gilmore had the instincts and energy of a builder. During his tenure as manager of Gilmore Bros. department stores, he had instituted a unit stock control system, acquired property for parking lots, and expanded the store to include outlets in two other Michigan cities. As vice president of The Upjohn Company, he would help oversee an explosion of

(left) Donald S. Gilmore (1895-1979). When Gilmore joined the company in 1930, W.E. assigned him the task of opening the morning's mail. He went on to serve as Upjohn president (1944-1953), chairman (1953-1962), and vice chairman (1962-1969).

(izquierda) Donald S. Gilmore (1895-1979). Cuando Gilmore se incorporó a la compañía en 1930, William Erastus le asignó la tarea de abrir la correspondencia de la mañana. Continuó sirviendo como presidente de Upjohn (1944-1953), administrador (1953-1962) y viceadministrador (1962-1969).

(à gauche) Donald Gilmore (1895-1979). Lorsqu'il est entré à la société Upjohn en 1930, William Upjohn lui a confié le dépouillement du courrier du matin. Il est ensuite devenu président d'Upjohn (1944-1953), président-directeur général (1953-1962) puis vice-président (1962-1969).

（左）ドナルド S　ギルモア（1895～1979）。1930年にギルモアが入社したとき、W．E．アップジョンは、朝届いた郵便を開封する仕事を割りあてた。のちにギルモアは、アップジョン社社長（1944～1953）、会長（1953～1962）、そして、副会長（1962～1969）を歴任した。

branch offices, from three in 1930 to eleven by the outbreak of WWII. Like W. E., Donald Gilmore was warm with intimate company but reserved in public, preferring to work behind the scenes. He was also a good listener, with a ready ear for people's ideas, and a shrewd evaluator of their proposals. Moreover, if an associate had a good idea and convinced Gilmore it was good, he followed through on it.

Another trait Gilmore had in common with the founder was a mechanical bent. Gilmore was a tinkerer, and he had a love of electrical gadgets. Although not medically trained, and not even a college graduate, Donald Gilmore would be a staunch supporter of the growing research department.

The third family member in the early-1930s executive lineup, Dr. E. Gifford Upjohn, had joined the corporation in 1930 at the age of 26. As L. N.'s son, he grew up amid the sights and sounds of Upjohn business affairs. During his high-school days, he worked summers at the downtown-Manhattan sales office, crating gallon and five-gallon bottles of fluid extracts and tinctures. Strengthened by this and possessing natural athletic ability, he won a state high-school shot-put title and later turned to tennis, a game he was still playing in his 80s.

(right) Upjohn executives gathered for a meeting at Donald Gilmore's summer cottage in August 1933. Pictured are (l-r): Merrill Hart and Fred Heyl, the company's senior scientists; Lew Crockett, superintendent of construction and maintenance; Harold Adams, plant superintendent; and Will Little, tablet department head.

(derecha) Grupo de ejecutivos de Upjohn que asistieron a una reunión en la cabaña de verano de Donald Gilmore, en agosto de 1933. En la foto aparecen, de izquierda a derecha: Merrill Hart y Fred Heyl, principales científicos de la compañía; Lew Crockett, superintendente de construcción y mantenimiento; Harold Adams, superintendente de la planta; y Will Little, jefe del Departamento de Tabletas.

(à droite) Réunion des cadres de la société Upjohn à la maison de campagne de Donald Gilmore, au mois d'août 1933. De gauche à droite, sur la photo : Merrill Hart et Fred Heyl, experts scientifiques de la société Upjohn, Lew Crockett, surintendant de l'usine, Harold Adams, et Will Little, chef du département de production de comprimés.

（右）1933年8月、アップジョン社の役員たちは会議のため、ドナルド・ギルモアの夏の別荘に集まった。写真左から：シニア研究員のメリル・ハートとフレッド・ヘイル。建設管理部長のルーイ・クロケット、工場長のハロルド・アダム、錠剤部門長のウイル・リトル。

The Older Guard

Vice President and Treasurer John McColl had come to work for Upjohn in 1900, four years before Gifford Upjohn was born; so had Will Little, the versatile production man. Fred Heyl, a 1904 Yale graduate, had joined the firm in 1913. Longtime employee Malcolm Galbraith, sales director, turned 56 the year of the founder's death, while 47-year-old Lew Crockett had already figured prominently in completing or renovating 13 Upjohn buildings. (In his time, the dapper Crockett was to have a big hand in completing more than 50 of them.)

All these men had earned the respect of W. E. Upjohn. McColl had chaired the first executive committee and was named an executor and trustee of Dr. Upjohn's estate. Crockett had designed a number of the buildings at Brook Lodge and had seen to the construction of a major gift by Dr. Upjohn to the community, the Civic Auditorium. As for Galbraith, when he came to Upjohn as Kansas City branch manager in 1909, overall company sales stood at $645,085; by 1941, the year before he died, they had climbed to

$19,376,000. That, wrote L. N., was evidence that Galbraith had "lived up to expectations."

Dr. Harold S. Adams, Phi Beta Kappa graduate of Williams College and holder of a doctorate in chemistry, started out in 1926 as an assistant to S. R. Light, then succeeded him in 1930 as plant superintendent. Scholar, scientist, voracious reader, the company's ranking expert in matters of English language usage, poet, musician — Dr. Adams brought this versatility, and intense dedication, to his work for Upjohn.

Other capable men carried leadership burdens in the early 1930s. Chemist Merrill C. Hart had come in to be Fred Heyl's first assistant in 1914. Genial C. V. (Pat) Patterson, an Upjohn salesman since 1925 and a man known for his marketing instinct, moved from Kansas City to Kalamazoo in 1932 and continued a steady climb through the sales ranks.

Still others were coming along, men like William Fred Allen, assigned to head the Dallas branch office when it opened in 1935. D. Gordon Knapp was assigned to John McColl's office in 1934 as an accountant, eventually succeeding McColl as the number one financial man.

Leslie D. Harrop, a former journalist who shifted to law, came to Upjohn in 1937 and in time not only established himself as general counsel but also built the legal division. Emil H. Schellack, Upjohn sales representative since 1919, was named Kalamazoo sales manager in 1930 and continued to move up the ladder. A few years later, Personnel Manager Franklin Varney took on as his assistant (and ultimate successor) Harry E. Turbeville. And J. Bryant Fullerton, a stout ex-Marine and the third man hired by Fred Heyl, was named the first director of the new Control Division, in 1936.

The executives managing Upjohn in the early 1930s could not have forecast another world war and how it would reshape their enterprise, but they were well aware of the Great Depression and were concerned about the future. They surely saw that to stay competitive they would have to uncover new products, and that meant an increased commitment to research.

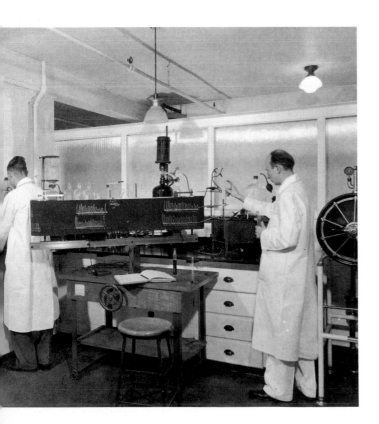

(left) The "round table" in the Kalamazoo branch credit and collection department was a way of organizing data before the age of computers. The table revolved, putting the account books within easy reach. In the foreground are depression-era word processors, cast-iron typewriters.

(izquierda) La "mesa redonda" en el departamento de crédito bancario y recaudación de Kalamazoo, era un método de organizar la información antes de la edad de las computadoras. La mesa giraba, colocando los libros de cuenta al alcance de la mano. En primer término aparece el equipo de procesamiento de texto, de la época de la Depresión: máquinas de escribir de hierro fundido.

(à gauche) Table ronde à la section de crédit et recouvrement de la société Upjohn, à Kalamazoo. C'était un procédé de collecte des données avant l'ère des ordinateurs. Table tournante, mettant les livres comptables à la portée de chacun. Au premier plan, machines à écrire et système de traitement de données à l'époque de la dépression.

（左）カラマズーの本社の信用管理部門の"丸テーブル"は、コンピューター時代以前の帳簿整理の手段であった。丸テーブルを回して、会計簿を手の届く距離まで動かした。手前には大恐慌時代のワードプロセッサー、鋳物製のタイプライターが見える。

(right) The Upjohn Research Fellowships awarded in 1933 brought an influx of young scientists. Many of them were involved in medicine's most exciting new field — hormonal research. These men are conducting a biological assay on pituitary extracts, using a smoke-tracing device.

(derecha) Las Becas de Upjohn para Investigaciones, otorgadas en 1933, trajeron consigo una afluencia de jóvenes científicos. Muchos de ellos estaban participando en un campo de la medicina estimulante: la investigación hormonal. Estos hombres llevan a cabo un ensayo biológico en extractos de pituitaria, utilizando un sistema de rastreo por medio de humo.

(à droite) Les bourses de recherche Upjohn ont permis, en 1933, à de jeunes scientifiques de se perfectionner dans une science nouvelle et passionnante : la recherche hormonale. Ces boursiers font des travaux biologiques sur des extraits de glandes pituitaires.

（右）1933年に、アップジョン特別研究員制度ができ、奨励金が与えられるようになると、若い科学者たちが、アップジョン社に続々と入社してきた。その多くは、当時の医学の大きな関心事であり、最先端の分野であったホルモン研究に従事した。スモークトレーシング機を使って、脳下垂体抽出物の生物分析を行なう研究員たち。

(left) These animal colonies were maintained for performing assays for fat-soluble vitamins in the nutrition research laboratories. At far left is Ed Wise, Ph.D., head of nutrition science (1934). Out of these experiments came a flood of important vitamin products.

(izquierda) Estas colonias de animales eran mantenidas para realizar ensayos con vitaminas solubles en grasa animal, en los laboratorios para investigaciones sobre alimentación. A la extrema izquierda aparece Ed Wise, Ph. D., jefe de ciencias de alimentación (1934). De estos experimentos se derivó un torrente de importantes productos vitamínicos.

(à gauche) Ces colonies d'animaux étaient réservées pour des tests de laboratoire pour l'utilisation de vitamines riches en matières grasses solubles dans les laboratoires de recherche sur la nutrition. A l'extrême gauche, Ed Wise, Ph.D., chef du département des sciences de la nutrition (1934). Résultat de ces expériences: une avalanche de produits riches en vitamines.

（左）栄養研究所の油溶性ビタミンの分析のために飼育されていた動物。左端は1934年当時の栄養科学部長のエド・ワイズ博士。この研究所から、多くの重要なビタミン製剤が生まれた。

(right) Super D Cod Liver Oil was the leading Upjohn product of the depression era. Here, pints of Super D are flushed with compressed air, filled with fluid under vacuum, and sealed by caps with cellulose liners, a sophisticated mechanical process for 1934.

(derecha) El Aceite de Hígado de Bacalao Super D fue el principal producto de Upjohn durante la Depresión. Aquí los envases (1/8 de galón) de Super D son limpiados con aire comprimido, llenados con líquido al vacío y sellados con tapas con revestimiento de celulosa, un sofisticado proceso mecánico para 1934.

(à droite) L'huile de foie de morue, Super D, était le principal produit Upjohn à l'époque de la grande dépression. Sur cette photo, des bouteilles d'huile de foie de morue Super D sont nettoyées à l'air comprimé, remplies de fluide sous vide, et cachetées à la cellulose, selon un procédé mécanique complexe qui était employé en 1934.

（右）スーパーD肝油は、大恐慌時代のアップジョン社の主要商品であった。何リットルというスーパーD肝油が圧縮空気によって押し出され、真空パックされた後、封印される。1934年当時としては非常に精巧な工程である。

INTO A NEW ERA OF RESEARCH

The 1930s did little to cure the world's economic problems and even less to spread peace among nations. By contrast, the decade showed to the amazement of professional and layman alike what medical and pharmaceutical research could do. For millions of ill people, it was a time of unprecedented hope.

Surveys by medical historians point out that between 1920 and 1940, all research grew by a factor of ten. The same pattern occurred in the pharmaceutical industry — 11 labs in 1920, 96 two decades later. In five drug firms surveyed, those 20 years saw an increase in total research personnel from 100 to 300; four of them had a total of 26 chemists in 1920 and 147 in 1940.

What propelled this growth of research? For one thing, World War I. It had shown U.S. pharmaceutical houses, cut off from the big European drug firms, that they did not need to depend on foreign sources for new products or raw materials. For another, American universities had begun to recognize that in addition to teaching, one of their responsibilities was to carry out basic research. Also, the concept of industrial research had evolved from the "Edisonian" type, which featured individuals working alone, to a team approach, promising greater strength.

At the same time, the desirability of more fundamental research in industry was beginning to draw increasing attention, and the pharmaceutical industry reached for top-grade scientists. Various firms started offering fellowships to academic scientists. Out of that collaboration came significant new compounds in the two decades after World War I.

The Upjohn Company moved ahead with its peers. In 1932, Fred Heyl had all of 15 people, including himself, in his research department, scarcely more than one percent of the company's 1,186 employees. And most of his staff was engaged primarily in control operations. Hardly a massive research force. But the company was poised for a period of great development of its research capability, and the framework for that growth was already in place. Dr. Merrill Hart headed the chemists. Dr. George C. Cartland had accepted the company's invitation to attend the University of Chicago's graduate school, then came to work for Fred Heyl in charge of pharmacology. And when the vitamin field had grown more interesting in 1926, Heyl had arranged to have Edwin C. Wise, a chemist from the University of Kansas, concentrate on that activity in nutrition.

It remained only for a masterful stroke by Fred Heyl to open Research's trail to the future. Heyl won the company's approval to hire ten research fellows for one year's work in Upjohn labs. He advertised in May 1933 for candidates for 10 postgraduate fellowships: one at $5,000, three at $3,600, and six at $1,800. Each fellow could choose his own subject to investigate. The only obligation for those engaged in this basic research would be to publish the results of their work as coming from the Upjohn laboratory. And any technical achievements having commercial application would have to be "first offered to The Upjohn Company."

In no time at all, Heyl's desk was swamped with applications — as many as 570 of them. Picking his way through the harvest, Heyl selected his ten. The candidates converged on Kalamazoo from the universities of Rochester, Pittsburgh, Illinois, Cincinnati, Michigan, and Yale, as well as from Rockefeller Institute, Zurich. They gave Upjohn research a very salutary shot in the arm. In one fell swoop, Heyl had put Upjohn into a new kind of medical research.

The impending arrival of the new scientists gave Fred Heyl and Lew Crockett a housekeeping problem: where would the young men work? The Upjohn Company's patchwork of aging buildings in downtown Kalamazoo had very little stretch left in it. After touring the premises, the two executives decided to house the laboratories for the newcomers on the top floor of Building 20, part of what was called the "old card factory."

This plan for locating the Class of '33 fellows was a temporary solution at best. In fact, the company suffered from space that was too small, too old, and too risky. People did not need to be reminded of the night a few years earlier when an upper floor gave way and Phenolax bottles crashed through to the packaging department below. Fortunately the 25-woman staff had left for the day.

L. N., Donald Gilmore, and their associates knew something had to be done to change the Upjohn plant, and not just to accommodate the expanding Research Department. This was Vice President Gilmore's kind of challenge. Industrial designer Albert Kahn of Detroit was invited to develop a solution that would overcome the all-too-numerous drawbacks: inadequate floor-loading capacity, only one building fireproofed, old and unsafe elevators, poor ventilation. Upjohn needed 50,000 square feet of added space.

On May 8, 1934, Donald Gilmore sent his fellow directors a 20-page memo ticking off the problems and the solution. Among many points, he took note of the fact that Dr. Heyl's Research Department, apart from the fellows in Building 20, occupied the "sooty basement" of two other structures. The overall remedy called for more than $1.5 million in new construction. Gilmore reminded his colleagues, "We are in such wonderful financial condition and have such old buildings that it seems wise to go ahead with the program at the earliest possible moment."

By the middle of May, directors and stockholders voted their approval, and construction soon began. That spelled the end of the White Office. In its place rose the executive offices on Henrietta Street, the seven-story research tower on top of new production areas, and other facilities. Financing came partly from invested surplus, partly out of profits, and did not interfere at all with dividends.

Pre-WWII Research

Dr. Fred Heyl shaped and ran Upjohn research for 31 years, turning over the responsibilities in 1944 to his longtime deputy, Dr. Merrill C. Hart. During Heyl's three decades in charge, pharmaceutical science made a historic shift from producing mixtures of medicines largely out of plant extracts (quinine, the opiates, digitalis) to medicines extracted from animal tissues, such as endocrine gland substances. The change presented a great challenge to the ingenuity and perseverance of the researchers.

At Upjohn, the shift gained impetus from the batch of fellows brought in by Heyl in 1933. A good many of them arrived itching to push ahead with hormone projects they had begun at their respective universities. They found a ready ally in Gifford Upjohn, who had already been pushing for investigation of newer possibilities in medicine. Extracts of the ovaries, the adrenal cortex, liver, beef lung, the endocrine glands — they all merited intensified research. That thrust came in the 1930s, paralleled by accelerated efforts in nutrition, and, later, sulfanilamide, penicillin, and other chemotherapeutic compounds with marked product potential. This was the scope of the company's research in the decade leading up to World War II:

VITAMINS: Upjohn entered the vitamin field when the competition was very young. In 1930, vitamins accounted for 10 percent of Upjohn's sales. Doing well with oil-soluble vitamins A and D, principally Super D and Super D Concentrate, Research set to work on the water-soluble vitamin B. The first B product, Accessorone (short for "accessory food factors") did not catch on, but Myeladol (cod liver oil plus B-rich malt) did. As of 1935, vitamin products contributed one-third of Upjohn's sales revenues.

Success with these products did more for the firm than increase its profits. It gave Upjohn a new stature among its peers. In Gifford Upjohn's words, "Primarily, I think it was the rapid, fortuitous development of the vitamin field that got us into prominence, because we were into it early... We grew along with the vitamin business."

(left) This aerial view of the Upjohn plant, taken in 1935, shows Building 24 under construction. The company's aging collection of buildings was bursting at the seams, causing the need for rapid expansion. This new building was to house general administrative offices.

(izquierda) Esta vista aérea de la planta Upjohn, tomada en 1935, muestra el Edificio 24 en construcción. La colección de viejos edificios de la compañía ya no daba abasto, y se hacía necesaria una rápida expansión. Este nuevo edificio se destinaría a servir de sede a las oficinas generales de administración.

(à gauche) Vue aérienne de l'usine Upjohn, prise en 1935, montrant les chantiers du bâtiment No. 24 en construction. La situation des vieux bâtiments de l'entreprise était critique, créant la nécessité d'une extension rapide. Ce nouvel édifice devait loger les bureaux de l'administration générale.

（左）1935年に撮影したアップジョン社工場。24号館が建設中である。アップジコン社の建物はみな古くなって来ており、早急な拡張が必要であった。新しい24号館には、一般管理部門が入ることになっていた。

(right) Building 25 was completed in 1936. The 13-story tower was a dramatic addition to the Kalamazoo skyline, symbolizing the rapid growth of the company. The top floors of the tower were reserved for research laboratories and the bottom floors for production.

(derecha) El Edificio 25 se completó en 1936. La torre de 13 pisos fue una espectacular adición al conjunto de edificios de Kalamazoo, que simbolizaba el rápido crecimiento de la compañía. Los pisos superiores de la torre se reservaron para laboratorios de investigación y los pisos inferiores para producción.

(à droite) Le bâtiment No. 25 fut achevé en 1936. Sa tour de 13 étages se profilait dans le ciel de Kalamazoo, symbole de la croissance rapide et spectaculaire de l'entreprise Upjohn. Les derniers étages au sommet de la tour étaient réservés aux laboratoires de recherche, et les premiers à la production.

（右）1936年に25号館が完成した。この十三階建てのビルは、アップジョン社の急成長ぶりを象徴するものとして、カラマズーに劇的に出現した高層ビルであった。上の方の階は研究室に、下の方の階は生産設備に当てられた。

One thing led to another. Ed Wise traveled to Norway, then Iceland, to tie up a source of extra-strength fish oil; before long, barrels of Super D Cod Liver Oil by the thousands were being stockpiled at the North Pitcher Street warehouses. Wise's researchers also recognized a growing interest in vitamin B complex and developed a product in tablet form, Cerelexin, made from extracts of yeast and liver. This was another marketing success story. Here was the first American compound with all the B-complex vitamins anyone would need in a day.

Upjohn now found itself in a race with the competition. Great progress was being made in isolating and then synthesizing not only vitamin C but also the various components of the B complex. Who would be the first to combine in one dosage form all the vitamins — fat soluble as well as water soluble — recommended for an adult's daily use? The company gave its answer in 1940: Unicap. It was not advertised to the lay public when it went on the market, but sales jumped anyway, and Unicap took over the lead among all vitamins. After one year, the product accounted for one-seventh of the company's entire sales; by 1943, it represented one-fifth of the total. By 1945, one-half of Upjohn's business came from its nutrition supplements, led by Unicap. Meanwhile, the benefit to Americans everywhere was extraordinary. Science writer Leonard Engel asserted that these Upjohn products gave the U.S. "standards of nutrition second to none in the world."

HORMONES: One of Fred Heyl's 1933 research fellows, Marvin H. Kuizenga, a biochemist, had worked on adrenal cortex extract in graduate school. In time, isolating and analyzing the chemistry of the adrenal hormones brought him into national prominence.

Moving to a bench in Building 20, Marvin Kuizenga first set about the task of producing an improved adrenal cortex extract. He managed to steer through the challenges, and in 1935 Upjohn brought to the market its product ACE, the first standardized and sterile adrenal cortex extract; it was used for specific treatment of Addison's disease, and for lesser degrees of corticoadrenal deficiency. Thus, Upjohn could justly claim that it pioneered in developing these extracts some 15 years before the advent of cortisone.

Between 1934 and 1940, Dr. Kuizenga and his associates arrived at other findings of note. They learned that a number of steroids could be isolated from the adrenal cortex. Particular emphasis was given to isolating and identifying each and then measuring and comparing the biological activity. The researchers managed to come up with small amounts of Compound E — cortisone — and Compound F — hydrocortisone — but scientists elsewhere actually hit that target first. Subsequently, other Upjohn researchers brought distinction to the company by facilitating the synthesis of these compounds.

In these same years, Upjohn scientists also searched for heightened understanding of the gonadotropic and sex hormones estradiol, progesterone, and testosterone. Here, too, medical studies in the 1920s had hinted at possible commercial potential in this area. There was reason to suspect that these hormones might relieve disorders and ailments of the reproductive system, both male and female.

Distant lines of research converged. In 1928, European researchers found estrogenic hormonal activity in the urine of pregnant women and animals. A few years later,

gonadotropic hormones were discovered in the blood of pregnant mares, closely resembling the hormone produced by the human anterior pituitary gland. High toxicity, however, prevented its use in humans.

Upjohn researchers, most of them 1933 fellows, took up the project in earnest. Collecting the blood serum of pregnant mares stabled at Upjohn Richland Farms, they discovered a practical method of preparing a standardized, safe, and highly stable sex hormone for humans. Gonadogen, introduced in sterile solution in 1934, was used in the treatment of sterility, amenorrhea, delayed puberty, and other hormonal abnormalities.

At the same time, estrogenic hormones were discovered. After six years of research work, clinical studies, and bumping into another institution's patent, Upjohn introduced Urestrin in 1940. Using Upjohn Richland Farms' horses as the source of the raw material — pregnant-mares' urine — Urestrin quickly became a success in the treatment of menopausal symptoms and menstrual disorders. In fact, its quick acceptance posed quite a problem — demand outstripped supply. For a while the company had to import mares' urine from a number of stables. To Upjohn chemists, the dilemma was not insuperable; they were on the verge of partially synthesizing the sex hormones, and total synthesis was only a bit farther down the road.

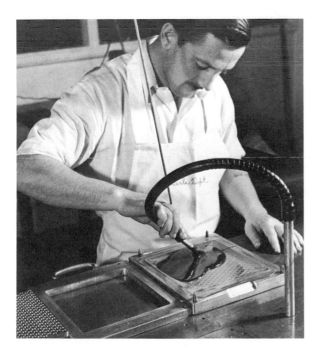

(left) Making friable pills in the 1930s was becoming a cumbersome task. They had to be rolled by one machine, then counted and bottled by another. Compressed tablets could be made, counted, and bottled by one rotary punch machine.

(izquierda) La fabricación de píladoras friables en los años 30 se estaba convirtiendo en una tarea tediosa. Tenían que ser enrolladas por una máquina, luego contadas y embotelladas por otra. Las tabletas comprimidas podían fabricarse, contarse y embotellarse por una máquina de punzón rotativo.

(à gauche) Fabriquer des pilules friables dans les années 30 était une tâche ardue. Il fallait les confectionner dans une machine, puis les compter, et les mettre en flacon dans une autre machine. Les comprimés pouvaient être fabriqués, comptés, et mis en bouteille par une seule rotative.

（左）崩れる丸薬の製造も1930年代には面倒な仕事と考えられるようになってきていた。最初の機械でコーティングをし、もう一つの機械で数を数える。錠剤であれば、製造し、数を数え、包装するという工程が、ロータリー・パンチ機一台でできた。

(right) Soft elastic capsule production began in earnest in late 1935 when Upjohn began experimenting with the dosage form for use in several vitamin formulations. By 1937, Concentrate B and G capsules debuted, and a small production unit was working two shifts.

(derecha) La producción de cápsulas elásticas blandas comenzó en serio a fines de 1935, cuando Upjohn inició los experimentos con la forma de dosificación para uso en varias fórmulas de vitaminas. Para 1937 aparecieron las cápsulas concentradas B y G, y una pequeña unidad de producción trabajaba en dos turnos.

(à droite) La production de capsules de gélatine commença vers la fin de 1935. Upjohn commençait à expérimenter le dosage de diverses formules de vitamines. En 1937 débuta la production de capsules B et G concentrées, et deux équipes furent affectées à la production sur une petite échelle.

（右）1935年の後半、柔らかく弾力性のあるカプセルの生産が本格的に始まった。このとき、アップジョン社ではちょうど各種ビタミン剤の剤型についての研究を開始していた。1937年には、濃縮BおよびGカプセルが登場し、小さな生産施設は、二交代制で稼動していた。

(left) In the mid-1930s, the bacteriological research department supervised the production of sterile solutions and vaccines, managed bacteriological control, and conducted research experiments on new compounds. The woman in the foreground is working with vaccine cultures.

(izquierda) A mediados de los años 30 el departamento de investigaciones bacteriológicas supervisaba la producción de soluciones estériles y vacunas, dirigía el control bacteriológico, y realizaba experimentos de investigación sobre nuevos compuestos. La mujer en primer plano está trabajando con cultivos de vacunas.

(à gauche) Au cours des années 1930, la section de recherche bactériologique supervisait la production de solutions stériles et de vaccins. Elle supervisait également le contrôle bactériologique et menait des recherches expérimentales sur de nouveaux composés. Au premier plan, des femmes faisant des cultures de vaccin.

（左）1930年代の中頃、細菌学研究部門は滅菌溶液とワクチンの製造を監督し、新薬開発のための研究活動を続けていた。手前の女性は培養ワクチンを取り扱っている。

(right) Inspecting finished soft elastic capsules in the 1930s required fine attention to detail, a tolerance for tedious work, and good eyesight. These women searched for "leakers" and "imperfects" with tweezers.

(derecha) La inspección de las cápsulas elásticas blandas ya terminadas, en los años 30, exigía una fina atención a los detalles, tolerancia para el trabajo tedioso y buena visión. Estas mujeres buscan "pérdidas" e "imperfecciones" con pinzas.

(à droite) L'inspection des capsules de gélatine, dans les années 1930, exigeait une attention à tous les détails, une tolérance du travail ardu et une vision excellente. Ces femmes cherchaient des "imperfections" et des "fuites" à l'aide de petites pinces.

（右）最終工程を終えた軟カプセルの検査では、1930年代には、細部への注意、こまかい仕事に対する忍耐力、そしてよい視力が必要であった。女子社員たちがピンセットで、漏れや不良品をチェックする。

HEPARIN: In Kalamazoo, Marvin Kuizenga built a reputation as a bridge-player of memorable deftness. This may have served him well when he reported for work, because he had to play several research hands at the same time. Apart from his concentration on adrenal cortex hormones, he set out to find a better way of extracting heparin, which can be used to slow the clotting of blood, from fresh beef lung. That effort not only succeeded but also pointed out how the yield of heparin could be tripled from a given quantity of beef lung.

Fueled by this line of study, Upjohn scaled up the lab work and in 1942 brought its product Heparin into the marketplace. The company was among the earliest to achieve this goal. Heparin qualified as the first anticoagulant in physicians' hands. Had it been available 14 years earlier, it might have saved the life of Harold Upjohn.

KAOPECTATE: This product marked its 50th anniversary in 1986, but its origins go back to ancient times. Its active ingredient, kaolin, a fine clay, was used to stop diarrhea by ancient generations of Chinese and by Cherokee Indians when they inhabited what is now Georgia.

In 1935, Gifford Upjohn came across a journal article about the antidiarrheal effectiveness of kaolin. "Since there weren't any major kaolin-based products like this on the market," he recalls, "we decided to make one." Kaolin was available in England, China, and Georgia. The company decided to buy it from England, and did so until the early stages of World War II, when Georgia became the source.

Although Kaopectate had all the potential of a good over-the-counter seller, Upjohn marketed it through the physician, much as it had so many times in the past.

Early sales were hardly vigorous. In 1937, Kaopectate's $36,653 reflected less than one percent of net sales. The next year, it edged up to almost one percent. By 1949, the product broke over the $1 million mark, and in 1985, sales totaled more than $20 million. Its age notwithstanding, Kaopectate remains a leading antidiarrheal.

OTHER RESEARCH ROUTES: Dr. Merrill Hart and Upjohn's bacteriologists gave prolonged attention to the perfection of antiseptic and germicidal agents. One of these, a combination of an organic mercurial and pentacresol, went into distribution in 1936 as Mercresin, designed for use by physicians in preparing patients for surgery.

In 1933, Upjohn hired the city of Detroit's Director of Laboratories Dr. John F. Norton to succeed Wilbur Payne as head of the bacteriologic lab. Norton soon learned about Fred Heyl's outlook on institutional cooperation in research. "The greatest source of intellectual advance," said Dr. Heyl, "stems from the free, untrammeled, and generously supported work of our great state universities and other scientific organizations." And what was the role of a company like Upjohn? It was "largely to reduce these discoveries to better and better productive practice." John Norton subscribed to this view. He was soon working closely with the Michigan State Department of Health. Out of their joint efforts came a modified whooping cough vaccine in 1936.

Further Transfusions for Research

Dr. Heyl's gamble on the research fellows in 1933 had paid off so well that in 1941 the company created 14 more of these research positions. One of the winners, Dr. Dwight J. Ingle, came to Kalamazoo from the Mayo Clinic Research Laboratories. At Upjohn, he concentrated on studying the physiology and chemistry of the adrenal cortex. His work drew national attention: in 1947, he received the first Roche-Organon award in endocrinology.

But research accomplishments at Upjohn came from hands other than those of the fellows. Farm-reared Floyd A. Eberly, a Ph.D. and organic chemist from the University of Kansas, joined Upjohn production in 1935 and later shifted to Fred Heyl's area. One of his early targets in research was to define ways of testing the toxicity of the brand new sulfanilamides. During World War II, he worked in other areas — with serum albumin, immune serum globulin, and fibrin foam. Eberly later rose to be a corporate executive vice president, and served the company for 32 years.

In the mid-1930s researchers were leaving plant extracts behind and making increasing use of animal extracts. But the pendulum kept swinging toward the complete synthesis of drug compounds. In 1935, Upjohn began marketing its first synthetic medicinal, Bismuth Ethylcamphorate, used in the treatment of syphilis.

CORPORATE GROWTH, VITAMIN-FORTIFIED

Company sales climbed each year of the 1930s, more than doubling between 1930 and 1940. The Great Depression may have hit hard elsewhere but not at Upjohn. No one was laid off for lack of work. Workers were paid for a full 40-hour week, even if production called for fewer hours; insurance and vacation benefits stayed in effect. The 1,128 Upjohn employees of 1930 grew to 1,307 in 1933. By mid-decade the total passed 1,500. And as the years of depression turned to years of war, Upjohn personnel numbered nearly 2,000.

An aggressive marketing effort keyed Upjohn's growth during those troubled years. Upjohn's sales network, largely stimulated by vitamin product success, expanded noticeably from 1931 to 1941. Malcolm Galbraith set up a Memphis branch in 1931 and gave Kalamazoo separate branch status in 1934. After that, branch offices opened in quick succession — in Dallas in January 1935, Toronto ten months later, Atlanta in April 1936, and Cleveland in January 1938. Boston's branch office opened in early January 1940, and the Minneapolis branch set forth in December 1941.

Sales representatives fanning out from those offices and from the older branches (New York, Kansas City, and San Francisco) carried an impressive bag of samples. Phenolax, that durable winner, may have peaked in 1924, but it sold an average of 60 million tablets a year in the 1930s. Citrocarbonate sold well, too; as the decade began, the product generated 27 percent of total sales. The following year, it hit a peak volume of almost $2.1 million. And then there were the vitamins, awakening Americans to a better sense of how vital food supplements were to the health and growth of their families.

The closer the end of the depression decade came, the more Upjohn put advertising and promotion to work in support of its sales campaign in the field. But before those tactics could be applied with any zeal, there had to be

some fence-mending with the American Medical Association's Council on Pharmacy and Chemistry, and its publication, *Journal of the American Medical Association (JAMA)*.

The relationship had been strained for some time. In 1905, the AMA refused to accept Upjohn ads in *JAMA* because it felt the company did not detail its products ethically, and that some Upjohn advertising was misleading. W. E. Upjohn was offended and felt the company didn't have to advertise. Upjohn representatives could call on the doctor directly and tell their story. There was no need for journal advertising. For nearly 35 years Upjohn placed no ads in the influential trade publications.

When Gifford Upjohn, not long out of medical school, arrived at the company in 1930, he saw "a bad situation. The AMA thought we were not a good company. They thought we had developed a technique of selling the doctor by detailing with our own scientific rationale, and that wasn't necessarily what they knew to be true... Therefore, it was unethical as far as they were concerned."

Young Gifford felt this made no sense, so he spoke up — in fact, he "insisted" that Upjohn mend its approach. He believed that Upjohn had to "change the nature of our research... We were going to have to change the character of the products so that we could get them approved by the Council on Pharmacy and Chemistry."

(left) The company's first sterile solutions were produced in 1917, through methods established by Fred Heyl and the small staff of the bacteriology lab under Wilbur Payne. By the mid-1930s, this elaborate arrangement of filtration equipment was being used in sterile fluid manufacturing.

(izquierda) Las primeras soluciones estériles de la compañía se produjeron en 1917, mediante los métodos establecidos por Fred Heyl y el pequeño personal del laboratorio de bacteriología bajo la dirección de Wilbur Payne. A mediados de la década de los 30, este complicado equipo de filtración se utilizaba en la fabricación de líquido estéril.

(à gauche) En 1917 débuta la production des premières solutions stériles, par des méthodes conçues par Fred Heyl et une équipe du laboratoire de bactériologie sous la direction de Wilbur Payne. Dans les années 1930, ce système complexe de filtration était utilisé dans la production de fluides stériles.

（左）1917年に、アップジョン社初の滅菌溶液が生産された。フレッド・ヘイル、ウイルバー・ペインが率いる細菌学研究室の小さな研究グループが開発した方式によって生産されたものであった。1930年代中頃までには、この濾過器が精巧に組み立てられ、滅菌溶剤の生産に使われていた。

(right) In 1936, the Control Division was established with J. Bryant Fullerton (third from left) as director. Fullerton and his staff improved Upjohn products by initiating important quality control changes both on the production line and in the laboratory.

(derecha) En 1936, se estableció la División de Control con J. Bryant Fullerton (tercero de izquierda a derecha) como Director. Fullerton y su personal mejoraron los productos Upjohn al iniciar importantes cambios en el control de calidad, tanto en la línea de producción como en el laboratorio.

(à droite) En 1936, la division de contrôle fut fondée avec pour directeur J. Bryant Fullerton (troisième, à partir de la gauche). Fullerton et le personnel ont amélioré la qualité des produits Upjohn, en apportant des réformes importantes à la procédure de contrôle tant à la production qu'au laboratoire.

（右）1936年、管理分析部門はJ．ブライトン・フラートン（左から3人目）を長として発足した。フラートンとスタッフは、生産工程や研究室における管理分析の重要な仕事を担当し、アップジョン製品の品質向上の原動力となった。

He was convinced that the company had to recognize that fundamental medical advances in the future were going to come from university medical schools, and therefore it would be smart to maintain a good relationship with the AMA and the leaders of the medical profession.

The nature of Upjohn research and the character of its products had changed dramatically during the past two decades; it was time to approach the AMA.

Part of a solution existed right within the Upjohn camp. Production head Dr. Harold Adams had gone to Williams College with the council's new secretary, Dr. Paul Leech. They got together and talked, with the result that Dr. Leech suggested Upjohn submit for the council's approval some simple products (e.g., "uncombined pharmaceuticals without trade names"). With pharmacologist George Cartland as conduit, Upjohn presented some simple items to the council in December 1937, won its approval of a "small list," and gradually the council withdrew its objections to Upjohn advertising in the JAMA.

As a starter, however, the company decided in 1939 to place in the JAMA a series of institutional ads, which made no mention of specific products. These were followed the next year by a generous schedule of ads and mailings to physicians. This 1940 thrust included 12 four-color inserts detailing "Studies in the Avitaminoses" (vitamin deficiencies). Reaching beyond the AMA's publication, Upjohn placed ads in 80 medical and drug magazines. The next year the company lengthened its stride, placing institutional ads with the theme "Why Your Doctor Knows" in lay publications such as *Time* and *Saturday Evening Post*. A sequel to this, "Your Doctor Speaks," told of progress physicians were making in treating specific diseases. Four-color fine art paintings ran as companions to these messages. During these same years Upjohn began to put out a scientific periodical, *Scope*, edited by Dr. Garrard MacLeod of the Medical Department, for mailing to physicians. Prominent New York artist-designer Will Burtin laid out the first issues.

Upjohn also revived an old strategy from the glory days of Phenolax, which called for reaching the public in a professional manner that would not offend physicians. It decided to package window displays on vitamins and distribute them to drugstores all over the country. Each display unfolded around a central painting which showed a familiar family scene and a few vitamins, as well. Thinking big, the company commissioned the widely admired illustrator Norman Rockwell to do one of these paintings a year. Rockwell's inaugural work in 1939 depicted "Super D Tommy" measuring himself on a doctor's scale. Rockwell's and other artists' work throughout the 1940s and 1950s created a small gallery of illustrations relating to the health needs of the lay public and the medical community. For the promotion-minded, this program had a happy postscript: for years Upjohn found itself obliged to meet a fairly large number of requests from doctors and druggists for reprints.

The drive to expand advertising came mainly from one man, C. V. Patterson. Beginning as a salesman and later serving as secretary to Sales Director Malcolm Galbraith, "Pat" Patterson joined sales management during the late 1930s. He brought with him a firm conviction about the need to broaden Upjohn's advertising reach. His views gained reinforcement in 1941 when the versatile Jack C. Gauntlett, son-in-law of the founder's daughter Dorothy Upjohn Dalton, joined the firm. Gauntlett first worked in the export department, then transferred to the advertising department, where he was to become director in 1955, and later headed Marketing.

(left) The Medical Division was established in 1937 with a staff of one — its director E. Gifford Upjohn, M.D. (left). Soon, new staff members were monitoring scientific literature, supervising the writing of product labels, helping instruct salesmen, and arranging for product testing.

(izquierda) La División Médica se estableció en 1937 con sólo una persona su director, E. Gifford Upjohn, médico (izquierda). Pronto nuevos miembros del personal estaban vigilando la literatura científica, supervisando la redacción de las etiquetas de los productos, ayudando a instruir a los vendedores y haciendo arreglos para la prueba de productos.

(à gauche) La division médicale a été créée en 1937, avec une seule personne : son directeur, Gifford Upjohn, médecin (à gauche). Peu de temps après, le personnel s'agrandit pour s'adonner à des tâches diverses : information scientifique, supervision de la rédaction des étiquettes des produits, aide à la formation des agents de vente, et planification des tests de produits Upjohn.

（左）学術部門は1937年に設立された。部員はたった1人、部長のE．G．アップジョン医博であった（左）。まもなく新しい部員が次つぎと入社し、学術文献の検索、製品添付文書のチェック、営業部員の指導、製品試験などを行なっていた。

(right) Upjohn introduced three ointment products, a new specialty for the company, in 1902. By 1939, when this woman was working on the ointment tube filling line, the company marketed more than 40 ointments.

(derecha) Upjohn introdujo tres productos de ungüento, una nueva especialidad para la compañía en 1902. Para 1939, cuando esta mujer estaba trabajando en la hilera en donde se llenaban los tubitos de ungüento, la compañía estaba vendiendo más de 40 ungüentos.

(à droite) La société Upjohn a lancé sur le marché trois types de pommades, nouvelle spécialité de l'entreprise, en 1902. Vers 1939, à l'époque où cette femme travaillait à l'usine de mise en tube, la société Upjohn avait déjà commercialisé plus de 40 types de pommade.

（右）1902年、アップジョン社は3種類の軟膏剤を発売し、外用剤の分野にも進出した。これは軟膏をチューブに入れる工程で、この写真が撮影された1939年当時、アップジョン社は40種類以上の軟膏剤を発売していた。

(left) In 1939, this Upjohn worker employed a wooden tablet sorter little different from equipment used in the 1890s. For small lots, this kind of hand work was still widely used. The difference was the hat and rubber gloves that production now required.

(izquierda) En 1939 este operario de Upjohn empleaba un separador y contador de píldoras de madera que difería poco del equipo usado en la década de 1890. Para pequeños lotes esta clase de trabajo a mano se usaba mucho todavía. La diferencia consistía en el sombrero y los guantes de goma que la producción ahora requería.

(à gauche) En 1939, cet employé de la société Upjohn utilisait une palette de bois servant à trier les comprimés, mais légèrement différente de celle qu'on utilisait dans les années 1890. Pour les petits lots de comprimés, ce type de travail manuel était très courant. La différence : le chapeau et les gants de caoutchouc, dont on se sert en production, de nos jours.

（左）1939年、アップジョン社では、1890年代のものとほとんど変わらない、木製の錠剤仕分け器を使っていた。小さなロットの場合には、まだ手作業が広く行なわれていた。違いは、帽子、手袋の着用が義務づけられるようになったことである。

(right) Whether it's 1886, 1936, or 1986, some basic production processes just can't be improved. These revolving pans for coating pills and tablets were modeled after W.E.'s original friable pill machine. Similar pans are still on the job throughout the company today.

(derecha) Ya sea en 1886, en 1936 o en 1986, algunos procesos básicos de producción no pueden mejorarse. Estos recipientes rotativos para revestir pastillas y tabletas siguieron el modelo de la máquina original para pastillas desintegrables de William Erastus. Recipientes similares siguen aún desempeñando su tarea en la compañía hoy.

(à droite) Que ce soit en 1886, en 1936 ou en 1986, certaines méthodes de production ne peuvent être améliorées. Cet appareil qui sert à enrober pilules et comprimés a été fabriqué d'après le modèle inventé par William Upjohn, la première machine à pilules friables. Le même appareil est toujours en usage aujourd'hui dans tous les centres Upjohn.

（右）1886年であっても、1936年であっても、1986年であっても、基本的な生産工程の中には、あまり変わらないものもある。錠剤を糖衣錠に仕上げる回転皿は、W.E.アップジョンの作った"崩れる丸薬"のための回転皿が原型となっている。同じような機械が、今日なお社内の各所で使われている。

ORGANIZATIONAL CHANGE

Several dimensions were added to Upjohn's administrative structure in 1937. The Personnel Department opened its doors officially, with the former preacher, Franklin Varney, in charge.

Then there was the proposal of Gifford Upjohn to establish a medical department and thus upgrade contacts with the medical profession and perhaps, in the process, give sales a legitimate boost. The department would establish rapport with medical schools and the AMA. University physicians would be encouraged to evaluate Upjohn products and publish their observations. The department would cultivate doctors and urge them to write articles that might have "commercial value." Then, too, it should arrange for field testing to define product safety, usage instructions, and toxicity warnings. Department staff would also seek product approvals from nonofficial entities, supervise the writing of product labels, and help instruct salesmen.

All in all, it was a big order. When E. G. U. got the go-ahead on the proposal, he asked if he could leave the production area and become head of the Medical Department. His request was granted. At first it was a department of one — E. G. U. — but soon Drs. William Murray and William Wenner came in to help.

The timing could scarcely have been better because a tragedy made such activity imperative. On October 19, 1937, the worst kind of news for drug firms came out of Tulsa, Oklahoma. Nine people had died of kidney damage after taking a new medicine called Elixir of Sulfanilamide. Normally, elixirs have an alcohol base, but sulfa did not dissolve well in alcohol, so an unwitting scientist used diethylene glycol — the main ingredient in automobile antifreeze, and a deadly poison — but the label failed to mention that. By November 11, more than 73 people were dead. Sad to say, even a minimum of testing before the product was marketed would have picked up the deadly component, but that analysis wasn't made.

Reacting with urgency, Congress drafted the Food, Drug and Cosmetic Act of 1938. Its main requirement stemmed from the Elixir of Sulfanilamide disaster: from then on, no company could sell a new medicine until it had demonstrated to the Food and Drug Administration that people could safely use it.

"You couldn't do that without having some clinical testing," says Gifford Upjohn — and a medical department to take charge of it.

AG-VET BEGINNINGS

Meanwhile, a Kalamazoo St. Bernard named Prince figured in launching another activity at Upjohn. Prince belonged to Sales Director Malcolm Galbraith, and a day came when the dog needed the attention of a veterinarian. That brought Galbraith to the doorstep of Dr. J. Lavere Davidson, a local D.V.M. The two men found they liked each other's brand of talk, and Davidson took to visiting at the Galbraith home even when Prince had no complaints.

One conversation led to another, and in 1940, Galbraith proposed that Davidson do a market survey of adapting Upjohn's product line to the needs of the veterinary doctor. Accepting the challenge, Davidson toured midwestern cities, found the market wide open, and even wrote orders from 10 percent of the vets he called on. That satisfied Galbraith that a market existed among veterinarians for Upjohn items, so Dr. Davidson was hired part-time to go after the business. Making up a catalog, answering letters from the field, devising new

veterinary products — these tasks absorbed his early months on the job. Then, in 1941, events in a wartorn world caught up with him. As a Reserve Army captain, he was called to active duty. That and the company's war commitments led Upjohn to put off temporarily further talk of assembling a full-fledged Department of Veterinary Medicine. But the seeds had been sown.

REWARD AND CONCERN

Life at The Upjohn Company in the waning years of the 1930s had a special quality. By today's standards, the company was still a small enterprise — employment crested over 2,000 for the first time in 1940-41. Some who were still active could remember what Upjohn had been like in 1900, with scarcely more than 50 employees.

The founder had always watched for those, in L. N. Upjohn's words, "who could do things." He had appreciated people like that and wanted them to know it, so much so that he addressed the matter in his will. A block of stock was left to the company; the income was to be available annually for use as prizes "for special accomplishment of any employee, except members and relatives of the Upjohn family." Any income not used in a given year would go to the Kalamazoo Foundation. This was the charter for the W. E. Upjohn Prize Awards, as he called them.

The awards were presented for the first time in 1938. They went to three men who had contributed, as the founder had hoped, "to the stability of the business by more than routine services." These three — with a total of 91 years as Upjohn employees — were Vice President and Treasurer John S. McColl, Sales Director Malcolm Galbraith, and Director of Research Dr. Frederick W. Heyl. Since then, more than 1,300 employees have received Upjohn Awards. They are presented each year on October 18, the anniversary of W. E. Upjohn's death.

SERVING A NATION AT WAR

At eight o'clock on Monday morning, December 1, 1941, Upjohn's new branch office in Minneapolis opened for business. It was a festive occasion. Baskets of roses and chrysanthemums sent by the other branches adorned the desks and cabinets. Lester Tritle, Jr., a 20-year Upjohn veteran trained in Kansas City by Malcolm Galbraith, presided as sales manager, while Office Manager Harold White probed the first morning's mail. In short order, his people set to work processing invoices.

With their colleagues elsewhere in the nation, the Minneapolis sales representatives were reaping another fine harvest. The American physician and his patients were buying more Upjohn products every year.

On Wednesday of that week, back in Kalamazoo, Upjohn's sales manager for government accounts, Fernen E. Fox, received an order for 153 ampules of S.S. Ephedrine Sulphate (used in treating asthma). The contract wasn't very large — $56 in all — but at least the company was beginning to get some defense business from the military. That same day, 1,000 miles south of the Aleutian Islands, the six carriers of Vice Admiral Nagumo's First Air Fleet plowed deep furrows southward through the gray Pacific seas.

Four days later, at the end of the long and fateful Sunday of December 7, America was catapulted into war. The nation's medical and scientific resources were marshaled as they never had been before. Science writer Robert Burlingham judged in his *Odyssey of Modern Drug Research* that these activities "raised the whole medical research and development effort in this country . . . to a new and permanently higher plane." New techniques and

new forms of cooperation between companies accelerated progress in unprecedented ways. The result was greater medical advance than the world had ever seen in a comparable period.

Shifting to Wartime Status

The war had not been wholly unexpected. As early as 1938, as the world situation worsened, Upjohn executives had learned that the military wanted to look over key industries in America. On October 27, 1939, an agent of the War Resources Board surveyed the Upjohn facilities in Kalamazoo.

Upjohn and its competitors began to bid on contracts for "defense" business. Time and again, Upjohn finished as an also-ran. In November 1940, Donald Gilmore reviewed the situation in a memo to C. V. Patterson.

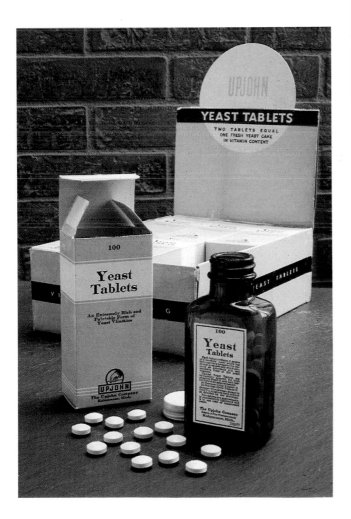

(left) The 1940s brought research and development methodologies that required sophisticated new equipment and specially trained personnel. This man is testing a substance to determine its exact melting point, a way to establish its identity and purity.

(izquierda) En los años 40 surgieron métodos de investigación y desarrollo que requerían nuevo equipo más sofisticado y sobre todo personal especialmente capacitado. Este hombre está probando una substancia para determinar su punto exacto de fusión; una forma de establecer su identidad y su pureza.

(à gauche) Les années 1940 ont marqué l'avènement de techniques et de méthodologies nouvelles, en matière de recherche théorique et pratique, exigeant un équipement moderne et un personnel qualifié. Cet homme vérifie une substance afin de déterminer son point exact de fusion, un moyen d'établir son identité et sa pureté.

（左）1940年代に入ると、新しい研究開発の方法論が確立され、より高度な、新しい研究施設や、専門的な教育訓練を受けた研究員が必要となってきた。物質を同定し、その純度を測定するために、正確な融点を測っているところ。

(right) "TWO TABLETS EQUAL ONE FRESH YEAST CAKE IN VITAMIN CONTENT" points out this retail display for Upjohn Yeast Tablets. The tablets, sold from 1937 to 1967, contained vitamins B and G.

(derecha) "Dos tabletas equivalen al contenido vitamínico de un pastel de levadura fresca" —esta frase aparecía en un desplegado para las Tabletas de levadura Upjohn, que contenían vitaminas B y G y estuvieron a la venta de 1937 a 1967.

(à droite) "DEUX TABLETTES EGALENT UN GATEAU DE LEVURE FRAIS VITAMINE", lit-on sur cette annonce pour tablettes de levure Upjohn. Ces tablettes, en vente de 1937 à 1967, contenaient des vitamines B et G.

（右）「できたてのイーストケーキ1個のビタミンが、この2錠で」と、小売店用のディスプレーでアップジョン社はイースト錠を宣伝した。1937年から1967年まで販売されたこのイースト錠剤は、ビタミンBとビタミンGを含んでいるものであった。

Upjohn had lost out on 54 straight biddings. Why? Simply, its bids were too high. That dictated a new policy: prices on government business would be set close to standard costs, and its army-navy bids would omit most overhead charges. This approach worked. On February 11, 1941, Upjohn received its first defense order, $221.40 worth of Vitamin C Concentrate Caps. Other orders followed, the first sizable one coming in January 1942 for 50 million aspirin tablets for the Naval Supply Depot in Brooklyn.

To handle these affairs, the company transferred Salesman Fernen Fox from Denver to the home office, and from May 1, 1940, until January 15, 1945, he served as Upjohn's contact for all government business, keeping in touch with a dozen or more national offices and many military supply depots.

Kalamazoo may have seemed a long way from the combat zones, but a wartime psychology soon took hold. Little more than two months after Pearl Harbor, an Army Procurement official urged tightened security. Guards should be posted and employees fingerprinted and equipped with badges. Visitors' passes should be registered, packages checked in and out, fire drills scheduled, identifications required from all outsiders, flood lights and window barricades installed, and unknown cars banned from the plant area.

Gifford Upjohn, who directed civilian mobilization in Kalamazoo County, testifies to the mood of the times. "There was a real sense of urgency about sabotage," he says. "There were stories about the Japanese submarines going up and down the West Coast. The German navy was up and down the East Coast. The feeling was that we ought to be ready if something happened."

Awareness of the emergency sharpened in the spring of 1942. A red-bordered War Department letter arrived on May 15, a Friday. Upjohn was ordered to go into three shifts on all war work. Production head Harold Adams was out of town, so his number two man, Will Little, called a night meeting to plan the changeover. A three-shift schedule would begin in Dr. Floyd Eberly's Sterile Solutions and Vaccines Department. It was too late to reach the affected personnel, so management told individuals as they came to work Monday morning. Some were directed to go home and return for the 3 P.M. shift, others, to come back for the 11 P.M. graveyard shift. If anyone had a gripe, Floyd Eberly never heard about it. At the same time, the plant swung into a stepped-up schedule for turning out 17 million antimalarial tablets for the army.

Money and manpower soon emerged as other compelling issues. A long telegram arrived on May 27, 1942, from Treasury Secretary Henry Morganthau, Jr., urging the firm to do whatever was necessary to get employees to subscribe to war bonds at the level of 10 percent of gross payroll. And the sense of emergency heightened when Selective Service told employers in October 1942 that they could expect to have all their able-bodied men drafted. The company began immediately to train women as their replacements.

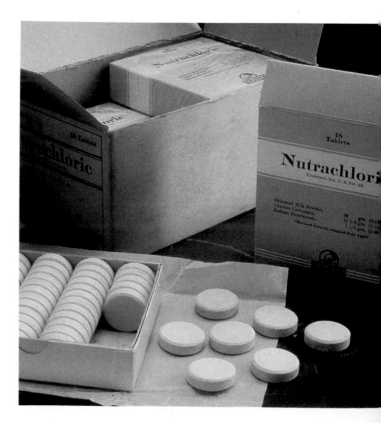

Products for the Fighting Forces

From start to finish, Upjohn supplied great quantities of products to the armed forces. In 1941 alone, 87 different items were produced for the military. Greatest volume throughout the war was in serum albumin, penicillin, sulfadiazine, sterilized sulfanilamide, aspirin, sodium bicarbonate tablets, and chemical pellets (used to cut the flash of naval guns firing at night). Producing these items for the war effort demanded high dedication, and it often entailed a measure of drama.

PENICILLIN: Alexander Fleming's discovery in the late 1920s finally found its proper role in serving mankind during World War II. At Upjohn, Dr. J. F. Norton and his associates first made penicillin in March 1942, using a culture from the U. S. Department of Agriculture.

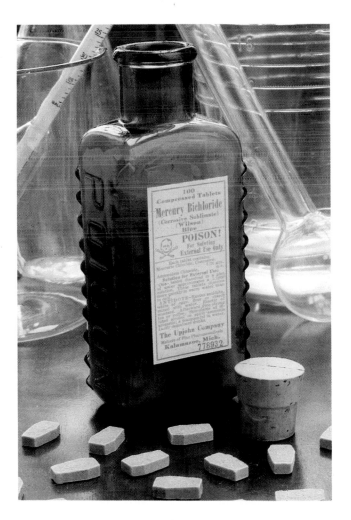

(left) The company's Nutrition Research Laboratory, established in 1927, created such products as Super D Cod Liver Oil (1928), Unicap multivitamins (1940), and Nutrachloric tablets (1937). Nutrachloric tablets were used as a pediatric dietary supplement.

(izquierda) El Laboratorio de Investigaciones sobre Alimentación, establecido por la compañía en 1927, creó productos tales como Aceite de Hígado de Bacalao Super D (1928), multivitaminas Unicap (1940) y tabletas Nutrachloric (1937). Las tabletas Nutrachloric se usaban como suplemento dietético pediátrico.

(à gauche) Le laboratoire de recherche en matière de nutrition, créé en 1927, a préparé des produits comme l'huile de foie de morue Super D (1928), les tablettes de Nutrachloric (1937), et les comprimés Unicap de multivitamines (1940). Les tablettes de Nutrachloric servaient de complément d'alimentation en pédiatrie.

（左）1927年に設立したアップジョン社の栄養研究所からは、スーパーD肝油（1928）、ユニキャップ総合ビタミン剤（1940）、ニュートラ・クロリック錠（1937）などの製品が開発された。ニュートラ・クロリック錠は、幼児の栄養補助剤として使われた。

(right) If the label warning "POISON" didn't clue you in that Upjohn's Mercury Bichloride was not meant for internal use, then surely the coffin-shaped tablet did. These tablets were dissolved in a solution used to sterilize lab instruments.

(derecha) Si la etiqueta que dice "VENENO" no le indicaba que el Bicloruro de mercurio Upjohn no era para uso interno, seguramente que lo indicaba la tableta misma en forma de féretro. Estas tabletas se disolvían en una solución usada para esterilizar instrumentos.

(à droite) Si l'étiquette POISON ne suffisait pas à indiquer que ce produit Upjohn, le bichlorure de mercure, n'était pas pour usage interne, le comprimé en forme de cercueil, lui, accomplissait certainement ce but. Ces comprimés étaient dissous dans une solution servant à stériliser des instruments de laboratoire.

（右）アップジョン社の塩化第二水銀剤のラベルには「毒薬」という表示があり、これは服用禁止を意味しているわけだが、うっかりそれに気がつかない場合でも、錠剤が柩のかたちをしているので、それが一つの目印の役割を果たした。この錠剤は、溶かして実験器具を消毒するのに使われた。

(left) By the end of World War II, sulfadiazine "Wound Tablets" turned out to be by far the largest of Upjohn's war orders. Some 21,184,384 plastic packages were produced, containing more than 169 million 7.7-gram tablets. Upjohn also designed and milled the package.

(izquierda) Para finales de la II Guerra Mundial, las "Tabletas para heridas" de sulfadiazina se convirtieron, por mucho, en los mayores pedidos a la casa Upjohn durante la guerra. Se produjeron cerca de 21.184.384 paquetes plásticos, que contenían más de 169 millones de tabletas de 7,7 gramos. Upjohn diseñó y elaboró el paquete.

(à gauche) Vers la fin de la seconde guerre mondiale, les "tablettes" de sulphadiazine "pour blessures" absorbaient le plus gros volume des commandes de guerre passées à la société Upjohn. Chiffre de production: 21.184.384 sachets de plastique, contenant plus de 169 millions de tablettes de 7,7 grammes. Upjohn a également conçu et préparé l'emballage.

（左）第二次世界大戦の終る頃には「傷口用の錠剤」サルファジアジンは、アップジョン社の非常に大きな戦時商品となっていた。7.7 グラム錠1億6,900 万個が2,118万を越えるプラスチックのパッケージに詰められ、出荷された。アップジョン社は、この軍用包装材料のデザインや印刷も行なった。

(right) When Upjohn introduced Unicap multivitamins in 1940, it did not advertise them to the public, but detailed them to physicians. It worked. By 1943 Unicap accounted for nearly one-fifth of the company's annual sales and became Upjohn's first $5 million product.

(derecha) Cuando Upjohn introdujo las multivitaminas Unicap en 1940, no las anunció al público, sino que las describió a los médicos. Esto dio resultado. Para 1943 Unicap representaba cerca de una quinta parte de las ventas anuales de la compañía y llegó a ser el primer producto de Upjohn en lograr $5 millones por este concepto.

(à droite) Lorsque la société Upjohn lança sur le marché les comprimés de multivitamines Unicap, en 1940, elle n'avait fait aucune annonce publicitaire pour le public, mais elle les avait expédiés aux médecins. C'était la bonne formule. En 1943, Unicap représentait près d'un cinquième des ventes annuelles de la société, et fut le premier produit qui rapporta 5 millions de dollars à cette firme.

（右）1940年、アップジョン社が総合ビタミン剤ユニキャップを発売したとき、一般向けの広告は行なわず、医師にだけ宣伝活動を行なった。これは成功した。1943年までには、ユニキャップはアップジョン社の年商の5分の1近くを占め、はじめての500万ドル商品となった。

Studies of product and process edged up slightly that August, and for a period of months company scientists on the 11th floor of the research tower looked at different ways of cultivating the mold, extracting the active substance, and purifying it. But all this activity was largely limited to the lab bench.

On May 25, 1943, Department of Agriculture representatives asked Upjohn executives if they would be interested in making penicillin for the military. Upjohn thought it could turn out 200 million units a week, using the early surface-culture technique. Dr. Harold Adams got the assignment to coordinate the project, and top management agreed to invest $50,000 in the start-up. Upjohn took over the old Ruud Building, formerly a furnace factory, on North Rose Street in Kalamazoo, and began brewing the mold in 120,000 bottles in the basement. By July 1943, the company's first shipment was ready for the army — 100 vials of 100,000 units each.

Normally, rival manufacturers do their utmost to guard their respective secrets, but this was a war situation and antitrust laws were temporarily suspended. As a result, Eli Lilly & Co., Abbott Laboratories, Parke Davis Group, and Upjohn formed the Midwest Group in November 1943. The aim was to pool research on penicillin structure and possible synthesis, as well as on the submerged-culture technique for making the antibiotic. As 1944 began, Upjohn had learned enough to begin small-scale production by submerged culture. One steel tank had been ordered; planning called for three more (each with a 2,000-gallon capacity) for the pilot installation.

Along with others in the Midwest Group, Upjohn signed a contract in December 1943 with the Office of Scientific Research and Development to advance the quest for a way of making penicillin synthetically. At that point, 21 American and 17 British labs were working toward this same goal; Upjohn put 20 of its own chemists to the task. There was great urgency about their work. To the armed services, penicillin was just as important as the latest weaponry.

Upjohn completed its first large delivery of the drug to the army in February 1944 — 3,550 vials of 100,000 units each. The production curve edged up, jumped to 23,000 vials in June 1944, and peaked at 24,000 vials that September. During the entire year of 1944, the company turned out 15.6 billion units, against 1,591 billion from the drug industry as a whole, and during the last half of that year Upjohn also supplied 16.2 percent of the penicillin units for the U.S. civilian population.

Upjohn could do little more: the racks in the Ruud Building only held 120,000 fermentation flasks. Of course, as production took off, unit cost decreased. The first shipment going out of Kalamazoo in July 1943 carried a price of $20.05 a vial; for Upjohn's last army shipments in May 1945, the figure had dropped to $1.90; and by October 1945, a 100,000-unit vial was going for 60 cents.

Upjohn scientists learned a great deal about the chemistry of penicillin. As early as 1944 they had a deep-vat fermentation tank in place, and it became obvious that this was a much more efficient method than the bottle-by-bottle procedure.

By the fall of 1945, Dr. John Norton, head of bacteriology, and his associates knew that streptomycin loomed as the next major antibiotic. Building a deep-vat production unit of eight 5,000-gallon tanks would mean that Upjohn could begin making it for the civilian market. However, if streptomycin failed commercially, Upjohn could turn out penicillin in the same plant. Donald Gilmore liked the concept, and the Upjohn board gave it formal approval. The company's war experiences were going to be very useful in retooling for a peacetime world.

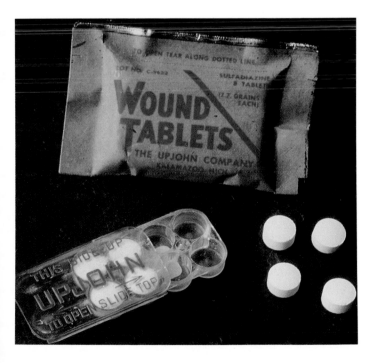

SERUM ALBUMIN: In March 1942 the navy requested that Upjohn make serum albumin. The substance substituted effectively for whole plasma in treating shock and severe burns. And it had a big advantage: 100 cc of a 25 percent solution equaled 500 cc of plasma. That meant less had to be administered for the same results. Further, serum albumin did not need to be refrigerated as did plasma and could be packaged for immediate use.

Upjohn representatives visited the laboratories of Harvard Medical School's Dr. Edwin J. Cohn. For more than two decades he had worked to fractionate human blood into its components. He and his associates were coming to understand such parts of whole blood as serum albumin, gamma globulin, and fibrinogen. The Cohn laboratory offered vital guidance.

Convinced it could do the job, Upjohn ordered equipment to begin manufacture. However, delivery delays kept the company from producing pilot lots until January 1943. Meanwhile, supplies of whole blood funneled in from the American Red Cross's Blood Donor Service, first from Detroit, and later from Chicago. Overall, the company received 324,714 pints for its production line.

By May, Upjohn was ready to ship finished serum albumin. And from then until the project ended in December 1944, the company delivered almost 83,000 units to the navy. (A unit amounted to 100 cc of a 25 percent solution of serum albumin packed in a sealed tin can with sterilized components for transfusion.)

Upjohn's 43 plasma-processing people worked a three-shift day, and the line operated seven days a week. Once again there was a promising spin-off. Making serum albumin yielded by-products — immune serum globulin, fibrin foam, and thrombin. The Harvard laboratory of Dr. Cohn had been instrumental in achieving this result, but Upjohn scientists such as Ed Wise and John T. Correll had helped materially in working out the techniques, particularly with fibrin foam. With new awareness of the importance and potential of these blood fractions in modern surgery, Correll began to study the possibility of whipping purified gelatin and thrombin into a foam from which patches could be made to control bleeding. The product was Gelfoam. Dr. Richard U. Light, grandson of W. E. Upjohn and a company director since 1937, and Dr. Hilger P. Jenkins played a prominent part in its clinical development. Their tests proved that Gelfoam worked in surgery, and the product reached the market in late 1945.

SULFA PRODUCTS: One of the heroes of damage control during the Pearl Harbor attack was the antibacterial agent sulfanilamide. Its efficacy led the army to order huge supplies for what lay ahead. But suddenly the Food and Drug Administration learned of a serious problem: sulfa powder, from which sulfanilamide was made, was not self-sterilizing, as the agency had thought. The FDA saw no solution in sight.

At that very time, Upjohn's C. V. Patterson and General Counsel Les Harrop had gone to Washington to meet with the FDA on an unrelated matter. FDA Commissioner W. G. Campbell confided in his Kalamazoo visitors the dilemma on sulfanilamide; he wanted no publicity — it might shake public confidence in the drug. Returning to their hotel, Patterson and Harrop telephoned John Norton, in the bacteriology lab, to see what he could do. Norton thought it would be possible to come up with a sample of sterilized sulfa in a few days, and when the sample was delivered to army officials, they were grateful. Upjohn got a contract to

produce one-half of the army's emergency need for 5-gram envelopes of sulfa to be used in dusting the antibiotic on an open wound. The company prepared almost 42 million of these envelopes.

Later, the army saw it had to have an allied medication, a punch-board package of eight 7.7-gram sulfadiazine tablets. A wounded soldier should be able to open the packet and swallow the tablets, even if he could not use one arm. The proposed package turned out to be a real headache. It had to be tapped hard to get the tablets to spill out, and even slight pressure could jam or pulverize the medication. Even so, as of July 6, 1943, Upjohn had a contract to make 500,000 of these punch-board packages and tablets. Some alternative had to be devised, and Upjohn's production specialists proposed a plastic slide-top container. Upjohn could design and mill that package itself.

The Surgeon General's representatives enthusiastically approved the concept and asked the company to deliver the product in bulk as quickly as it could. Specifications were refined in September 1943, and Upjohn got an order for more than 16 million packages. By war's end, sulfadiazine tablets turned out to be by far the largest of Upjohn's war orders. Some 21,184,384 plastic packages were produced and, along with them, more than 169 million 7.7-gram tablets. Dr. L. N. Upjohn computed that the tablets in one army contract, placed end to end, would reach from Kalamazoo to the embattled island of Guadalcanal.

Employees in the War Effort

The civilian society that remained at home during WWII mobilized for support of the uniformed services in a way that was remarkable. The legendary "Rosie the Riveter," with hundreds of thousands beside her, turned out 296,000 planes, 86,000 tanks, 71,000 naval vessels, and 5,400 merchant ships (among them, a Liberty Ship christened *The Upjohn*, after the prolific nineteenth-century church architect Richard Upjohn, who was a first cousin of the founder's father, Uriah).

At Upjohn, employee ranks grew from 2,164 in 1942 to 2,668 four years later. From those numbers, 460 left to enter the services — 21 percent. At war's end, 87 percent of those in uniform came back to jobs with the Michigan drug-maker. Twelve men were killed in action or died in the line of duty.

In the Kalamazoo plant, certain controls affected employment during the war emergency. In March 1944, the War Manpower Commission ordered Upjohn to go to a minimum 48-hour workweek, the industry standard for all factory and maintenance personnel. After an appeal, the commission allowed the company to set a 44-hour week for office and research people. As for wages and salaries, these were frozen at the levels of September 15, 1942, until the ceilings were lifted in August 1945. But Upjohn continued granting merit and promotional increases.

(left) During World War II, Upjohn produced nearly 42 million 5-gram envelopes of sterilized sulfanilamide powder for the U.S. Army. These envelopes, representing one-half of the army's emergency need, were used to dust the medication on an open wound.

(izquierda) Durante la II Guerra Mundial Upjohn produjo cerca de 42 millones de sobres de 5 gramos de polvos de sulfanilamida esterilizada para el Ejército de Estados Unidos. Estos sobres, que representaban la mitad de las necesidades de emergencia del ejército, se utilizaron para espolvorear el medicamento sobre una herida abierta.

(à gauche) Pendant la seconde guerre mondiale, la société Upjohn a produit près de 42 millions d'enveloppes de 5 grammes de poudre de sulfanilamide stérilisée pour les Forces Armées américaines. Ces enveloppes, représentant la moitié des besoins d'urgence de l'armée, servaient à panser les blessures.

（左）第二次世界大戦中、アップジョン社は、アメリカ陸軍向けに4200万袋近くの5グラム入り滅菌サルファニラミド粉末を生産した。これは、陸軍の救急用医薬品の半分を占める分量で、傷口に振りかけて使用された。

(right) Beginning in June 1943, this three-story building in downtown Kalamazoo housed Upjohn's first penicillin production plant. Its basement shelves contained more than 75,000 two-quart flasks in which the penicillin was grown.

(derecha) Comenzando en junio de 1943, este edificio de tres pisos en el centro de la ciudad de Kalamazoo fue la sede de la primera planta para producción de penicilina de Upjohn. En los anaqueles del sótano se conservaban más de 75.000 frascos de dos cuartos de galón donde se producía la penicilina.

(à droite) A partir de juin 1943, cet édifice de trois étages au centre-ville de Kalamazoo abritait la première usine de production de pénicilline d'Upjohn. Le sous-sol contenait sur des étagères plus de 75.000 flacons de 2 litres servant à conserver la culture pour la pénicilline.

（右）1943年6月、カラマズーの市街地に建てられたこの3階建の建物の中に、アップジョン社の最初のペニシリン製造設備が設置された。この地下室の棚には、ペニシリンを培養するフラスコが、75,000個以上並べられていた。

Upjohn faced a special problem when it came to the military's demand for manpower. The company needed certain specialists, too. Up to May 1, 1946, it filed 1,366 requests for deferment (the list included nine appeals for one individual). Of all the claims, 92 percent were granted. Upjohn was able to have 380 key individuals deferred and lost no technical personnel whose absence might have seriously interfered with operations.

As for its men in uniform, Upjohn did not forget them. The wife of every serviceman without children received a check covering the premium on his National Service Life Insurance policy. If a man had children, his wife got a monthly check for $50, as well as the N.S.L.I. premium. And at Christmas, each Upjohn man in the military had his own company bonus: a $25 money order.

By and large, executive and employee alike at Upjohn supported the war effort by subscribing to the war bond drives. By March 1943, almost two-thirds of the employees had agreed to buy bonds through payroll deduction, and when the final figures were assembled in 1947, the men and women of Upjohn had invested a total of $2,078,000 to support their country in time of war.

The war did not halt change in Upjohn's executive offices, and sadness accompanied some of it. On April 10, 1942, Sales Director Malcolm Galbraith died at 66; he had been a valued employee since 1910. The company replaced him with joint sales managers, C. V. Patterson and Emil H. Schellack, an arrangement that went into effect October 21, 1942.

The following fall, other shifts were set in motion. At their November board meeting, directors named Donald Gilmore as president, and L. N. moved up to the chairmanship, a position that had not been filled since W. E.'s death. Three new vice presidencies were established — Dr. Gifford Upjohn as vice president and medical director, Dr. Harold Adams as vice president and director of production, and Patterson as vice president and director of sales. Emil Schellack was designated general sales manager.

Less than three weeks later, the entire company was shocked at the sudden death of Dr. Adams at age 55. The *Overflow* had its own explanation for his premature demise, noting that "his willingness to accept new responsibilities led him all too readily to assume the mounting burdens of a staggering load during recent months in which he undoubtedly gave himself to the war effort." Navy Captain L. R. Newhouser responded to the news by saying that Dr. Adams had died "as a result of the present war just as the man who dies on the battlefront."

Closing ranks, the Upjohn management switched Patterson to Dr. Adams' position in charge of production and made Schellack vice president and director of sales. Although Patterson had no production experience, he did have a B.S. in chemical engineering, and he had impressed Gilmore with his knowledge of the company. Fred Allen, sales manager for both Dallas and Kansas City, was brought to Kalamazoo to be Schellack's assistant. (When Emil Schellack died in February 1946, Fred Allen was elected to the board and named vice president and sales director.)

The Company Goes On

The war put heavy demands on the company. Overtime work and night shifts were costly; lights, fences, and security guards added to the expense of doing business. It was difficult to travel, and with some frequency Upjohn executives were called to take spot duty elsewhere for the industry or the nation. (General Counsel Les Harrop, for instance, went to Washington for a two-year stint as chief of the Safety and Technical Equipment Section, Production Division, Headquarters, Army Service Forces.)

(left) Growing penicillin in bottles (the surface-culture method) was costly and time consuming. In February 1944, when these women were filling sterile bottles with the medium on which the mold would be grown, the finished product cost $20.05 per vial.

(izquierda) La producción de penicilina en frascos (método de cultivo en superficie) era costosa y consumía mucho tiempo. En febrero de 1944, cuando estas mujeres llenaban los frascos esterilizados con el medio ambiente en el cual el moho se producía, el producto acabado costaba $20,05 por frasco.

(à gauche) Préparer la pénicilline en bouteille (méthode de culture en surface) était à la fois coûteux et difficile. En février 1944, lorsque ces femmes remplissaient des bouteilles stérilisées avec la culture pour préparer la pénicilline, le produit fini coûtait 20 dollars 5 par fiole.

（左）表面培養法で、瓶の中にペニシリンを培養する方法は、コストがかさみ、時間もかかつた。1944年2月、ペニシリン菌を植えつける培地を無菌瓶に詰める作業。最終製品は、1バイアル当たり20ドル5セントにもなつていた。

(right) After allowing the penicillin bacteria to grow for about five days, a technician would "harvest" it. By 1949, when the company perfected the process of growing penicillin in large tanks (submerged-culture method), the price dropped to just a few cents per vial.

(derecha) Después de dejar que la bacteria de la penicilina se desarrollara por cinco días aproximadamente, un técnico la "cosecharía". Para 1949, cuando la compañía perfeccionó el proceso de cultivar penicilina en grandes tanques (método de cultivo sumergido), el precio bajó a sólo unos centavos por frasco.

(à droite) Après avoir cultivé la bactérie de la pénicilline pendant environ cinq jours, un technicien la "récolte". En 1949, lorsque fut mise au point la méthode de culture de la pénicilline dans des récipients volumineux (méthode de culture par submersion), les prix baissèrent à quelques centimes par flacon.

（右）ペニシリン菌は5日間培養した後に、技術者が"収穫する"という方法をとつていたが、1949年、大型タンクによるペニシリン培養の方法（水中培養法）をアツプジョン社が完成すると、ペニシリンの価格は1バイアル数セントまで下つた。

With it all, sales kept climbing, even though the sales force had lost 136 men to war service. For Upjohn, as L. N. wrote afterward, the war years became a "seller's market." Sales of Unicap, other vitamin preparations, and some new products received "an extraordinary stimulus." Sales in the war period added up to a total of $142.7 million. Of that, just 10 percent ($14.4 million) was from government business. Upjohn's average margin (before taxes) on its war contracts was 5.01 percent. Looking back, Treasurer Gordon Knapp, who replaced a retiring John McColl in 1947, reported, "In no instance were our profits on Government business deemed to be excessive."

Upjohn was "complimented repeatedly," in Knapp's words, "on the completeness of our records, the availability of information, and our fairness in computing costs applicable to Government business." And it had produced in ways that counted — so well, in fact, that in 1944 it received the Army-Navy Production Award for "high achievement" in making materials for the services. At a half-hour ceremony that November 24, the Army-Navy "E" flag was raised. Throughout the company, *(top) This window display appeared in pharmacies throughout the U.S. in the fall of 1944. Entitled "Pharmacy in the War," it was an Upjohn tribute to the thousands of pharmacists called into service during World War II.*

(arriba) Esta exhibición en la vitrina aparecía en las farmacias para todos los Estados Unidos en el otoño de 1944. Se titulaba "la farmacia en la guerra" y era un tributo de Upjohn a los miles de farmacéuticos llamados al servicio militar durante la II Guerra Mundial.

(en haut) Etalage de pharmacie aux Etats-Unis à l'automne 1944. "Pharmacie en temps de guerre" était un hommage de la société Upjohn à des milliers de pharmaciens enrégimentés pendant la seconde guerre mondiale.

（上）このウインドウ・ディスプレーは、1944年秋全米の薬局に飾られた。「戦争協力薬局」と表題のつけられたこのディスプレーは、第二次大戦中、軍務に服した何千人もの薬剤師に対するアップジョン社からの贈り物であった。

(bottom) Between 9:30 and 10:15 a.m., Friday, November 24, 1944, Upjohn's 1,503 Kalamazoo employees gathered around radios installed throughout the company for a special broadcast. The occasion was the presentation to Upjohn employees of the Army-Navy "E" Award for wartime production excellence.

(abajo) Entre las 9:30 y las 10:15 a.m. del viernes, 24 de noviembre de 1944, los 1.503 empleados de Upjohn en Kalamazoo se reunieron alrededor de radios instalados en toda la compañía para una transmisión especial. La ocasión era la presentación a los empleados del Premio "E" del Ejército y la Marina, por su excelencia en la producción durante el tiempo de guerra.

(en bas) Entre 9 h 30 et 10 h 15 du matin, le vendredi 24 novembre 1944, à Kalamazoo, les 1.503 employés de la société Upjohn étaient à l'écoute d'une émission spéciale à la radio. C'était l'heure de la remise du prix Armée-Marine aux employés d'Upjohn pour leur excellence dans la production en temps de guerre.

（下）1944年11月24日金躍日、午前9時30分から10時15分、アップジョン社のカラマズー地区に勤務する 1,503名の社員は、社内各所に配置されたラジオの前に集まった。それは、アップジョン社社員の戦時生産協力に対する合衆国陸海軍の"E賞"授与式の特別放送であった。

employees gathered by department in front of radios to listen to a special awards broadcast.

Then, hostilities finally ended, the uniformed employees of Upjohn turned in their military gear and put on civilian clothes once again, and people of national stature sent along their closing commendations to the Kalamazoo drug-maker. The commander of Army Service Forces, General Brehon Somervell, wrote to express appreciation for Upjohn's "magnificent achievements . . ." And a distinguished man of science added his official compliments. Vannevar Bush, director of the Office of Scientific Research and Development, wrote in May 1946 to applaud Upjohn and its industrial compatriots for their "outstanding contribution" to winning the war. He spoke too of going forward "into a world in which peace has been won through this concerted effort . . ."

For some time, Upjohn's top executives had been talking about how to move the company forward into that peacetime world. Anyone driving on Portage Road, south of Kalamazoo, in the summer of 1946 could begin to see below Bishop Road the hard evidence of what Donald Gilmore and his builders had determined to do.

POSTSCRIPT TO THE WAR: BUILDING FOR THE FUTURE

The sounds of world war had been stilled for several years, but voices of anger growled on, and a cold war had now succeeded the hot one. The Marshall Plan had been installed to rebuild ravaged Europe. America was moving aid to Greece and Turkey. Talks had started on forming the North Atlantic Treaty Organization. And planes were droning eastward once more, this time to haul food and coal to Berlin citizens encircled by a Communist blockade.

On Portage Road, six miles south of downtown Kalamazoo, a vast crater in the cornfields was slowly filling up with the I-beam skeleton of an innovative modern factory, Upjohn's manufacturing complex for tomorrow. A well-traveled visitor from New York viewed the construction with amazement. He remarked to Jack Gauntlett, "This is a stroke of genius! Donald Gilmore's got perfect timing. Here the economy's growing and new industries are popping up all over the place, and he decides to go ahead and build this huge factory. It's genius!" Gauntlett thought Gilmore might enjoy this appraisal and passed it along.

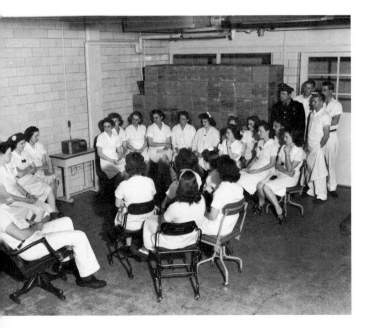

Donald Gilmore, a practical man for all seasons, took the judgment in stride. "The main reason we're putting up the plant is that we need more room," he told Gauntlett.

And that was that. No fanfare was necessary. By tradition, Upjohn people have always preferred the low-key way, and Gilmore was no exception. Always professing to know little about medicine, technology, or the nuts and bolts of production, Gilmore once said, "What I contribute is organization, systems of doing things." Put simply, he was a leader, cut from the same cloth as his father-in-law, W. E. Upjohn. Creating that huge structure — Building 41 — was hard proof.

Dr. W. E. Upjohn always knew his company would grow, but his projection somewhat undershot the mark. He thought the firm would need a new building every five years. As of 1909, it had seven. Using his yardstick, Upjohn would have occupied another seven by 1945. Actually, 30 buildings were in use that year, and their 838,000 square feet of floor space still were not enough. Production department heads estimated they needed at least 40 percent more space.

Perhaps the company could have stayed in the center of the city. Before the war, at Donald Gilmore's request, architect Albert Kahn had come up with a plan to accomplish that kind of expansion, and it had been approved by management. Basically, it would have continued the traditional vertical method of making products, that is, the raw materials were taken to the top of a building, mixed and shaped into product form on lower floors, and then packaged and shipped out at the bottom. However, during World War II, says Gifford Upjohn, "We grew so rapidly that it was perfectly clear the plan wasn't good enough. There wasn't any place to go." Further, Donald Gilmore and his associates recognized a decided trend toward one-story, ground-level plants with air conditioning, ventilation, and fluorescent lighting.

Any planning discussions at the time also had to take into account the fact that a new era in medicine was at hand — and Upjohn belonged in that era. Early research had led to the sulfas, the antibiotics, the endocrine hormones, and the beginnings of drug synthesis. Who could tell where the road ahead would lead?

President Donald Gilmore and his planners weighed all these matters and arrived at a decision. "It now seems to those of us on the inside here," Gilmore wrote to Dr. S. R. Light in late July 1945, "that we should replace our fifteen old wooden manufacturing buildings with a modern one-story plant in the country." They should be thinking of the future 15 to 20 years out and allow "plenty of room" for expansion, he added. Gilmore and Lew Crockett had been scouring the surrounding countryside for a site and would make a proposal at the September board meeting. Meanwhile, he cautioned, all this was to be treated as "strictly confidential within the inner circle." Upjohn did not want to have land values skyrocket because of premature disclosures.

When the board met on September 25, the directors of the company approved the plan and told management to go ahead and buy the needed land on Portage Road — 1,500 acres in all. This was no small venture, and supervising it did not happen to suit the makeup of Chairman L. N. Upjohn, now 72 years old. The whole project was turned over to Donald Gilmore, and from that point on, he and Crockett, as vice president and director of engineering, were in charge. Together, they worked with an architect and an engineer from the construction firm, The Austin Company of Cleveland.

That quartet brought off the whole job. Says Ward Nay, who retired as vice president for engineering and maintenance in 1986, "If we did that project today, we'd probably have a 100-man team. In those days, the management style was different. Decision-making was different." Of course, Crockett did not try to handle all the minutiae as the project unfolded. Laverne Hansen and Walker Sisson were assigned as liaison men between Upjohn and Austin. By the time Building 41 was finished, those two knew just about every pipe and valve in the entire structure.

Economy of operations and flexibility were the key demands facing the design team. They decided to break up the space into four big sections from south to north — incoming warehouse, production, packaging, and outgoing warehouse. That, said Production Director Patterson, would enable Upjohn for the first time ever to "accomplish everything in one motion."

The huge facility encompassed 870 x 1,360 feet of space. Enclosing it took almost 57,000 cubic yards of concrete, 9,436 tons of steel, and enough bricks to put up 642 five-room homes. The company landscaped 50 of the surrounding acres with 6,000 trees and shrubs and trucked in 5,000 yards of topsoil and 2,000 square yards of sod.

One after another, other Portage Road structures rose. Building 38, dedicated to producing antibiotics, went on line in 1946. Next came number 39, the adrenal cortex building, said at the time to be the only building in the world devoted exclusively to processing adrenal cortex hormones. Number 43, the main power plant with three 700-horsepower coal-fed boilers, began in 1949 to produce its target of 60,000 pounds of steam an hour.

Building 41 was fully occupied by April 1951 — with 33 acres of floor space. All production was housed there, except for antibiotics and adrenal cortex hormones. *Architectural Forum*, sizing up the facility in its April 1951 issue, noted: "To a remarkable extent, the mammoth new plant . . . is like some precision-engineered laboratory instrument. To accomplish this kind of precise accommodation in a plant where some 33 acres are under one roof is an assignment big enough to stagger even today's building technology: here the normal mechanical services have been so highly developed as to point some new directions for all kinds of industrial building."

oller

The magazine noted with seeming endorsement that in Building 41 provisions had been made for "a complete flexibility of future operations — room to expand, room to install new machines, room to convert quickly from one product to another." Once the word got around, Upjohn's competitors came to see this wonder of a new industrial age. Imperial Chemical Industries of England borrowed the blueprints for its own factory.

All in all, it took a full six years to plan, design, construct, and occupy 41 and the surrounding facilities. And Upjohn met the entire cost of $36 million from earnings and reserves. Completion of this major project put Upjohn in excellent position on the threshold of an exciting future, a future that would be forever indebted to Donald Gilmore's bold vision.

Says former engineering chief Ward Nay, "The biggest testimony to 41 is the fact that we moved in in 1949, finished moving in 1951, and until the Control labs were added in 1983 we did not have to expand the building by one square foot. Yet production has gone up a hundredfold. That testifies to good long-range planning."

(left) Until the advent of steroidal chemistry in the 1950s, all Upjohn hormonal products were biologically extracted from animal substances. These men are working in the Control Lab of the Adrenal Cortex Building (Building 39), now known as the Biological Extracts Building, in 1949, where most of this work took place.

(izquierda) Hasta el advenimiento de la química esteroide en los años 50, todos los productos hormonales Upjohn se extraían biológicamente de substancias animales. Estos hombres están trabajando en el Edificio del Laboratorio de Control de Cortezas Suprarrenales (Edificio 39) el año 1949. Este edificio, donde se realizaba la mayor parte de este trabajo, se conoce actualmente como Edificio para Extractos Biológicos.

(à gauche) Avant l'apparition des stéroïdes dans les années 50, tous les produits hormonaux Upjohn étaient biologiquement extraits de substances animales. On voit ici les employés du laboratoire de l'Adrenal Cortex Building (bâtiment No. 39), où se font toutes ces opérations, en 1949. Ce bâtiment est aujourd'hui appelé Centre d'extraits biologiques.

（左）1950年代にステロイドが合成できるようになるまでは、アップジョン社のホルモン製剤はすべて、動物から抽出されていた。動物抽出棟と呼称されていた副腎皮質研究棟（第39棟）の、分析管理研究室で働く人たち。1949年当時、動物抽出はほとんどこの建物で行なわれた。

(right) Because of Building 41's "remote" location, Upjohn offered employees bus service to their homes in Kalamazoo. Upjohn was one of the first companies to provide such a service.

(derecha) Debido a la "remota" ubicación del Edificio 41, Upjohn ofrecía a sus empleados servicio de autobús a sus hogares en Kalamazoo. Upjohn fue una de las primeras compañías que proporcionó tal servicio.

(à droite) Transport en commun offert aux employés par la société Upjohn, à cause de l'éloignement du bâtiment No. 41. Upjohn est l'une des premières entreprises à offrir un tel service.

（右）41号館はカラマズー市街地から離れているためアップジョン社では社員用に送迎のバスを用意した。アップジョン社は、こうした社員のためのサービスを行なった最初の企業であった。

CHAPTER FOUR

JOURNEY INTO PROMINENCE

Somewhere in 1949 or 1950, The Upjohn Company crossed the threshold into the era of modern pharmaceuticals. No one event signaled that passage, no memo marked the date. Yet the basic change happened in those months. From then on, Upjohn was outward bound toward the worldwide enterprise it is today.

Actually, the company was an elixir of old and new ingredients in those early postwar years. The sales results for 1949 tell part of the story. Seven products sold more than $1 million apiece in a $61.4 million sales year. One of them, Solu-B, was strictly a prescription product. The other six would be classified as over-the-counter items today — Unicap, Zymacap, Cheracol and Cheracol D, Citrocarbonate, Orthoxicol, and Kaopectate. Only one, Orthoxicol, was brand-new. The others were at least five years old, and Citrocarbonate and Cheracol had been launched in the 1920s.

If the product line suggested an earlier time, so did some of the upper-level managers. On V-J Day in August 1945, Chairman L. N. Upjohn, 71, looked back on four decades with the company. Builder Lew Crockett had engineered 34 years of growth and change in the Upjohn plant, and the research head, Dr. Merrill Hart, had been on the scene for 31 years. As for Will Little, he was going to be celebrating half a century with the firm in 1950. Each remembered the founder and his influence. His example "of always striving for improvement," said Little, "was our guiding star."

Memories of that vanished star lingered on in 1949 and 1950, but a new time was at hand. Two Henrietta Street executives also remembered W. E.'s role, yet they had a sense of the future, too. President Donald Gilmore, who would be 55 in 1950, knew Upjohn had to have a better physical plant for whatever the years ahead might dictate, and he was willing to lead in that direction. Since joining the company at W. E.'s request in 1930, the thin, shy businessman had put himself through a vigorous self-training, learning not only the technical details but learning to gauge the men who made things work at Upjohn. By 1943, when he became president and general manager, he had surrounded himself with a cadre of knowledgeable managers.

Gilmore said once that his greatest satisfaction was "being part of the team of harmonious executives, other members of which are specialists who know more than I do, and in encouraging them and watching them develop their organizations."

But his second satisfaction was in spurring physical expansion. It was Gilmore who championed the move to Portage Road and the construction of Building 41, committing the company's resources to providing not just for the next decade, but for many decades to come.

E. Gifford Upjohn, who had also joined the company in 1930, was looking hard at the future, too. Upjohn's medical director, and nine years Gilmore's junior, E. G. U. had maintained since the late 1930s that the company must grow out of simple formulations and basic compounding into a new range of more modern, sophisticated medicines. He had played an important role in renewing Upjohn's ties with the AMA and was an advocate of international expansion.

These two men symbolized the thinking that crystalized at Upjohn in the wake of World War II.

A crucial synthesis had begun. New people were coming on board, better facilities were taking shape, and far more challenging research was preoccupying the scientists at their lab benches. A sales force of proven accomplishments was converting innovative items into market dominance and revenues to fuel continued growth. It was an exciting time.

RESEARCH:
IN THE EXPRESS LANE

In pharmaceutical research and development, or PR & D, there is no exception to the rule: the brass ring goes to the one who gets there first. And after World War II, PR & D turned into a fast, tense race throughout the industry. Half the drugs prescribed in 1953 did not exist 10 years earlier; 90 percent were unknown 15 years before. Medical science and technology were advancing very rapidly. Researchers put in very long days and nights to get new cures on the market fast — and first.

Donald Gilmore had an ear for the pleas of the new breed of researcher. He believed the company had to make the sizable investments that R & D calls for, a conviction still shared by his successors. In 1953, Upjohn spent eight percent of sales on research. By 1962, the commitment had swelled to 11 percent, and it stands at 14 percent of sales today, the second highest percentage of the top ten drug firms in the U.S. In the last three decades, Upjohn has invested more than $2 billion in hunting for new pharmaceuticals — and that does not include expenditures for major construction of PR & D facilities.

New products were marketed in the four postwar decades as an outgrowth of Upjohn innovation or adaptation of the discoveries of others: antibiotics,

steroids, antidiabetes agents, nonsteroidal anti-inflammatory drugs, central nervous system agents. In the process, Upjohn put behind its reputation as a mere compounder or manufacturing pharmacist. It could now create a product entirely through synthesis and manufacture its own drugs and chemicals.

But before that happened, there was much to be learned.

Turning Points

The year 1949 was filled with events that would prove to be of significance to Upjohn. Swedish researcher Dr. Sune Bergstrom reported that there was more than one prostaglandin, substances which help to regulate a great many physiological functions. On April 13, 1949, Dr. Philip Hench announced the use of cortisone in the treatment of rheumatoid arthritis, a "hormonal bombshell" to many. That same year, an Upjohn team made the essential vitamin folic acid. L. N. Upjohn called this accomplishment "the first really significant venture of this company in the field of synthetic chemical manufacture."

An important new face joined Upjohn on January 24th of that year as associate director of research. Dr. Richard S. Schreiber, an Illinois native, left a promising career at Du Pont to join a company he had never heard of before. "The people convinced me," he told his Du Pont colleagues. Donald Gilmore made it clear that he needed someone who in time could replace Merrill Hart as research head. He was primed to answer when Schreiber asked if he were committed to research. "Yes," said Gilmore. "That is why I'm hiring you."

Upjohn people soon found that organic chemist Schreiber was one of a kind. He was given to answering his own phone, never wearing overcoats, and speaking out freely on most topics. He believed in people and preferred to give his researchers their head whenever he could. And as a man who had worked with long-chain molecules at Du Pont, he knew from his own experience where chemical research was headed.

In May 1950 the company named Schreiber to succeed Dr. Hart. At 41, Schreiber was Upjohn's youngest vice president. At the time, Research had some 297 staff-members — 65 in pharmacology and endocrinology, 53 in antibiotics, and lesser numbers in eight other departments.

On his arrival, Dick Schreiber had set out to get to know his scientists. Some were old hands; others had only recently joined the company. Dr. George Cartland, credited with persuading Upjohn to stick with fermentation after World War II, had been an employee since 1924. Dr. Marvin Kuizenga was one of Fred Heyl's 1933 fellows. A star among the 1941 fellows, Dr. Dwight J. Ingle, "really had a big importance to Upjohn," says Gifford Upjohn, "because he was perhaps the world's leading authority on the physiology of hormones of the adrenal cortex and carbohydrates metabolism." Biochemist Dr. Durey H. Peterson had accepted an Upjohn post in antibiotic research in 1946, after establishing a name for himself by developing nylon surgical sutures and formulating the Toni home permanent for Raymond Laboratories.

One of Schreiber's stronger scientists was David Weisblat, who had come to Upjohn in the spring of 1943 fresh from a two-year postdoctoral fellowship at Ohio State University. His work on the project team that synthesized folic acid helped him win the Upjohn Award in 1949. Weisblat was named vice president of pharmaceutical research and development in 1968, a post he held until his retirement in December 1981.

After only a short time at Upjohn, Dr. Weisblat got a clear sense of what lay ahead from an old hand, Ed Wise. As Weisblat recalls, "He said to me, 'Someday we're going to have to come up with some new products, and I don't see anything. In the way we're doing it, we're never going to get anything. Because every department's like a country unto itself.'"

In Weisblat's opinion, Dr. Schreiber's arrival marked the beginning of the modern age for the firm. Certainly Schreiber moved quickly to expand the scientific base. By 1952, Research had 421 people, almost one-quarter with Ph.D's. On December 1 that year, Schreiber announced that Upjohn research was "the best of any pharmaceutical house in the United States, exclusive of Merck & Company."

Antibiotic Developments

Once the war was behind them, Upjohn managers debated hard over staying in antibiotic research and production. Why not buy product from others, some argued. Management listened, then said no. The company would put in deep-vat fermenters and keep going because doing meaningful research would be next to impossible without big manufacturing capacity. And so it was that the engineers planted the vats of Building 38 in the cornfield on Portage Road.

While Upjohn had come out of the war with invaluable experience in antibiotic research, so had its main competitors. By the early 1950s, the industry had screened hundreds of thousands of microbe-laden soil samples in a pell-mell drive to find antibiotics to rival penicillin and streptomycin. Out of them all, only six were effective and nontoxic enough to make it into production. For its part, Upjohn devised Cer-O-Cillin in 1951 for those allergic to penicillin.

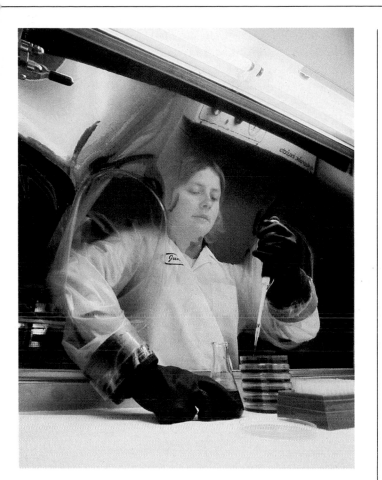

Persisting in its search, PR & D in Kalamazoo finally found a new antibiotic with world-market potential. Salesman Larry Bersin had sent in five soil samples from around his New Jersey home. The odds were 100,000 to 1 against finding a winner, but Research began to get excited about one batch. The assessment and testing shifted into high gear, and in June 1956 the company went public with its first highly promising antibiotic — Albamycin. Substance "66A," its lab name, proved very potent in treating pneumonia, wounds, skin infections, and diseases resistant to penicillin and other antibiotics. It was as effective orally as it was by injection, and it could be manufactured in Upjohn's big-bellied fermenters. Would Upjohn have tracked down 66A if it had not told sales reps in 1953 to send in soil samples for the colossal microbe hunt under way? Perhaps so. The irony is that, separately, Merck came up with an antibiotic exactly like Albamycin. But the Upjohn product took firm root in the physician market anyway.

(left) Steroid research, 1952. When Upjohn announced that a process had been developed to mass-produce cortisone, it was hailed as an event rivaling the discovery of penicillin. The big break had come when a culture plate placed on a laboratory windowsill yielded a microbe needed for the process.

(izquierda) Investigación de esteroides, 1952. Cuando Upjohn dió a conocer el descubrimiento de un proceso para la producción en masa de cortisona, el evento fue aclamado tan sensacional como el descubrimiento de la penicilina. La culminación del evento aconteció al dejarse una bandeja de Petri sobre la repisa de una ventana, la cual produjo un microbio requerido para el proceso.

(à gauche) Recherche sur les stéroïdes, 1952. Lorsqu'Upjohn annonça la mise au point d'un procédé pour la production de masse de la cortisone, cet événement fut salué comme devant être aussi décisif que la découverte de la pénicilline. La clef de ce procédé fut trouvée lorsqu'une plaquette de culture, placée sur la fenêtre d'un laboratoire, se mit à produire le micro-organisme nécessaire à son développement.

（左）ステロイド研究、1952年。アップジョンによるコーチゾン大量生産方法の開発は、ペニシリンの発見に匹敵すると言われた。開発のきっかけは、窓際に置かれた培養皿に発生した微生物によってもたらされた。

(right) Steroid research, 1986. Upjohn remains the world leader in steroid research and development. But today, company researchers can begin their search for new compounds by using microbes that have been genetically engineered to offer the best results.

(derecha) Investigación de esteroides, 1986. Upjohn continúa ocupando el primer lugar en el mundo en investigación y desarrollo de esteroides. Pero hoy en día, los investigadores de la compañía pueden iniciar su propia investigación de nuevos compuestos usando microbios que han sido genéticamente diseñados para obtener los mejores resultados.

(à droite) Recherche sur les stéroïdes, 1986. Upjohn est toujours le leader mondial en recherche et développement de stéroïdes. Mais aujourd'hui, les chercheurs peuvent commencer leurs travaux à partir de micro-organismes conçus par le génie génétique pour obtenir les meilleurs résultats.

（右）ステロイド研究、1986年。ステロイドの研究開発において、アップジョンは今だに世界最先端のレベルを保持している。アップジョンの研究者は今日、遺伝子工学によって作られた微生物を使って、新化合物を追求している。

Not long after Albamycin was marketed, Upjohn PR & D showed its adaptability. To create a compound with the widest possible range of antibacterial effectiveness, the scientists combined Albamycin with Upjohn's Panmycin, the firm's name for tetracycline (which was purchased from another manufacturer). The name for the new antibiotic was Panalba. Introduced in 1957, it was soon one of the most prescribed of all antibiotics. Demand was so universal that at one point Upjohn had to stop making all other antibiotics just to meet the call for Panalba.

About this time, Dave Weisblat took over the fermentation work. As chief of antibiotic research, he went to meet his key personnel in the lab — John Evans, Don Collingsworth, and George Savage. Weisblat found himself facing an organizational puzzle. "We would have to do things differently," he said, "if we were going to discover any new antibiotics." So a reorganization began. "We started the modern chemical pilot plant in research," says Weisblat. "I give Dick Schreiber a lot of credit for that."

The winding trail of PR & D was not always smooth. Upjohn made the "first kilo or two" of erythromycin, according to Dr. Weisblat, then shared it with Abbott and Lilly. They belonged to the Midwest Group of competitors that had joined together in wartime to try to synthesize penicillin. The war was over, but for the time being, the group continued to trade research information on projects begun during the war. Upjohn concluded that erythromycin was only a "weak penicillin." Lilly and Abbott thought otherwise and capitalized on it. Erythromycin turned out to be one of the leading antibiotics of the time.

Upjohn could have used a drug like erythromycin, because there were some lean years in antibiotics after Albamycin's initial market surge. It wasn't until 1965 that the company put a newcomer, tradenamed Lincocin, into the catalog. It had taken researcher George Savage and his team six years to refine and test the product, derived from another salesman's soil sample. *Medical World News* called Lincocin "the first major nonsynthetic antibiotic isolated in this country since Albamycin." It was brand-new and quite unlike a thousand antibiotics known to Upjohn. And here again ample debate accompanied its PR & D journey. At one point, Research was told to forget it because it was "so controversial." (One unpleasant side effect associated with all antibiotics is diarrhea. Some reports, later disproved, suggested that the drug caused *severe* diarrhea.) But Research refused to give up on it. Two decades after its launch, the payback from Lincocin has justified that faith.

The pursuit of still other antibiotics as weapons against unconquered diseases has continued. In 1968, Upjohn science developed Cleocin, synthesized as a derivative of Lincocin and potent against a host of deadly organisms. In 1971, Trobicin was introduced. It has made possible an impressive rate of gonorrhea cures among men and women. Cleocin Phosphate, a powerful injectable agent against anaerobic infections, went on the market in 1972. Its sales today top $100 million. More recently, other Upjohn antibiotics have gone on sale — E-Mycin E Liquid, for children, in 1979; and in 1980, Cleocin T, used in the treatment of acne.

Today, there is no talk at Upjohn about shelving its four decades of commitment to the search for useful drugs from soil-derived fermentation and the big fermenters. For one thing, the industry has not begun to exhaust the soils in which active microbes are sure to be multiplying.

As for the fermenters, they have uses beyond antibiotic production. They will enable Upjohn to produce in volume the products that result from the new biotechnology, or genetic engineering. Large-scale fermentation is needed to make substances in bulk quantities using biotechnology methods and cultures. And Upjohn fully intends to produce those substances in the years ahead.

Learning to Synthesize Steroids

Upjohn had learned a thing or two in the mid-1930s about extracting hormones from an animal's adrenal cortex. Drs. Cartland and Kuizenga had developed a method of manufacturing a stable extract of adrenal cortex, marketed in 1935 as ACE. Their unit of measure for adrenal hormone potency, the Cartland-Kuizenga unit, became the worldwide standard. But it was painfully slow work, demanding prodigious supplies of animal glands. Upjohn's other hormonal products, Gonadogen and Urestrin, were likewise derived from animal substances. The breakthrough came when the active principles of these products were found and they were synthesized by steroidal chemistry.

Then Merck synthesized cortisone in 1946, using a highly complex 37-step process extracting the substance from cattle bile. Its product was the one used by Dr. Philip Hench in 1949 with such telling effects on 14 rheumatoid arthritis patients. The new substance showed a remarkable ability to reduce inflammation but the price per gram was prohibitive.

Hench's announcement touched off a first-class chase scene to overtake Merck. In time, more than half of Upjohn's researchers were working on the case, split into seven teams. The most exotic assignment fell to a team that was sent on a six-month expedition covering more than 11,000 miles through a dozen Central African territories in search of a particular species of the strophanthus vine, whose seed was reported to contain a substance from which cortisone might easily be made. None was found.

Another group was given the task of employing microorganisms to synthesize cortisone. And this group, in Dave Weisblat's view, was distinctive. It included biochemist Durey Peterson, microbiologist Herb Murray, and biologist Samuel Eppstein. Other members were L. M. Reineke, R. H. Levin, Marian Leigh, P. D. Meister, and Adolph Weintraub. The team worked seven

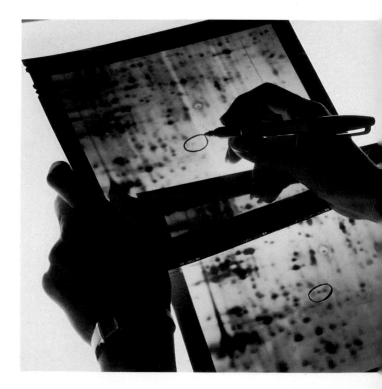

days a week, often until the early hours of morning. And along the way, as Dave Weisblat recalls, "We had a lot of fun."

They also got results. The object was to add an oxygen atom to a critical position in the steroid nucleus. Peterson and crew had to teach themselves the brand-new technique of filter-paper chromatography, a critical tool in checking sample brews to see what progress they were making. Herb Murray spotted culture plates around the lab and on the windowsill — "As good a way to search for microbes as any," he said. One of those plates grew the lead they needed: a Rhizopus mold often found on rotting fruit. The mold got them very close to the steroidal intermediate they needed in order to make cortisone. Peterson and Murray had a hunch that their problem would be solved by an organism in the same family. A shipment of similar Rhizopus molds was ordered from a Washington, D.C., culture bank, and one of them, Rhizopus nigricans, performed beyond the team's wildest hopes. It made possible the conversion of almost 100 percent of the chosen starting material, the simple steroid progesterone, into active cortisone. This latest finding, *Medical World News* later asserted, was "perhaps the greatest achievement of Upjohn research." Herb Murray and lead-man Durey Peterson became heroes almost overnight.

Getting a supply of progesterone posed a problem. Returning to the lab bench after his retirement, Dr. Fred Heyl, along with Milton E. Herr, had discovered a key path to changing a sterol in soybeans directly into progesterone. Dr. Schreiber was all in favor of trying the full-scale process with a small but expensive batch of raw material. Donald Gilmore had other ideas. He and General Counsel Les Harrop traveled east to meet executives of Syntex, another pharmaceutical company, which had a big source of progesterone in the form of Mexican yams. Soon Gilmore was on the phone with Schreiber. "I can get a bargain," he reported. "They dropped the price 5 cents a gram if we buy $3 million to $5 million worth. I want to know from you," he told Schreiber, "if you think it will work." There was no way to be sure, but Schreiber thought it would. Gilmore decided to take $5 million worth of progesterone. Schreiber spread the word. "We're under the gun now," he told his people. "This has to work. You're going to have to work your butts off!"

(left) Diabetes research, 1957. Upjohn's Orinase was the first oral antidiabetes agent approved for the U.S. market. By 1960, more than one-third of all known diabetics in the U.S. were using it. Upjohn efforts have led to two more anti-diabetes agents, Tolinase (1966) and Micronase (1984).

(izquierda) Investigación de la diabetes, 1957. Orinase, producto de Upjohn, fue el primer agente antidiabético oral aprobado para la venta en los Estados Unidos. En 1960, más de una tercera parte de los diabéticos conocidos en los Estados Unidos tomaban el fármaco. Los esfuerzos de Upjohn han producido otros dos agentes antidiabéticos, Tolinase (1966) y Micronase (1984).

(à gauche) Recherche sur le diabète, 1957. Orinase a été le premier anti-diabétique autorisé aux Etats-Unis. En 1960, plus d'un tiers des diabétiques américains identifiés l'utilisaient. La poursuite des recherches a permis la mise au point de deux autres anti-diabétiques : Tolinase (1966) et Micronase (1984).

（左）糖尿病研究、1957年。アップジョンのオリナーゼは、米国市場で最初に承認された経口血糖降下剤。1960年には、米国の糖尿病患者の⅓以上がこの製品を使用していた。オリナーゼに続いて、アップジョンは2つの血糖降下剤、トリナーゼ（1966年）とマイクロナーゼ（1984年）を開発した。

(right) Diabetes research, 1986. The long-range goal of Upjohn diabetes research is prevention of the disease. One step toward this end might be probing cellular tissue for genetic markers that could indicate a person's predisposition to diabetes.

(derecha) Investigación de la diabetes, 1986. La meta a largo plazo de la investigación de la diabetes en Upjohn es la prevención de la enfermedad. Un paso hacia esta meta podrá ser la investigación del tejido celular para detectar indicadores genéticos que pudieran advertir la predisposición de una persona a la diabetes.

(à droite) Recherche sur le diabète, 1986. A long terme, l'objectif des recherches d'Upjohn sur le diabète est la prévention de la maladie. Un pas pourrait être fait dans cette direction en recherchant dans les tissus cellulaires des marqueurs génétiques indiquant la prédisposition au diabète chez un individu.

（右）糖尿病研究、1986年。アップジョンの糖尿病研究の長期的な目標は、この病気の予防である。このゴールへ向けての研究として、糖尿病にかかりやすくなる素質を形成する、細胞中の遺伝要因が探求されている。

(left) Prostaglandin research, 1960s. For more than 25 years, Upjohn has supplied most of the world's samples of these hormone-like substances — even when the raw material, sea whip coral, had to be hand-harvested from Caribbean waters.

(izquierda) Investigación de las prostaglandinas en la década de 1960. Por más de 25 años, Upjohn ha suministrado la mayoría de las muestras en el mundo de estas sustancias tipo hormonal — aún cuando la materia prima, el coral con forma de látigo, tenía que ser recogido manualmente de las aguas del Caribe.

(à gauche) Recherche sur les prostaglandines, 1960-1970. Pendant plus de 25 ans, Upjohn a fourni la plupart des échantillons disponibles dans le monde de ces substances comparables à des hormones, même lorsque la matière première, un corail, devait être récolté à la main dans les Caraïbes.

（左）プロスタグランジン研究、1960年代。アップジョンは25年以上にわたって、このホルモン状物質のサンプルを世界に供給してきた一時にはカリブ海のサンゴから原料を取り出して。

(right) Prostaglandin research, 1986. Improving breeding-management in cattle, combating congenital heart disease in newborns, raising or lowering of blood pressure, reducing inflammation, and inhibiting stomach ulcers are only some of the broad product uses for which prostaglandins are used or show potential.

(derecha) Investigación de las prostaglandinas, 1986. Algunos de los usos generales en los cuales se aplican las prostaglandinas o para las cuales poseen potencial, son en el cruce de ganado bovino, en enfermedades cardíacas congénitas en recién nacidos, en el control de la presión arterial, la reducción de la inflamación e inhibición de úlceras estomacales.

(à droite) Recherche sur les prostaglandines, 1986. Une meilleure gestion des troupeaux bovins, la lutte contre les malformations cardiaques congénitales du nouveau-né, la régulation de la pression artérielle, le traitement des inflammations, la réduction des ulcères gastriques sont quelques-unes des nombreuses applications actuelles et futures des prostaglandines.

（右）プロスタグランジン研究、1986年。家畜の飼育、血圧の調整、新生児の先天性心臓病、炎症、胃潰瘍など、プロスタグランジンは幅広い分野での応用が期待されている。

Meanwhile, the company told Durey Peterson and his team they could formally report their discovery. They chronicled it in the April 7, 1952, issue of the American Chemical Society's *Journal.* Seven weeks later, Upjohn had its own cortisone on the market, followed in 1953 by hydrocortisone. The company had successfully leapfrogged Merck, a "tremendous event," in Dick Schreiber's words. "This was a big thing."

Despite their stunning success in anti-inflammation therapy, cortisone and hydrocortisone could have less-than-desirable side effects in patients, such as salt and water retention. Aware of that, Upjohn scientists under Dr. John Hogg's leadership went back to the lab bench, modified the hydrocortisone molecule, and in 1957 offered physicians Medrol, a more potent anti-inflammatory with fewer side effects. Today, Upjohn makes all of its own starting materials from soybean sterols and remains the world leader in steroid production.

Finding an Antidiabetes Agent

The steroid story echoed through PR & D's labs and offices for a long time. But it wasn't the only game in town. Other Upjohn scientists had their sights set on finding alternatives to insulin as a therapy for diabetes. Their search had started years earlier. In fact, the first paper by an Upjohn scientist on diabetes was published in 1929. Seventy articles were written in PR & D's labs over the next 25 years, a number of them by Dr. Dwight Ingle. But no product-related breakthroughs occurred.

Then, in 1955, the wind changed. A Detroit newspaper ran a squib about a new German antidiabetes drug, code-labeled BZ-55. Medical Director Dr. Earl L. Burbidge immediately called Farbwerke Hoechst headquarters in West Germany. Not only was the story correct but Hoechst had an even better agent of its own, tolbutamide — code-named D860. Under an existing agreement with Hoechst, Upjohn was able to gain exclusive rights to market a tolbutamide product in America and Canada.

First, though, the medication had to run the gamut of tests in the States. Thus began what has been called "one of the most careful investigations undergone by any substance in modern medical history." By late 1955, a number of diabetes specialists had received supplies of the

product, which the company had named "Orinase." In all, Upjohn gave away 19 tons — 1.5 million doses — of Orinase. Some 20,000 diabetics took the oral medication for the study, and records of use by 9,168 were analyzed at Upjohn. The chief conclusion was that Orinase was notably safe and effective at lowering blood sugar. Only 1.5 percent of the patients had any side effects. And when the product was used in cases of maturity-onset diabetes, it restored blood sugar essentially to normal and controlled other symptoms in 70 to 95 percent of the patients.

Orinase was approved by the FDA in June 1957. By the end of 1959, it was being used daily by more than one of every three known diabetics in the United States. Orinase continued as a major Upjohn product for two decades. In the meantime, metabolic research at Upjohn pushed on. It developed its own oral antidiabetes compound, Tolinase, introduced in the U.S. in 1966, and licensed from Hoechst a third-generation option, Micronase, marketed in the U.S. for the first time in April 1984. The long-range goal of Upjohn diabetes research, of course, has been diabetes prevention. Work toward this end continues as one of the main lines of PR & D.

Converting Ibuprofen into Major Success

Soon after Orinase went on the market, Upjohn's scientists learned of several intriguing substances under study in the United Kingdom. This series of compounds held promise for countering inflammation. PR & D heard about them as a result of Upjohn's alliance with the British pharmaceutical house Boots Pure Drug Company, Ltd., an arrangement enabling each to share in the research findings of the other.

The professionals in PR & D looked carefully at all the compounds in the Boots series, then, in 1962, fastened on one of them, ibuprofen, as having the most evident potential. A team led by Dr. E. Myles Glenn began basic studies of this substance, knowing that to gain FDA approval for an eventual product, they would have to build their own base of supportive data, regardless of what the Boots researchers might have accumulated.

This process of investigation went on for five years in Kalamazoo, with results that were sometimes less than encouraging. Some in the company tagged ibuprofen as "just another aspirin," but PR & D's interest in the compound remained high. When the reorganization of PR & D took place in 1968, the new Hypersensitivity Diseases Research cluster, headed by Dr. Norman B. Marshall, took on the challenge of developing ibuprofen. Dr. Carter Brooks set to work demonstrating that this pharmacologically active compound would be useful in treating human disease.

By early 1969, PR & D had scheduled human tolerance tests on ibuprofen. In England, Boots launched the distribution of its ibuprofen product, Brufen. That step activated Upjohn's determination to nail down more exact contract terms with Boots. The resulting agreement gave Upjohn a nonexclusive license to sell the new compound in the Western Hemisphere. Nonexclusivity meant that, if it chose, Boots could decide to market the medication in the Americas, or license others to do so. (In 1977, Boots did exactly that.)

The R & D process on ibuprofen accelerated in 1970. As many as 200 investigators began tests on more than 5,000 patients with arthritis, a process supervised by Carter Brooks as medical monitor. By now the compound had been given a trade name, Motrin. Evidence accumulated that Motrin, in contrast to possible competitors among anti-inflammatories, caused little if any irritation of the stomach wall.

The researchers developed enough evidence in 1970 for management to conclude that ibuprofen should be designated a "product candidate." The following year, Marketing worked up a preliminary sales forecast, and exploratory market research and planning got under way. But the matter of dosage still had to be resolved, and there Upjohn found itself facing a perplexing phenomenon. International sales of Motrin in Mexico, Brazil, and Canada found quick market acceptance, only to be followed by a precipitous drop in demand. A team went to Canada to study this puzzle and returned with the conviction that sales declined because the product was not effective at the 200 mg/three-times-a-day dosage recommended by Boots.

Carter Brooks wasn't surprised at the report the investigators brought back from Canada. He had found that at the Boots dosage the compound acted simply as an analgesic, not as an anti-inflammatory. Since the drug was well tolerated, Upjohn investigators increased the dosage to 400 mg, four times a day. Efficacy of treatment increased markedly.

Almost at the same time, Upjohn submitted its New Drug Application (NDA) to the FDA, which in 1974 agreed to accept the company's recommended dosage of 300 to 400 mg, taken four times a day. Motrin became the first new agent to be approved by the FDA in nine years for treating osteoarthritis and rheumatoid arthritis.

Tests on 3,000 patients had shown that the compound could effectively relieve pain, stiffness, and swelling in joints. And side effects were few and far between.

Motrin went on the market on October 7. In the first two months, sales doubled the forecast. By February 1975, 110 million tablets had been sold, and demand obliged Fine Chemicals in Kalamazoo and North Haven, Connecticut, to put on three shifts a day, seven days a week, producing bulk ibuprofen. When the product's first year concluded, Upjohn had marketed more than 500 million tablets. Initially, production centered in Building 41. However, once the Upjohn Manufacturing Company facility was in high gear in Puerto Rico (*see* pages 126-28), a decision was made to transfer Motrin to that plant. The changeover occurred in December 1976. By then the operators in Building 41 had produced more than 1.7 billion tablets of the anti-inflammatory, and Motrin was Upjohn's leading product.

Meanwhile, researchers had gone back to the bench. If 400 mg Motrin was good, maybe a 600 mg version would be even better, and so researchers began bioavailability and stability tests of the product at a 600 mg dosage level. At the same time, other investigators looked into the effect of Motrin on menstrual pain. In 1979, the FDA authorized sale of the compound in the 600 mg dosage; it also allowed added indications for relief of pain in

(left) Cancer research, 1963. Upjohn testing resulted in a bank of more than 12,000 potential anticancer compounds. Some showed promise when tested in lab animals. But, as was all too common in the frustrating field of cancer research, none proved effective in humans.

(izquierda) Investigación del cáncer, 1963. Los ensayos conducidos por Upjohn resultaron en un banco de más de 12.000 compuestos anticancerosos potenciales. Algunos fueron prometedores en ensayos con animales de laboratorio. Pero, como es tan común en el desalentador campo de la investigación del cáncer, ninguno resultó ser eficaz en humanos.

(à gauche) Recherche sur le cancer, 1963. Les essais réalisés par Upjohn ont permis de constituer une banque de plus de 12.000 agents potentiellement anticancéreux. Certains ont révélé leur potentiel lors d'essais sur des animaux. Mais comme il est habituel dans ce domaine de la recherche, l'efficacité chez l'homme n'est pas pour autant donnée.

（左）癌研究、1963年。アップジョンの研究により発見された可能性のある抗癌性物質は、12,000以上にのぼる。そのうちのいくつかは、 動物実験で効果を上げたが、困難な癌研究分野でよくあるように、人間の癌に対して効能を示した物質はなかつた。

(right) Cancer research, 1986. Following the successful development of Cytosar (1969) and Zanosar (1982), Upjohn cancer researchers and clinical investigators are now screening many chemotherapeutic compounds in search of new anticancer agents.

(derecha) Investigación del cáncer, 1986. Después del gran éxito obtenido en el desarrollo de Cytosar (1969) y Zanosar (1982), tanto los investigadores del cáncer de Upjohn como los investigadores clínicos, ensayan en la actualidad muchos compuestos quimioterapéuticos en busca de nuevos agentes anticancerosos..

(à droite) Recherche sur le cancer, 1986. Les travaux ayant déjà abouti à la mise au point de Cytosar (1969) et de Zanosar (1982), les chercheurs et les cliniciens d'Upjohn recherchent maintenant de nouveaux agents anticancéreux.

（右）癌研究、1986年。サイトザー（1969年）とザノザー（1982年）の開発に続いて、アップジョンの臨床研究者は、今日も新しい抗癌物質を求めて、化学療法用の化合物をふるい分けしている。

menstruation, after dental extractions and surgery, and in cases of injury to soft tissue. Within three years, the 600 mg dosage ranked as one of the most frequently prescribed nonsteroidal anti-inflammatory drugs (NSAIDs) in the U.S. (In 1985, Upjohn introduced Motrin 800 mg; *see* page 123.)

This kind of success drew attention. Acting within the original agreement, Boots began in 1977 to market its own brand of ibuprofen in the U.S.

Then, in 1984, it licensed a 200 mg version for nonprescription sale to American Home Products Company. Upjohn manufactures its own 200 mg ibuprofen analgesic, Nuprin, with Bristol-Myers & Company the sole distributor.

Motrin has been Upjohn's most successful product to date. Its development resulted from thousands of Upjohn employees pulling together in one of those impressive team efforts that have characterized Upjohn operations from W. E.'s time to the present.

The Versatile Prostaglandins

The discovery of prostaglandins dates back to 1930, when a gynecologist and a pharmacologist in New York observed that a factor in human semen triggered relaxation or contraction in the uterus. Five years later, Sweden's Ulf von Euler, a 1970 Nobel laureate, gave these hormone-like substances their name. And then, for almost 20 years, the prostaglandins, which play a key role in regulating cellular metabolism and function, dropped from sight.

The fact that they came to Upjohn's attention at all can be linked to an acquaintance between Swedish Professor Sune Bergstrom and Dr. David Weisblat, going back to the latter's years as a postdoctoral chemist at Ohio State University in the early 1940s. Bergstrom arrived at Ohio State to lecture on his heparin research. The two men met, and a lasting friendship formed. In October 1957, when Dave Weisblat was director of chemical research at Upjohn, he got an enthusiastic letter from Bergstrom, who would soon join Sweden's renowned Karolinska Institute. "I am now involved and excited about 'prostaglandins and sheep prostate glands,'" Bergstrom wrote. "We are collecting some data on the structure — but keep it under your hat. One is smooth muscle stimulating and one also blood pressure decreasing. The main trouble now is supply of raw materials." Upjohn, responded Weisblat, was "extremely interested." Perhaps it could help Bergstrom get a larger store of prostate glands.

That was the start of a new link between Bergstrom, Weisblat, and Upjohn. Over the next 25 years, Bergstrom was to visit Kalamazoo 75 times. And when he and two others received a 1982 Nobel prize for their prostaglandin work, Bergstrom underscored how important Upjohn's collaboration had been.

Studies beginning in mid-1958 discerned that there were at least 14 different prostaglandins (PGs) in human tissue. But what could be done to overcome the shortage of raw materials? By 1961, it was clear that an attempt

had to be made to synthesize the molecules, an awesome challenge. However, Upjohn had a distinct in-house strength to call upon: its experience with biosynthesis in the giant fermenters on Portage Road. The clue, various researchers proposed, might be a fatty substance found in the body, arachidonic acid. Under the right conditions, it seemed to be convertible to a PG.

Upjohn jumped on that lead. Soon a pilot plant was converting the acid into two PGs. It was a "godsend," says Weisblat. "It provided the materials for nearly all the prostaglandin studies in the world for almost five years."

PR & D kept working to perfect total synthesis. Then another clue came to light. PGs could be found in concentrations in a Florida coral, sea whip. Upjohn chemists solved extraction problems, and the PG supply worldwide expanded. Finally, total synthesis was achieved, an Upjohn process accomplished by researchers Robert Kelly, Verlan VanRheenan, David White, Joel Huber, and others. Now PG supplies were ensured. And Upjohn continued to offer scientists elsewhere free supplies. In 1979 alone, it gave away 5,675 samples. That same year, 4,900 reports on PG implications appeared in print.

Those findings have been extraordinary. Early investigation centered on PGs in reproductive physiology, but the PGs can do much more. One Upjohn PG product introduced in the U.S. in 1981, Prostin VR Pediatric, has saved the lives of "blue babies," infants afflicted with congenital heart disease. The prostaglandins have also shown themselves effective, as Dr. Weisblat wrote in 1981, in lowering or raising blood pressure, dilating or constricting bronchi, stimulating or relaxing intestinal and smooth muscle, shrinking nasal passages, mediating inflammation, and inhibiting gastric secretion. Viewed broadly, the PGs would seem to have product potential in a number of areas.

Other Directions

Upjohn has been in the war against cancer for more than a quarter of a century. Starting in the late 1950s, PR & D sent trial steroids to the National Institutes of Health for antitumor testing. By 1965, more than 170 compounds had been offered to that program. New products resulted, too. Cytosar, launched in 1969, achieved remissions in significant numbers of leukemia patients during clinical trials. Zanosar, launched in 1982, is prescribed for metastatic islet cell carcinoma, a rare form of cancer.

The scientists in PR & D have had an equally long track record in fertility research. Dr. Jake Stucki, currently corporate vice president for pharmaceutical research, came to Upjohn in April 1957 as an

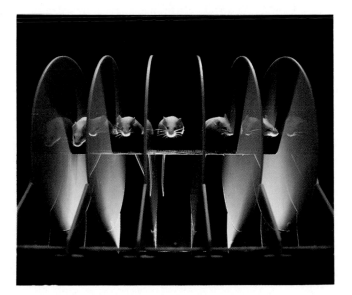

(left) CNS research, 1958. Upjohn's early efforts in this field met with limited success. But company chemists and pharmacologists measured and recorded a critical mass of basic research which proved to be a valuable stepping stone to later products — Halcion (1977) and Xanax (1981).

(izquierda) Investigación del SNC, 1958. Los esfuerzos iniciales de Upjohn en este campo tuvieron un éxito limitado. Pero los químicos y farmacólogos de la compañia evaluaron y recogieron una gran cantidad de investigación básica, la cual resultó ser un valioso escalón para productos posteriores — Halcion (1977) y Xanax (1981).

(à gauche) Recherche sur le système nerveux central, 1958. Les premiers travaux d'Upjohn dans ce domaine ont rencontré peu de succès. Mais les chimistes et les pharmacologues de la société en ont tiré une somme de données fondamentales qui a constitué les fondations de la mise au point de produits: Halcion (1977) et Xanax (1981).

（左）中枢神経系の研究、1958年。アップジョンによるこの分野の初期の研究は、実を結ばなかった。しかし、アップジョンの化学者・薬理学者による基礎研究の積み重ねは、近年の製品開発—ハルシオン（1977年）、ザナックス（1981年）—に貴重な貢献をした。

(right) CNS research, 1986. Research is still dependent on the ability to measure and record. How long these mice remain on the steadily rotating rod may give insights into the effects of certain drugs on the animals' central nervous system.

(derecha) Investigación del SNC, 1986. La investigación todavía depende de la habilidad de evaluar y registrar. El tiempo que estos ratones permanezcan en la constante barra giratoria puede aportar conocimientos acerca de los efectos de ciertas drogas sobre el sistema nervioso central de los animales.

(à droite) Recherche sur le système nerveux central, 1986. Le succès de la recherche dépend de la capacité à mesurer et à enregistrer des données. La durée pendant laquelle les souris sont capables de rester sur ce cylindre en rotation permet d'élucider les effets de certains médicaments sur le système nerveux central de l'animal.

（右）中枢神経系の研究、1986年。研究の成果は、測定と記録の良し悪しによって左右される。回転を続ける棒の上にマウスがどのくらいの時間乗っていられるかによって、薬剤の中枢神経系への影響が観察される。

Designing molecules, 1958 and 1986. Creating models helps researchers understand how molecules work and to develop more effective drugs. Though researchers still employ blackboards and hand-held models, computer imaging offers increased speed and accuracy.

Diseño de moléculas, 1958 y 1986. La creación de modelos ayuda a los investigadores a definir cómo actúan las moléculas y a desarrollar fármacos más eficaces. Aún cuando los investigadores aún se valen del uso de pizarras y modelos que sostienen en las manos, las imágenes en computadoras proporcionan mayor celeridad y exactitud.

Conception de molécules, 1958 et 1986. La création de modèles aide les chercheurs à comprendre comment les molécules fonctionnent et à concevoir des médicaments plus efficaces. Bien que les chercheurs utilisent encore le tableau noir et les maquettes, l'imagerie informatique leur permet plus de rapidité -et plus de précision.

分子デザイン、1958年、1986年。研究者はモデルによって分子の働きを理解し、より効果的な薬品の開発に役立てる。黒板と組立モデルは今も使われているが、モデルの精度とスピードは、コンピューター画像処理によって大幅に進歩している。

endocrinologist. After getting his bearings, he asked Dr. Schreiber to let him look for hormonal leads to fertility control. Schreiber took the matter to the company's board "not once but twice," says Stucki. The board concurred, and research began. The search went quickly. The scientists found that the substance medroxy-progesterone acetate had a remarkable ability to maintain pregnancy. Study led to trials, and in 1959 the FDA approved marketing the compound as Provera. At first it was intended for maintaining pregnancy. Further analysis showed it could be used in uterine and renal cancer treatment and as an injectable contraceptive. Today, Provera is available domestically and internationally for treatment of cancer and uterine bleeding; internationally, it is sold as a contraceptive.

Depo-Provera, for use by injection as a contraceptive, went to the FDA in 1967 as a new drug application. The agency has yet to act on this request, which led to prolonged debates and objections. Meanwhile, Depo-Provera has been approved as a contraceptive in more than 80 countries.

On March 10, 1985, Upjohn officials announced that fertility research was being terminated. The company chose to allocate its resources to areas where it saw the possibility of greater return on investment. It was also concerned about an adverse regulatory environment. However, executives said Upjohn would continue its efforts to get Depo-Provera registered for contraception in the U.S.

Central nervous system research has come to be one of Upjohn's most important research areas. This line of study began in 1950 and reached its first success in the late 1960s in the search for differently structured variations of benzodiazepines, chemical compounds which were being used to treat anxiety and other psychological disorders. Out of this investigation came Xanax, the antianxiety agent, and Halcion, the anti-insomnia agent. They are only the beginning of the payback on Upjohn's three-decade commitment.

Not all PR & D ventures are successful. Life in pharmaceutical research can have more than a normal ration of peaks and valleys. And PR & D professionals know what it's like to wind up in a valley. For example, the company's first solid candidate in the psychotherapeutic field, Monase, was launched in late 1961. After less than a year, it had to be withdrawn — every sample, every bottle — because of some suspected cases of agranulocytosis, a potentially fatal blood disease distinguished by destructive and severe decreases of certain blood cells. It was a real setback. "We had every reason to believe that the drug would be free of toxic effects," said Dick Schreiber. "Clinical tests couldn't show that one out of 30,000 to 40,000 patients might get agranulocytosis."

Fortunately for all concerned, such mistakes are rare. One means PR & D has employed to minimize the possibility of error as well as increase productivity had its genesis nearly 20 years ago. Then, PR & D professionals were grouped by profession, and the tendency, recalls Dave Weisblat, was for one group to war against another.

The decision was made in 1968 to reorganize along different lines. Product research units were established around specific disease areas. Each unit had a few biologists, chemists, pharmacologists, and physicians. Each unit was charged with the entire responsibility for making, identifying, and developing compounds to the point of an effective NDA.

Essentially, Upjohn PR & D staffing still sticks to this kind of matrix organization. Each group operates in one of eight disease groups, and each, in turn, has its own disease-therapy goals — for the Central Nervous System unit, depression, pain, psychosis, neurological deficit, and so on. This system, says Dr. Stucki, gave people "a new feeling of ownership of projects."

Drug discovery has taken a definite turn toward complexity in the years since 1968. So, when it seems necessary, the units can call in staff specialists, such as biotechnologists or computational chemists. Inevitably, other changes have been made. The Medical Division focuses on new indications and formulations. Pharmacy research on drug delivery systems has been stepped up. In

New facilities need new equipment. One-quarter of the equipment that newly hired scientists call for did not exist two decades ago. However, equipment that might have cost $100,000 some 15 years back may now cost $1,000. Although it takes nearly $250,000 to equip a new investigator, Upjohn is actually getting more data per dollar. This increase in information-gathering ability goes hand in hand with an increase in demand for equipment. Several years ago, equipment needs generated some 300 purchase orders annually. Now there are 700 a year. Small wonder that PR & D has 500 electronic balances, 300 microscopes, 100 Liquid Scintillation Counters, and almost one computer terminal for every scientist.

Case Study: PR & D on Xanax

With its product Xanax, Upjohn has earned a solid place among medical practitioners seeking to deal with the anxious moods of man.

Anxiety, according to some professional observers, ranks as the number one mental health disorder of the 1980s. Fortunately, due to work going on since 1950, this condition and other mental health problems can be treated with medication. French researchers in 1952 discovered chlorpromazine, the first antipsychotic compound. Iproniazid, the first antidepressant, came next. And then scientists came upon a new family of antianxiety agents, the benzodiazepines. Hoffman-LaRoche, the giant Swiss drug firm, brought out the first of these, Librium, in 1960, and followed it three years later with the current market leader, Valium.

At Upjohn, a lively curiosity about formulating medications for central nervous system (CNS) disorders materialized at about the time Dick Schreiber joined Research in 1949. By the next year, PR & D was probing for leads in neuropharmacology. Dr. Jacob Szmuszkovicz, who joined Upjohn in 1954 and was a Distinguished Scientist on his retirement in 1985, recalls that his fellow chemists and he were broadly deputized to "solve problems in areas including mental disease, arthritis, and hypertension."

During the 1960s, tranquilizers found a ready reception in an uneasy society. One day in the mid-1960s, two of Upjohn PR & D's "barons" (as heads of departments were sometimes called) discussed this very matter. The two

short, innovative as it was, the 1968 scheme is still being improved upon.

If organizational charts can age, so can the professional researcher's facilities and equipment. For Upjohn, a dynamic, growing research program has demanded not only the latest in scientific tools but also more and better space. In the mid-1960s, the company spent $6.5 million to build a three-story addition downtown for 100 scientists. Then, in 1976, came seven-story Building 209, $43 million worth of new PR & D facilities; it offered work areas for 850 employees. In 1984, Building 267, an eight-story structure, was erected next to 209 at a cost of $55 million. Building 267 houses Upjohn's biotechnology research.

Today, Upjohn has still more growth on its mind. Site preparation will probably begin in 1987 on a $75 million drug research structure — which could run to seven stories in height — as part of the Kalamazoo research complex, and construction is under way on a 240,000-square-foot pharmaceutical research facility in Japan.

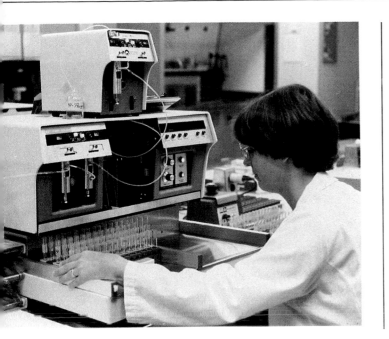

men, Dr. John Hogg, chief of the chemists, and Dr. Jake Stucki, then top pharmacologist, well knew of the market success of Librium and Valium. "We decided that we ought to get into the benzodiazepine business," Dr. Stucki recalls. "There was patent coverage all over the place. We said we ought to carve out an area of chemistry that is different."

A decision was formalized, and section head Dr. Richard Heinzleman promptly assembled the chemists and told them they were to start looking for "novel and useful benzodiazepine derivatives." And so the CNS researchers — Drs. Szmuszkovicz, Art Hanze, Jackson B. Hester, Jr., Thomas Lemke, and Bruce Moffitt — changed gears and set to work. They first scoured the literature on relevant patents to learn everything known about benzodiazepines so that, in Dr. Hester's words, "We could do things that were novel." They were looking for ways to modify the benzodiazepine molecule without losing its antianxiety activity. And it was a highly complex molecule, with a number of what chemists call "points of attachment." Recalls Dr. Szmuszkovicz, "We decided to play with the seven-member ring, which has five positions available for substitution. Jackson Hester got involved with attachments of small rings to the one and two positions. I was involved with attachments to the four and five positions. We made compounds, but we found we were losing biological activity."

The project had one real strength going for it: good relationships between the chemists and biologists assigned to it. The biologists quickly geared up to run tests on trial compounds. "It wasn't unusual," says Dr. Szmuszkovicz, "for a chemist to make a compound, diagnose what he had, take it down to the pharmacologist, and get results of the testing within a day." The biologists' team that carried out the testing, grouped under section head Dr. Hugh Keasling, included James R. Collins, Garland Johnson, Allan Rudzik, Robert N. Straw, and Andrew H. Tang, all Ph.D's.

The efforts of Dr. Hester in particular angled toward adding a "triazolo ring" of atoms to the benzodiazepine molecule. His colleagues recognized his unusual talents for such an assignment. "He not only knows how to synthesize compounds," explains Dr. Szmuszkovicz, "but is also very creative as a medicinal chemist. Not too many people can do that very effectively."

The search for a benzodiazepine molecule that would have biological activity and yet not invade existing patents was neither quick nor smooth. The breakthrough came in May 1968. Team members found a patent-free compound with as much activity as Valium. Its active ingredient was named ketazolam, now marketed abroad as Unakalm. The discovery gave the researchers a real lift. Other compounds followed. By October 9, the scientists were able to note another benchmark, the first equation for the molecule that was to be Xanax. Dr. Hester's assistant, Robert Green, put it into writing that day.

Dr. Hester and his group completed the conversion of formula into compound on January 15, 1969. For two weeks, fellow chemists analyzed and purified the substance. That led to the next step: testing on animals. At the same time, Dr. Hester went to the Chemical Process Research and Development unit to enlist their help in producing large quantities of the compound's starting materials.

The biological assayists had no easy time in running animal tests with the new formula. Finally, on February 12, Drs. Al Rudzik and Jim Collins showed up excitedly at Dr. Hester's lab. "You've got something," they exclaimed. "We know it works. It's the best compound we've ever run through our system. It's at least ten times as potent as Valium."

Meanwhile, the molecule for what would become Halcion was also taking shape. The CNS unit's goal had been to find a new antianxiety agent. The researchers' resultant compound, given the generic name alprazolam, would eventually go on the market as Xanax. With that achievement in hand, the scientists pursued close analogs, one of which, a halogen-modified derivative, was tested on animals. It did not have the sedative effect of Xanax or Valium. But when it was tested on humans, the results were quite different. The compound showed itself to be remarkably effective as both sedative and hypnotic. "It was unexpected," says Dr. Hester. And that is how Halcion came on the scene as a prospective Upjohn product.

In October 1969, alprazolam was officially labeled a new drug candidate, and on the 29th of that month, the company applied for a patent. Seven days later, the U.S. Patent Office received a patent submission from abroad. Takeda Chemical Industry, Ltd., the Japanese pharmaceutical firm, was following up in America its Japanese filing of one year earlier for a process very familiar to Upjohn's PR & D: attachment of a triazolo ring to the benzodiazepine molecule. The news jarred Upjohn researchers.

Not willing to wait for a decision before proceeding with development, Upjohn and Takeda signed an agreement that gave each company rights to the other's patents in this class of antianxiety agents. Then, on September 24, 1975, the Board of Patent Interference decided that Dr. Hester's patent had precedence over Takeda's.

Meanwhile, development effort by both companies was proceeding rapidly. In the U.S., PR & D was accumulating the clinical experience needed to define the drug's medical utilities and demonstrate its safety in humans and in laboratory animals. In Japan, Takeda and the Upjohn subsidiary, Japan Upjohn Limited, were cooperating in the development of Xanax. In October 1981, the U.S. NDA was approved, and shortly thereafter Xanax was marketed and rapidly became an important Upjohn product in the U.S. and in many other countries. In Japan, the drug is marketed by Japan Upjohn Limited under the tradename Solanax.

MEDICAL: PR & D's Staunch Ally

There is a resolute bond between PR & D in its downtown-Kalamazoo site and another part of Upjohn, the Medical Affairs Division, housed west of Building 88 in the six-year-old Building 243. When PR & D finishes its work on a new product, Medical and Marketing undertake parallel activities to maximize that product's success in the field.

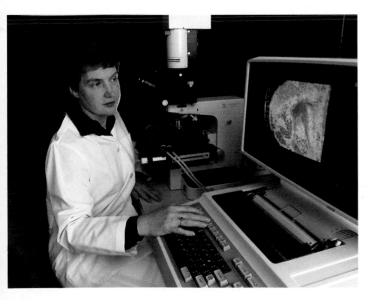

(left) Drug tracing, 1960. Where does it go? How much of it goes? These are questions researchers must ask about a drug before a patient takes it. This researcher is attaching a low-level radioactive isotope to a drug which will be used to trace the drug's route through a laboratory animal.

(izquierda) Localización del fármaco, 1960. ¿Hacia dónde y qué cantidad va? Estas son preguntas que los investigadores hacen acerca de un medicamento antes que el paciente lo tome. Este investigador adhiere un isótopo de bajo nivel radioactivo a una droga que será usada, para seguir su pista a través del sistema de un animal de laboratorio.

(à gauche) Métabolisation du médicament, 1960. Où va-t-il? Dans quelle quantité? Voilà deux des questions auxquelles les chercheurs doivent répondre avant qu'un médicament ne soit prescrit au patient. Ce chercheur fixe une petite quantité d'un isotope radioactif à un médicament afin de suivre son parcours dans l'organisme d'un animal de laboratoire.

（左）薬剤追跡研究、1960年。薬剤は体内のどこへ、どれだけ吸収されるのか？これは薬剤開発研究の重要な問題である。実験動物の体内での吸収経過追跡のため、放射性アイソトープを薬剤に取り付ける研究者。

(right) Drug tracing, 1986. This researcher at the console of a brain-imaging instrument has called up a section of brain tissue to demonstrate localization of drug binding to receptors — crucial information about the pharmacodynamics of a potential CNS drug.

(derecha) Localización del fármaco, 1986. Este investigador, trabajando en una terminal que produce una imagen del cerebro, ha ubicado una sección del tejido cerebral para demostrar la localización de la droga cuando se une a los receptores — información crucial acerca de la farmacodinámica de una droga de uso potencial en el SNC.

(à droite) Métabolisation du médicament, 1986. Installé devant la console d'un matériel permettant de visualiser le cerveau, ce chercheur fait apparaître une section de tissu cérébral afin de montrer la localisation d'un médicament fixé à des récepteurs. Cette information est cruciale pour comprendre la pharmaco-dynamique d'un médicament destiné au système nerveux central.

（右）薬剤追跡研究、1986年。中枢神経系薬剤の薬理学的作用を知る上で重要な、薬剤の脳内レセプターでの局部化を観察する研究者。

(left) Clinical testing, 1957. Upjohn researchers and 420 U.S. physicians amassed 23 volumes of clinical data for the Orinase New Drug Application to the FDA. Here, Medical Division personnel check over the results of what was then the industry's largest clinical trial.

(izquierda) Ensayos clínicos, 1957. Los investigadores de Upjohn y 420 médicos norteamericanos acumularon 23 volúmenes de datos clínicos para la solicitud de nuevo medicamente para Orinase, sometida a la Administración de Drogas y Alimentos. En la foto, personal de la División Médica verifica los resultados de lo que fue en aquella época el ensayo clínico más grande en la industria.

(à gauche) Essais cliniques, 1957. Les chercheurs d'Upjohn et 420 médecins américains ont amassé 23 volumes de données cliniques pour le dossier de demande d'autorisation d'Orinase destiné à l'administration américaine. Ici, le personnel de la division médicale vérifie les résultats de ce qui fut alors le plus vaste essai clinique jamais réalisé.

（左）臨床テスト、1957年。アップジョンの研究者と420人の米国の医師は、オリナーゼを新薬として米食品医薬品管理局（ＦＤＡ）へ申請するため、23巻にのぼる臨床データを集めた。当時としては、業界最大規模の臨床試験の結果をチェックする、アップジョン社医学部門の社員。

(right) Clinical testing, 1986. To ensure that new medications are safe and effective in the prevention and treatment of disease, Upjohn now maintains Clinical Investigation Units in Kalamazoo and Jackson, Michigan, and London, Ontario, Canada.

(derecha) Ensayos clínicos, 1986. Para asegurar que los nuevos medicamentos son seguros y eficaces en la prevención y tratamiento de enfermedades, Upjohn mantiene ahora unidades de investigación clínica en Kalamazoo y en Jackson, Michigan y en Londres, Ontario, Canadá.

(à droite) Essais cliniques, 1986. Afin d'assurer l'efficacité et la sécurité de nouveaux médicaments, Upjohn dispose d'unités de recherche clinique à Kalamazoo et Jackson, dans le Michigan, ainsi qu'à London (Ontario) au Canada.

（右）臨床テスト、1986年。新薬が安全で、病気の予防と治療に効能のあるものであることを保証するため、アップジョンは現在、ミシガン州（カラマズー、ジャクソン）とカナダ（オンタリオ州ロンドン）で臨床調査室を運営している。

Medical's present leader, Corporate Vice President for Medical Affairs Alan B. Varley, M.D., came to Upjohn in 1957. At the time, the 20-year-old medical office was headed by Medical Director Earl Burbidge, M.D. Burbidge, who succeeded Gifford Upjohn as medical director in 1951, directed some 30 people, 18 of whom were physicians. They provided the data, which then consisted basically of safety information to get a new drug application registered by the FDA. As late as 1961, federal law did not require that a new drug be proved effective in order to be approved. Additionally, pharmaceutical makers needed to wait only 60 days after filing an NDA before they could begin to sell their product. Medical also answered inquiries from physicians, monitored what salespeople were doing, and watched over the safety of products in use. Then came the 1962 Kefauver-Harris amendments to the Food, Drug and Cosmetic Act of 1938, leading to major modifications in the industry (*see pages 163-64*).

That same year, Dr. Burbidge died. He was replaced by Dr. Harold Hailman, who was given the title director of scientific relations. He was overseer of an expanded medical department that included a larger clinical research staff and a medical services group acting as liaisons to the FDA and physicians.

At this time Medical was given greater status when Harold L. Upjohn, M.D., son of then-Chairman Gifford Upjohn, was promoted to vice president for medical affairs. The 1968 reorganization saw the medical affairs team now interacting with many aspects of Pharmaceutical Research, Production, and Marketing. Varley, named medical director, pharmaceutical marketing, in 1970, and medical director, domestic pharmaceutical medical affairs, in 1974, was appointed to his current position in 1981.

As responsibilities stand today, PR & D is concerned with any steps needed to get a drug approved by the FDA; from that point on, Medical Affairs takes over. Its staff of 350 deals with the rest of a drug's life cycle — all new uses, all new formulations, any adverse reactions, and questions of safety and continued efficacy.

The nonsteroidal anti-inflammatory and analgesic agent Motrin is a case in point. Medical Affairs took on the job of developing it as an analgesic in addition to its original anti-inflammatory indication. In the process, Dr. Varley's associates found that the analgesic was a lot better than anything else available to treat dysmenorrhea (painful menstruation). That led to Motrin being the first prescription drug indicated in the U.S. for treating this condition. Medical Affairs is also at work on developing further extensions of the Motrin product line to help bolster the product's performance since it went off patent in May 1985. Immediately after Motrin went off patent, generic imitations began to be seen. They were available at 400 mg and 600 mg. Realizing well ahead of time that this would happen, Upjohn had decided to come up with something that would make it more difficult for another company to pursue. This meant creating product line extensions. The key one would be Motrin 800 mg tablets, followed by a sustained release 800 mg form. Upjohn submitted the appropriate data on Motrin 800 to the FDA and, after more than two years' wait, received approval in May 1985 to begin selling the new strength. The product's first year on the market produced excellent results.

Extended uses like this are not to be dismissed. Dr. Varley expects that 80 percent of Upjohn's growth over the next decade may well come from such evolutions as these.

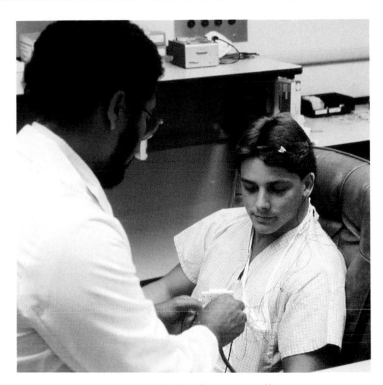

Another activity of Medical Affairs is equally important — in Dr. Varley's words, "keeping the company out of trouble." To him, Upjohn does very well in that respect. In fact, he ranks the company's adverse-reaction monitoring unit in the "top drawer" of those in the industry. The Medical Affairs staff went to work quickly when a few reports came in that some Motrin users were gaining excessive weight, while others encountered vision difficulties. Analysis showed that the latter did not stem from Motrin. As for the weight gain, Motrin, like aspirin, can cause weight increases among individuals bordering on congestive heart failure. Medical Affairs thereupon rewrote the package insert to warn physicians.

Of necessity, Medical Affairs keeps abreast of the latest developments and leads. One way they do this is to stay in touch with Marketing's Medical Science Liaison people, the "MSLs" (see page 146). Through the MSL chain, new ideas reach Medical Affairs, and sometimes new formulations or uses sprout from that stimulation.

Of the 30 physicians in the Medical Affairs unit, most are divided into five Clinical Investigation Units — endocrinology/cancer, infectious diseases, anti-inflammatory research, cardiovascular and gastrointestinal conditions, and psychopharmaceutical research. When one of these groups launches a field study of drug-use results — "postmarketing surveillance," they call it — big numbers can be involved. Recently, Upjohn began a study of 8,000 New Zealand women using Depo-Provera, the injectable contraceptive. The company paid for physical exams every six months in an effort to compare the Depo-Provera group with those using intrauterine devices or oral contraceptives. Numbers of that size do not dismay the Medical Affairs planners. They want information *before* problems boil up. Maybe only 500 patients out of 1 million have trouble with a certain drug. "The trick," says Dr. Varley, "is to find those 500 and study them intensely. We are working out better ways of identifying those people."

THE PRODUCTION PROCESS: A PERFORMANCE OF PEOPLE

In the huge spaces of Building 41, change is routine. The reasons for change seem almost limitless. A production line has to be shut down to switch over to a new product, a different label, a special run of sample packages, a display box. A different insert has to be put into an over-the-counter item, or a coupon offer is to be added. A new FDA regulation calls for an amended insert. Or products are being introduced in new dosages, new formulations, new delivery systems. The line starts, turns out a stream of packages, stops to adjust to new requirements, then starts once more. It's happening all the time. At every step of the way, hands, eyes, and experiences of people have been instrumental. Upjohn may be more automated than ever before, but its people stand as the movers and mixers, appraisers and analysts, innovators and problem-solvers.

Of course, production was not always automated. Retiree Elsie Kline remembers being on the line in the 1920s. "They had big tanks up on the next floor," she recalls, "and they put a hole through the ceiling. We had a garden hose come down, with a glass tube on the end. I had my tray of bottles, and I would have to suck the tube to get it started and fill the bottles. Then we had to wet the corks and pound them in with a wooden mallet."

Production has changed many times over since then. So has the Upjohn catalog. A century ago, it had 186 pill and granule formulas. That number gradually increased to more than 1,000 entries, most of them botanically or biologically derived products. By 1961, the last of these

old-timers, HT Morphine Sulphate 1/4 grain, was discontinued. Meanwhile, nutrition products, which represented 54 percent of sales in 1945, ebbed to 9.3 percent 25 years later. As of 1984, these substances accounted for only a little more than one percent of sales.

The newer products have brought with them new challenges for production: potent CNS drugs require elaborate protection for the worker; procedures to maintain a sterile environment have become so stringent for injectables that Sterile Products Production has begun to look like a futuristic movie set; over-the-counter products require flexible response to demand and innovative and tamper-resistant packaging. Further, as Upjohn became a worldwide enterprise, manufacturing could not remain a one-site operation. Facilities sprung up around the world, and major installations were constructed in Belgium and Puerto Rico.

The current head of manufacturing at Upjohn is John C. Griffin, Ph.D., corporate vice president for pharmaceutical manufacturing. Griffin, in 1978, replaced Louis C. Schroeter, Ph.D., who was elevated to the post of vice president and general manager, domestic pharmaceutical division. Schroeter, who in 1974 replaced James K. Traer as head of production, now serves as corporate vice president for worldwide manufacturing and engineering.

No one knows about change better than Schroeter and Griffin. Over a span of 30 years, Griffin says, there has been "almost total change" in how things are done. The most significant updating has come about in sterile product technology. "What was acceptable 15 years ago," he explains, "is completely unacceptable now." It has meant new job descriptions, a completely new physical area, and retraining of employees.

"It never ends," adds Schroeter. "There's a continual movement of technology."

The National Aeronautics and Space Administration offered the model for one newer component of Building 41 in Kalamazoo, the Potent Drug Facility, designed to protect personnel working with extremely potent chemicals. The chief ingredient in Halcion, for example, could put an unprotected worker to sleep if he were to inhale only a few particles of dust generated in mixing or transferring product. Individuals in this facility don what look like space suits before entering the room. Air is piped to the "Tyvec" suit through a tube, and communication is by radio. Thus clad, employees can go into the facility and begin diluting potent raw materials or turning them into finished products with no fear of contaminating the outside environment, the product, or themselves.

Portage manufacturing complex, 1953 and 1986. Although some have been demolished or moved, more than 140 buildings have been constructed at the company's main manufacturing site since 1946. More people work at this site than were employed at the entire company 40 years ago.

El complejo de manufactura en Portage, 1953 y 1986. Desde 1946 se han construido más de 140 edificios en el sitio principal de manufactura de la compañía, aunque algunos de ellos han sido derribados o trasladados. En este sitio, trabaja más personal que el que la compañía en total tenía 40 años atrás.

Usine de Portage, 1953 et 1986. Plus de 140 bâtiments ont été construits depuis 1946 sur le site industriel principal de la société. Certains ont été détruits ou déplacés. Ce site emploie aujourd'hui à lui seul un nombre de personnes supérieur à l'effectif total de la société il y a 40 ans.

ポーテジの製造工場、1953年、1986年。1946年以来、140 以上の建物が この敷地に建てられた。現在ここで働く従業員の数は、40年前の全社員数を上回っている。

There have been times when a problem faced by a competitor's product has touched off responsive change in Upjohn production. In 1982, when seven people died after using cyanide-laced Tylenol, Upjohn and other drug manufacturers went on emergency schedules to develop tamper-resistant packaging for their over-the-counter products. The prospect was sobering, to say the least. Upjohn manufactured 57 different O-T-C products — nearly 7 million packages — and all had to be repackaged. They began with Kaopectate. Four million bottles needed to be wrapped in plastic and sealed. Manufacturing employees opened up every single case in inventory and hand-sealed each bottle. People traveled to all 20 distribution centers in the country to seal bottles there. They worked seven days a week and in six weeks they were done. Every consumer product Upjohn sold met the new FDA guidelines for tamper-resistant packaging before the guidelines went into effect.

©Ezra Stoller

Puurs Manufacturing

The second-largest of Upjohn's major manufacturing facilities operates in Puurs, Belgium, some 20 miles from the company's business office in Brussels. It is a pivotal point in the production and distribution of Upjohn products for as many as 130 countries around the world.

Some 800 individuals, a good half of them women, work at this highly sophisticated Belgian production installation. The growth curve at the 23-year-old plant tells its own story. Since its 1963 dedication, Puurs has expanded five times. In 1968, Puurs was turning out 10 million units a year. Today, the figure is climbing above the 90-million mark. The $21 million expansion in 1982 and 1983 made Puurs second only to Building 41 in size and Upjohn the second largest of 125 pharmaceutical companies producing in Belgium. When the Puurs plant was erected in 1963, it encompassed 5,000 square meters; today it's 40,000 square meters. The latest expansion has an outer limit: 150 million units a year. At its current rate of growth, Puurs could reach that ceiling in the early 1990s.

Such growth has received a big assist from computerization, which has increased at Puurs by 54 percent a year for the past five years. Everything at Puurs begins with a forecast from 130 countries. Computers plug in right there, guiding each production, packaging, or shipping step for the basic categories of corticosteroids, antibiotics, and central nervous system compounds that Puurs handles.

The recent expansion gave Puurs managers a chance to review other equipment as well. As a result, the facility, with the most up-to-date manufacturing equipment in the world, is fully the equal of Kalamazoo's Building 41, even surpassing it in certain ways. Purified air circulates in sterile areas through filters perfected by the space industry. Sterile water, destined for use in injectables, is produced at Puurs and piped through a stainless-steel distribution system. Raw materials for certain tablets are dry-mixed for a length of time carefully determined and controlled automatically to avoid risks of overmixing. Small electronic sensors regulate the exact amount of powder to make a tablet and the pressure needed to shape

(top) Control Division, 1958. As the Upjohn product line expanded, quality control requirements also expanded. Production control labs were outfitted with the latest equipment and staffed by medical technologists, pharmacists, and chemists.

(arriba) División de Control, 1958. A medida que se ampliaba la línea de productos de Upjohn, también el control de calidad requería ampliación. Los laboratorios de control de producción fueron equipados con los aparatos más modernos bajo la vigilancia de técnico-médicos, farmacéuticos y químicos.

(en haut) Contrôles, 1958. Upjohn produisant un nombre croissant de médicaments, la fonction du contrôle de qualité a pris également une dimension croissante. Les laboratoires de contrôle en production ont reçu les équipements les plus modernes, au service de spécialistes des technologies médicales, de pharmaciens et de chimistes.

（上）品質管理部門、1958年。アップジョンの製品種類の増大とともに、品質管理、の必要性も大きなものとなった。生産コントロール研究室は、当時としては最新の器具を整え、医療技術者、薬学者、化学者を研究員として配置していた。

(bottom) Control Division, 1986. The division still uses the newest equipment and most sophisticated methodologies, but now Control gets involved early in the process. Even before a new drug goes into clinical trials, Control helps to establish the standards the final product must meet.

(abajo) División de Control, 1986. La división todavía está equipada con el equipo más moderno y las metodologías más complejas. Pero ahora, la división participa en el proceso mucho más temprano. Aún antes de que una nueva droga pase a ensayos clínicos, la División de Control colabora en el establecimiento de los requisitos que el producto final debe llenar.

(en bas) Contrôles, 1986. La division Contrôles dispose toujours des équipements les plus récents et des méthodes les plus perfectionnées, mais son intervention s'est étendue vers l'amont. Avant même qu'un nouveau médicament n'entre dans la phase d'essais cliniques, la division participe à la définition des normes que devra respecter le produit dans sa forme finale.

（下）品質管理部門、1986年。この部門は、現在も最新の機器と、洗練された方法を用いているが、近年では生産初期の段階で、製品の品質管理を始めている。新薬が臨床試験を始める前の時点で、品質管理部門は最終的な完成医薬品の基準設定を始める。

(left) Fine Chemicals, 1957. Prior to creating the division, Upjohn bought bulk drugs from others, mixed them into Upjohn formulas, and shipped the product off to market. This changed when the company started to employ production processes unique to the company, such as deep-vat fermentation.

(izquierda) Agentes Químicos Grado Farmacéutico, 1957. Antes de establecer esta división, Upjohn adquiría las drogas a granel de otros fabricantes, las mezclaba en fórmulas de Upjohn y enviaba los productos al mercado. Todo esto cambió cuando la compañía inició el uso de procesos de producción originales de la compañía, tales como fermentación en tanque profundo.

(à gauche) Chimie fine, 1957. Avant la création de cette division, Upjohn achetait à d'autres sociétés ses produits chimiques fins en vrac, procédait à la préparation de ses formules puis livrait ses médicaments. La société a ensuite mis en place ses propres processus de production, tels que la fermentation en cuve.

（左）ファインケミカル（精密化学）部門、1957年。この部門が設立される以前、アップジョンでは他社から買った薬剤を自社の調合薬と混ぜて、製品として出荷していたが、この方式は、アップジョン社が大型タンクでの発酵など、独自の生産方法を使用し始めたことにより、大きく変化した。

(right) Fine Chemicals, 1986. The roles of Fine Chemicals have expanded to include not only the bulk fermentation of Upjohn antibiotics and steroids but the production of other bulk pharmaceuticals, agricultural chemicals, and specialty chemicals sold to other companies.

(derecha) Agentes Químicos Grado Farmacéutico, 1986. Las responsabilidades de esta división se han extendido a tal grado que ahora no solamente incluye fermentación a granel de los antibióticos y esteroides de Upjohn, sino también la producción de otros agentes químicos grado farmacéutico, para la agricultura y otras especialidades de agentes químicos que se venden a otras compañías.

(à droite) Chimie fine, 1986. La division chimie fine a vu son rôle s'accroître de la fermentation d'antibiotiques et de stéroïdes Upjohn à la production d'autres produits pharmaceutiques, de produits pour l'agriculture et de produits chimiques spéciaux pour d'autres sociétés.

（右）ファインケミカル部門、1986年。ファインケミカル部門の役割は、アップジョン社の抗生物質とステロイドの発酵生産に加えて、他社へ売られる薬剤、農薬、特殊化学製品を含むようになった。

it — in a process that turns out 360,000 tablets an hour. In the new sterile "tunnel lines," automated equipment has reduced to 45 minutes the steps of washing, heating, cooling, filling, stoppering, and capping vials. In prior practice, this sequence took two to three days.

Continued updating of new technology and procedures has made the Puurs operation a model among production facilities throughout the pharmaceutical industry. As Upjohn continues to expand its worldwide business, Puurs' future growth will keep pace.

Puerto Rico Manufacturing

Further testimony that change is an overriding fact of life for Upjohn's production processes comes from a 300-acre site some 30 miles due west of San Juan, Puerto Rico, sitting on the border between the towns of Arecibo and Barceloneta. There, in what used to be a pineapple field, stand the ten primary buildings of the Upjohn Manufacturing Company (UMC).

The first of these buildings was dedicated in 1974. Today, some 830 employees — only one of them, Corporate Vice President John D. Martin, the man in charge, is from the continental U.S. — use the latest technology in a $131 million plant to produce Lincocin, Cleocin, Motrin, Xanax, and Halcion. And there is room for other products as well. Change is everywhere — from $8 million in renovations for water and tablet coating improvements to the new warehouse where computer impulses drive forklifts to stack pallets six stories above ground, to the recent aeromatic fluid-bed equipment that dries Motrin granules in 90 minutes, rather than the customary 14 hours.

Upjohn had growth on its mind in the late 1960s, and attractive tax exemptions made Puerto Rico a judicious choice as backup manufacturing site to the Portage Road plant. In late spring of 1971, after considering other possible locations, management determined to build in the Commonwealth. That December, UMC was

incorporated and given the board's formal blessing. At the same time, John Martin, then general manager of Upjohn International's marketing for Puerto Rico and the Caribbean, was selected to be general manager for pharmaceutical manufacturing, control, and various administrative functions; the late Robert Grindatti would be parallel general manager of chemical and engineering functions. In 1973, Martin became sole general manager.

The project moved out on a fast track. Lincocin fermentation and isolation came first, in six 45,000-gallon fermenters. Other facilities, such as Cleocin production, followed quickly. Says Martin, "On a lot of the work, the designs were brought out to the site the day they were doing the construction." Meanwhile, hiring began in August 1972. Some 30 Puerto Rican candidates were sent to Kalamazoo for training that lasted as long as a year. A nucleus started trial runs on October 3, 1973, and released the first lot late the next month, just a little more than two years since the site had been selected in July 1971. Early in October, management agreed that

Motrin, once approved, would be manufactured in Puerto Rico when an additional facility was completed. The production crew there turned out its first Motrin lot in January 1976, and UMC was fully under way. In 1985, manufacture of Xanax and Halcion was moved to Puerto Rico as well. The products made there are a measure of its importance and its capability.

Upjohn is keenly concerned about its kinship to the environment, both in the U.S. and in Puerto Rico. UMC's facilities call for 17 million gallons of water from an on-site artesian well. But what do you do with the 10 million gallons flowing out of the various processes as waste? For a time, the water was shipped at considerable cost out to sea for dumping. As an alternative, UMC shared in financing a joint municipal-industrial secondary waste treatment plant which was turned over to the Commonwealth when construction was completed.

In many ways, UMC is much like Upjohn in Kalamazoo. There are no time clocks for full-time employees. A company industrial health clinic, dedicated in 1984, is staffed by a full-time physician and three registered nurses. For those looking to the future, in-house training is available — 17 courses were offered in 1984. Yet basic cultural differences remain. The Puerto Rican culture is composed of a Spanish influence, with different traditions from Indians and blacks. Principles, values, and interests of the people may differ from those on the mainland. These differences have been respected as UMC has matured, and the result has been a highly productive member of the Upjohn manufacturing family.

The spirit of UMC is perhaps best summarized by something that happened in 1984, when the facility was gearing up to celebrate its tenth anniversary. Someone on John Martin's planning committee suggested that there be a theme. It happened that ten years before, a construction welder had shaped some scrap steel parts into a small statue of Don Quixote, one of literature's greatest dreamers about meeting impossible challenges. This should be the anniversary symbol, committee members said. "Fine!" John Martin replied. "He is very Spanish, but why do you feel that he is so representative of our operation?" The answer may be found on the commemorative silk-screened print of the statue which bears the inscription: *Lograr lo imposible es nuestro ideal* — To do the impossible is our ideal.

Chemicals for Pharmaceuticals

The Chemical Division, comprising facilities in Kalamazoo and North Haven, Connecticut, has been manufacturing fine chemicals for Upjohn since the 1940s. Fine Chemicals Manufacturing was set up as a production department in 1949 under the direction of Assistant Superintendent Harry F. Meier and Archibald B. "Arch" Spradling, department head.

The first important chemical synthesis was with folic acid in the same year. There followed a rapid succession of important synthetic assignments, not the least of which was making antibiotics. Working in the new complex on Portage Road, Fine Chemicals soon gained a great deal of experience in fermentation as well as chemical synthesis. Throughout the next four decades, the Fine Chemicals facility in Kalamazoo would expand nearly every year as demand for products such as cortisone skyrocketed.

The unit gained division status in 1957, with Keith H. Edmondson director. When Edmondson took on larger duties with the company's Polymer Chemical Division, Fine Chemicals was led by Vice Presidents A. W. Schneider (1970) and Robert Donia (1979).

The division's output is varied, ranging from agricultural, photographic, and diagnostic chemicals to dyes and pigments, as well as any of the raw materials needed in the manufacture of Upjohn's drugs. Without Fine Chemicals in Kalamazoo, Upjohn would face the very difficult problem of sourcing all its raw materials from the outside; Fine Chemicals in Kalamazoo takes care of those needs routinely and effectively. Says the man in charge since 1982, Corporate Vice President and General Manager for Chemicals Dr. Chong Y. Yoon, "We maintain a low profile but serve the vital interests of the company."

Fine Chemicals in Kalamazoo has three missions. First of all, it does R & D on its own to find better ways of making chemicals. In that respect, "better ways" is shorthand for methods that will enable Upjohn to produce quality chemicals in the safest, most timely, and most economical way possible. Fine Chemicals' R & D is divided into three segments: synthetic chemical process R & D, biotechnology and fermentation process R & D, and analytical methods development and assay services.

(left) Handling bulk drugs, 1957. Few potent drugs were handled by employees in the 1950s; hence the few safety precautions in place then were safety glasses, gloves, the occasional dust mask, and vacuum tubes to control dust.

(izquierda) Drogas a Granel, 1957. En la década de 1950, muy pocas drogas potentes eran manejadas por los empleados; de manera que las pocas precauciones de seguridad utilizadas en aquel entonces eran lentes de seguridad, guantes, máscaras contra el polvo y pequeños tubos extractores.

(à gauche) Principes actifs, 1957. Peu de molécules étaient manipulées par le personnel dans les années 1950. Il suffisait alors de respecter un petit nombre de mesures de sécurité: lunettes, gants, éventuellement masque anti-poussière et disposition de tubes à vide pour le contrôle des poussières.

（左）薬剤の取扱い、1957年。当時は効力の強い薬剤を従業員が取扱うことはまれだったため、安全のための予防策も、防護メガネ、手袋とマスク、吸塵パイプに限られていた。

(right) Handling bulk drugs, 1986. Potent drugs such as Halcion and Xanax call for safety precautions such as those found in the Potent Drug Facility in Building 41, where employees work amid elaborate air and water filtration equipment and wear special suits and breathing apparatus.

(derecha) Drogas a Granel, 1986. Las potentes drogas tales como Halcion y Xanax requieren precauciones de seguridad tales como las que se encuentran en las Instalaciones de Drogas Potentes en el Edificio 41 en Kalamazoo, donde los empleados trabajan rodeados de equipos complejos para filtración de aire y agua y usan indumentaria y aparatos especiales para respirar.

(à droite) Principes actifs, 1986. Des principes actifs puissants comme ceux d'Halcion et de Xanax nécessitent des précautions de sécurité telles que celles en vigueur dans l'unité Principes Actifs. Le personnel y travaille dans un milieu dont l'air et l'eau sont contrôlés par des équipements perfectionnés et porte des vêtements spéciaux ainsi que des appareils respiratoires.

（右）薬剤の取扱い、1986年。ハルシオンやザナックスなど効力の強い薬剤を取扱うには、第41棟の強力薬取扱い施設のような、水と空気のフィルター設備と特別の防護服、呼吸装置が必要になる。

When called upon, these units conduct scientific investigations to support the company's pharmaceutical and agricultural product research.

In addition, this division manufactures bulk pharmaceutical chemicals for Upjohn's use, as Dr. Yoon says, "using that better method which we develop." And, finally, Fine Chemicals sells to other companies the specialty chemicals that it manufactures.

Prior to creating a Fine Chemicals Division, Upjohn bought bulk drugs from others, mixed them into Upjohn formulas, and shipped the product off to market. Things changed, says Dr. Yoon, when Upjohn "started inventing its own drugs unique to the company. Then Upjohn discovered that it was not always possible to find an acceptable source of bulk drug." In 1984, the division produced for the first time $100 million worth of bulk chemicals in Kalamazoo and $30 million worth of goods

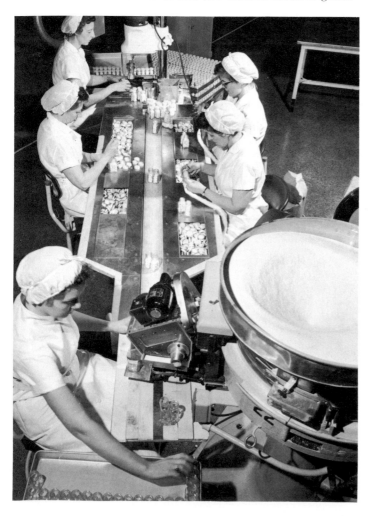

in North Haven. Some 60 percent of Kalamazoo's production went into making Upjohn products — 30 percent for pharmaceuticals, 30 percent into agricultural items. The balance was sold to others. Currently, the Kalamazoo operation purchases from $40 million to $50 million in raw materials a year for product manufacture.

The Chemical Division has more than 900 employees, approximately 100 of them with Ph.D.'s. When a technology question arises, production managers in Kalamazoo, Puerto Rico, or Cuernavaca, Mexico, know that Dr. Yoon's division is the place to call. It is the Chemical Division's responsibility to see that they have the right process for their needs. At the same time, the Kalamazoo Fine Chemicals representatives participate as working members of New Product Project Teams. That way, there is no guesswork when it comes time to scale up for production.

Fine Chemicals-North Haven is considerably smaller than the Kalamazoo facility sprawling next to Building 41 in Portage, but it accounts for production and sale of some $45 million worth of products. Over the years, the plant has produced agricultural chemicals and isocyanate for the manufacture of plastics. North Haven's most important product today is the dye and pigment intermediate "DCB" (dichlorolbenzidine dihydro-chloride), which goes into yellow pigments for printing inks used on textiles and paper (*National Geographic*'s yellow cover is a classic example).

Engineering: Putting It Together and Keeping It That Way

At the close of WWII, the company employed only a few engineers, most of them scattered through various divisions. Each division took care of its own engineering problems, except for construction and maintenance. Lew Crockett had been in charge of that since joining the company in 1911. Crockett had been a local architectural draftsman and a friend of Harold Upjohn's. Though not strictly speaking an engineer, he had a native genius for construction and had a great deal of influence with the board of directors on building matters throughout his 50 years with The Upjohn Company. In 1946 he was made vice president and director of engineering. His group consisted of "an architect and a few engineers."

A formal engineering division did not appear until 1957, when a coordinated group was formed. Engineers from many different disciplines, including chemical engineering, were brought under one organizational roof. Lew Crockett headed this up until his death in 1962, at the age of 77. During his tenure, Crockett had supervised the planning and construction of more than 75 Upjohn buildings across the U.S.

Because Crockett was very ill toward the end of his life, Chemical Engineer Bruce Lane served as nominal head of Engineering and Maintenance during the late 1950s. In 1959 Lane was made director of engineering and maintenance, and in 1970 he became vice president, a post he held until his retirement in 1975.

Lane was faced with the challenge of an expanding and diversifying company. Engineering was charged with doing construction work for the agricultural division, for instance. This proved to have very different requirements than pharmaceutical construction. The Chemical Division was in charge of most of its own engineering — except in Fine Chemicals-Kalamazoo, where there was constant expansion in chemical production and fermentation production facilities throughout the 1950s and 1960s.

In the 1970s, the division began experimenting with something called the "client engineer" strategy. Faced with a great many demands from diverse areas within the company, Engineering began assigning engineers or groups of engineers to service these clients on a permanent basis.

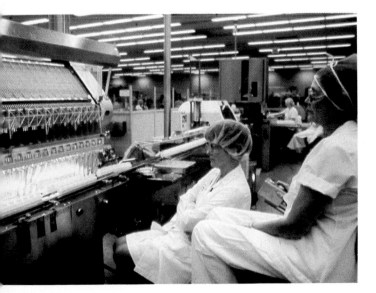

(left) Tablet packaging, 1957. Bottle filling, cottoning, capping, and cap tightening required five sets of hands — then the bottles went to another line where ten more operators labeled, cartoned, inspected, and packaged the bottles. Top speed was about 30 bottles per minute.

(izquierda) Envase de tabletas, 1957. El proceso para llenar frascos, insertar algodón, poner la tapa y apretarla requería cinco pares de manos. Después los frascos pasaban a otra línea donde otros diez operadores etiquetaban, encartonaban, inspeccionaban y envasaban los frascos. La velocidad máxima era de unos 30 frascos por minuto.

(à gauche) Conditionnement de comprimés, 1957. Mise en flacon, bourrage, bouchage et serrage occupaient les mains de cinq personnes. Puis les flacons passaient sur une autre chaîne où dix autres personnes procédaient à l'étiquetage, l'encartonnage, l'inspection et l'emballage. Vitesse maximum : 30 flacons par minute.

（左）錠剤包装、1957年。びん詰め、綿入れ、フタの取り付けが、作業員5人によって行なわれた後、びんは次のラインで作業員10人により、ラベル貼り、箱詰め、検査、包装の各工程を終える。当時の最高スピードは、1分間に30びん程度だった。

(right) Tablet packaging, 1986. This line automatically bottles, cottons, seals, caps, labels, cartons, adds package inserts, and packages bottles at a rate of up to 240 bottles per minute. Of the nine people attending the line, seven are inspectors.

(derecha) Envase de tabletas, 1986. Esta línea automáticamente enfrasca, inserta el algodón, sella, etiqueta, encartona, inserta prospectos y envasa frascos a una velocidad de hasta 240 frascos por minuto. Siete de las nueve personas al cuidado de la línea son inspectores.

(à droite) Conditionnement de comprimés, 1986. Cette chaîne automatique effectue toutes les opérations, y compris l'insertion de la notice, à une vitesse pouvant atteindre 240 flacons/minute. Des neuf personnes employées sur la chaîne, sept remplissent des fonctions de contrôle.

（右）錠剤包装、1986年。このラインでは、びん詰め、綿入れ、フタの取付・密封、ラベル貼り、使用説明書挿入、箱詰め、そして包装が自動的に1分間240びんのスピードで行なわれる。ラインの作業員9人のうち7人は検査員。

(left) Sterile production, 1955. After a surgical scrub-up, employees put on gowns, masks, and shoe and hair covers before they entered an aseptic room — but most of the filling task was accomplished by hand.

(izquierda) Producción estéril, 1955. Despés de una limpieza estéril, los empleados usaban guardapolvo, máscaras y cubiertas de zapatos y pelo antes de entrar a una sala estéril — pero la mayoría de las tareas de llenado eran manuales.

(à gauche) Production stérile, 1955. Après des ablutions chirurgicales, le personnel revêt blouses, masques, chaussures et coiffure avant de pénétrer dans une salle stérile. Mais la plupart du conditionnement était encore manuel.

（左）滅菌生産設備、1955年。外科手術準備の時と同等に手を洗った作業員は、無菌室に入る前に、ガウン、靴カバー、頭髪カバーを着用したが、注入作業のほとんどは、手で行なわれた。

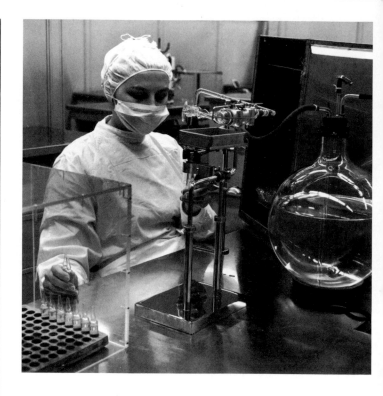

(right) Sterile production, 1986. Today, similar, though more sophisticated, standards of sterility exist to protect employees, products, and the environment from contamination. The production process itself is much more automated.

(derecha) Producción estéril, 1986. Hoy en día, existen normas similares de esterilidad, pero más refinadas, para proteger contra la contaminación de empleados, productos y el ambiente. El proceso de producción en sí es mucho más automatizado.

(à droite) Production stérile, 1986. Aujourd'hui, des normes de stérilité plus perfectionnées protègent le personnel et les produits ainsi que le milieu contre toute contamination. Et le processus de production est très automatisé.

（右）滅菌生産設備、1986年。作業員、製品、環境の汚染を防ぐため、今日の無菌作業は、自動化を取り入れた、洗練された設備によって行なわれている。

Ward Nay, who served as corporate vice president for engineering from 1975 until his retirement in 1986, says, "We approached areas like Pharmaceutical Research and Development and told them, 'We will dedicate a nucleus of engineers and architects to serve your needs . . . we'll send a manager and he'll be your person. He'll have bottom line responsibility to you, will live with you, have coffee with you, and serve your needs.' "

Rather than planning new facilities strictly from an engineering point of view, Nay says, representatives from among the various groups that would actually be using the building were brought together with the client engineers to form building planning committees. This strategy was more effective in designing buildings and facilities that would receive the maximum use from the people they housed. The first use of the client engineer concept was in the construction of the Building 209 research facility in Kalamazoo, which was completed in 1974.

In 1980 the client engineering concept was formally recognized and extended to PR & D, the Ag Division, and Puerto Rico. It is expected that in 1986 it will be extended to include pharmaceutical production and fine chemical production areas.

Today Engineering and Maintenance is headed by Charles E. Bell, who has been with Upjohn since 1965. The unit is staffed by 960 people, including 150 professionals. Engineering projects include everything from designing multimillion dollar building projects, to researching the use of robotics in production, to making sure the millions of square feet of office space in the company are dusted and vacuumed and the wastebaskets emptied. Water and air effluent monitoring, security, landscape maintenance, utility usage — all come under the E & M umbrella.

The division does nearly $200 million worth of projects a year, mostly in facilities construction. The company estimates that Upjohn engineers have supervised about $2.5 billion worth of construction since 1946.

The Roles of Control

Wherever Upjohn has a manufacturing operation, it also has a Pharmaceutical Control unit to ensure product safety and quality. In Kalamazoo, the company's main Control unit resides in Building 259, which is grafted on to the eastern flank of 41. There, the people of Control interact directly with the men and women of Production, Fine Chemicals, and Research.

There's nothing particularly new about that fundamental relationship. Control had its start at Upjohn back in 1899, when Art Crooks set up an analytical laboratory to inspect products for proper color, size, friability, and the like. Fred Heyl's arrival in 1913 signaled the beginning of modern chemical control. Heyl introduced analytical control methods to the various production departments, and developed many assays. Biological control began at this same time with the hiring of Will Perkins in 1912 as the company's first bacteriologist. Just before World War I, Wilbur Payne reorganized Upjohn bacteriology for the production of sterile products and vaccines, and instituted animal assays.

In 1926, the control laboratory was made a separate department under J. Bryant Fullerton, who had been hired in 1920 as a research assistant to Heyl. Ten years later the Control Division was formed with Fullerton as its director.

As product lines changed, so did the company's control techniques. Assays and equipment that worked well for friable pills and botanicals became outmoded for soft elastic capsules and animal extracts; these in turn gave way to hard-filled capsules and synthetic chemicals.

But equally important was the effect of legislation. Just as the 1906 Food and Drug Act had helped precipitate Heyl's coming, the 1938 amendments expanded the role of Control. Soon, the division was engaged in testing permissible variation from stated strength, time of disintegration in gastric fluids, viscosity, specific gravity, and performing other sophisticated measures.

When J. Bryant Fullerton retired as head of Control in 1960, he had seen his area grow from a desk top in the basement of W. E.'s White Office to a major division within the company, separate from Research and Production.

Following Fullerton, Glenn C. Bond, Ph.D., directed the division until his death in 1965, after which James L. Johnson, Ph.D., assumed the directorship. Bond and Johnson served during a period of great change, stimulated by the 1962 Kefauver-Harris amendments (*see* pages 163-64), which required much closer reporting to the FDA, and by the exponential increase in scientific knowledge.

Today, Corporate Vice President Dr. Anthony J. Taraszka, in charge of Control since 1970, directs the activities of worldwide Control operations that have undergone immense technical changes but have remained the same in terms of mission. That mission, explains Tony Taraszka, is two-part: defining and building the quality into a product, and then ensuring that it is there on a continuing basis. "You have to have both those steps," he says, adding that Control's main function is "to make sure that the product we are selling relives the clinical experience."

With that as a given, the division has seen a marked change of focus in the past two decades. Today, Control is what Dr. Taraszka defines as a "big component" of the product development process. Twenty-odd years ago, 95 percent of Control's efforts were directed toward production activities, the remaining five percent toward drug development. Now, about 65 percent of the manpower focuses on end-product testing. And as much as 35 percent concentrates on help in the development of new pharmaceuticals.

Control now gets involved early in the process, before a potential new product goes into clinical trials on humans. The basic characteristics of the new drug substance and the formulation are determined in order to establish the standards the product must meet. Early characterization of these critical product properties helps shorten development time.

Product standards change, too, propelled by technological advances and by regulations. For example, 50 years ago, standard industry practice for injectable drugs was hypodermic tablets, which were dissolved in water and injected. "No drug company or regulatory agency would condone that practice today," Taraszka says. "Our knowledge of the contamination potential resulted in the development of aseptically prepared products for injectable use."

Analytical standards have also continued to advance, requiring sophisticated equipment and highly trained personnel. In order to ensure that Upjohn products remain competitive in a global marketplace, product specifications are designed during development so that the products can meet increasingly tougher standards anywhere in the world.

An impressive array of complex instrumentation, computers, and electronic process monitors are now in use throughout Control's laboratories and Quality Assurance areas. Yet even with this array of sophisticated equipment, people remain pivotal to the Control process. After all the data have been evaluated, it is a Control employee who may need to tell his counterpart in another division that a product batch does not meet Upjohn's standards. A key element in maintaining high quality standards is this personal relationship.

Sterile inspection, 1959 and 1986. The image of a lone inspector steadfastly scrutinizing the company's wares is as constant today as in earlier times. But today's inspector is backed up by sophisticated robotic and computer technology that her predecessors could not have imagined.

Inspección estéril, 1959 y 1986. La imagen de un inspector aislado que constantemente y con todo cuidado examina los productos de la compañía, es en la actualidad lo mismo que antes. Pero el inspector de hoy en día es respaldado por refinada tecnología automatizada y computarizada que sus predecesores nunca se imaginaron.

Inspection des produits stériles, 1959 et 1986. L'inspection individuelle minutieuse des produits est toujours d'actualité. Mais aujourd'hui, cette inspection utilise des technologies issues de la robotique et de l'informatique, inimaginables il y a encore peu d'années.

滅菌検査、1959年、1986年。製品を検査して回る検査員の姿は、今も変らないが、今日の検査官はロボットやコンピューターなどの最新技術の恩恵を受けることができる。

Case Study:
The Manufacturing of Xanax

More than 20 months before the FDA authorized the sale of Xanax, the people of production began looking ahead to the day when the green light might set the Xanax lines rolling in Building 41. In January 1980, the first lot of alprazolam was trucked into 41 for trial runs to scout for any manufacturing problems that might emerge. It is always a learning experience the first time a product goes through the plant. A process that worked well with 2 kilos might not work well with 200 kilos. Processes are constantly evolving.

By the time Xanax went on the market in November 1981, Production had worked the bugs out of producing alprazolam in large volume, then converting it into a distributable product. The process started in Fine Chemicals. The raw material entered as a yellow crystal and left as a white, sugar-like substance. To make that conversion, the chemical engineers exposed the raw material in a four-step process to solvents, various active reagents, and heat. Those steps attached the extra rings to the molecule. The result: alprazolam.

Employees learned very early that safety would have to be given the highest priority; the chemicals in alprazolam were extremely potent. Hence, Fine Chemicals, in concert with Upjohn's Occupational Health and Safety professionals, laid down strict rules. Every operator had to have two to three years of training. Fire extinguishers, eye wash stations, and emergency showers were installed all around the site. Air flows would be regulated to pass over employees first, then over the equipment and chemicals, and finally into a wall filter system before being vented outside. In spite of the restrictions, operators developed a strong esprit de corps as they turned out both quality product and an excellent safety record.

After manufacture in Fine Chemicals, the alprazolam, sealed in drums, moved to Building 41 and into the Controlled Substance Vault, where devices monitored it continuously for any irregularities. When the time for processing arrived, the drums were taken to the Potent Drug Facility. There, the material was ground into a fine powder and mixed with other ingredients and magnesium stearate to lubricate the granules so they would flow well and compress into a firm tablet. The crew in Tablet Compressing had to make sure that walls, floors, and all equipment were meticulously cleaned and recleaned before the operation could start. At first it often took three to four days to clean and inspect the equipment, but the time was reduced to less than one day — a major productivity plus.

The next destination for the medication in the production sequence was Dry Products Packaging. Newly compressed tablets were locked in a vault with steel doors and cement-block walls until the line operators were ready for them. On the line, the crew packaged 100- and 500-count plastic bottles and 3-count "blister packs" (physicians' samples). At least one of the three lines operated 24 hours a day. During this phase, Quality Assurance came along every 20 minutes to inspect.

After Packaging, the product rode by truck from 41 to Building 212 on Milham Road for warehousing and shipment. Here too, tight controls went into effect the minute the vehicle arrived at the unloading dock. Men ran the boxes into the 10,300-square-foot cage to be guarded before delivery to the 15 distribution centers in Upjohn's system. At least a dozen individuals counted the items at seven different points in this last sequence. Finally, the truck was on its way, with next-day delivery guaranteed at all but a few of the 15 centers.

This was how Xanax production flowed for the product's first four years. Then, as it so often does, change came to the production lines. Almost all the intricate process, with its lengthy list of security precautions, was to be shifted to Upjohn's Puerto Rico operation. And by January 1986, Xanax tablets were cascading from the line at the Arecibo-Barceloneta facility.

MARKETING: A TOUGH ACT TO FOLLOW

Upjohn's marketing tradition goes back to the company's first fine salesman, the founder. A succession of strong sales executives has built and sustained Upjohn's reputation for marketing abilities. A Wall Street pharmaceutical specialist said in 1984 that Upjohn has a "remarkably effective" sales force, which has made it "one of the very strongest marketing companies in the U.S. drug business."

That didn't just happen. Hardworking leaders met the challenge more than halfway. The company's first sales director, Malcolm Galbraith, trained his representatives and started branches in seven cities. C. V. Patterson and Emil Schellack succeeded him in 1942 as joint sales directors. Then, Schellack had his run at sales direction when Patterson shifted to the helm of production in November 1942. Fred Allen, named assistant sales director on January 1, 1946, was elevated to the number one spot on Schellack's death six weeks later.

Puurs, Belgium, 1986. When the Puurs plant was erected in 1963, it encompassed 5,000 square meters; after five major expansions, it now covers 40,000 square meters, making Upjohn the second largest of the 125 pharmaceutical companies doing business in Belgium.

Puurs, Bélgica, 1986. Cuando en 1963 se inauguró la planta en Puurs, ésta tenía 5.000 metros cuadrados; después de cinco importantes expansiones, la instalación tiene ahora una superficie de 40.000 metros cuadrados, haciendo Upjohn la segunda en tamaño de las 125 compañías farmacéuticas que realizan actividades en Bélgica.

Puurs (Belgique), 1986. Lors de sa construction en 1963, l'usine de Puurs couvrait 5000 mètres carrés. Après cinq extensions importantes, elle en couvre maintenant 40.000, conférant à Upjohn la deuxième place, quant à la superficie, parmi les 125 sociétés pharmaceutiques de la Belgique.

ベルギー、プールス、1986年。1963年に建設された時、プールス工場の敷地は5平方キロメートル。その後5回の拡張工事を経た工場は、40平方キロメートルに広がり、ベルギーで営業している125の医薬メーカーの中で、第2の規模を誇るようになった。

(left) Upjohn Manufacturing Company (UMC), 1976. After 1.7 billion Motrin tablets were produced at the Kalamazoo manufacturing site, Motrin production moved to the UMC facility in Arecibo-Barceloneta, Puerto Rico.

(izquierda) Upjohn Manufacturing Company (UMC), 1976. Después de haberse fabricado 1.700 millones de tabletas Motrin en las instalaciones de manufactura en Kalamazoo, la producción de Motrin fue trasladada a las instalaciones de Upjohn Manufacturing Company en Arecibo-Barceloneta, Puerto Rico.

(à gauche) Upjohn Manufacturing Company (UMC), 1976. 1,7 milliard de comprimés de Motrin avaient été produits à l'usine de Kalamazoo avant que la fabrication ne soit transférée à l'unité de production UMC construite à Arecibo-Barceloneta, à Porto-Rico.

（左）アップジョン製造会社（ＵＭＣ）、1976年。モートリン錠剤170億個をカラマズーで生産した後、モートリンの製造は、プエルトリコ、アレシボーバルセロネタのＵＭＣ生産施設に移された。

(right) Upjohn Manufacturing Company (UMC), 1986. The products made at UMC are a measure of its importance. Today, some 830 UMC employees produce Motrin, Xanax, Halcion, Lincocin, Cleocin, and other important Upjohn products.

(derecha) Upjohn Manufacturing Company (UMC), 1986. Los productos fabricados en UMC son representativos de su importancia. En la actualidad, alrededor de 830 empleados en UMC fabrican Motrin, Xanax, Halcion, Lincocin, Cleocin y otros importantes productos de Upjohn.

(à droite) Upjohn Manufacturing Company (UMC), 1986. L'importance de cette unité de production tient à la gamme des médicaments qui y sont préparés. Aujourd'hui, quelque 830 personnes y produisent Motrin, Xanax, Halcion, Lincocine, Cléocine et d'autres grands médicaments Upjohn.

（右）アップジョン製造会社（ＵＭＣ）、1986年。ＵＭＣでは今日、830人の従業員がモートリン、ザナックス、ハルシオン、リンコシン、クレオシンなどの重要なアップジョン製品を生産している。

Allen served in that position until 1963, when he took on greater responsibility and was succeeded by Jack C. Gauntlett. Gauntlett resigned in 1969, and Lawrence C. Hoff, who would go on to direct worldwide marketing operations before becoming president of the company, moved into the job. Today, Daniel D. Witcher, corporate senior vice president for worldwide human health businesses, is marketing's head man. His associates, Reed B. Peterson, corporate vice president and general manager for the domestic pharmaceutical division, who was succeeded in that position on his retirement September 1, 1986, by Harold Chappelear; and Selvi Vescovi, corporate vice president and general manager for International, and president, Upjohn International, Inc., support the U.S. and worldwide effort through their individual responsibilities.

In the late 1950s, writer Leonard Engel talked to a rival manufacturer. Upjohn, this competitor declared, "can get ten percent of the market in any drug it chooses to sell, even if half a dozen firms have the drug out first." Upjohn's salespeople had accomplished this by doing their homework very, very carefully — by looking for the opportunity, in Larry Hoff's words, "to separate yourself from the pack."

In 1985, roughly two-thirds of the corporation's sales were posted by prescription pharmaceutical and consumer drug products. The executives directly responsible for the worldwide marketing operations are a seasoned trio.

Changes in Drug Marketing

Back in 1950, the physician was king. He made up his mind what drugs he wanted, and the hospital hopped fast to stock them in its pharmacy. Then, hospital administrators began to insist for cost reasons that the hospital would have one tetracycline, not five. Medicare and Medicaid came along, complicating matters considerably, and doctors had to face issues of medical liability that had never been so intense.

In the 1950s, support for sales reps in the field was not nearly as sophisticated as it has become, with strong inside marketing teams behind them every step of the way (*see* pages 226-29). Most physicians were general practitioners — they treated the skin and all its contents — so Upjohn's salespeople could be generalists, too. But when the physician started specializing, the sales rep had to follow suit. Upjohn's first move was to set up an organization of specialists in hospital sales. Today, 165 reps concentrate on some 1,200 teaching hospitals. Upjohn reached another conclusion. It would develop a program that, in Hoff's words, "would allow us to work from inside out, from the top down." That was the germ of the idea for what was to become the Medical Science Liaison (or MSL) program (*see* page 146).

The 1962 Kefauver-Harris amendments (*see* pages 163-64) led to further refinements. Before that time, the scientific data supporting pharmaceutical products had been much less complex. Then, in the 1960s, very sound controlled studies began appearing, and having more solid reports gave a firmer basis for a representative's claims.

Changes of a different character also began to be seen in Upjohn's marketing operations in the 1960s. Advertising was beefed up, the product manager concept and long-range planning were introduced, and a more sophisticated level of market research was implemented.

One example of the new visibility that Upjohn sought was a series of huge models — a cell, a chromosome, a blood vessel, and the brain — for display at trade shows. Visitors were fascinated at being able to walk inside these giant futuristic mock-ups.

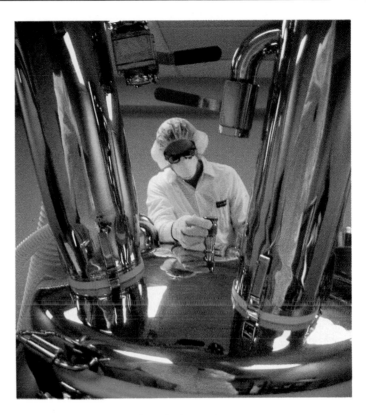

The Training of a Sales Force

Out of 100 applicants for the job of Upjohn sales representative, only one will be accepted for the position. Upjohn detailers are well educated before they ever join the company — many have master's degrees, and a few even possess Ph.D.'s. But even the most qualified are not allowed to rest on their laurels. All Upjohn sales reps are given an intensive two-and-a-half-month training period; they continually update that training through conferences, at-home study courses, and course sessions in Kalamazoo.

Sales training officially began at Upjohn during L. N. Upjohn's tenure as New York branch manager. L. N. perceived a lack of real medical knowledge among the salesmen at a time when he was looking to expand the force. As a former college instructor, L. N. naturally turned to developing ways to educate his detail crew, and by 1908 he had introduced the conference system of sales training. This soon spread throughout the company, and as the Upjohn scientific staff grew, it began to take an active role in helping to keep the salesman abreast of the rapid advances in medicine.

By 1925, Warren K. Allen was assigned to the Kansas City branch as the company's first "sales instructor." His function evolved steadily until, in 1940, a "Sales Education Department" was set up under his leadership.

Today the company has a Professional Training and Development unit dedicated to the ongoing education of the more than 1,000 sales reps in the domestic pharmaceutical marketing force. The unit makes sure each rep has the training necessary to detail the physician on new products and new product indications. When an Upjohn sales rep is first hired, he or she is given a month of training in the sales area office, working on everything from anatomy, physiology, and applied therapeutics to the pharmacologic characteristics of Upjohn products and the development of selling skills. This lays the foundation for a month spent at the sales training facilities in Kalamazoo, where the new recruits cover subjects in more detail.

From there the sales reps go back to the field, spending about two weeks with a district manager, learning to call on physicians. The key is to organize the information efficiently, and to make sure that a product is presented as a solution to a problem the physician is confronted with in his daily practice.

"The sales rep has to be diplomatic," says Reed Peterson, "and he has to help the doctor see that we are involved in the health care process together."

After his or her initial education, the sales rep has little time to worry about becoming complacent. The rep attends area and district sales conferences, and after 18 to 24 months returns to Kalamazoo for further instruction.

"The rep will be going to meetings for the rest of his or her life," says one sales trainer. "It's like getting a Ph.D., slowly."

The academic comparison is apt. The curriculum can cover the latest information on OB/GYN, surgery, or internal medicine, as well as subjects like microbiology and pharmacology. The company uses a combination of internally developed material, professionally designed training programs, and standard medical textbooks. Sales trainers put the material together and conduct the classes, including overseeing the evaluation process.

To rise in the sales career path, a rep must pass a series of study courses. These include, for the first level in general sales, anatomy and physiology, pathophysiology, and pharmacology. The material becomes more complex as a sales representative advances through the career pathway.

"The Upjohn sales rep never stops learning, and that's one of the real pluses of the job," says Peterson.

It usually takes new recruits six or seven months to determine if Upjohn sales work is for them or not — but once they decide to stick with it, they are around a long time. Figures for the last decade testify that turnover in the sales force for all reasons runs only five to ten percent a year.

Reaching the Thought Leaders

There was a time some 20 years ago when Upjohn Marketing began picking up negative rumbles from the teaching hospitals, where it was increasingly possible to hear a Ph.D. endocrinologist say to his students, "Don't use oral drugs for the diabetic; use insulin only." Upjohn had to do something to counter this advice because, in all too short a time, these medical students would be out in the real world, writing prescriptions for insulin and perhaps ignoring Upjohn's Orinase.

This unsettling turn of events was in part the result of a misunderstanding about oral antidiabetic drugs; it had been created by the University Group Diabetes Program (UGDP), a massive study undertaken in the 1960s that severely threatened oral antidiabetes therapy.

(left) Detailing, 1957. Upjohn sales reps had three exciting new products — code named "MOP" — to offer physicians and druggists this year: Medrol, the anti-inflammatory steroid; Orinase, the oral antidiabetes agent; and Panalba, the Panmycin/Albamycin combination antibiotic.

(izquierda) Los representantes, 1957. En este año, los representantes de ventas de Upjohn contaban con tres prominentes productos nuevos — la palabra clave "MOP" — para ofrecer a los médicos y farmacéuticos de la época: Medrol, un esteroide antiinflamatorio; Orinase, el agente antidiabético oral y Panalba, la asociación antibiótica de panmicina/albamicina.

(à gauche) Ventes, 1957. Les visiteurs médicaux d'Upjohn disposaient alors de trois produits nouveaux très prometteurs, connus sous leurs initiales : "MOP". Il s'agissait de l'anti-inflammatoire stéroïdien Médrol, de l'anti-diabétique oral Orinase et de l'antibiotique Panalba composé de Panmycine et d'Albamycine.

（左）ディテール活動、1957年。この年、アップジョンの販売員には、抗炎症用のメドロール、経口血糖降下剤ォリナーゼ、そしてパンマイシンとアルバマイシンを化合した抗生物質、パナルバの三つの新製品があった。これらの製品は、頭文字をとって「ＭＯＰ」と呼ばれた。

(right) Detailing, 1986. Sales reps now have an array of antibiotic, anti-inflammatory, central nervous system, anticancer, cardiovascular, antidiabetes, and other drugs that they detail to doctors, pharmacists, and hospitals.

(derecha) Los representantes, 1986. Ahora, los representantes de ventas cuentan con un gran número de antibióticos, agentes antiinflamatorios, agentes para el sistema nervioso central, anticancerosos, cardiovasculares, antidiabéticos y otras drogas para ofrecer a los médicos, farmacéuticos y hospitales.

(à droite) Ventes, 1986. C'est toute une gamme d'antibiotiques, d'anti-inflammatoires, de médicaments pour le système nerveux central, de produits cardio-vasculaires, d'anti-diabétiques et d'autres classes thérapeutiques que les visiteurs médicaux présentent aujourd'hui au corps médical.

（右）ディテール活動、1986年。今日のアップジョン販売員には、抗生物質、抗炎症、中枢神経系、抗ガン、循環器系、血糖降下など、広い分野にわたって、医師、薬剤師、病院に活用されている製品がある。

Before it was marketed in 1957, the oral antidiabetes agent Orinase made it through a clinical obstacle course more rigorous than any earlier compound had faced. The reports of 420 physicians on trial uses in 7,000 patients were filed with the FDA. But questions lingered. Could an oral agent safeguard an individual's health as well as insulin? What side effects might be revealed? The FDA and the National Institutes of Health thought those questions should be answered, and so the UGDP was funded. Adult diabetics began to enter the program in 1961. The process moved very slowly. By late 1968, some answers appeared to have materialized: patients on Orinase seemed to have a higher cardiovascular death rate than those on other medications.

Seeing trouble looming, Upjohn retained two independent specialists, who concluded that the study had flaws. But study results began leaking out to the press. The headline of one story in May 1970 speculated that the investigation was likely to be "Unfavorable to Upjohn's Orinase." Thousands of users made panicky phone calls, and very quickly the world of the diabetic resounded with angry voices.

Walter S. Ross, in his book *The Life-Death Ratio* (1977), observed that the UGDP study was "not designed in accordance with the most basic clinical requirement — that treatment be tailored to the patient's condition." The study might even be considered "unethical," he added.

What resulted, he observed, looked very much like a "medical war." And the hostilities raged on. The FDA, meanwhile, insisted that Orinase's package inserts warn about possible cardiovascular risks to users. But studies other than the UGDP demonstrated that patients on oral agents had *lower* mortality rates than those on other therapies. In due course, a court fight held that the UGDP appraisal was questionable. But unfortunately, the well had been polluted, doctors began to doubt the safety of oral antidiabetes agents, and it would be several years before these compounds returned to favor.

The situation called for a special kind of damage control. To that end, representatives of Upjohn and the American Diabetes Association (ADA) came together and agreed to start a Clinical Education Program. The goal was to come up with uniform standards of care that would be in the best interest of the diabetic. A means to that end was to be a physicians' guidebook. With Upjohn's assistance, 25 doctors convened in November 1983 to see how they could collaborate on writing chapters of the book. Some 120 other physicians reviewed the manuscript, and *The Physician's Guide to Type II Diabetes* went to press. Today it stands as the bible on diabetes treatment.

This only began the process of getting the message across to medical practitioners. On April 11, 1984, 19,000 physicians at 27 different sites watched a satellite telecast on the new guidelines for diabetes treatment. To further buttress this effort, the ADA lined up 120 specialists to be local sources of information in handling inquiries. Since then, more than 63,000 physicians have gone to symposia on diabetes care.

It took a very long time indeed to counter the faulty conclusions of the UGDP study; it wasn't until the mid-1980s that the oral antidiabetes compounds returned to favor. Fortunately for the nation's Type II diabetics, the ADA was prepared to take the lead in defining a new spectrum of standards for patient treatment. But the UGDP experience will serve long as a reminder that divisive situations can arise from possibly flawed studies and/or incomplete understanding of their results.

Upjohn was developing other means during the 1960s to point up the advantages of oral therapy for certain diabetic patients. The intent was to try to give the "thought leaders" influencing the practicing physician special materials, offer them slides for their lectures, talk to them about new developments on the horizon. Any of these steps, taken cautiously and diplomatically, might help to put other views, other data, before the medical leadership. It would be theirs to evaluate; all Upjohn wanted was for them to be aware of it.

(left) Upjohn advertising, 1955. "Doctor and Boy Looking at Thermometer" is the title of this Norman Rockwell painting commissioned by Upjohn. Works by Rockwell and other contemporary artists graced magazine ads and pharmacy window displays in the 1940s and 1950s.

(izquierda) Publicidad de Upjohn, 1955. "El Médico y el Niño Mirando al Termómetro" es el título de este cuadro del renombrado pintor, Norman Rockwell, quien fue comisionado por Upjohn. A través de las décadas de 1940 a 1950, los trabajos de Rockwell y de otros artistas comtemporáneos adornaban los anuncios en revistas y escaparates en farmacias.

(à gauche) Publicité Upjohn, 1955. "Le médecin et l'enfant consultant le thermomètre" : cette peinture de Norman Rockwell avait été commandée par Upjohn. Des oeuvres de Rockwell et d'autres artistes ont illustré les publicités dans la presse et dans les vitrines de pharmacies pendant les années 1940 et 1950.

（左）アップジョン社広告、1955年。アップジョンがノーマン・ロックウエルに制作を依頼したこの絵は、「体温計を見る医師と少年」と題されている。ノーマン・ロックウエルと他の芸術家、イラストレーターによる広告は、1940年代、1950年代の雑誌や薬局を飾った。

(right) Upjohn advertising, 1964. Sent to all general practitioners and pediatricians in the U.S., this Cheracol cough syrup ad — "Picture of a Cough" — was drawn by a ten-year-old New York girl. Three years earlier, Unicap was the subject of Upjohn's first TV commercial.

(derecha) Publicidad de Upjohn, 1964. Este anuncio de Cheracol, jarabe para la tos — "Retrato de la Tos" — obra de una niña de Nueva York de diez años de edad, fue enviado a todos los médicos de familia y pediatras en los Estados Unidos. Tres años antes, Unicap fue el tema del primer anuncio de Upjohn en la televisión.

(à droite) Publicité Upjohn, 1964. Adressée à tous les généralistes et pédiatres des Etats-Unis, cette publicité pour le sirop contre la toux Cheracol, "Image de la toux", a été dessinée par une fillette new-yorkaise de 10 ans. Trois années plus tôt, Unicap avait donné lieu à la première publicité télévisée d'Upjohn.

（右）アップジョン社広告、1964年。全米の一般開業医師と小児科医師に送られたこの、チエラコルせき止めシロップの広告「せきの絵」は、10才のニューヨークの少女が描いたもの。この3年前にアップジョンは最初のテレビコマーシャルで、ユニキャップの宣伝をした。

(top) Upjohn advertising, 1974. Motrin was originally advertised to physicians whose patients suffered mild to moderate cases of osteoarthritis and rheumatoid arthritis. This 1974 medical journal ad for Motrin depicts the inflamed knee joint of an arthritis sufferer.

(arriba) Publicidad de Upjohn, 1974. Motrin fue originalmente presentado a los médicos cuyos pacientes padecían de casos leves a moderados de osteoatritis y artritis reumatoidea. Este anuncio de Motrin publicado en una revista médica en 1974, muestra una articulación de la rodilla inflamada de un paciente artrítico.

(en haut) Publicité Upjohn, 1974. Le Motrin était à l'origine promu auprès des médecins pour le traitement de leurs patients souffrant d'ostéoarthrite légère et d'arthrite rhumatoïde. Cette publicité pour Motrin parue en 1974 dans une publication médicale montre l'inflammation du genou chez un arthritique.

（上）アップジョン社の広告、1974年。モートリンは初め、変形性関節症と関節リウマチによる痛みに悩む患者を持つ医師に向けて、広告された。1974年の医学雑誌に載ったモートリンの広告は、関節炎患者の炎症を起こした膝関節を描いている。

(bottom) Upjohn advertising, 1986. As indications for Motrin use multiplied, ads for the drug became more specialized. This Motrin medical journal ad, one of a series depicting skiers, football players, and other athletes, is directed at specialists in the growing field of sports medicine.

(abajo) Publicidad de Upjohn, 1986. A medida que las indicaciones para el uso de Motrin se multiplicaron, las piezas publicitarias para el fármaco se hicieron más especializadas. Este anuncio de Motrin en una revista médica, es de una serie que muestra esquiadores, futbolistas y otros atletas, dirigida a especialistas en el creciente campo de la medicina deportiva.

(en bas) Publicité Upjohn, 1986. L'accroissement du nombre des indications de Motrin a conduit à produire des annonces plus spécialisées. Cette publicité destinée à la presse médicale fait partie d'une série sur le thème du ski, du foot-ball et d'autres sports. Elle s'adresse aux spécialistes, de plus en plus nombreux, de la médecine sportive.

（下）アップジョン社の広告、1986年。モートリンの効能が増えて行くに従って、この薬品の広告も専門化してきた。この医学雑誌に載った広告は、スキー、フットボールなどの運動選手を扱ったシリーズのひとつで、伸び続けるスポーツ医学分野の専門家を対象としている。

This was the skeleton of what grew into the Medical Science Liaison (MSL) program. Upjohn Marketing people had observed that their program paid little attention to physicians until they were out of school. The new thinking in Marketing said: why not establish a rapport with the doctor before he writes prescriptions, while he is still a student?

Clearly, the best of the sales force would be needed to do this kind of missionary work. In 1967, the novel MSL program got under way. A survey of medical students showed that Upjohn was not well known to them. MSLs began distributing monographs to every medical school in the country. They visited medical school deans and faculties. Six years later, survey results indicated that Upjohn was among the best-known, and many monographs had become required reading for future physicians.

Gradually, the MSL became visible as someone teaching and practicing physicians could ask for almost any kind of assistance — scientific literature, access to Upjohn researchers, help in setting up a symposium, invitations as a guest lecturer.

Today there are 125 MSLs, divided into groups paralleling PR & D's disease targets. By and large, it has taken these men and women at least 10 years in sales to be considered for MSL work. They must have an intense interest in science, have high social skills, and must recognize that they are no longer detailing products. Today, the MSLs have evolved into specialists immersed in a disease area, offering medical thought leaders insights, perspective, and assistance in their respective specialties. They do not sell products.

Case Study: The Marketing of Xanax

For many years now, Upjohn has adhered to the practice of involving its Marketing people in the early stages of product development. It may be long months, even years, before a medication is finally approved for sale, but Marketing's planners have innumerable steps to take to prepare for a first-class product launch.

The Xanax New Product Project Team (NPPT) was formed once alprazolam was officially declared a new drug candidate in October 1969. Its task was to coordinate all the corporate energies essential to prepare the drug for the market.

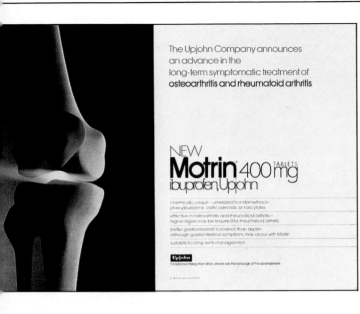

There were more than a few challenges to overcome. To start with, the Upjohn drug would face formidable competition. Prescribing physicians already had at least six benzodiazepines to choose from. Moreover, drug-makers were looking at a declining market for antianxiety medications, down one-third from the 1975 peak of 90 million benzodiazepine prescriptions. The 1975 designation of these drugs as controlled substances under federal law shrunk prescription refills. Then, too, adverse publicity about benzodiazepines curtailed their use.

Complicating matters, Upjohn was about to get into the most promotion-intensive market it had ever entered, a move demanding the most expensive push in the history of Upjohn product launches. The company had to overcome the apparent tendency of many doctors to see all benzodiazepines as the same. And if psychiatrists represented a key element in this marketplace, then Upjohn had to reckon with the fact that there were 30,000 psychiatrists in the U.S. who really did not know the company. This meant that Upjohn had to learn more about how psychiatrists prescribed compounds for their patients.

"Our strategy was to work from the top down," says Larry Hoff. "So we spent time and effort to get to the psychiatrists, because if they agreed that Xanax was different from the other benzodiazepines and started to use it, the word would trickle down." It was an ideal challenge for the Medical Science Liaison specialists. Sixteen of them went into action two years before Xanax was introduced. Their main target was academic thought leaders in the crucial field of psychopharmacology.

At the same time, Upjohn fielded another team of special-duty people, the Medical Specialty Representatives, trained solely for CNS business. It was their assignment to call on the community-based psychiatrists. In parallel, the Marketing staff, building on a growing acquaintance with the American Psychiatric Association, offered to support a number of its educational programs; that helped make the Upjohn name more familiar among its membership.

Out of these coordinated efforts came an aggressive marketing plan. Its main objective was to bring this unique product Xanax to the attention of 130,000 physicians in general practice, family practice, and internal medicine, as well as in psychiatry. Sales reps were instructed to compare Xanax directly with the market leader, Valium, comparing it head to head on clinical efficacy and safety parameters to show its superiority. In detailing, emphasis was to be given to the product's uniqueness. This was *not* a "me-too" medication. Rather, it was distinctive in chemical structure, pharmacology, and ability to treat anxiety and anxiety associated with depression, the main indications for which FDA approval was being requested. What made Xanax different from any other benzodiazepine was the indication for "anxiety associated with depression." Further, sales reps were to accent a disease concept approach which recognized that a physician rarely sees a patient with just anxiety. In seven out of ten cases, the anxious patient also has accompanying depressive symptoms.

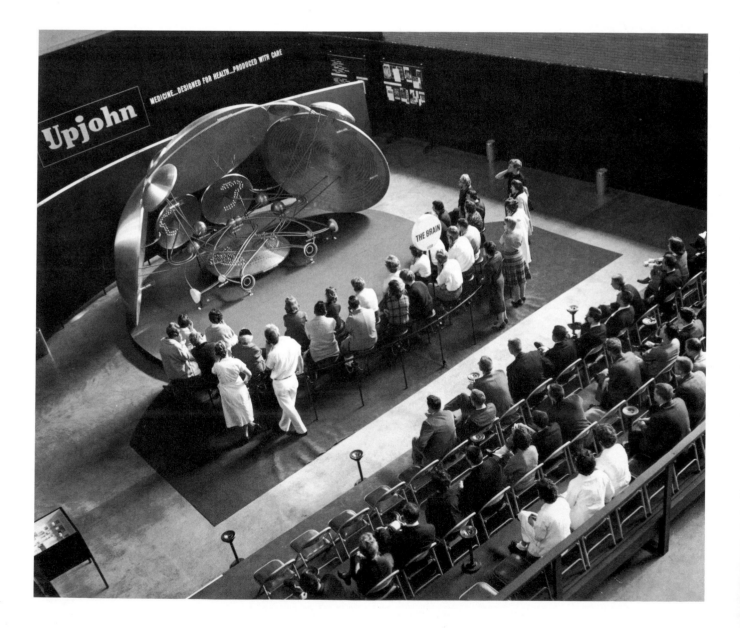

These were the main points of attack in the marketing plan devised for Xanax. Xanax first went on sale in foreign markets — Brazil, Canada, Colombia, Mexico, and Switzerland. Then came the FDA's authorization in October 1981 for marketing in the U.S., 12 years after Dr. Hester had discovered how to achieve greater therapeutic potential by adding a triazolo ring of atoms to the diazepam molecule. One month later, the Upjohn sales force moved out. They were to make 360,000 details on Xanax in its first year (in comparison, they accounted for 1.4 million details on *all* products in 1979). The launch demanded a determined push by everyone. Upjohn had no use for an indecisive, fainthearted approach. Xanax was too good for that.

The results were exhilarating. By year's end, $2.7 million of Xanax had been sold. In 1982, sales jumped to $12.6 million, and the product won a modest 3.2 percent share of the market. The next year, sales almost quadrupled, and the share fattened to 8.1 percent. The year 1984 saw even greater success — Xanax sales of $91.9 million gave Upjohn a 13.7 percent segment of overall benzodiazepine use. That share climbed to 17 percent in 1985, with sales of $164 million.

CHAPTER FIVE

CITIZEN OF THE WORLD

Upjohn's success in the demanding decades since World War II has come about by using wisely the lessons of the past, by looking ahead, and by giving full rein to the competitive spirit. Thus it is that today Research, Production, and Marketing scarcely look anything like their old selves of 1945.

The new look reaches beyond those three important areas. It has meant changes as well in company leadership, in the way the company now operates as a public enterprise, and in the challenges it faces. The past, while treasured, does not dominate Upjohn's future.

The leadership of Upjohn in 1945 was L. N. Upjohn, chairman of the board; Donald Gilmore, president; and Gifford Upjohn, vice president and medical director. At the close of 1952, L. N. passed the chairman's portfolio to Gilmore, and Gifford Upjohn came into the presidency in January 1953. Meanwhile, C. V. Patterson, not an Upjohn-Gilmore family member but an employee since 1925, was named executive vice president.

The prime mover, Donald Gilmore, would be 65 in 1960. Well before then, he decided to begin training the next generation of Upjohn leaders. And he had a particular group of candidates in mind, five young men referred to as "The Quintette," four of whom had married granddaughters of the founder:

Robert M. Boudeman, senior of the five, had married Donald Gilmore's oldest daughter, Carol, and had joined Upjohn in 1940.

Harold James Maloney was the husband of the second of Gilmore's daughters, Jane, and an employee of the firm since 1942.

Preston S. (Pete) Parish was married in 1948 to Suzanne Delano — daughter of the founder's daughter Dorothy Upjohn Delano Dalton — and then started to work for Upjohn in 1949 at age 30.

Ray T. (Ted) Parfet, Jr., husband of the youngest Gilmore daughter, Martha, came to Upjohn in 1947.

William John Upjohn, Harold Upjohn's son, was the youngest of the five men. He was born in 1925, three years before his father's death. He worked for the company intermittently from 1943 to 1948, then joined it full-time in '49.

Donald Gilmore had it in mind that the future leadership of Upjohn should come from "The Quintette." Hence, in the words of an explanatory memo, he "felt it advisable to provide [for them] special facilities for expediting training in and information about the Company history and affairs." Accordingly, during 1949 and 1950, the five rotated through various departments to "acquire familiarity with operations in general."

A few more years passed before the shape of the succession came into view. (Of the five, Maloney left the company in September 1960 and William John Upjohn left in November 1962.) Then, in January 1960, C. V. Patterson retired as executive vice president. Both Ted Parfet and Pete Parish were made executive vice presidents, reporting to Gifford Upjohn as president. The next step occurred at the end of 1961. Donald Gilmore resigned from the chairmanship and was succeeded by Gifford Upjohn. Ted Parfet was named president and general manager, effective January 1, 1962. Donald Gilmore kept in touch by serving as vice chairman of the board. In 1967, Executive Vice President Floyd Eberly resigned and he was replaced by Bob Boudeman.

The next major changes came in 1969. Gifford Upjohn and Donald Gilmore retired from their posts on November 1. Ted Parfet was elected chairman and chief executive officer. Pete Parish was named vice chairman, and Bob Boudeman stepped up to the presidency. In addition, other nonfamily members joined the top executive ranks as the company moved through the 1970s and into the next decade.

Robert M. "Bob" Boudeman

By all accounts, Bob Boudeman was a unique and engaging human being, remembered with affection by the many people who knew him.

A Kalamazoo College graduate, Boudeman had returned to Upjohn in 1945 after service as a naval officer. He was among the earliest engaged in building Upjohn International and was appointed its president in 1962. The next year, the board named him company vice president. He later was an executive vice president before becoming Upjohn president in 1969.

Bob Boudeman had a tremendous rapport with people. He was dynamic, intelligent, and well liked throughout the company. His door was open to anybody, anytime. Boudeman would tour the production lines in Building 41, would remember people's names, and the next time through would recall what individuals had been doing the last time he had seen them.

As a manager, Boudeman had little interest in details and often made decisions fast. He gave International a real boost, just as he did the idea of spending millions to set up a production plant in Puerto Rico.

One weekend in late 1973, Boudeman went skiing. Returning, he complained of a backache and headed for his doctor. There, a checkup revealed a spot on his lung. He had cancer. Boudeman died four months later on March 23, 1974, at age 56.

Preston S. "Pete" Parish

Pete Parish joined Upjohn in 1949 as a production engineer. His career covered a number of activities in Buildings 41 and 88 — training and publications in Personnel in 1952; production superintendent two years later; an administrative assistant in 1956; a vice president and administrative assistant in 1958. Later that same year, he was elected a director of the corporation. Two years afterward, Donald Gilmore thought the time had come for him to move up to an executive vice presidency, and then on November 1, 1969, Parish received the title of vice chairman.

During his time as an executive vice president, Parish was instrumental during negotiations leading in 1968 to Upjohn's purchase of Asgrow Seed Company, a major building block in the Kalamazoo firm's strategy to diversify (*see* pages 182-84). He also was one of the key individuals engaged in the late 1950s and 1960s in systematically expanding International into foreign markets.

(left) Donald S. Gilmore, Upjohn President from 1944 to 1953; Chairman of the Board, 1953 to 1962; and Vice Chairman of the Board, 1962 to 1969. He died in 1979.

(izquierda) Donald S. Gilmore, Presidente de Upjohn de 1944 a 1953; Presidente de la Junta Directiva de 1953 a 1962; y Vicepresidente de la misma, de 1962 a 1969. Falleció en 1979.

(à gauche) Donald Gilmore, président de la société Upjohn, de 1944 à 1953. Il fut président du Conseil, de 1953 à 1962, et vice-président du Conseil, de 1962 à 1969. Il est mort en 1979.

（左）1944年から1953年までアップジョン社社長、1953年から1962年まで会長、1962年から1969年まで副会長を務めたドナルドS．ギルモア。ドナルド・ギルモアは1979年に死去した。

(right) Robert M. Boudeman, Upjohn President from 1969 until his death in 1974.

(derecha) Robert M. Boudeman, Presidente de Upjohn desde 1969 hasta su muerte en 1974.

(à droite) Robert Boudeman, président de la société Upjohn de 1969 à sa mort, en 1974.

（右）1969年から1974年に死去するまで、アップジョン社の社長を務めたロバートM．ブーデマン。

Urbane and stylish, Pete Parish chaired the board's executive committee and such other critical bodies as the public affairs committee. As the man in overall charge of public relations, he also devoted a lot of his time and energy to serving the community on behalf of Upjohn. He was instrumental in bringing to life the Kalamazoo 2000 and Portage 2000 projects, local efforts to ensure the reasoned growth of the two communities in ways desired by their citizens.

Although his combat service in WWII was as an infantry officer with the First Marine Division on Guadalcanal and Peleliu, he also learned to fly during the latter stages of the conflict. An enthusiastic pilot still, he advocated regional airport development in the Kalamazoo area.

In his time, Parish came to be seen as the symbol of the corporate conscience. Says Parish, "I merely recognized that there are some things that are unique about our company, most of which stem from the attitudes and philosophy of W. E. Upjohn and those who followed him, L. N., and Donald Gilmore. Quality of the product, integrity of business dealings, dedication to medicine and science, concern and compassion for people — these are philosophies and traditions, more than conscience, that have stood us well over 100 years."

Parish helped keep these traditions alive, especially where employees were concerned. He was ultimately responsible for Employee Relations and thus had primary concern for how the men and women of Upjohn were treated. The respect and dignity that Upjohn employees enjoy today are in part a result of Pete Parish's efforts.

Parish retired in October 1984, although he remains a member of the board of directors. He was succeeded by Dr. Theodore Cooper.

Dr. William N. Hubbard, Jr.

The man who followed Boudeman in the company's presidency could not have been less like him. Dr. William N. Hubbard, Jr., was a physician, an erudite North Carolinian as steeped in classical literature as he was in the science of his profession.

A graduate of Columbia and, in 1944, of the New York University Medical School, Hubbard saw firsthand how truly wonderful the wonder drugs were as he worked with patients in the wards of New York's Bellevue Hospital. He taught others the art and science of medicine as an N.Y.U. faculty member from 1950 to 1959, then accepted appointment as dean of the University of Michigan Medical School, where he served until joining Upjohn in 1970.

Dr. Hubbard had been invited in 1968 to serve on Upjohn's board. Two years later, he went to work for the company as vice president and general manager, pharmaceutical division. That, in turn, was followed in 1972 by his promotion to executive vice president. On April 16, 1974, he succeeded Bob Boudeman as president.

Once on board at Upjohn, Hubbard took his part in the further development of drugs in a decade that put Motrin on the market and completed the design of Xanax and Halcion. It also fell to him to stand for the defense of the antibiotics Lincocin and Cleocin before the U.S. Senate. Upjohn's Lincocin, launched in 1964, was widely proving itself a winner over many potent bacteria. Then in late 1973 came unexpected and unwanted word: a few people who had been treated with Lincocin had contracted severe diarrhea, and as far as they were concerned, Lincocin was the cause. Cleocin, the antibiotic synthesized from Lincocin, was also implicated.

The issue wound up before a Senate committee and Dr. Hubbard appeared to respond to the allegations. There could be no question about the diarrhea cases. But Upjohn thought interpretations of these reports were, in Dr. Hubbard's words, "open to very serious question." There seemed to be a "clustering pattern" in the data, suggesting a variable that was external to patient and drug. Upjohn vigorously pursued that lead, supporting scientists interested in this line of study. The investigators discovered that the cause of the diarrhea was not Lincocin but a certain bacterium. With that knowledge, doctors could quickly cure the diarrhea.

The matter had put Upjohn in some turmoil for months. But, says Dr. Hubbard, "We were able to proceed from a scientific base, and we were successful. You have to defend from the science, not from anecdotal reports or popularity."

As an administrator, Dr. Hubbard worked at eliminating the separation between major components of the business. Looking back, he takes satisfaction from having become "part of an evolving system that is more collaborative and less wastefully competitive." On October 1, 1984, he retired, succeeded in the presidency by Larry Hoff. Hubbard remains a member of the board of directors.

(left) Preston S. "Pete" Parish, Upjohn Vice Chairman of the Board, 1969-1984.

(izquierda) Preston S. "Pete" Parish, Vicepresidente de la Junta Directiva de Upjohn, de 1969 a 1984.

(à gauche) Preston "Pete" Parish, vice-président du Conseil de la société Upjohn, de 1969 à 1984.

（左）1969年から1984年までアップジョン社副会長を務めたプレストンS．パリシ。

(right) William N. Hubbard, Jr., M.D., Upjohn President, 1974-1984.

(derecha) William N. Hubbard, Hijo, Médico, Presidente de Upjohn, de 1974 a 1984.

(à droite) Le Dr. William Hubbard Jr., président de la société Upjohn de 1974 à 1984.

（右）1974年から1984年までアップジョン社社長を務めたウイリアムN．ハバードJr．医博。

(left) Lawrence C. Hoff, Upjohn President, 1984 to the present.

(izquierda) Lawrence C. Hoff, Presidente de Upjohn, desde 1984 hasta la fecha.

(à gauche) Lawrence Hoff, président de la société Upjohn depuis 1984.

（左）1984年以来社長の任にあるローレンスC．ホフ。

(right) Theodore Cooper, M.D., Ph.D., Upjohn Vice Chairman of the Board, 1984 to the present.

(derecha) Theodore Cooper, Médico, Ph.D., Vicepresidente de la Junta Directiva de Upjohn, desde 1984 hasta la fecha.

(à droite) Le Dr. Theodore Cooper, Docteur en médecine, vice-président du Conseil de la société Upjohn, de 1984 à nos jours.

（右）1984年から副社長、テオドール・クーパー医博。

Lawrence C. Hoff

A native of Fresno, California, Larry Hoff received his A.B. degree in economics from Stanford in 1950, where he was co-captain of the track team, and went to work the next morning as a sales trainee for Upjohn. He was given five days' briefing, then dispatched to detail some of the best of San Francisco's physicians. He compensated for his lack of extensive scientific education by a program of persistent self-indoctrination in medical libraries.

Eight years after hitting the streets with his alligator bag of samples, Hoff was named a sales supervisor. Two years later, he moved to Kalamazoo for a post in Sales Education. Other promotions followed — from assistant sales manager to sales manager to regional sales manager in 1965, director of domestic pharmaceutical sales the following year, and vice president for domestic pharmaceutical marketing in 1969. He was elected to Upjohn's board in 1973 and a year later became vice president and general manager for domestic pharmaceutical operations. Designated executive vice president in 1977, Hoff was selected to succeed Dr. Hubbard as president in 1984.

Apart from his long career in sales work, Larry Hoff has held a number of posts in industry and educational organizations. The Pharmaceutical Manufacturers Association elected him to its board of directors in 1984 and he will assume the chairmanship of that organization in 1987. He has also served as chairman of the board and executive committee of the National Pharmaceutical Council and is on the board of Kalamazoo's Borgess Hospital.

Dr. Theodore Cooper

Succeeding Pete Parish in 1984 as vice chairman of Upjohn's board, Dr. "Ted" Cooper had first been elected a director in 1978. Two years later, he joined the company as executive vice president.

Prior to that time, Dr. Cooper had held posts of distinction in medicine and government. A physician and physiologist by education, he served as professor of surgery at St. Louis University, and as professor and chairman, Department of Pharmacology, and professor of surgery, University of New Mexico School of Medicine.

Moving into the federal government, he directed the National Heart and Lung Institute of the National Institutes of Health. In the Department of Health, Education and Welfare, he held an appointment as assistant secretary for health in the Ford administration.

Returning to teaching, Ted Cooper held an appointment as professor of surgery and pharmacology at Cornell University Medical College. He was also named adjunct professor, Rockefeller University, and visiting physician, Rockefeller University Hospital. Dr. Cooper was selected as dean of Cornell University Medical College in 1977. His many awards and honors include the Schwartz Award in Medicine, American Medical Association; the Albert Lasker Special Public Service Award; and the Department of Defense Distinguished Public Service Medal. Among his affiliations, he is a member-at-large of the American Red Cross's board of governors and serves on the boards of two other corporations.

RTP — The Chairman

Ted Parfet, a man in shirt sleeves with a smile to match his big six-foot-plus frame, flew 60 missions over Italy and Austria as a B-25 pilot in WWII, then attended the University of Michigan. He joined the company in 1947 after graduating from Michigan with a degree in finance. He has been on the firing line at Upjohn since his 1962 election as president.

In large measure Parfet came up through the financial side. In his adult years, numbers have been his prime tools, replacing the implements of ranching that so appealed to him as a younger man.

Parfet is known as a hard worker who has a warm, generous nature. His style is to seek consensus, but he is unafraid to make the hard decisions alone when he must.

"My experience has been that the more people you get to support a decision, the better decision it is," says Parfet. "I don't like to see dissension detract from the decision-making process. The decisions we make affect not only our shareholders but the lives of our employees and the public as well. We have to make them in as cooperative and rational a way as possible."

The chairman looks back over almost 40 years with a company that has, during that time, become worldwide in scope. He ticks off certain satisfactions, some of them shaded by the realities of constant growth and change. "I find pleasure in knowing that dedicated employees have positioned themselves for corporate expansion without surrendering an ethical sense." He sees, too, that "the team effort at Upjohn has continued to turn out the highest quality products." There also has been an ongoing, "heavy" investment in research under his direction. "My predecessors always emphasized the importance of research," he says. "I also feel that way, and this whole team that manages this company feels that way."

As chairman, Parfet has guided the evolution of the company into the multinational, highly respected business it has become. He continued support for areas of the company "that were the real providers of strength for us," while at the same time providing for growth.

During Parfet's tenure as president and chairman, Upjohn expanded internationally to take advantage of growing worldwide opportunity; it diversified in order to exploit the synergistic relationships between pharmaceuticals and other activities, such as polymer chemicals and the agricultural seed business; it developed new approaches to financing the heavy capital development required by the growing business; and its sales, earnings, and employee count increased dramatically.

"We planned for growth," Parfet says. "We have to have growth. Our survival depends on it." Always, however, he has been concerned that the growth be quality growth. "This company is now 100 years old, and I want to be sure that it's prepared to go another hundred," he says. "The effects of the job I've done will continue long after I retire."

Parfet feels the job he has done and his preparation for the future are sound. "Good management people have been brought in to lead the company into its next century," he says. Three men have filled the presidency in his time, and each one, in his words, "made positive contributions to the company's development." A new structure, the Office of the Chairman, now comprising Parfet, President Hoff, and Vice Chairman Cooper, was established in 1983 and, says Parfet, "I'm extremely pleased with the way that's working."

The chairman makes one other comment about achievement that takes him back through the years of his apprenticeship as a "number-cruncher" and demonstrates his concern for people and understanding of today's workplace. It is well and good, Parfet feels, for Upjohn to have thrust itself extensively into the latest technology, including full-scale computerization. "Our people and this whole company are benefiting a great deal from this," he observes. "It is now, and it is the future." And yet, the younger people, who adapt so quickly to technology, cannot assume "that once they have the information from the computer, they have the experience. The two dovetail together at some point, but it takes hours of blood, sweat, and tears behind a desk or at a work station before you get the experience." Older hands face the job of ensuring that younger ones get the experience to match their technological finesse. That, says Ted Parfet, is a major challenge for the years ahead.

UPJOHN GOES PUBLIC

The three-column *Wall Street Journal* article of June 2, 1954, presented a little-known view of Upjohn. The headline summed up the contents: "Upjohn Co., Privately-Owned and Run by a Family Of Doctors, Sells $100 Million of Drugs Through M.D.'s."

This company, the lead sentence related, was "one of the few remaining major American enterprises still mostly owned by one family." It was a happy condition, but it could not last. As early as 1955, family members talked about the benefits and drawbacks of "going public."

On the minus side, Upjohn managers would wind up in a fishbowl, with all their corporate actions on display. On the other hand, Upjohn needed to know what its stock was worth for gift-tax and inheritance-tax purposes. The U.S. Treasury, entering the picture in 1955, decided that an Upjohn share looked to be worth $282.50. This determination was compromised when some Upjohn shares sold in over-the-counter trading for $2,050.00 apiece.

(left) Ray T. Parfet, Jr., Upjohn Chairman of the Board, 1969 to the present.

(izquierda) Ray T. Parfet, Hijo, Presidente de la Junta Directiva de Upjohn, desde 1969 hasta la fecha.

(à gauche) Ray T. Parfet, Jr., président du Conseil de la société Upjohn depuis 1969.

（左）1969年から現在まで、代表取締役会長レイ T. パーフェット Jr.

(right) The Office of the Chairman (1986). Lawrence C. Hoff, President; Theodore Cooper, M.D., Ph.D., Vice Chairman; and Ray T. Parfet, Jr., Chairman and Chief Executive Officer.

(derecha) La Oficina del Presidente de Upjohn (1986). Lawrence C. Hoff, Presidente; Theodore Cooper, Médico, Ph. D., Vicepresidente de la Junta Directiva; y Ray T. "Ted" Parfet, Hijo, Presidente de la Junta Directiva y Principal Funcionario Ejecutivo.

(à droite) Le Bureau du président, 1986. M. Lawrence C. Hoff, directeur général; M. Theodore Cooper, M.D., Ph. D., vice-président; M. Ray T. Parfet, Jr., président et "Chief Executive Officer".

（右）1986年会長室で社長ローレンス C. ホフ、副会長テオドール・クーパー代表取締役会長レイ T. パーフェット Jr.

The realities of going public came a step closer in 1958 when San Francisco-based salesman Dick Sellman, who had been left a handsome block of Upjohn stock by his father, Waters Sellman, decided to improve his estate-tax situation by selling his shares.

His decision implied risk. Family members managing the company in Kalamazoo could have resented his intention, and that might have ended his days as assistant director of sales for the western branches. But Sellman went ahead. He arranged to sell 1,327 shares at a price of $1,080,000. Further, no one asked him to step down. In retrospect, he probably did Upjohn a service.

Now the action shifted to a larger stage. Upjohn's 20-member board convened on October 24, 1958; 11 of the directors were related directly or by marriage to the founder. Be that as it may, the board voted to recommend public ownership for Upjohn. On November 21, stockholders endorsed that decision, and, after a 25-for-1 stock split, the sale began on December 11 at $45.00 per share. On January 5, 1959, The Upjohn Company was formally accepted for listing and trading on the New York Stock Exchange. Its symbol: UPJ.

Upjohn's chairman and managing director, Donald Gilmore, considered it important to explain to employees both the sequence of events and the meaning behind them. In an *Overflow* article, he wrote that going public gave Upjohn a way of determining the fair value of a share of stock. At the same time, listing the shares on the NYSE board added to Upjohn's prestige. And it also created an organized market for buying and selling company stock. That, said Gilmore, would make it easier for a shareholder to sell shares and would simplify things in estate settlements.

So at last Upjohn was a public corporation, and outsiders, now that the company had opened its doors, began investigating this heretofore remote business. Herbert Solow, writing in *Fortune* in 1959, reached the conclusion that Upjohn was "the very model of the modern successor to the old pill-rolling establishments: a chemical house producing 'fine chemicals' as well as drugs, with a first-class research organization and a smart merchandising outfit that yields impressive profits."

Wall Street analysts could also get a sharper look at the company now. After studying the books and talking to Upjohn people in mid-1959, the firm of Adams & Peck declared, "This is one of the great companies of America." Beyond that, the investigators considered Upjohn "one of the most desirable equities available in our market and [it] deserves a rating better than most other drug stocks." In short, one new face on the stock exchange board had already proven itself worthy to at least some of the specialists on Wall Street.

Since it was going to be on display as it had never been before, the company would have to set up a mechanism for keeping the public properly informed, a realization that led to forming a public relations office. Upjohn had already ventured into product and event P.R. Low-key activities had accompanied the opening of Building 41, the firm's commitment to bioconversion, and its crucial achievement in finding a shortcut for making steroids. In 1958, Upjohn formalized the function under William Bayliss, a man already experienced in drug public relations at the national level.

In June 1970, Bayliss left, and Charles T. Mangee, who had begun his Upjohn career as an ag/vet sales representative, succeeded him. Now corporate vice president for public relations, Mangee has assembled a network of support agencies for International in major cities of the world (the lineup today amounts to 20 local P.R. companies) and has reorganized corporate public relations in a functional way, to offer "full-service support to the businesses." It is what he calls "a very flexible, project-oriented, issue-oriented approach to public relations."

Meanwhile another, more tangible aspect of Upjohn's changing public image was taking shape. The vintage-1930s Henrietta Street executive office no longer accommodated the fast-growing postwar corporation. Donald Gilmore and his associates concluded that the place for a new headquarters should be on the west side of Portage Road, across from Building 41.

(left) After a 25-for-1 stock split in December 1958, Upjohn stock was formally accepted for listing and trading on the New York Stock Exchange. Company president E. Gifford Upjohn, M.D., is shown with stock exchange officials at the listing ceremony, January 5, 1959.

(izquierda) Después de una división de acciones 25-por-1, en diciembre de 1958, las acciones de Upjohn fueron formalmente aceptadas para inscripción en la lista de compraventa en la Bolsa de Valores de Nuevo York. El presidente de la compañía, E. Gifford Upjohn, médico, aparece con funcionarios de la bolsa de valores en la ceremonia de inscripción en la lista, el 5 de enero de 1959.

(à gauche) En décembre 1958, les actions Upjohn sont introduites à la Bourse de New York, le New York Stock Exchange. Le président de la société, le Dr. Gifford Upjohn, est entouré des cambistes lors d'une cérémonie, le 5 janvier 1959.

（左）1958年12月の1対25の株式分割後、アップジョン社はニューヨーク証券取引所に上場を認可された。1959年1月5日の上場記念式典で、証券取引所の役員と並ぶ社長E．G．アップジョン医博。

(right) E. Gifford Upjohn, M.D., Upjohn President from 1953 to 1962; Chairman of the Board from 1962 to 1969.

(derecha) E. Gifford Upjohn, Médico, Presidente de Upjohn de 1953 a 1962; Presidente de la Junta Directiva de 1962 a 1969.

(à droite) Le Dr. Gifford Upjohn, président de la société Upjohn, de 1953 à 1962. Il fut président du Conseil, de 1962 à 1969.

（右）1953年から1962年までアップジョン社社長、1962年から1969年まで会長を務めたE．G．アップジョン医博。

(left) Ground-breaking ceremony for Bldg. 88, September 25, 1958. Donald Gilmore (seated), Lew Crockett, vice president for engineering (with shovel), E. Gifford Upjohn (lower left), Coy V. Patterson, executive VP (top left).

(izquierda) Ceremonia de la excavación inaugural para el Edificio 88, el 25 de septiembre de 1958. Donald Gilmore (sentado), Lew Crockett, vicepresidente de ingeniería (con la pala), E. Gifford Upjohn (abajo a la izquierda), Coy V. Patterson, vicepresidente ejecutivo (arriba izquierda).

(à gauche) Pose de la première pierre du bâtiment 88, le 25 septembre 1958. Donald Gilmore (assis), Lew Crockett, vice-président chargé de l'ingénierie (tenant une pelle), E.Gifford Upjohn (en bas à gauche), Coy V. Patterson, directeur général adjoint (en haut à gauche).

（左）1958年9月25日、88号館の起工式。着席しているのがドナルド・ギルモア、手にシャベルを持つ技術部門担当副社長ルー・クロケット、左下がE．G．アップジョン、左上が取締役副社長コイV．パターソン。

(right) When the general administrative office in downtown Kalamazoo became overcrowded in the late 1950s; a new building was constructed on Portage Road across from Building 41. Two years in the planning and two years under construction, "Building 88" was dedicated in August 1961.

(derecha) Cuando la oficina administrativa general en la ciudad de Kalamazoo se vio atestada de personas a fines del decenio de 1950, se construyó un nuevo edificio en Portage frente al Edificio 41. Después de dos años de planificación y de dos años de construcción, el "edificio 88" fue inaugurado en agosto de 1961.

(à droite) Quand les locaux du bureau de l'administration générale du centre-ville de Kalamazoo s'avérèrent trop étriqués à la fin des années 1950, on construisit un nouvel édifice sur la rue Portage, en face du bâtiment 41. Après deux ans de planification et deux ans de construction, le "Bâtiment 88" fut inauguré au mois d'août 1961.

（右）1950年後半、カラマズー市街地の本社事務所が手狭になり、ポーテージ通りの41号館の向い側に新しいビルを建てることになった。計画に2年、建設に2年をかけ、1961年8月に88号館が完成した。

The company hired the internationally known architectural firm Skidmore, Owings & Merrill in July 1957 to lay out a building concept. O. W. Burke of Detroit won the bidding for general contractor, and on March 30, 1959, construction began. The process of construction took more than two years. Now and then, labor stoppages and plan revisions slowed progress, and crews even had to contend with a fire main failure under the cafeteria site, just days before the moving date. Building 88, one of the most striking constructed in the U.S. at that time, was occupied August 1961.

A PIVOTAL EVENT

The U.S. drug industry as we know it today was shaped in large part by an event that occurred as America entered the 1960s. The investigation of the pharmaceutical industry by the U.S. Senate's Antitrust and Monopoly Subcommittee, led by Democratic Senator Estes Kefauver of Tennessee, rocked the drug-makers back on their heels.

Senator Kefauver had decided to look into drug industry pricing methods on antibiotics and steroids, and he called for the inquiry to begin in December 1959. Testimony revealed that at a cost of 14 cents per bottle of 100 tablets, Upjohn manufactured prednisolone (one of the Upjohn family of corticosteroids, used in treating rheumatoid disorders, allergic states, and female hormonal conditions). Upjohn sold the 100-tablet bottles to another firm for $1.57 each. When these same tablets finally reached patients, the cost had escalated to more than $15.00 — a markup in excess of 10,000 percent! Right away, the industry and Upjohn looked bad.

Upjohn's president, Dr. Gifford Upjohn, a calm, soft-spoken health care professional, appeared before the committee to try to clarify the company's position. E. G. U. could not account for what had happened to the product's price after Upjohn had sold it, but he could explain Upjohn's price. He pointed out that the raw material represented only a fraction of the product's cost. The time, the manpower, the many steps and years involved in pharmaceutical R & D — all these elements were included in determining Upjohn's price. In all, Upjohn's president testified for five hours.

The Senate hearings lasted from that December until October 1960. Along the way, they piled up 16,000 pages of testimony. And the outcome was a bill to lower industry prices and profits. The newly elected President John F. Kennedy bypassed the proposed act in favor of a weaker bill brought forward by Rep. Oren Harris. Then the matter became clouded by the issue of thalidomide, one of the saddest chapters in the history of drug manufacture.

A German product, thalidomide had gone on the market in West Germany in 1957 as a sedative. Signs of irreversible nerve damage appeared, and in 1960 came even worse news: babies whose mothers had taken the medication during pregnancy were being born with severe deformities. Before much could be done, more than 8,000 deformed infants had been delivered.

In America, the FDA never formally approved distribution of the product. Even so, Senator Kefauver's staff had built up quite a clipping file on it. And at a key moment, Kefauver released these stories to the news media, hoping this would revive his legislation on drug industry practices. His forecast was correct. A furor swelled, and soon the White House was listening. President Kennedy thereupon instructed that a new bill be drawn to protect the public against future thalidomide-type situations.

The new legislation required that drug-makers set forth "substantial evidence" that a drug was both *safe* and *effective* before the FDA would allow it on the market. Greater emphasis than before would be given to testing and long-term clinical study not only to prove safety, as already required, but also to prove efficacy. Both houses of Congress approved the measure without dissent, and Public Law 87-781, commonly known as the 1962 Kefauver-Harris amendments to the Food, Drug and Cosmetic Act of 1938, became the law of the land. The Food, Drug and Cosmetic Act of 1938 did not provide that a drug be demonstrated effective. Although there were proponents of proof of efficacy when the act was debated, their arguments failed. Leonard Engel, in his *Medicine Makers of Kalamazoo* (1961), expressed the climate of opinion just prior to the Kefauver-Harris amendments. "If a provision for proof of effectiveness had been written into the 1938 law," Engel says, "the FDA, the pharmaceutical industry and the entire profession of medicine would soon have been bogged down in helpless debate, for the effectiveness of a drug can be extremely difficult to define or measure."

Clearly, although the new law complicated the approval process considerably, the "helpless debate" did not materialize, nor was a drug's efficacy as difficult to demonstrate as had been feared. Still, for the drug industry the new restrictions and increased costs of testing and development presented major challenges. Drug approval time was also lengthened, which meant that precious years of patent protection were eroded. All told, the new law was the single most important nonscientific event to affect the industry and Upjohn in the years following WWII.

DIVERSIFYING FOR A WORLD MARKET

Over the last 36 years, while Upjohn was enlarging and improving its operations in its major business, pharmaceuticals, and meeting the challenges of going public and new legislative forces, it was also changing its approach to business in a world marketplace. Prior to 1950, the company served primarily the U.S. market; now it sells products in more than 150 countries and has operations in nearly 50 of them. In addition, since midcentury it has added an Agricultural Division, a HealthCare Services subsidiary, and a Fine Chemicals Division. From 1962 until July 1985, the firm also was a major polymer chemicals manufacturer.

Upjohn's full commitment to explore worldwide markets may not have come until the 1950s, but Upjohn products were available in England as early as 1890 and in Latin America not long after. As for diversifying, Dr. W. E. Upjohn and his key associates were debating that when their friable pill was still in its infancy. Through the years, Upjohn made occasional stabs at diversification, never with great enthusiasm, until the brave new postwar world of the late 1940s presented opportunities that could not be ignored.

A check of the corporate balance sheet shows what a difference these ventures into expansion have meant. In 1984, the first year Upjohn's consolidated sales exceeded

$2 billion, one-third, or $746 million, came from foreign sales. The agricultural and chemical businesses accounted for one-third of consolidated sales. And HealthCare Services, an Upjohn property since 1969, contributed $177 million, or 12 percent of the corporation's Human Health Care sales total. (These figures reflect actual sales in 1984 prior to the divestiture of the worldwide polymer chemical business in 1985.) In 1985, after divestiture of the polymer chemical business, consolidated sales still exceeded $2 billion; foreign sales accounted for 34 percent, agricultural for 21 percent, and Upjohn HealthCare Services for nine percent.

Going international and developing new enterprises, give or take some growing pains, have for the most part enhanced the corporation's performance.

BUILDING THE INTERNATIONAL ENTERPRISE

Upjohn first dipped its toe in international waters before the turn of the century. In June 1890, the company put on a "creditable display" at the British Medical Society meeting in Birmingham. The founder had had it in mind "to give the detail men employed by our representatives in London [probably John Timpson & Company] an opportunity to become conversant with our methods of showing our goods to the profession."

But most of Upjohn's earliest learning experiences in the export field occurred at the New York branch, during its management by F. L. Upjohn and his successor L. N. Upjohn. At one point, F. L. made contact with an Egyptian physician-pharmacist named Dr. Nikola Nimr, who bought a full line of pills and granules. Gratified, F. L. had the Upjohn catalog printed in Arabic. However, Egyptians scarcely benefited from the transaction. Several decades later, Upjohn learned that Dr. Nimr's inventory still lingered untouched on his shelves.

(left) Friable pills even traveled as far as Egypt at the turn of the century. A physician, Dr. Nikola Nimr, purchased a full line of pills and granules from the New York Office. Nimr placed this advertisement in an Egyptian newspaper in 1894.

(izquierda) Las píldoras desintegrables llegaron a países tan lejanos como Egipto, a la vuelta del siglo. Un médico, el Dr. Nikola Nimr, compró todo un lote de píldoras y gránulos en la oficina de Nueva York. Nimr insertó este anuncio en un periódico egipcio en 1894.

(à gauche) Les pilules friables ont même atteint l'Egypte au tournant du siècle. Un médecin nommé Dr Nikola Nimr acheta une série complète de pilules et de granulés de la filiale Upjohn à New York. Cette annonce publicitaire, faite par le Dr Nimr, a paru dans un journal égyptien en 1894.

（左）19世紀の終り頃、崩れる丸薬は、遠くエジプトにまで販売されるようになっていた。ニコラ・ニムル医師は、アップジョン社のニューヨーク支社から錠剤や顆粒の全製品を購入し、1894年、エジプトの新聞にこの広告を出した。

(right) In the 1890s, the company's New York office did a booming export business with Mexico. Quinine made up the bulk of the orders, and the company had special labels printed in Spanish. By 1903, an export manager had been hired to coordinate this business.

(derecha) En el decenio de 1890, la oficina de la compañía en Nueva York logró una floreciente exportación a México. La quinina constituía el grueso de los pedidos, y la compañía tenía etiquetas especiales impresas en español. Para 1903 se contrató un gerente de exportación para coordinar este ramo.

(à droite) Dans les années 1890, la filiale de la société Upjohn à New York connut un boom de ses exportations vers le Mexique. La quinine était en tête de liste des commandes et Upjohn avait fait imprimer des étiquettes spéciales en espagnol. En 1903, un responsable des ventes à l'exportation fut recruté pour coordonner ces affaires commerciales de la société.

（右）1890年代、ニューヨーク支社からメキシコへの輸出事業はブームを迎えていた。その大部分がキニーネ剤で、ラベルはスペイン語で印刷された。1903年、この仕事のために新しい輸出担当部長が採用された。

Early in the new century, much of the New York branch's business abroad consisted of quinine pills shipped to Mexico. As early as 1903, New York had an export manager, a Mr. Charles F. B. Rudolph. Rudolph, a German who had emigrated to Mexico as a young man, single-handedly kept track of all foreign orders — calculated exchange rates, tariffs, and duties; chased invoices through customs; and kept lengthy correspondence with Latin American customers and with the few far-flung salesmen of The Upjohn Company. Rudolph's health deteriorated in the late 1920s, and he died in 1930. His obituary in the *Overflow* called him the "father" of export.

When L. N. started working at the New York branch in 1904, export sales peaked for about a year at the level of $75,000. The Mexican shipments accounted for $50,000 of that total. These figures declined considerably following the Mexican Revolution in 1911.

Then came Harold Upjohn's effort of the early 1920s. He proposed having nurses in England go from door to door selling Mylax, a version of Phenolax. This venture failed miserably and very probably hardened for years to

come the mind-set of Upjohn management against a wide-open commitment to export. A corporate historian wrote two decades later that foreign sales "grew up as an unwanted child"; that, in fact, from the earliest days, the founder "had looked askance at foreign business." This skepticism was shared by many of the executives who came after him.

All this may have been so, but from the early 1920s on, "Export" at Upjohn slowly created a life of its own. The "home office" may have "passively discouraged export business," as L. N. noted, but it still complied with requests for foreign goods from both New York and San Francisco salespeople. Some of those orders presumably came from wholesalers overseas who needed Upjohn specialties requested by travelers.

There are references in the *Overflow* volumes to sales offices in Mexico, Cuba, and Puerto Rico in the 1920s, and to several traveling salesmen in Central and South America. Typical of the "international salesman" was Ernesto Inderbitzen, a Swiss who spoke Spanish, French, German, and Italian, plus a number of Mexican Indian dialects. Hired in 1926, Inderbitzen became senior salesman in Mexico, after weathering natural disasters and a revolution. He first worked out of the Kansas City branch, which apparently handled the northern Mexico export business from around 1925 to 1930.

By the mid-1930s, Upjohn salesmen were regularly detailing in Panama, Ecuador, Venezuela, and Central America. The hours were long, the conditions often primitive, but the worst part of the job was the slowness of communication. Salesmen on extended trips didn't receive news from home — or their paychecks — for months at a time.

In the 1930s, the San Francisco office began actively to explore sales to the Far East. There was already some activity — in 1929, for example, there is reference to an Upjohn agent in Tokyo — and the branch had had a sales office in the Hawaiian Islands for many years. In 1931, Tse Wei Wu of Shanghai was engaged as an Upjohn representative to China, opening the door to a potentially enormous market. Wu, intelligent and strikingly handsome, was equally at home in a Western suit or a traditional Chinese robe and fan: he carried the Upjohn name through his offices in Shanghai and Hong Kong for many successful years, and even visited Kalamazoo.

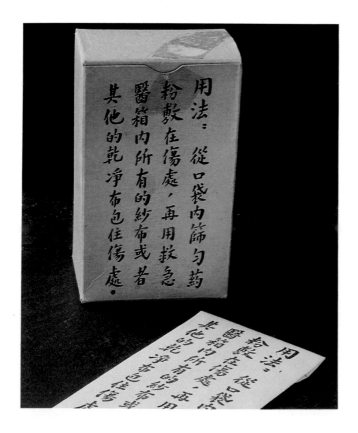

World War II put a halt to the sales activity in the Hong Kong and Shanghai offices. After hostilities ceased, Wu attempted to revive his business, but ran afoul of the Communists. Shanghai operations ceased in 1947, and trade with China did not resume until the late 1970s. The Hong Kong office, under new management, thrived and became a branch office in the 1960s.

In October 1931, San Francisco arranged for the T. M. Thakore Co., of Bombay, to become the company's sole representative for India, Burma, and Ceylon. This resulted in a successful relationship for many years, until Thakore failed in 1952.

By the mid-1930s, Upjohn salesmen also were being assigned to the "Philippine Islands territory."

Closer to home, the history of Upjohn selling in Canada is a long and illustrious one. Upjohn pharmaceuticals had undoubtedly been exported to Canada from 1927 on, but the company's active sales presence began in earnest when Malcolm Galbraith was named director of sales in 1929. Galbraith, a Canadian by birth, set up a Toronto branch in 1935. This was Upjohn's first foreign sales branch. Two years later, cashier Violet Braiden was appointed Toronto office manager, very probably the first of Upjohn's female executives.

(left) Export to the Far East began through the San Francisco office. In 1931, Waters Sellman engaged Tse Wei Wu of Shanghai as Upjohn's sole agent in China. Wu carried on operations from this office in Shanghai and from another in Hong Kong until 1947.

(izquierda) Las exportaciones al Lejano Oriente comenzaron por medio de la Oficina de San Francisco. En 1931 Waters Sellman contrató los servicios de Tse Wei Wu de Shanghai como agente único de Upjohn en China. Wu llevó a cabo las operaciones desde esta oficina en Shanghai y desde otra en Hong Kong hasta 1947.

(à gauche) Les exportations en Extrême-Orient commencèrent par San Francisco. En 1931, Waters Sellman choisit Tse Wei Wu, de Shangaï comme agent exclusif d'Upjohn en Chine. C'est de ce bureau, situé à Shangaï , et d'un autre, situé à Hong-Kong, que Wu dirigea ses affaires jusqu'en 1947.

（左）極東への輸出は、サンフランシスコ支社を通じて開始され、ウォルターズ・セルマンは、1931年に上海のシェ・ウェイ・ウーをアップジョン社の中国総代理人として契約した。ウー氏は上海のこの事務所と、香港の事務所で1947年までアップジョン社の仕事を行なった。

(right) In the late 1930s, Upjohn opened several sales offices throughout Latin America. Gerald V. Littig was hired in 1937, trained for 10 days, and sent to Puerto Rico. When he needed to meet with the New York office he traveled by steamer — a four-day trip.

(derecha) A fines del decenio de 1930, Upjohn abrió varias oficinas de ventas en toda la América Latina. Gerald V. Littig fue contratado en 1937, adiestrado durante diez días y enviado a Puerto Rico. Cuando necesitaba reunirse con el personal de la oficina de Nueva York, viajaba por barco en un viaje de cuatro días.

(à droite) Vers la fin des années 1930, la société Upjohn ouvre plusieurs succursales de vente en Amérique latine. Gerald Littig fut recruté en 1937, et suivit un stage de formation pendant 10 jours, avant d'être nommé à Porto Rico. Pour rencontrer les cadres de la société à New York, il effectuait une traversée de quatre jours.

（右）1930年代の後期、アップジョン社はラテンアメリカの各地に販売事務所を開発した。ジェラルド V. リティグが1937年に採用され、10日間の教育訓練ののち、プエルトリコに派遣された。ニューヨーク支社の会議に出席するためには、蒸気船で4日の船旅であった。

With such expansion, management had to do something to cope with the paperwork of increasing foreign orders. With that in mind, in April 1937 they picked Sid W. Steensma to coordinate all export activity on both East and West Coasts. The next year, his base was moved from New York to Kalamazoo, where all export was centralized by 1940. Steensma was credited by L. N. with waging "quite courageously" a good fight within the firm for export, and was "fortunate in being able to show considerable growth in sales during his incumbency."

During WWII, business at the Toronto branch slowed to a trickle because of border restrictions. The Canadian sales force was reduced to four men at one point. But two more foreign sales offices hung out the Upjohn sign (Caracas, Venezuela, 1944; and Cali, Chile, 1945). In the South Pacific, export was suspended when Japanese troops flooded into the islands. Upjohn's representative in the Philippines, Stuart R. Barnett, was taken prisoner, along with his staff. Three employees died during the ordeal, and the business was not revived until 1948.

For more than two decades, export had been gradually expanding. A hint of what lay ahead came in November 1945 when Sales Director Emil Schellack named two assistant sales directors, Fred Allen and Robert S. Jordan.

For Jordan, a seasoned Upjohn salesman since 1923, there was a special responsibility: export sales. Three months later, Schellack died. Allen became vice president and director of sales, and Jordan was made general sales manager. Jordan had lost the race for the top sales spot, and that did not sit well with him. Brilliant, dynamic, hardworking, Bob Jordan needed a challenge as consolation. He asked to be assigned fully to export. Management concurred, and Jordan started what International is today.

Late in 1946, Chairman L. N. Upjohn, President Donald Gilmore, and others convened to stake out a larger commitment to export. It was "the first occasion," L. N. wrote, "on which we seriously — and favorably — discussed the possibility of providing for evolution of the export business." Then, in retrospect, L. N. added a telling admission: "As a matter of fact, it has grown more or less in spite of us."

One of the agenda items at that important December 9, 1946, conference had to do with picking an export sales manager. The man selected to carry the banner was 42-year-old H. B. (Hank) Roberts, a 17-year veteran of Upjohn sales who had risen through the ranks to divisional sales manager. The inside counterpart to Roberts was Sid Steensma, export office manager.

The work of export's nucleus began in earnest in 1947, a year in which one-third of Upjohn's entire liver extract output went to India and in which Gelfoam became the company's first product to be labeled in three languages (French, Spanish, and English). In late February, Bob Jordan and longtime salesman Robert G. White set out on a contact-building tour in Latin America. Roberts recalls that his "first real assignment came early in 1948 when [he] was asked to make an extended trip around the world" — the first such tour for anyone in export. One of Roberts' tasks was to visit Manila, find Upjohn employees who had been imprisoned by the Japanese, and pay them their back salary from the war years. That January, Upjohn had 22 salesmen abroad — nine in Cuba, four each in Mexico and Venezuela, two each in Puerto Rico and Central America, and one in Colombia.

Birth of the Export Division

Upjohn's foreign trade finally gained full corporate commitment in 1952 when, at its January meeting, the board of directors approved formation of the Export Division, with Bob Jordan as general manager. He would report to Executive Vice President C. V. Patterson.

Jordan knew all the ins and outs of his sales trade, and he was ably assisted by such men as Hank Roberts, Richard D. Tedrow, William H. DeCou, and Bob White. These men laid the first row of bricks for International.

The company's first foreign subsidiary was in Canada, where the Toronto branch office formed the nucleus for The Upjohn Company of Canada, incorporated on July 24, 1952.

Next, Jordan shifted his attention across the Atlantic. Upjohn had no European presence, so Bill DeCou, an experienced sales rep, was dispatched to England to open the window. Upjohn of England, Ltd., began operations in London's West End in 1953. Within two years, DeCou had hired 27 employees and was showing a profit. Salesmen were trained the same way as their American counterparts, and DeCou bought them all automobiles, throwing in lessons for those who didn't know how to drive.

So 1952 launched what Jordan called a "renaissance" for Upjohn's overseas operations. Actually, it wasn't that strong a year from a numbers standpoint. Antibiotic prices hit the skids. The new division made a skimpy profit of $53,000 on sales of $2.85 million. And, worst of all, the largest customer, Thakore of India, failed. At one time, Thakore's purchases had been upwards of $250,000 a year; now bankrupt, they owed Upjohn more than $375,000. Upjohn management, leery of further involvement, declined to take over the business and liquidated it.

There were added considerations in all sizes. Boots Pure Drug Company, Ltd., of England was one of them. Boots was doing business in 78 countries, it had 1,290 pharmacies in the United Kingdom, and it also had three manufacturing plants, a capacity that Bill DeCou's English subsidiary lacked. Upjohn and Boots worked out a deal. Boots would draw on Upjohn's experience in fermentation and manufacturing at Kalamazoo and modernize its own production. In exchange, it would make Upjohn items in England for DeCou's salespeople to market. A crucial clause in the agreement gave the firms the right of first refusal on each other's new products — an agreement which, two decades later, would result in spawning Motrin (*see pages 111-13*).

Expansion of Export

Export steamed into 1953 with 141 employees and big designs on the future. Agents had to be found and subsidiaries formed. Having entered the postwar international market later than other companies, Upjohn's Export had plenty of lost ground to make up, and it wasted no time in doing so. To back up the subsidiaries, a number of plants were built, all under the direction of engineer Leonard T. Cookson, a son-in-law of L. N. Upjohn and protégé of Lew Crockett. The first plant outside the U. S. opened in Toronto's Don Mills section on July 10, 1954. The second started in Crawley, England, in 1956 and the third in Australia in 1959. Later, in the 1960s, seven more started up, among them Belgium in 1963. Nine came on line in the 1970s: two in 1970, four in 1972, two in 1974, and one in 1978. Two more have been added since then — Taiwan in August 1981 and South Korea in November that same year. Further, science liaison offices opened in various sites, including India, Pakistan, and Egypt.

Upjohn's export people learned by doing. Sometimes the situation could be traumatic. Hank Roberts was trying to line up agents in China in 1949 when guards knocked on his hotel door at dawn. "You are leaving," they said. "I'm not ready to go," he replied. "You are leaving now," they told him. By 7 A.M. he was on a flight to Hong Kong. The Communists were taking over.

Country by country, the system differed. In pre-Castro Cuba, Upjohn had what Roberts calls a "propaganda-office operation." The office stirred up retail business for the company which, in turn, sold to the wholesalers, who sold to the retailers. In Puerto Rico, Export worked exclusively through wholesalers. In Mexico, the company manned a "propaganda office" and dealt through an agent. One lesson that Roberts brought home with him was the importance of "understanding merchandising within the country, then doing business the way it is done in that country, because if you don't, you never succeed."

The Cuban operation was succeeding until Fidel Castro came to power in 1959. The situation deteriorated rapidly and the decision was made to close down the Cuban operation. Upjohn had about a dozen distributors on the island. The distributors paid the banks what they owed the company, but the banks never remitted the funds to Upjohn.

By 1960, Upjohn International, Inc. (the name had changed from Export in 1956) had its stakes firmly in place. It had a work force of 700, more than 80 of them in Kalamazoo, and it was contributing almost 10 percent of total sales. Fourteen subs were operating, 10 of them wholly owned by Upjohn; eight of the 14 were scarcely two years old.

The operation had sprouted so fast in the 1950s that snags and snarls in management were almost inevitable. At Pete Parish's behest, Jack Gauntlett wrote a job description for someone to untangle the situation. Parish then tracked down Gauntlett on a fishing trip to Michigan's Upper Peninsula and told him, "I just wanted you to know that I found the guy for the job. It's you." Replied Gauntlett, "You've just ruined my vacation." Nevertheless, he transferred to International, where his friend Bob Boudeman had been working for some years.

(left) When the Toronto, Canada, branch sales office opened in 1935, it was the first company office located outside the U.S. Two years later, branch cashier Violet Braiden was appointed Toronto office manager, very probably the first of Upjohn's female executives.

(izquierda) Cuando la oficina de ventas de la sucursal en Toronto, Canadá, abrió en 1935, fue la primera de la compañía localizada fuera de Estados Unidos. Dos años después Violet Braiden, cajera de la sucursal, fue nombrada gerente de la oficina de Toronto, probablemente la primera mujer ejecutiva de Upjohn.

(à gauche) Lorsque la succursale de Toronto (Canada) fut ouverte en 1935, ce fut le premier bureau de la société hors des Etats-Unis. Deux ans plus tard, Violet Braiden, caissière de la succursale, s'en vit confier la direction, devenant ainsi très probablement le premier cadre féminin de la société.

（左）1935年、カナダのトロントに開設された支社は、海外に設立された最初の支社であった。2年後、カナダ支社の経理課長であったバイオレット・ブレイデンは、トロント支社長に任命された。アップジョン社初の女性役員であった。

(right) Upjohn of England, Ltd., began operations at No. 4 Alford Street, London, in 1953. This was the new Export Division's first subsidiary outside North America and its second international operation. Upjohn of England later relocated to Crawley.

(derecha) Upjohn de Inglaterra, Ltd., comenzó sus operaciones en el No. 4 de la calle Alford en Londres en 1953. Esta fue la primera subsidiaria de la nueva División de Exportaciones fuera de Norteamérica, y su segunda operación internacional. Upjohn de Inglaterra fue posteriormente reinstalada en Crawley.

(à droite) Les Laboratoires Upjohn en Angleterre, Upjohn of England, Ltd., ont ouvert leurs portes au No. 4, Alford Street, à Londres, en 1953. C'était la première filiale de la division exportation, en dehors de l'Amérique du Nord, et la seconde succursale internationale hors des Etats-Unis. La filiale britannique d'Upjohn devait s'installer par la suite à Crawley.

（右）1953年、英国アップジョン社がロンドン市アルフォード街4番地で営業を開始した。新設されたばかりの輸出部門にとって、英国アップジョン社は、北米以外で初めての子会社であり、2番目の海外事業所であった。英国アップジョン社は、後にクローリー市に移転した。

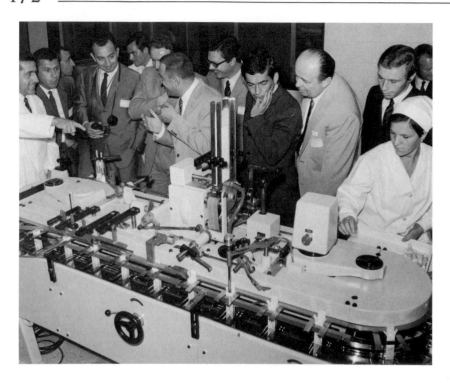

Change in the Management Team

As the new alignment shaped up in 1960, Boudeman would head International on the inside, Gauntlett would take charge of the subsidiaries, and Bob Jordan would report to Gauntlett. Jordan saw Gauntlett as "a nice fellow" but didn't want any part of the arrangement. For his part, Gauntlett wanted to run the operation "like a business, not like a sales office." Jordan resigned. Still, the man who had put International on the express track in the first place, Bob Jordan, retained pride in what he started. Back in 1952, he recalled, management budgeted $100,000 to launch International and "they never, never, never regretted it."

The command shifted several times thereafter. For a time, Bob Boudeman served as president. Dick Tedrow moved up from head of the International Legal Department to president (1967) and chairman (1971) of Upjohn International; later, in 1977, he switched to the corporate business development sphere. Meanwhile, Daniel D. Witcher, who had joined Upjohn in 1960,

progressed through several steps to the presidency of Upjohn International in 1972. In May 1979, he was retitled vice president and general manager for International and president and general manager, Upjohn International. On Witcher's appointment in April 1985 as corporate vice president for worldwide human health businesses, Selvi Vescovi succeeded him as corporate vice president and general manager for International. Vescovi had started with Upjohn in 1954 as a New York-area salesman and had held a series of assignments in International in the years after 1965.

This succession of leaders took International a long way. There was a time in 1952 when its staff of 141 operated two subsidiaries and brought in $2.85 million in sales. By contrast, International today consists of 45 subsidiaries and branches, with 16 overseas pharmaceutical manufacturing plants. Its 8,000 employees — the sales force numbers about 2,800 — produce, distribute, and sell products in more than 150 countries. Of further interest in a company always concerned about its people is a footnote offered by Dan Witcher. "We don't have a single American citizen who is a manager of one of our overseas offices," he points out. "We have produced a true international company."

Selvi Vescovi, the man currently in charge of International, must take into account the marketplace shifts and trends, as well as the individual political, economic, and social differences in the division's sales areas. At the same time, Vescovi must look at his far-ranging territory with truly broad international perspective. What he sees is generally reassuring. "When you look at the problems that International has had," he says, "and you look at the successes we've enjoyed, you become more optimistic as you develop the organization and the people in it. To me, that's the key — developing people who can handle problems, who have ideas about doing things differently. The future looks bright. We know what most of the problems are going to be, and we've already started to figure them out."

A DRUG-MAKER'S SIDE VENTURES

The year was 1907. A special meeting of the Upjohn board of directors had convened to discuss a prospective new product. It had a name to tease the taste buds — Richard's Buffet Bouillon — and it stimulated a spirited discussion. One director spoke out heatedly, saying that this was not a pharmaceutical item; it could not be sold through druggists or to physicians; it would detract from the salesman's ability to sell the regular line; and, besides, the company was too much in debt to attempt this "divided effort." When the time came to vote, the board approved — with that one dissent — the expenditure of up to $10,000 to manufacture and sell the product. Richard's Buffet Bouillon was sold for several years prior to World War I, then vanished.

This bit of Upjohn history happened almost 80 years ago. Such discussions have accompanied other Upjohn decisions to diversify, and other nonpharmaceutical products have followed Richard's Buffet Bouillon just as rapidly into history.

In 1912, Upjohn took a flyer on another product just as remote from its primary line of pharmaceuticals — Kazoo Mints, which ended in "disaster," as L. N. Upjohn put it (see page 44).

(left) Scenes like this were common in the 1960s and 1970s as Upjohn opened a series of manufacturing facilities throughout the world. These Upjohn salesmen toured the company's new Italian manufacturing plant, Upjohn S.p.A., in Caponago, Italy, during open house ceremonies in September 1968.

(izquierda) Escenas como ésta eran comunes en los años 60's y 70's a medida que Upjohn abría una serie de instalaciones manufactureras en todo el mundo. Estos agentes de ventas de Upjohn recorrieron la nueva planta manufacturera de la compañía en Italia, la Upjohn S.p.A., en Caponago, durante las ceremonias inaugurales en septiembre de 1968.

(à gauche) De telles scènes étaient courantes dans les années 1960 et 1970, Upjohn ouvrant une série d'unités de production dans le monde entier. Les délégués médicaux d'Upjohn visitent la nouvelle usine de la société en Italie, Upjohn S.p.A., à Caponago, lors de portes ouvertes inaugurales en septembre 1968.

（左）アップジョン社が世界各地に生産工場を開設しはじめた1960年代と1970年代には、こうした光景がしばしば見られた。1968年9月のイタリア・カポナゴにおけるアップジョンS．p．A．で行なわれた開所式。イタリアのアップジョン社の社員たちが新しい工場を見学する。

(right) The 8,000 employees of Upjohn International, Inc., produce, distribute, and sell products in more than 150 countries. The manufacturing plant in Puurs, Belgium, is the second largest Upjohn plant, after Kalamazoo.

(derecha) Los 8.000 empleados de Upjohn Internacional Inc., producen, distribuyen y venden productos en más de 150 países. La planta manufacturera en Puurs, Bélgica es la segunda planta en importancia de Upjohn después de Kalamazoo.

(à droite) Les 8.000 employés des laboratoires Upjohn International, Inc., produisent, distribuent et vendent leurs produits dans plus de 150 pays. L'usine de fabrication des produits à Puurs, en Belgique est la seconde par ordre d'importance des laboratoires Upjohn, après Kalamazoo.

（右）アップジョンインターナショナルの8000人の社員は、世界150カ国以上でアップジョン社の製品を生産し、流通にのせ、販売している。ベルギーのプールスの生産工場は、カラマズーの本社工場に次いで大規模な工場である。

(left) Not everything The Upjohn Company has attempted to market has been a resounding success. Pictured are some long-forgotten early products (clockwise from top): Pantomime Chocolates; Worm Syrup; Borated Soap; Ferrophyll (a powdered spinach product); and Skeet-Skoot Powder (an insect repellent).

(izquierda) No todo lo que la Compañia Upjohn ha tratado de vender ha sido un éxito rotundo. En la foto aparecen algunos productos fabricados al principio, por largo tiempo olvidados (desde arriba, siguiendo las manecillas del reloj): Chocolates Pantomime; Ferrophyll (espinaca en polvo); Jabón Boratado; Polvo Skeet-Skoot (un producto contra los mosquitos); y Jarabe Vermífugo.

(à gauche) Tout ce que les Laboratoires Upjohn ont essayé de commercialiser n'a pas forcément eu un succès retentissant. Ci-contre, quelques anciens produits qui sont tombés dans l'oubli; de gauche à droite, Chocolats Pantomime; un sirop vermifuge; Ferrophyle (une poudre d'épinards); Savon à l'eau boriquée; et Poudre Skeet-Skoot (un insectifuge).

（左）アップジョン社が市場化しようとした製品のすべてが営業的に成功したものばかりではなかった。写真はそうした初期の製品のいくつか。（上から右回りに）フェロフイル、硼酸塩石鹸、スキート・スクート粉末（蚊よけ）、虫下しシロップ。

(right) Upjohn's Chemical Division manufactured polyurethane foams for construction (shown here) and the auto industry. In the early 1980s, construction starts plummeted, auto sales lagged, and so did polyurethane sales figures. The division was sold in 1985.

(derecha) La división de Productos Químicos de Upjohn fabricó esponjas plásticas de poliuretano para la industria de la construcción (según aparece en la foto) y para la automotríz. A principios de la decada de 1980 la construcción decayó drásticamente, y las ventas de automóviles decayeron, lo mismo que las cifras de venta de poliuretano. La división fue vendida en 1985.

(à droite) Fabrication de mousse de polyuréthane pour l'industrie du bâtiment (photo ci-contre) et l'industrie automobile par la division chimique d'Upjohn. Au début des années 1980, la crise dans l'industrie du bâtiment et dans les ventes d'automobiles entraîna la chute des ventes de polyuréthane. La division a été vendue en 1985.

（右）アップジョン社の化成品部門では、ポリウレタンフォームを建設会社向けに、また自動車産業向けに生産していた。1980年代初めに、建設業界が不振になり、自動車産業も売り上げが頭打ちになって、そのあおりを受けてアップジョン社のポリウレタンの売り上げにも陰りが出てきた。1985年に化成品部門は売却された。

Eight years later, Upjohn was ready to diversify again, and this time Harold Upjohn played a role. Lew Crockett and he combined with owner Bert Kitchen of The Chocolate Shop in Kalamazoo to make and market Pantomime Chocolates with the Upjohn label. Company people rated the product "first-class," but tasters detected a hint of "a pharmaceutical odor." Soon Pantomime Chocolates had gone the way of Kazoo Mints.

In more recent times, Upjohn has taken a few more runs at marketing items unrelated to the purely medicinal. Twice it went afield through International. In 1964, when other pharmaceutical firms were buying cosmetic companies, Upjohn International decided to follow suit. Mexico offered a likely prospect in C. P. Continental S. A., a firm known chiefly for its Missuky line of cosmetics. Lipstick in 68 colors and nail polish, priced at the lower end of the scale, were the firm's sales leaders. Upjohn stuck with the venture for ten years, but, unwilling to promote the products at the level of its competitors, the firm liquidated the operation.

Upjohn's next unorthodox venture was north of the border in Canada. In 1967, the company ran a pilot project in Ontario on "party plan" direct selling to consumers. Amway was doing it. So was Tupperware. Why not Upjohn?

The vehicle for this enterprise was The Kenral Company, bought by Upjohn in September 1969. The products — mainly housewares and domestic items — wore the Anora label. Perhaps one-third were Upjohn goods, such as Clocream, a hand cream. Another segment of the inventory amounted to Upjohn formulations manufactured by other firms. Kenral's waxes and floor polishes came entirely from outside sources. But the pilot venture did not work out, and in 1968 it closed. (Kenral, still an Upjohn subsidiary in Ontario, today sells ibuprofen.)

The corporation has also made acquisitions closer to its main-line pharmaceutical business. One such venture was the 1967 purchase of Laboratory Procedures, Inc., of King of Prussia, Pennsylvania, a clinical reference lab where technicians accumulated test results to aid physicians and hospitals in diagnosing patients' conditions. After operating this business for 14 years, company management realized that staying competitive would require a heavy infusion of capital investment, primarily for new high-tech machinery. In November 1981, Upjohn decided to sell Laboratory Procedures to SmithKline Corporation and to focus its resources on the personnel and capital needs of its basic businesses.

Today the Office of the Chairman determines strategies that will serve the company's long-term growth objectives and develops criteria for evaluating all Upjohn operations. According to chairman Parfet, "A business acquired by Upjohn must meet demonstrable, significant market needs, whether for a new seed or an unmet medical need. It should have a strong science basis, preferably biological or biochemical. Its products or service should have the potential to be global in use. In addition, it should be capable of establishing a research base within a reasonable time period and should possess the potential for interfacing with the other businesses. Broad though they are," he says, "these guidelines give considerable strategic focus to our plans for the future."

UPJOHN SCIENCE ENTERS THE AGE OF PLASTIC

It was a marriage that seemed to have been made in chemical engineers' heaven. Upjohn needed a house source of n-butyl-isocyanate, a vital component of its highly promising antidiabetes medication Orinase. In connection with its plastics manufacturing operation, The Carwin Company of North Haven, Connecticut, made the material that Upjohn wanted. In 1962 Upjohn acquired Carwin and integrated it into the Orinase supply pipeline.

Carwin's founder, Carl Van Winkle, founded his company in 1932 to manufacture perfume. He followed with interest the evolution of polymer chemistry which was taking place in Europe. By the early 1950s, the technology had emigrated to America to replace foam in bedding and cushioning. Carwin, improving its own science, was able in 1960 to build a plant in LaPorte, Texas, to produce polymeric isocyanate.

Meanwhile, Upjohn had already advanced its understanding of chemistry during the war. Keith H. Edmondson, who in 1986 retired as corporate vice president and general manager of Upjohn's Chemical Division and a member of the board of directors, took a job at Upjohn in 1949 and saw firsthand what it was doing. Back of Building 41, Upjohn had mastered deep-vat fermentation; it was on its way to ranking as the top steroid producer in the world. For all practical purposes, it had set up its own chemical business.

BETTER FOODS
FOR THE WORLD'S FIVE BILLION

The roots of the comparatively young Agricultural Division actually run deep in Upjohn's history. They reach back more than half a century to Richland Farms and a time when Dr. W. E. set out to turn that acreage into a depression-era work project. A corporate division with sales today of more than $400 million has grown from that soil. The division's harvest helps to feed not only this nation but also many peoples of the world. The founder would have welcomed that unexpected yield from his farm.

Dr. W. E. bought the 1,262-acre site in December 1931, and it has been added to over the years. Known as Upjohn Farms today, its 2,043 acres accommodate 17 animal facilities in 41 buildings, while corn, small grains, and hay crops grow on 1,300 acres and the rest is used for permanent pasture. In season, there are 150 beef cattle, more than 600 feedlot and dairy cows, perhaps 500 pigs, 200 sheep, and some 50 horses, as well. In one or another of the project areas, there is a vast sea of chickens (70,000 were bought in 1984). These animals and crops are studied by agricultural scientists with the aim of finding new products to protect their health and increase their yield of vital foods.

At the western flank of the property stands Building 190, the Agricultural Division's administrative hub. From it radiate programs that span the world, including seed development, poultry breeding, and animal health. Little more than two decades ago, the division's employment numbered less than 100. Today, 2,600 employees do the worldwide work of "Ag," as the division is known. Some produce vegetable seeds — 85 million pounds in 1985 alone grown on more than 75,000 acres located around the world. Others draw a yield of agronomic seeds (approximately 400 million pounds) from 200,000 total acres. The division's animal health unit, with a research and marketing staff of more than 350, develops and sells almost 100 different products — TUCO (for The Upjohn Company) feed additives for treating and preventing illness and promoting growth in cattle, hogs, and poultry; veterinary items, some for companion animals such as house pets and horses; and other packaged products for large animals. Cobb, Inc., a producer of broiler chicken breeding stock joined with Tyson Foods, Inc., in 1986 to serve the growing poultry market.

In less than 25 years, the Ag Division has matured into a major force in its industry.

The Beginnings

Use of W. E.'s farm as a source of food and labor for Kalamazoo's unemployed lasted throughout the Great Depression. By 1940 its more than 1,500 acres had become a diversified farm collective. Resident families raised feed crops, vegetables, cattle, sheep, horses, and ran a commissary on site. In the late 1930s, however, activity of a different sort developed at the farms.

Scientists had learned that hormonal substances in the urine of pregnant mares could provide relief to women suffering menopausal and fertility disorders. The Upjohn

Richland Farms, still under the auspices of the W. E. Upjohn Unemployment Trustee Corporation, acted in concert with Upjohn researchers to collect urine from the farm's stable of pregnant thoroughbred mares. They also contracted with other horse breeders in Michigan, Ohio, and Canada to obtain more pregnant-mares' urine. Upjohn then established a laboratory at the farms to do the necessary extractions for producing the primary hormonal products for humans, Gonadogen and Urestrin (see pages 76-77).

Meanwhile, veterinarian J. Lavere Davidson, the man who had begun his association with Upjohn by taking care of Malcolm Galbraith's St. Bernard, Prince, went afield to see if Upjohn's product line could be adapted to the needs of veterinarians. His survey produced positive answers, and he was developing a market when he was called to serve in World War II. At that, Upjohn's young veterinary program slowed to a walk.

(left) ECP, Upjohn's estrogen compound used to treat infertility or delayed fertility in cattle, was introduced in March 1952. It was the company's first product developed solely for veterinary use.

(izquierda) ECP, compuesto de estrógeno de Upjohn, usado en el tratamiento de la infertilidad o fertilidad tardía en el ganado, se introdujo en el mercado en marzo de 1952. Fue el primer producto de la compañía desarrollado únicamente para uso veterinario.

(à gauche) ECP, composé oestrogène d'Upjohn pour le traitement de l'infécondité ou des retards de fécondité chez les bovins, a été lancé en mars 1952. C'était le premier produit à destination exclusivement vétérinaire mis au point par la société.

（左）1952年3月、牛の不妊治療薬としてアップジョン社が開発したエストロゲン製剤ＥＣＰが発売された。これはアップジョン社が家畜用に開発した最初の製品であった。

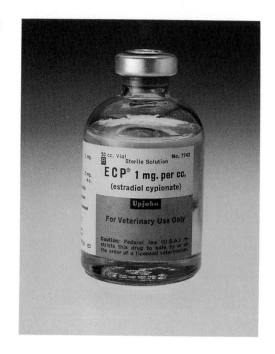

(right) Swine management is made easier with Upjohn animal health products, such as Lincomix, which helps fight mycoplasmal pneumonia in hogs. A strong research effort at Upjohn is working to bring new medicines and growth promotants to the food producers of the world.

(derecha) El manejo de los cerdos se hace más fácil con los productos Upjohn para la salud animal, como Lincomix, que ayuda a combatir la neumonía mycoplásmica en los puercos. Upjohn lleva a cabo un vigoroso esfuerzo de investigación para llevar nuevos medicamentos y estimulantes del crecimiento a los productores de alimentos en el mundo.

(à droite) L'élevage de porcs est facilité par l'utilisation des spécialités Upjohn, telles que le Lincomix, qui aide à combattre la pneumonie mycoplasmique chez les porcs. Les spécialistes de la recherche aux laboratoires Upjohn travaillent à la mise au point de nouveaux médicaments et de produits stimulant la croissance des animaux, à la portée des éleveurs du monde entier.

（右）豚のマイコプラズマ肺炎治療薬のリンコミックスなど、アップジョン社の動物薬のおかげで、養豚経営が容易になった。アップジョン社の強力な研究活動の成果として、世界の食糧生産者たちには、有望な新薬や成長促進剤がもたらされた。

Dr. Davidson resumed his work for Upjohn in 1946. He set about writing the literature for pharmaceutical salespeople to use in marketing human products to veterinarians for animal ailments. On April 1 that same year, Dr. Gordon Stocking, a new Doctor of Veterinary Medicine (D.V.M.) from Michigan State, was hired by the farms to ensure compliance with health standards in the herd of mares. Three years later, he joined Dr. Davidson as an Upjohn employee. Another veterinarian, Dr. Kenneth B. Haas, joined the company, and an Upjohn pharmaceutical salesman was added to head up the marketing effort. Slowly Upjohn's Veterinary Medicine Department took shape.

At first, animal health products were, without exception, merely Upjohn's human products relabeled. A number of bottles would be removed from production lots and a veterinary label would be glued on them; except for the label, veterinary and human versions of the product were exactly the same. Then research began to focus on specific animal conditions. One target was the traditional incidence of infertility or delayed fertility in cattle. Upjohn biochemist Arnold Ott found an answer — "ECP," or estradiolcyclopentylproprianate, a long-acting estrogen compound. On the market in March 1952, it was the first product that Upjohn developed solely for veterinary use.

Development of neomycin in 1952 gave Upjohn another advantage; it could now enter the field with a strong weapon against mastitis, or inflammation of the udder. The product, Teatube Neomycin, broke important ground when it was launched in September 1952. Up to then, no effective medication for mastitis had been available to veterinarians. Today, America produces more milk from half as many cows as it did 30 years ago; the control of mastitis has been an important factor in that increased milk supply.

When six years of research launched the human antibiotic Lincocin in 1965, Upjohn had also produced another awesome candidate for bettering animal health. Lincomix, a feed additive containing lincomycin, was a new weapon against animal disease. Today, 20 years later, it remains one of the most important products in its field.

Commitment to Agricultural Products

Midway through the 1950s, Upjohn formalized its commitment to the fledgling animal health business. In 1954, the company published its first issue of *Veterinary Scope*, "to be of service to the medical professionals in the field of veterinary medicine," according to its inaugural statement of purpose. Like its human medicine counterpart, *Scope* magazine, its pages contain articles written by respected veterinary and animal health experts, on "specific topics and specialized fields in the profession."

In 1956 a new Veterinary Research Section was created and charged with carrying on the development of animal health products. At the same time, an experimental station opened on 25 acres at the farms. One year later the company announced the formation of the Veterinary Division, with Dr. Gordon Stocking as its head, and began hiring veterinary sales reps, who were dispatched to detail 12,000 veterinarians countrywide. In 1956 there was only one full-time veterinary salesman. One year later the total stood at 20. Through the years the number has risen to more than 130.

Further commitment to agriculture was evidenced in the decision to purchase the land for Upjohn Farms. The company had been leasing most of the acreage it needed from the W. E. Upjohn Unemployment Trust. Some thought the property too expensive to buy, but eventually Donald Gilmore agreed with the logic that the company was not buying farmland, it was buying a research facility. The purchase was wrapped up in 1963.

About this time, Upjohn faced a marketing quandary. It had built some good relationships with veterinarians, and virtually all company sales in the animal health field were being made to these professionals. But some products, such as Albamix, a feed additive for turkeys containing the antibiotic albamycin, were aimed at farmers and livestock producers. And there surely were other ways of getting them to these users — through feed manufacturers, animal health distributors, and the like. The strategy would be tricky because veterinarians would not like to be selling products that were also available at lower prices from the feed store down the street.

Upjohn met this problem in 1961 by forming a new enterprise, Michigan Agriculture Company, to handle nonvet selling. This gave field sales reps some in-house competition, but nobody wanted to offend the legion of veterinarians. Time passed, and management decided to be open about it with the veterinarians, convincing them that there was a place for both the veterinarian and the feed store. Upjohn also decided to get rid of the name it had contrived for the business. Using "Michigan" in the name down South did not enhance product popularity, so in 1965 the products got the new designation of "TUCO."

Building the Ag Division

Ted Parfet had been president and general manager of Upjohn for two years when the decision was made to move the company's Ag program into a bigger league. Some of the competition was chipping off impressive market shares, and this would not do.

One part of the strategy called for lining up an experienced front-line manager. That man was David A. Phillipson, then at Eli Lilly and a veterinarian by profession. Phillipson had been at Lilly for eight years when he was approached about switching to Upjohn. The appeal was that the Kalamazoo company earnestly wanted to build an agriculture division. Phillipson joined Upjohn in 1964. Today, he is senior corporate vice president and general manager for the Agricultural Division and a member of the board of directors.

Not long after arriving, Phillipson reached a sobering conclusion. Several Ag products were not as good as they had appeared to be. "I found myself with an Ag Division on paper only," he says, "so we began to think about what else we could do to create a division that would have products that would interest the farmers." First they looked at fertilizer potentials but concluded that was not for Upjohn. But what about seeds? That made sense. As Phillipson explains, "That is something used every year and which everybody has to use."

Phillipson and his associates boiled down a list of 600 seed companies to seven "that looked like they would be feasible and large enough for us to attempt to acquire." Then calls were put in to the general managers of those companies. In 1968, after 12 months of dialogue and courtship, much of it done by Phillipson and Pete Parish, Asgrow Seed Company came into the Upjohn fold. The Ag Division was now off and running.

Quality Joined to Quality

The Asgrow Seed Company began in 1856 when Everett B. Clark of Orange, Connecticut, faced one of those eternal hazards of the farmer's life. His cabbage crop had gone to seed ahead of its time. Rather than plow it under, he thought, he'd sell the seed the next spring. It was a good idea — he earned $350. Everett Clark saw that selling seed had a bigger future than farming, so he set to work in this new furrow.

It was more than a century before Clark's creation assumed the name of the Asgrow Seed Company. By that time, in 1958, the Clarks had gone into pea production in Wisconsin, bean production in Michigan, more pea growing in the state of Washington, and other operations in California. Asgrow had also ventured into the international market, and in 1955 it had taken over an existing retailer, converting it into The Asgrow Florida Company. The business Upjohn bought in 1968 was already a respected name in many agriculture regions.

Today, Upjohn's Asgrow unit has two basic businesses: growing 33 different species of vegetable seed and growing five main species of agronomic-crop seed (corn, sorghum, soybean, sunflower, and alfalfa) as well as various forage mixtures. Overall, Asgrow markets the seed of 550 to 600 varieties of plants in nearly 60 countries. Year in, year out, it is engaged in a massive operation that contracts with farmers worldwide to produce seed for its processing plants.

Why should anyone be concerned about producing ever-better seed? Dave Phillipson answers, "There is a decreasing amount of agricultural resources on the planet. We're using up farmland and covering it with housing developments. At the same time, we have more and more people. If we're to survive on the planet, we'll have to produce more and more food from a given amount of agricultural land."

To meet this challenge, plants have been totally re-engineered. Today's corn and tomatoes differ completely from what they were in the 1940s and 1950s. Farmers used to set out some 12,000 corn plants per acre. Now they can put in anywhere from 20,000 to 24,000. The leaves on the new hybrid corn, for example, have been developed to be more upright than in earlier days; this allows more sunlight to penetrate between stalks.

Research-oriented Upjohn does not take for granted the range of difficulties in producing the increasingly better plants that vast populations must have for survival. Thus, Asgrow operates 14 testing stations in various parts of the world. At Asgrow Brazil's Vegetable Research Station, for example, the staff has had specific aims, such as adapting existing Asgrow products to the Brazilian fresh vegetable market or breeding tougher plants that are able to survive tropical growing conditions. Since one-third of Asgrow's business comes from nations outside the

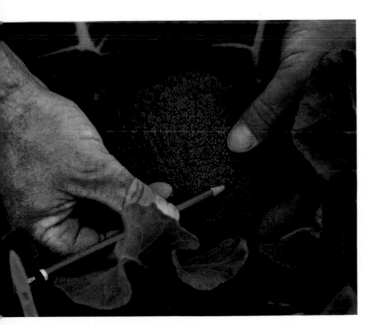

(left) TUCO (for The Upjohn Company) feed additives treat and prevent illness and promote growth in cattle, hogs, and poultry. This man is packaging Lincomix at the TUCO production facility in Orangeville, Canada. Lincomix is a cattle feed additive containing the antibiotic lincomycin.

(izquierda) Los aditivos alimenticios de TUCO (sigla de The Upjohn Company) tratan y previenen la enfermedad y promueven el crecimiento del ganado, los puercos y las aves de corral. Este hombre está empaquetando Lincomix en la instalación de producción de TUCO en Orangeveille, Canadá. Lincomix es un aditivo alimenticio para el ganado que contiene el antibiótico lincomycin.

(à gauche) Les additifs alimentaires TUCO (abréviation de The Upjohn Company) assurent le traitement et la prévention de maladies et sont des facteurs de croissance pour les bovins, les porcins et la volaille. Ici, conditionnement de Lincomix à l'usine TUCO d'Orangeville (Canada). Lincomix est un additif alimentaire bovin contenant un antibiotique, la lincomycine.

（左）TUCO社はアップジョン社向けに飼料添加剤を生産しており、この添加剤は、牛、豚、鶏の病気治療、予防、成長促進剤として使われている。カナダのオレンジビレにあるTUCO社の生産工場で、リンコミックスの包装作業中。リンコミックスは、抗生物質リンコマイシンを含有する牛用の飼料添加剤である。

(right) Vegetable breeding is a difficult process. Aside from the usual considerations of yield, disease resistance, response to climate, and ease of picking, the plant scientist also has to grade a hybrid on taste and appearance.

(derecha) El cultivo de vegetales es un proceso difícil. Aparte de las usuales consideraciones de rendimiento, resistencia a las plagas, reacción ante el clima y facilidad para la cosecha, el fitotécnico también tiene que calificar un producto híbrido por su gusto y apariencia.

(à droite) La culture de légumes est un procédé difficile. Hormis les considérations habituelles de rendement, de résistance aux maladies, d'acclimatation, et de récolte, le phytogénéticien doit aussi classer un hybride selon son goût et son apparence.

（右）野菜の品種改良は難しい。高い収穫量、病気に対する耐性、気候への順応性、収穫のしやすさといった通常の条件のほか、味や見栄えの点についても改良が必要である。

U.S., such considerations take on special importance. One important goal in all 14 Asgrow stations is to reduce the years it takes to come up with a new plant. Asgrow scientists have known for some time that they can bypass the use of seeds to speed things up. They know how to combine desired genes in a cell to make a hybrid, thereby eliminating six to 10 generations from the process of developing a new plant. On biennials like carrots or onions, that means a savings of 12 to 14 years.

With this heavy commitment to R & D has come important growth for Asgrow and the Ag Division. Asgrow has matured and expanded into very probably the largest seed supplier to food processors — to firms such as Del Monte Corp., Libby, McNeill & Libby, Inc., Campbell Soup Company, and The Pillsbury Company, maker of Green Giant brand vegetables. Its soybean program may be the best in agriculture anywhere. Its pea seed plant in Filer, Idaho, has the biggest output in the world (20 million pounds a year). Today, Asgrow employs 1,150, almost 170 of them full-time researchers. Abroad, it has branches in Japan, Spain, and Taiwan, as well as seven subsidiaries, in Argentina, Brazil, France, Germany, Italy, Mexico, and South Africa. For Upjohn, Asgrow sales have quadrupled since 1968, and the horizon is not yet in sight.

Chickens in Upjohn's Pot

In 1972, Asgrow headquarters moved from Orange, Connecticut, and took residence in Building 190 at the farms. Two years later, Upjohn made another step to broaden the scope of Ag, acquiring Cobb Breeding Corporation, a producer of chicken broiler breeders.

In the early 1900s, Harvard graduate Robert Cobb, Sr., had determined to be a dairy farmer. But after taking some agriculture courses, he found himself absorbed in the complexities of poultry breeding. One thing led to another, and in 1916 he founded in Concord, Massachusetts, a company to produce broiler breeder stock.

Cobb sold his chicks when they were a day old (ratio: 10-12 males to 100 females), so their heredity had to be managed precisely to yield an adult population which would produce well and yet effectively fight disease and stress. Careful mastery of genetic factors turned out to be the key to success. Cobb's approach worked, and by the 1970s, his company stood fifth in the world among producers of broiler breeder stock.

Upjohn bought the privately held Cobb Breeding Corp. in July 1974, and the scientific rationale remains solid today. Cobb and Upjohn shared a commitment to basic genetic research. Further, poultry consumption is skyrocketing.

In May 1986, Cobb, Inc., and Tyson Foods, Inc., the largest poultry integrator in the world, formed a 50-50 joint venture called Cobb-Vantress. This new company will allow expansion of the division's broiler breeder operations.

Adding O's Gold

For the farmer of the future, The O's Gold Seed Company offers several lessons of value on what it takes to build a successful venture, and on how a parent company's strategy can help it overtake the leaders in one important agricultural field.

Farmer J. Mansel Ocheltree of Parkersburg, Iowa, made a trial run in 1963 at producing single-cross hybrid seed corn. Skeptical neighbors finally agreed to try the seed the following year. They liked the results enough to ask Ocheltree to sell them more seed. Being an innovator at heart, he put together a crude seed processing plant in his barn. By 1966, annual sales added up to $20,000; Ocheltree was ready to hire his first two employees and put The O's Gold Seed Company into business. A decade later, O's Gold had a network of 2,500 dealers in 25 states and a balance sheet showing $12.5 million in annual sales. It ranked among the top ten seed companies in America and was still growing.

(left) This Asgrow seed sales representative in Indonesia must develop a strong relationship with his customer. The farmer's entire season's earnings may depend on his choice of seed variety, so the sales representative must help the farmer make an informed decision.

(izquierda) Este representante de ventas de Asgrow en Indonesia tiene que desarrollar una intensa relación con su cliente. Las ganancias del granjero durante toda la estación pueden depender de su selección de una variedad de semilla, de modo que el representante de ventas debe ayudar al granjero a hacer una acertada decisión.

(à gauche) Ce vendeur de semences Asgrow en Indonésie doit entretenir des contacts étroits avec sa clientèle. Les revenus et profits agricoles de toute une saison peuvent dépendre de son choix de variétés de semences. Le représentant doit aider l'agriculteur à faire un choix éclairé.

（左）インドネシアに駐在するアズグロー社のこのセールスマンは、顧客との間に強い人間関係をつくっておかなければならない。この農家のひとシーズンの収入のすべてが、種子の選択にかかっている。従ってセールスマンは、この農家の人びとが正しい決定を下せるように、しっかりした情報を提供しなければならない。

(right) In 1974 Upjohn purchased Cobb Breeding Corporation, the world's fifth largest producer of chicken broiler breeders. In 1986, Cobb and Tyson Foods, Inc., a poultry processing and marketing company, formed a joint venture to expand broiler breeder operations.

(derecha) En 1974 Upjohn compró la Corporación Cobb Breeding, el quinto productor de pollos para asar en el mundo. En 1986, Cobb and Tyson Foods, Inc., una compañía de preparación y venta de aves de corral, formó una empresa conjunta para expandir las operaciones de venta de pollos para asar.

(à droite) En 1974, les Laboratoires Upjohn ont acheté la firme Cobb Breeding, le cinquième producteur mondial de poulets. En 1986, Cobb et Tyson Foods, Inc., une firme de commercialisation du poulet, formèrent une entreprise commune pour augmenter la production de poulets à rôtir.

（右）1974年、アップジョン社は、世界5位のブロイラー飼育会社であるコッブ養鶏会社を買収した。1986年、鶏肉販売会社のタイソン・フーズ社とコッブ社は、ブロイラー関連事業拡張のために合弁会社を設立した。

(left) Asgrow Seed Company, a subsidiary of The Upjohn Company, is the world's largest producer of proprietary soybean products. Skilled plant breeders work year-round to produce soybean hybrids with vigorous yields and qualities such as disease or drought resistance.

(izquierda) La Compañia Asgrow Seed, una subsidiaria de la Compañía Upjohn, es la mayor fabricante mundial de productos patentados de frijoles de soya. Expertos horticultores trabajan todo el año para producir frijol de soya híbrido con vigorosos rendimientos y cualidades como resistencia a plagas y sequías.

(à gauche) La société Asgrow Seed, filiale d'Upjohn, est le premier producteur privé de soja au monde. Pendant toute l'année, des phytogénéticiens produisent des hybrides de soja, à haut rendement et de haute qualité, résistants à la sécheresse et aux maladies.

（左）アップジョン社の系列会社アズグロー社は、世界最大の大豆生産メーカーである。病気や旱ばつに強く、高い収穫性を持つ大豆の交配種を作るため、熟達した植物交配研究員たちが働いている。

(right) Upjohn HealthCare Services personnel often staff hospitals, clinics, health promotion programs, industrial health offices, rehabilitation centers, and nursing homes, filling in part-time where the demand occurs.

(derecha) Con frecuencia el personal de atención de salud de Upjohn presta servicios en hospitales, clínicas, programas de promoción de salud, oficinas de salud de las industrias, centros de rehabilitación y asilos de ancianos, desempeñando labores en jornadas parciales cuando hay mucha demanda.

(à droite) Le personnel d'Upjohn HealthCare Services est fréquemment employé par des hôpitaux, cliniques, programmes pour l'amélioration de la santé, services de santé dans l'industrie, centres de réhabilitation et maisons de repos pour des remplacements.

（右）アップジョン・ヘルスケア・サービスのスタッフは病院、診療所、健康増進プロジェクト、企業の健康管理室、リハビリセンター、養老院などで人手が必要になると、パートタイムで仕事を援助する。

By 1983 Upjohn's Ag Division had fixed O's Gold in its sights as what Dave Phillipson calls "a logical extension." Its sales were at the level of $25 million a year. Its product line was compatible with Asgrow's, and it had strength where the Asgrow line was weaker in the northern part of the country. As a second consideration, O's Gold had built a dealer organization of more than 3,000. Of further value to Upjohn, the O's Gold people had no soybean sales. "We are the largest seller of proprietary soybean seeds," Phillipson notes. "O's Gold would give us another outlet through its dealers for our soybeans, and we could pick up a product line with their corn."

The deal looked promising, so Upjohn made the purchase. Thus, it picked up 3,000 dealers who could now sell soybean seeds, and added not only a good product line but also two excellent production plants.

"The farmer," observes Dave Phillipson, "is the world's greatest gambler." If that is so, then the Ag Division to some extent gambles with him. It protects its bets by keeping one eye on the agricultural economy and the other on the competition. "The odds may not always be favorable," says Phillipson, "but the rewards are great. Being part of the worldwide process of feeding people is a wholly satisfying experience."

HOME CARE
FOR YOUNG AND OLD

On November 1, 1969, a number of important changes took place in Upjohn management. Gifford Upjohn retired as chairman; Donald Gilmore retired as vice chairman; Ted Parfet moved up from president to become chairman and chief executive officer; Pete Parish became vice chairman; and Bob Boudeman became president. The new management team also had a new business to develop. What is now known as Upjohn HealthCare Services was acquired the same month the executive changes took place.

Corporate Planning and Development, headed by Robert O. Stafford, Ph.D., had heard about the availability of an organization called Homemakers Inc. of Joliet, Illinois, a 43-office enterprise engaged mostly in housekeeping and nonhealth-related tasks. Stafford recommended that Upjohn acquire Homemakers, and Boudeman, president for just eight days, seized the opportunity. (Technically, the two corporations agreed to merge. Stafford was named chairman of Homemakers, a position he held until he retired in 1982. Dan Witcher succeeded Stafford.)

Boudeman, the spark behind other Upjohn moves to diversify, thrust his special kind of drive into this new venture. Budd J. Norris was brought on board in 1970 as Homemakers' vice president, moving up to the presidency half a dozen years later. Norris retired in 1983, and Upjohn hired David Cosgrove, veteran of 14 years' experience with IBM and, subsequently, executive director and chief operating officer of Kelly HealthCare Division, Kelly Services.

The timing was good for Upjohn's decision to enter the health care field. Society was entering an era when care for the homebound was to become increasingly important. Phasing out the housekeeping, babysitting, and other nonhealth aspects of the company, Upjohn has lifted Homemakers, renamed Upjohn HealthCare Services on September 1, 1978, to a dominant height. What had been a modest 43 offices have flowered into a field of 300 centers in 39 states, the District of Columbia, and seven Canadian provinces. UHCS has 233 employees in Kalamazoo and its two main regional financial centers in Tampa and Phoenix; 27 field managers; 1,560 full-time and part-time staff members at the 300 locations; and some 60,000 full-time and part-time "caregivers" who work in homes and institutions. Less than five years after the purchase, Upjohn turned this wholly owned subsidiary into the largest private full-service home care provider in the nation and the source of $182 million in corporate revenues in 1985, representing nine percent of Upjohn's overall sales in Human Health Care.

Without much question, what UHCS does is where a lot of the action will be for the foreseeable future in health care delivery. Count as one factor the public's effort to avoid potentially staggering costs of being in a hospital or nursing home. It is far less expensive to have a patient recuperate at home than in a hospital. Then, too, the American Medical Association has noted that "physicians generally agree that a majority of their patients are likely to prefer being in their own home and that improvement in their convalescence is likely to be more extensive and rapid."

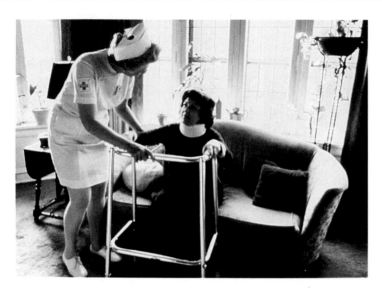

Another force is the cost-controlling system of "Diagnosis-Related Groups," or DRGs, federally mandated for Medicare patients. A schedule of illnesses has been set up to keep a lid on the expense of hospitalization. As an example, for a hernia operation on a 69-year-old male, the government has established a standard of 7.1 days stay in the hospital and a set rate of payment. If the patient remains longer, then the hospital must absorb the cost of care beyond 7.1 days. If the individual is discharged before 7.1 days are up, then the hospital may keep that part of the set Medicare fee not already spent. Hence, says Dave Cosgrove, "there is a considerable emphasis on getting people out of the hospital as quickly as possible." But the patient may still need care, perhaps an injection several times a week. "That is where we come in," says Cosgrove.

Social services operating in the 1980s and beyond will have to take into account another significant phenomenon: the graying of America. As of 1981, 48.2 million Americans were 55 or older. That translates into one out of every five citizens — 21 percent of the population, 29 percent of adults. By 1990, the over-55s will number almost 10 percent more than their total in 1980. By the year 2000, one person out of every eight will have reached the age of 65 or more. In its extensive May 6, 1985, cover story on what demographic trends are

doing to the American family, *Newsweek* concluded this way: "If a society can be judged by the way it treats its elderly, then we are not without honor — so far. But as we all grow older, that honor will demand an ever higher price." Once again, as Dave Cosgrove put it, this is where Upjohn HealthCare Service comes in — as well as all similar organizations. Cosgrove figures that the competition now numbers at least 10,000. In 1980, for example, Detroit had perhaps eight of these services; five years later, it had almost 100.

The Problems Confronting UHCS

Clearly, Upjohn arrived on the home health care scene at a golden time. But no one in management says that makes the job easy. This is a labor-intensive business (more than 60 percent of the expense goes for the caregivers) and margins are dramatically lower than in pharmaceutical sales. The price of the UHCS "product" can vary from town to town, and headquarters must rely on the local director to set that figure to reflect local competition. This can be complex. "We have in our computer more than 34,000 different pay and bill rates for all over the country," says Cosgrove.

In marked contrast to 1969, UHCS is now prepared to fill as many as 100 different types of jobs in the field. Aides who will cook meals and perform light housekeeping for the homebound; R.N.'s who specialize in chemotherapy or hyperalimentation or intravenous therapy or caring for ventilator-dependent children unable to breathe without help — these are only a few of the skills available in many UHCS locations. And the service will place its people in a wide range of settings. Often UHCS part-timers staff hospitals, clinics, health promotion programs, industrial health offices, rehabilitation centers, and nursing homes, filling in part-time where the demand occurs. And of course UHCS is an old hand at sizing up requirements of the patient at home, then assigning coverage that meshes with both technical and psychological needs.

For that patient, the cost of home care will fall well below comparable service in an institution. Currently, for example, UHCS personnel tend to 200 ventilator-dependent children at home. In a hospital, their care could run as high as $30,000 a month. At home, trained UHCS professionals do the same job for $12,000.

The Kalamazoo headquarters of UHCS mails out guidelines on various aspects of the business. This may mean specific lesson plans and study guides for in-service training courses. Or it could be assistance in Medicare matters; 120 of the service's locations are Medicare-certified — more than any of UHCS's competitors. In each of those offices, the nurses' credentials, their case records and notes, and their billing procedures have to pass inspection by a Medicare surveyor. UHCS in Kalamazoo helps the respective field locations meet the different standards set for certification.

The home office staff also stands behind the local representatives in their educational endeavors — in calling on hospitals, insurance companies, bank trust officers, ministers, community awareness programs, men's and women's groups, and, of course, doctors.

The Upjohn HealthCare Services nucleus in Kalamazoo can say with accuracy and pride that it serves more than 200,000 clients. In fact, however, it has no caseload at all. Rather, each local office has its list of patients and handles all the necessary administrative tasks such as hiring, training, managing, disciplining, and promoting. This decentralized approach has worked well because each office, like the UHCS professionals, is concerned with local people and problems; the office can tailor its services precisely to the area it serves. "This gives us a great opportunity to emphasize the 'care' in 'HealthCare,' " says Cosgrove. "And finally, that's what we're here for."

(left) Upjohn HealthCare Services has 300 offices in the U.S. and Canada, making it the largest private full-service home health care provider on the continent.

(izquierda) Los Servicios de Salud de Upjohn tienen 300 oficinas en los Estados Unidos y Canadá, haciendo de éste el mayor servicio privado completo de salud en los hogares, que se proporciona en el continente.

(à gauche) Upjohn HealthCare Services dispose de 300 bureaux aux Etats-Unis et au Canada, ce qui en fait la plus grande organisation privée de soins à domicile sur le continent américain.

（左）アップジョン・ヘルスケア・サービスは、アメリカとカナダに300 の事業所を持ち、北米で民間最大の、完全な訪問看護システムを持った機関である。

(right) Aides who will cook meals and perform light housekeeping for the homebound; R.N.'s who specialize in chemotherapy, hyperalimentation, intravenous therapy, or caring for ventilator-dependent children — these are only a few of the services provided by Upjohn HealthCare Services.

(derecha) Asistentes que prepararán la comida y realizarán menores quehaceres de casa para los internos en el hogar; enfermeras tituladas que se especializan en quimioterapia, hiperalimentación, terapia intravenosa o atención a niños dependientes por deficiencias respiratorias. Estos son apenas algunos de los servicios proporcionados por los Servicios de Salud Upjohn.

(à droite) Aide à domicile pour des patients immobilisés, personnel soignant spécialisé en chimiothérapie, hyperalimentation, injections intra-veineuses ou assistance respiratoire aux enfants sont quelques-uns des services rendus par Upjohn HealthCare Services.

（右）自宅療養の人のために食事作りや簡単な家事を手伝うホームヘルパー。化学療法、高栄養療法、ベンチレーター依存小児患者の看護などを専門とする州公認看護婦。これらはアップジョン・ヘルスケア・サービスによる種々のサービスの中の、ほんの数例である。

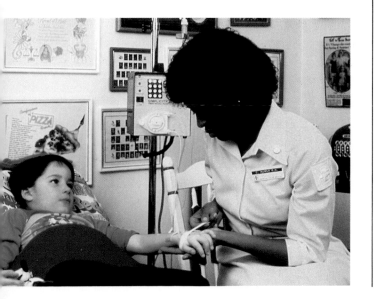

CHAPTER SIX

THE TRADITION OF A CONCERNED EMPLOYER

W. E. Upjohn greatly valued his employees. "Our primary resource is our people," he said early in the century. Dr. L. N. sensed that his uncle generally appreciated hard-working people. "He had a genuine concern," wrote Dr. L. N., "for the individual needs of employees who were raising large families, those who met with misfortune, and those who grew old." And from its very first years, the company made a practice of introducing benefits to help these individuals, to secure them against future need, make the workplace as happy as possible, and ease the worker's burden.

Clearly, that attitude has lasted at Upjohn. Today it is part of the company's character, and Upjohn continues to be a pleasant place to work. A recent survey of Upjohn pharmaceutical manufacturing employees underlined that feeling. Ninety-nine percent of the respondents said they rated Upjohn as a good or excellent place to work. Did the firm provide steady work and job security? Ninety-eight percent said it was "very good" or "pretty good" in those respects.

That Upjohn is a desirable place to work remains a clear and present reality for Employee Relations. One Saturday morning in March 1984, the department got all the proof it will ever need. Upjohn had decided to update its file of applications for jobs in production and maintenance.

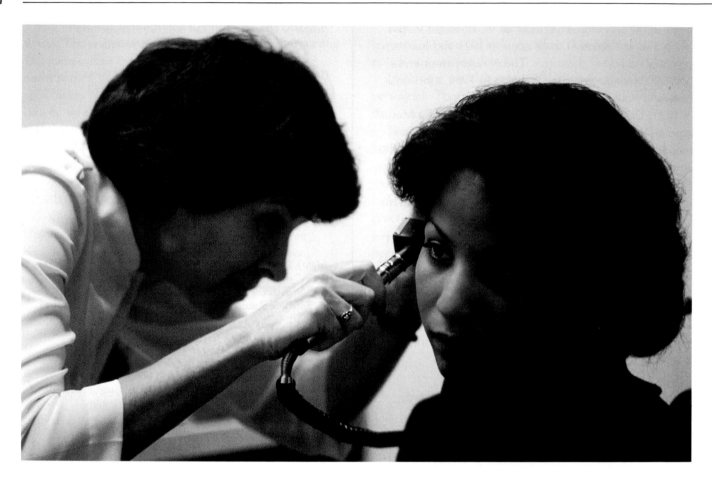

Upjohn's first personnel manager, Franklin Varney, was asked in 1938 to assess the shrinking workweek. It had not affected output, he asserted. "When we cut down from 50 to 45 hours, and from 45 to 40," he said, "we found that we were getting very nearly the same production per individual as we were when working longer hours, because of the workers' enthusiasm and desire for additional leisure. They made every effort to make each minute count."

1910: One day, Dr. W. E. asked Isabel Gillies, an assistant in Manufacturing (and later the second wife of W. E.'s brother James T. Upjohn), to give him a hand in Building 12. The founder wanted to offer free soup to employees who had brought their lunch with them. The setup was scarcely elaborate: two tables from the plant, two dozen bowls and spoons, and a soup kettle. That was the beginning of the company cafeteria. The following year it began operating regularly. Employees paid for food at cost, except for potatoes, which were free until 1953.

1915: The first formal benefit plan, probably worked out by Harold Upjohn, offered company-paid group life insurance. Each employee received a $1,000 policy after one year's service. After three years, the policy grew by $100 a year until it reached $2,000. The plan was improved as time went by. For employees without dependents, Upjohn made available in 1941 a company-paid $500 policy after one year's service. Employee-paid insurance was introduced, based on wage level; the company covered the premium cost above 50 cents a month per $1,000 of insurance. By 1946, these benefits had been modified so that both contributory and noncontributory insurance was offered after six months of employment, rather than one year.

1919: The first aid department was born as the "Red Cross Room" in Building 5. The company appointed Xanthippe E. Chase as the first nurse. In a few months Gertrude Bowen succeeded her, continuing for more than 20 years in that capacity. In 1936, Dr. George Caldwell transferred from Research and took up his duties as the first company physician. Today, the Occupational Health and Safety unit comprises approximately 60 employees, including registered nurses, physicians, a physical therapist, laboratory and X-ray technicians, safety specialists, a psychologist, industrial hygienists, toxologists, and medical records personnel. The Environmental Services unit conducts extensive health and safety surveys and environmental audits at Upjohn facilities around the world.

1937: The Personnel Department (renamed Employee Relations in 1975) was established formally, with Franklin Varney as manager. (Varney, a former minister, had been informally counseling employees since his hiring in 1913.) In this same decade of the 1930s, Upjohn hired its first safety engineer, T. Herbert Shenstone, four decades before the federal government launched its Occupational Safety and Health Administration.

1938: On October 18, the sixth anniversary of the founder's death, the first W. E. Upjohn Prize Awards were presented (see pages 85-86).

1941: This was a banner year in employee benefits. In the first place, time clocks, in use since the 1890s, were discontinued and replaced by a "Weekly Time Report." At the start of the year, a medical insurance plan went into effect. And the Upjohn Retirement Plan was activated on December 31. (Dental insurance was added to the medical plan on November 1, 1977.)

1944: Various production sections, acting on their own, had been allowing employees to take morning and afternoon rest periods. During this year, Upjohn decided to make rest periods a matter of policy.

During the decade of the forties, the organization of personnel services reached a higher level. Individuals with special training were assigned to handle the various functions — wage and salary administration, group insurance, training and publication, industrial health, safety, the cafeteria, recreation, and personnel research.

1950: The importance of the Personnel Department was acknowledged with the election of Harry Turbeville to the board of directors and his being designated vice president for personnel. Turbeville had been named personnel manager in 1945 on Franklin Varney's retirement.

The effective management of health, safety, and environmental issues is becoming increasingly important. As a result, Upjohn now conducts extensive health and safety surveys and environmental audits on a regular basis at its facilities around the world.

El manejo efectivo de las cuestinoes de salud, seguridad y ambiente es de gran importancia. Como resultado de esto, Upjohn realiza amplias encuestas sobre salud y seguridad, y audiencias sobre asuntos ambientales en forma regular en sus instalaciones en todo el mundo.

Une gestion efficace des problèmes de santé, de sécurité et d'environnement devient de plus en plus indispensable. Résultat : les Laboratoires Upjohn procèdent à des enquêtes et vérifications périodiques très poussées sur la santé, la sécurité et l'écologie dans tous ses centres à travers le monde.

社員の健康管理、安全確保、環境の整備といった課題は、ますます重要になってきている。アップジョン社では、世界各地の事業所で大規模な健康管理・安全管理の調査、環境査定を定期的に実施している。

As the department evolved, so did employee benefits. Today, for every dollar paid to each full-time employee in the U.S., almost 50 cents more go into benefit programs. Those programs include: group life insurance, medical and dental coverage, retirement, Christmas bonus, savings plan, and others; expenditures prescribed by law — unemployment insurance, workmen's compensation insurance, Social Security, and related plans; and salary expenses for time not worked — paid holidays, vacation, coffee breaks, and a reduced week in summers (workshifts end one-half hour earlier).

(top) Upjohn's Environmental Services unit conducts extensive health and safety surveys and environmental audits at all Upjohn facilities. These men are testing for toxic residue in a dismantled piece of production equipment.

(arriba) La Unidad de Servicios Ambientales de Upjohn lleva a cabo extensas encuestas sobre salud y seguridad, y audiencias sobre el ambiente en todas las instalaciones de Upjohn. Estos hombres están haciendo pruebas sobre residuos tóxicos en una pieza desmantelada de equipo de producción.

(en haut) Les services écologiques Upjohn mènent des enquêtes, des sondages et font des vérifications sur les conditions sanitaires, la sécurité et l'environnement dans tous les centres de production Upjohn. Ces techniciens examinent les résidus toxiques dans un équipement de production.

（上）アップジョン社の環境管理サービス部門は、会社のすべての事業所で、大規模な衛生管理、安全調査、環境査定を実施する。取り壊された製造機械の残留毒性検査を行なう。

(bottom) The Upjohn cafeteria in Building 18 was a center of company social life in the 1920s and 1930s. It was the scene of frequent lectures, dances, and parties after hours and was the prime meeting place for all Upjohn employees during the day.

(abajo) La cafetería Upjohn en le Edificio 18 era el centro de la vida social de la compañia en los años 20 y 30. Fue el sitio de frecuentes conferencias, bailes y reuniones sociales después de las horas de trabajo y fue el primer lugar de reunión para todos los empleados de Upjohn durante el día.

(en bas) La cafétéria Upjohn, au bâtiment No. 18, était un centre de loisirs et d'activité sociale dans les années 1920 et 1930. C'était le théâtre de conférences, bals et réceptions. C'était aussi le centre de réunion de tous les employés des laboratoires Upjohn, pendant la journée.

（下）1920年代と1930年代、18号館の社員食堂は、社員の社交場であった。勤務時間の終了後、ここで講演会、ダンスの会、パーティなどが開かれ、当時のアップジョン社員の交流の場となった。

With this parade of benefits came amenities in other forms. When Building 41 opened, one magazine called it a "Country-Club-Like Plant." Perhaps in some ways it was. The building offered its people a recreation lounge, three ample lunchrooms, an area for table tennis and shuffleboard, outside sports fields, and a health clinic that is virtually a modest hospital.

Organized Employee Growth

Employee Relations has changed a great deal since the day more than 70 years ago when Franklin Varney stepped in and opened a one-man shop. Up to then, Dr. W. E., then Dr. S. R. Light, had been the primary interviewers. By the 1930s, the approach had broadened: two people handled that job for Varney. When Varney retired in 1945, Harry Turbeville succeeded him as personnel manager. By mid-1954, Turbeville, as director of personnel, had an organization of four section heads and 18 individuals in subordinate roles (from employment, training, and publications to "Visitation and Counseling" and barber shop supervision).

That same year of 1954, Cass S. (Kit) Hough, Jr., now corporate vice president for employee relations, set out in his Upjohn career. At the time, the company had 4,419 people on its rolls; today Upjohn employs almost 7,200 men and women in the Kalamazoo area alone, with another 13,000 or more spread throughout the U.S. and various parts of the world. It should not be surprising that Kit Hough, who succeeded Harry Turbeville on October 1, 1970, has an organizational chart vastly more complex than Turbeville's of three decades ago. Not only is Upjohn five times bigger, but it functions in a world of intricate employment regulations of federal, state, and local origin, many legislated only in recent years.

One fact of life for Hough and his staff is that Upjohn has an annual turnover — for all reasons — of only about three percent. This means hiring annually, as a rule, no more than several hundred people for additions and replacements in jobs ranging from highly specialized scientific positions to entry-level posts in production and maintenance. "We try to build up a pool of candidates for each job," says Hough. "The size of the pool depends on our expected hiring needs."

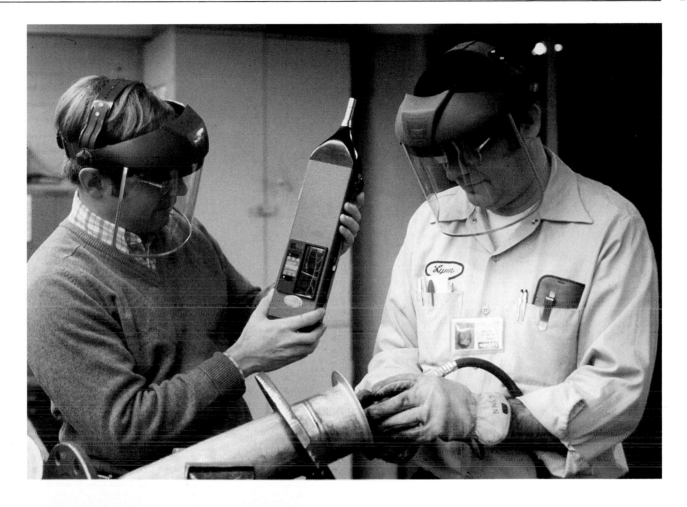

There's no question how Kit Hough feels about his employer. "It's a joy to work here," he says. "We care about our people, and the people care about the company. We appreciate the individual for being a contributor to our company."

Chairman Parfet has commented on the future employment needs of the company: "We will need an increasingly complex set of skills," he says. "To get them, we will need to recruit some personnel, but we will also be able to retrain our own people, giving them new skills and capabilities. We devote a lot of time and resources to continuing education and training."

Parfet echoes Hough's concern for the individual. "I want our employees to be proud that they are working for a blue-ribbon company committed to advancing itself and its employees to high levels of skill. And I want to back that up by showing our gratitude to the employees as individuals."

Minority Hiring

It was a number of years before the company made minority hiring a consistent practice. Upjohn hired few blacks in the early decades, but as with most of American businesses, no concerted effort was made to seek out minorities for employment. The situation changed after 1954 with the Supreme Court ruling against racial segregation in public schools. Personnel Director Harry Turbeville asked a number of Upjohn's executives whether the company should "deliberately" begin "gradually" to hire blacks? Turbeville "met with a favorable response on all sides," according to L. N.

Company interest in hiring blacks was heightened by a national tragedy, the assassination of Dr. Martin Luther King, Jr., on April 4, 1968. Shortly afterward, Vice Chairman Pete Parish spoke to fellow executives and all the operating directors. Upjohn needed to be more alert to the plight of minorities seeking work, he told them. Since then, Upjohn has worked hard at minority recruitment and hiring. The result has been that blacks and other minorities are now working in greater numbers and at higher levels throughout the company.

Upjohn and Collective Bargaining

At Upjohn, talk of unionization has come up now and then over a stretch of years. Back in 1941, the shipping department at the San Francisco branch office organized under the CIO and the union was in place for seven years. Generally, though, advocates of collective bargaining have been unsuccessful.

Harry Turbeville once addressed the union issue head-on, pointing out that many organizers assert that under union rules, employees are better off because they are treated the same. To that his response was, "We do not have rules and regulations to be sure that all people are treated alike at The Upjohn Company, because all people are *not* alike." And he made the further point that the firm chose to treat circumstances alike, not people. It strove for consistent response to the same circumstances, weighing each individual's situation.

In August 1966, an attempt was made to organize the plant on Portage Road, the first time this had been attempted since World War II. Ted Parfet, then president and general manager, sent an open letter to all employees. They could join if they wanted, he said, but

(left) The Upjohn Orchestra was a melodic feature in the cafeteria before World War II. The band often played at lunchtime and occasionally for dances in the evenings. The company provided the music sheets and the tuba — the rest was up to the amateur musicians.

(izquierda) La Orquesta Upjohn fue un aspecto melódico en la cafetería antes de la II Guerra Mundial. La banda a menudo tocaba a la hora del almuerzo y ocasionalmente para bailes por las noches. La compañía suministraba las piezas de música y la tuba — el resto quedaba a voluntad de los músicos aficionados.

(à gauche) L'orchestre Upjohn ajoutait un élément mélodieux à la cafétéria, avant la seconde guerre mondiale. L'orchestre jouait souvent à l'heure du déjeuner, et parfois animait les bals du soir. La compagnie donnait les partitions musicales et le tuba, et le reste était fourni par les musiciens amateurs.

（左）第二次大戦前、アップジョン・オーケストラは、社員食堂で美しい旋律をかなでたものであった。このオーケストラは、昼食時や社員のダンスパーティなどで演奏を行なった。会社が楽譜とチューバの経費を負担し、残りはアマチュア音楽家の社員たちが、それぞれ持ち寄った。

he did not think it was in their best interests. For 80 years, he pointed out, Upjohn had provided steady, uninterrupted work, good salaries, and good working conditions. It had developed benefits programs "among the best in industry." The company intended "to maintain this record," achieved "without necessity of any third party to bargain for employees."

That feeler fizzled, and no appreciable attempt to unionize in Kalamazoo has been made since. In North Haven, there is a union which was in place when The Carwin Company was purchased in 1962. It still exists at the Fine Chemicals facility, a nonaffiliated, independent union covering about two-thirds of the employees. Of course, Upjohn installations in other countries do have unions. Often they reflect standard industrial practice in a given nation. In Belgium, for example, more than 80 percent of all workers — including those at Upjohn's Puurs plant — are organized into unions on the basis of political party.

(right) This Upjohn employee at the Takasaki, Japan, production facility enjoys his lunch in somewhat different fashion than other Upjohn employees. Japanese workers traditionally pack their own lunch or have it catered, unlike U.S. employees who dine on food prepared in company cafeterias.

(derecha) Este empleado de Upjohn en la instalación de producción de Takasaki, Japón, disfruta de su almuerzo en forma algo diferente que otros empleados de Upjohn. Los trabajadores japoneses tradicionalmente llevan su propio almuerzo o lo sirve un proveedor de comidas, a diferencia de los empleados en Estados Unidos, que comen la comida que preparan las cafeterías de la compañía.

(à droite) Cet employé des Laboratoires Upjohn, au centre de production de Takasaki (Japon), déguste son déjeuner d'une façon différente de ses collègues de travail. Les travailleurs japonais ont l'habitude de préparer leur propre déjeuner ou bien ils en passent la commande, alors que les ouvriers américains prennent leur déjeuner à la cafétéria de l'entreprise.

（右）日本の高崎市にあるアップジョン社の包装工場の社員たちは、会社が運営する社員食堂で昼食をとるアメリカのアップジョン社社員たちと違って、自宅から弁当を持ってきたり、仕出しの弁当をとったりする。

The longstanding philosophy of trust in and respect for the individual employee, so familiar in the company's Kalamazoo facilities, also guides the policies of Upjohn throughout the world. Each of the worldwide locations has adopted specific employee practices in keeping with overall company policies. At the same time, those practices reflect legal and societal needs and customs at each site.

Concerned Community Member

On May 3, 1985, Upjohn made big headlines in its hometown press in a way that any corporation might envy.

The bold headline of the *Kalamazoo Gazette* spanned five columns: "Upjohn gives $2 million for math center." To mark its centennial, the firm pledged a two-part gift to set up an advanced math and science center for top students from 14 nearby public and private high schools. The first $1 million would renovate the old Kalamazoo Central High School, develop curriculum, and buy lab equipment. The second increment would endow the

programs of the new center, which enrolled its first students in September 1986.

The Upjohn of the 1980s, in supporting the math-science center, is doing no more than Dr. W. E. would have expected, or, for that matter, no more than he did at various times as city alderman, president of the Kalamazoo Hospital Association, longtime supporter of local churches, leader for change in the local government's structure, mayor, and philanthropist.

The founder supported his community deftly and with a soft pedal, a practice carried on by those who have come after him. "We have always tried to maintain a low profile," says former Vice Chairman Pete Parish. "We have not tried to throw our weight around to get people to do something because we felt it was a good idea."

Did older generations of management lecture to their apprentices about getting involved in supporting the community? It's not likely. Says Parish, "I don't ever remember anybody sitting you down and saying that this is something that you are expected to do." Nevertheless, Donald Gilmore, Gifford Upjohn, Ted Parfet, Bob Boudeman, Parish, and others knew the tradition and

believed in it; they led whenever possible and welcomed having subordinates do likewise. *Upjohn people serve.*

Upjohn and Its People Contribute

As a corporate citizen in Kalamazoo County, Upjohn stands taller than its downtown Research Tower. You may be a long way from Henrietta Street, but you still know the company is there.

Upjohn's 1985 payroll for its nearly 8,000 Kalamazoo-based employees was $352 million. The company buys a mound of goods and services — $97.3 million worth in '85. Its 1985 tax payments included $11.6 million on local property and $8.7 million to the state of Michigan (it also withheld $13.2 million in state taxes for those who work in Kalamazoo).

The corporation only does what other businesses must do in issuing these checks. But it also has long believed that it must go further as a citizen. Thus, it made worldwide charitable contributions in 1985 of $4.5 million. Of that amount, nearly $1.3 million was committed to nonprofit agencies in the Kalamazoo area — health and welfare organizations, schools and colleges, and cultural and civic agencies.

These contributions haven't always been a habit for Upjohn. Early in the century, institutions did not appeal to business very often for financial support. Still, Upjohn helped a local hospital, and Dr. W. E. did more than his share on his own. Then, when the Community Chest opened its door in 1926, the pattern of corporate contributions gradually turned into an annual routine.

(left) The Upjohn Company fielded this ten-man basketball team in two Kalamazoo Industrial Leagues in 1930. The squad, composed of production and research employees, won 14 out of 15 starts and more than doubled their opponents' scores.

(izquierda) La Compañía Upjohn inscribió este equipo de basquetbol de diez hombres en dos Ligas Industriales de Kalamazoo en 1930. El equipo, integrado por empleados de producción e investigación, ganó 14 de 15 juegos y anotó más del doble que sus contrarios.

(à gauche) Les Laboratoires Upjohn, en 1930, lancèrent cette équipe de basket-ball de dix membres dans deux Ligues industrielles et sportives de Kalamazoo. L'équipe, formée d'employés des centres de production et de recherche, remporta 14 des 15 premiers matches du championnat, et marqua deux fois plus de points que ses adversaires.

（左）1930年、アップジョン社はこの10人編成の男子バスケットボール・チームを、カラマズーの2つの実業団リーグに送った。生産部門の社員と研究者たちからなるこのチームは、15戦中14勝し、対抗チームの合計得点数の2倍の得点を獲得した。

(right) Upjohn's first women's softball team, organized shortly after the Upjohn workweek was reduced to 40 hours in 1931, provided an after-hours athletic outlet and a time for socializing for these employees. In the 1930s single women made up much of the production force.

(derecha) Primer equipo de softball femenino, organizado poco después de que se redujera la semana de trabajo en Upjohn, 40 horas en 1931; ésto proporcionó la oportunidad de practicar atletismo y la ocasión de establecer lazos sociales entre los empleados. En los años 30 la mujer soltera constituía gran parte de la fuerza de producción.

(à droite) La première équipe féminine de soft-ball, formée à l'époque où la semaine de travail fut réduite à 40 heures en 1931, était un foyer d'athlétisme et un lieu de rencontre pour ces employées des laboratoires Upjohn. Dans les années 1930, les femmes célibataires formaient une grande partie de la force de production.

（右）1931年、アップジョン社の勤務時間が週40時間に短縮された直後、女子ソフトボール・チームが結成された。終業後、社員たちはこうしたスポーツを通じて交流した。1930年代、独身の女性たちは生産現場の一大戦力であった。

(left) Table tennis, shuffleboard, cafeterias, lounges, a picnic area — even a movie theater and golf driving range — these were some of the amenities the company offered its employees with the opening of Building 41.

(izquierda) Tenis de mesa, plataforma para juego de tejo, cafeterías, salones sociales, un área para paseos campestres y aún una sala para cine y teatro y un mini-camp para golf — estos eran algunos de los entretenimientos que la compañía ofreció a sus empleados con la inauguración del Edificio 41.

(à gauche) Tennis de table, jeu de palets, cafétéria, salon, aire de pique-nique, et même une salle de cinéma et un mini-golf, tels sont les agréments que la société Upjohn offre à ses employés, depuis l'inauguration du bâtiment No. 41.

（左）卓球、シャッフルボード、カフェテリア、遊園地、映画館、ゴルフ練習所・・・41号館の完成と同時に、アップジョン社は社員のために、こうした施設を整えた。

(right) Soap, bread, and canned goods were sold to Upjohn employees and the public alike at the commissary located at the Upjohn Richland Farms in the 1930s. Crops and livestock raised at the farms were also offered for sale at cut-rate prices.

(derecha) Jabón, pan y artículos enlatados se vendían a los empleados de Upjohn y al público también en el almacén situado en las Haciendas de Upjohn en Richland, en los años 30. Los productos de la tierra y el ganado criado en las haciendas también se ofrecían a la venta a precios reducidos.

(à droite) Savon, pain et conserves étaient vendus aux employés de la société Upjohn et au public à la ferme de Richland, dans les années 1930. Cultures et bétail, produits de la ferme Upjohn de Richland, étaient mis en vente à des prix réduits.

（右）1930年代には、アップジョン社のリッチモンド農場に併設された売店で石鹸、パン、缶詰などが社員や地域住民に売られた。農場で収穫された作物や飼育された家畜も、安い価格で売り出された。

Over time, the corporation has worked up a definition of its role as a community citizen. First of all, Upjohn believes it should be successful in business so that it can keep on contributing in a positive way to the area's economy. Secondly, it should continue supporting nonprofit organizations and public service agencies that play key parts in community health and welfare. And, finally, Upjohn should respond reasonably to primary social issues touching the lives of its fellow citizens.

But the company's statements would look cold and artificial if the *people* of Upjohn did not also do their bit. Employees could easily fall back on variations of that old dodge, "I gave at the office." But in and around Kalamazoo and Portage, Upjohn men and women, in various ways, give again and again. The *Overflow* of more than 50 years ago said that Dr. W. E. "gave of himself with practically every gift." So do the offspring of his enterprise more than two generations later. Says Pete Parish, "Everybody has been involved as a citizen, but not necessarily as a corporate representative. We have had people on the Kalamazoo Commission, the Portage City Council, the county board of commissioners, the boards of local hospitals. Many have served on education committees and school boards."

During his vice chairmanship at Upjohn, Parish came more and more to be the corporate point man in top-level dealings with the community. An intriguing situation arose when Upjohn gave a sum of money to the city of Portage to help it undertake municipal planning for the year 2000 — the beginning of what became known as the Portage 2000 project. The leadership of Kalamazoo decided to set up a similar program, and with the help of Upjohn people and dollars, that planning effort — Kalamazoo 2000 — expanded to encompass the entire Kalamazoo County. Then-Vice Chairman Pete Parish and Charles Mangee, corporate vice president for public relations, served on the project's steering committee. As an outgrowth of Kalamazoo 2000's final report, a new committee, Kalamazoo Forum, was formed to help affected communities and appropriate municipal agencies carry out the broad recommendations developed by Kalamazoo 2000. In late 1985, Forum volunteers were analyzing the problems of solid waste management and current tax resources available within the county.

At another point, Parish and Gifford Upjohn took part in the area's lengthy consideration of whether a new regional airport should replace the local fields separately serving Battle Creek and Kalamazoo. The Upjohn representatives did not duck the hard questions. "We didn't actively oppose the regional program," recalls Parish, "but we stated that it didn't make a lot of sense to add a third airport, and the community felt that way also." The concept of a regional field, failing to stir up enthusiasm, eventually died.

What if top management and Upjohn employees serving on a local board wind up on opposite sides of an issue? "It *does* put them in an awkward position," Ted Parfet recognizes. "But it doesn't bother us if they vote against the company. The company has never taken measures against anybody who might take a position in the community contrary to what our corporate position is. We don't do things that way."

What Upjohn *does* do — with corporate contributions and with the attentive labor of so many employees — is help the area around it grow and prosper as much as possible.

Service on a Wider Front

In late 1904, W. E. Upjohn began to construct the framework of another Upjohn tradition: tending to the needs of the world beyond the banks of the Kalamazoo River. He had begun to grapple with the tough question of protecting depositors against bank failures. His pamphlet on *Bank Deposit Insurance* was his answer. Once again, Dr. W. E. was ahead of his time. It wasn't until 1933 that the nation finally had a Federal Deposit Insurance Corporation. Its formula differed only in minor ways from the one proposed by Dr. Upjohn three decades earlier.

Whether he knew it or not, the founder was, by his example, urging his successors to avoid provincialism. They have accepted that precept. In trade affairs, they have taken leadership roles in the key associations. Donald Gilmore headed the board of the American Drug Manufacturers Association. Gifford Upjohn served as president of the Pharmaceutical Manufacturers Association (PMA). Ted Parfet is a former director of the International Federation of the PMA and a former PMA board chairman. Dr. Hubbard chaired the PMA board in 1980-81. Larry Hoff has invested his energies in many trade assignments: chairman of the National Foundation of Infectious Diseases, chairman of the National Pharmaceutical Council, and vice president of the Proprietary Association. He will become PMA chairman in 1987.

Upjohn executives have also put time into other forms of national commitment. Vice Chairman Dr. Ted Cooper has been a consultant on health care procedures to U.S. Defense Secretary Caspar W. Weinberger, and is a member-at-large of the American Red Cross board of governors. Dr. Hubbard was a member of the Institute of

Medicine of the National Academy of Sciences and of the Science Board of the National Science Foundation.

A wider spectrum of corporate giving has also evolved. Often, donations go far from Kalamazoo to improve the well-being of those in distant regions of the world. Years ago, as a dominant vitamin-maker, Upjohn started shipping vitamins to leper colonies, and cod liver oil was sent to child welfare agencies as a supplement to the diets of the disadvantaged. Between 1982 and 1985, the company sent nearly one million dollars to agencies concerned with aiding drought-stricken nations of Africa. The corporation's donations of seeds to these same countries exceeded a total value of more than one-half million dollars from 1981 to 1985.

Few in the Western world in early 1983 knew how desperate the famine in Ethiopia was getting to be. Yet that year, as it had every year since 1977, Upjohn sent thousands of pounds of seeds to help ill-fed populations, including, through a religious organization, several tons of seeds to Ethiopia. An official observer estimated that Upjohn's gift fed 122,000 people in Ethiopia.

Today, the reach of the 100-year-old Kalamazoo drug-maker spans a far larger community than ever before, and its service role in the nation and the world will continue to take a variety of shapes. Along with its peers in the pharmaceutical industry, Upjohn will keep on singling out remaining areas of medical need, then designing compounds to meet them. In this corporation's lifetime, the level of health in the world has improved remarkably, in part because drug firms have provided physicians with the products that relieve suffering and cure disease.

Those who have been leaders of Upjohn in recent times believe that other corporate activities must expand in the future. These have to do with the company's participation in a vital world industry and in the swiftly changing field of health care delivery, and with its position as what former Vice Chairman Pete Parish calls "an ambassador of our nation."

One facet of this activity involves working to improve the relationship between the industry and government. At present, society has nowhere else to turn for its new medicines, except in restricted situations to the National Institutes of Health and to academia. But these two sectors can only provide discovery. Development must be done by industry. It alone has the means to turn discovery into product.

W.E.'s Depression-era farm project aimed at providing work and food for Kalamazoo's jobless. It has evolved into a private research foundation which studies the economic and social indicators relating to employment. The W.E. Upjohn Institute for Employment Research is based in Kalamazoo.

El proyecto de finca de William Erastus durante la época de la Depresión, encaminado a facilitar trabajo y comida a los desempleados de Kalamazoo. El mismo ha evolucionado en una fundación privada de investigación que estudia los indicadores económicos y sociales relativos al empleo. El Instituto W. E. Upjohn para Investigaciones sobre Empleo tiene su sede en Kalamazoo.

Le projet agricole de W.E. Upjohn, mis en oeuvre durant la crise de 1929, avait pour but de fournir du travail et de quoi manger aux chômeurs de Kalamazoo. Ce projet est devenu une fondation privée consacrée à la recherche sur les indicateurs sociaux et économiques de l'emploi. L'Institut W.E. Upjohn pour la recherche sur l'emploi a son siège à Kalamazoo.

大恐慌時代のW．E．アップジョンの農場プロジェクトは、カラマズーの失業者に仕事と食料を与えることだった。このプロジェクトは、その後、雇用に関する経済・社会指標を研究する民間研究機関として生まれ変わった。いま、W．E．アップジョン雇用研究所（上）としてカラマズ に現存している。

Dr. Cooper favors modification of the sometimes adversarial relationship between drug firm and government. "With technical changes and challenging social priorities ahead," he observes, "we will have to be much more willing early on to explore ways of making regulatory requirements more responsive." Inevitably, that will mean conferring more closely with the regulators. Says Dr. Cooper, "As best we can, we need to develop a greater sense of cooperation."

Thus, just as Upjohn urges its headquarters employees to thrust themselves into the affairs of the Greater Kalamazoo area, the company's leaders face a time of becoming more involved in national activities and in the world. As Ted Parfet sees it, "The general atmosphere today requires the input of managers of business so that things will be better understood and so that we can accomplish what's necessary not just for individual corporations but for the nation as a whole."

Upjohn's president, Larry Hoff, has a parallel view of where Upjohn is and where it's headed in this respect. "We are becoming increasingly an activist organization," he says. "We can't just go about our own affairs anymore. Our business is *everybody's* business." In the past, Upjohn has spoken out on the industry's role in society and on what Dan Witcher describes as "the very real contributions" to human health that pharmaceutical companies have made. There is every reason to believe that these activities will increase in tempo and on an international scale.

Hoff says that Upjohn's policy of what he calls "good global citizenship" has turned into an integral part of the firm's international operations. That kind of citizenship, he predicts, will expand to include "greater involvement with governments, industry, and international agencies and interest groups."

Upjohn stays in touch with the World Health Organization (WHO), the European Economic Community, and the Organization for Economic Cooperation and Development. As an outgrowth Upjohn has provided its facilities to help train Third World health officials in pharmacy and quality control. Through WHO, it has distributed an audiovisual resource catalog and has offered the anti-inflammatory corticosteroid prednisolone at a special price. Upjohn is also working with WHO to assess compounds that might treat or eradicate "river blindness," a disease devastating millions in developing nations. In addition, the company has sponsored symposia on medical science for Third World health personnel, offered health education poster programs in Kenya and Peru, and helped to build health care infrastructures in The Gambia and Sierra Leone so that drugs can reach patients who need them.

"The health care problems faced by the Third World are immense," says Hoff. "It will take this sort of cooperation if we are to continue with the kinds of gains made in international health care earlier this century."

The Upjohn Company has long been a good citizen in its hometown of Kalamazoo. In its second century, the corporation will push forward with the sensitive, yet essential task of serving as a good citizen of the world.

Following the example of founder W.E. Upjohn, The Upjohn Company and its employees have often contributed to the cultural, educational, and social well-being of Kalamazoo. One example is the Donald S. and Genevieve Gilmore Institute of Arts opened in 1961 in downtown Kalamazoo.

Siguiendo el ejemplo de su fundador W. E. Upjohn, la Compañía Upjohn y sus empleados han contribuido con frecuencia al bienestar cultural, educativo y social de Kalamazoo. Un ejemplo es el Instituto de Artes Donald S. y Genevieve Gilmore, abierto en 1961 en la ciudad de Kalamazoo.

Suivant l'exemple du fondateur, W.E. Upjohn, la société Upjohn et ses employés ont souvent contribué à la vie culturelle, éducative, et sociale de Kalamazoo. Voici par exemple le "Donald S. and Genevieve Gilmore Institute of Arts", fondé en 1961 au coeur de Kalamazoo.

創立者W．E．アップジョンにならって、アップジョン社とアップジョン社の社員たちは、カラマズー市の文化、教育、社会福祉にさまざまな貢献をしている。その一つが、1961年カラマズー市街地に開館したギルモア美術館である。

CHAPTER SEVEN

MARCH TOWARD A NEW CENTURY

There's a certain fascination in looking back at how a revolving pan of pills in rural Hastings, Michigan, grew over 10 decades into a worldwide enterprise. But a centennial birthday challenges a corporation to look ahead, not just at the past.

The Upjohn Company can look forward with a confidence built on the solid foundations of a century's achievements. At this writing, Upjohn is a $2 billion company. Construction totaling more than $180 million has been planned to assure continued growth. Every year Upjohn ranks first or second among leading drug-makers in its investment in pharmaceutical R & D, measured as a percentage of sales. The market curves of Xanax and Halcion have been climbing steadily. Sale of the polymer chemical business has enabled the firm to concentrate more of its resources on the primary human health care businesses. New drugs are in the wings, including one, topical minoxidil solution, which, says Vice Chairman Cooper, "could be an enormous commercial success."

In short, for Upjohn there are rich promises of things to come. "Not since our founder's discovery of the friable pill," says President Larry Hoff, "have there been as many opportunities as there are today."

(top) Through molecular biology, cell biology, and biopolymer chemistry, Upjohn's Biotechnology unit seeks to unlock the mysteries of life at its most basic genetic level. This researcher works under a laminar air-flow hood in the unit's cell biology research section.

(arriba) Mediante la biología molecular, la biología celular y la química biopolímera, la unidad biotecnológica Upjohn procura descubrir los misterios de la vida en su nivel genético más básico. Este investigador "biotécnico" trabaja bajo la cubierta de un flujo laminar aéreo en la sección de la unidad para investigaciones sobre biología celular.

(en haut) Par l'application de la biologie moléculaire, de la biologie cellulaire, et de la chimie biopolymère, l'unité de biotechnologie Upjohn cherche à élucider certains mystères de la vie, au niveau du code génétique. Ce chercheur travaille sous une hotte à aération laminaire à la section de recherche en biologie cellulaire.

（上）分子生物学、細胞生物学、バイオポリマー化学の技術を使って、アップジョン社のバイオテクノロジー部門は遺伝子のレベルで、生命の秘密を解き明かす研究を行なっている。細胞生物学研究グループの研究者。

(bottom) These two researchers in the Biotechnology unit's Molecular Biology section are studying a sequencing gel of a DNA molecule — the molecular basis of heredity in many organisms.

(abajo) Estos dos investigadores en la sección de Biología Molecular de la unidad de Biotecnología, están estudiando un gel en secuencia de una molécula DNA — la base molecular de la herencia en muchos organismos.

(en bas) Ces deux chercheurs de la section de biologie moléculaire de l'unité biotechnologique examinent un gel de séquence pour une molécule d'A.D.N-source moléculaire de l'hérédité dans beaucoup d'organismes.

（下）バイオテクノロジー部門分子生物学研究グループのこの２人の研究員は、多くの有機物の遺伝の基本分子 — ＤＮＡの連鎖ゲル — を研究している。

THE CHALLENGES BEFORE THE DRUG-MAKERS

If prospecting for these opportunities is to be a worthwhile exercise, it cannot be done in a vacuum. Where Upjohn goes in the years ahead will depend greatly on what happens in the world in which it works and serves.

Certain factors stand out. For one, more Americans are living longer. In 1940, less than seven percent of the nation was 65 or older. By 1990, about 13 percent will have reached that age level — and the population will be almost twice the size of half a century ago. That holds significant implications for a company such as Upjohn with its longstanding commitment to providing for the health care of human beings, elderly or otherwise.

Today, comments about trends in health care are everywhere. Dr. Richard Beinicke of the Harvard Community Health Plan states that 1983 health expenditures of more than $1,500 a person were nine times larger than those of 1965. By 1990, he projects, these payments will be as much as $3,000 per citizen. By then, more than three-quarters of our hospitals will have joined multihospital systems, and enrollment in health maintenance organizations (HMOs) — some 12.5 million in 1983 — will have hit almost 50 million. More physicians will join group practices, and home health care will continue growing at 13 to 20 percent a year. Dr. Beinicke concludes, "Health care is in the midst of a revolution . . . which will accelerate into the future."

Until recently, the costs of such care climbed seemingly without restraint. Then, individuals and institutions dug in their heels to fight the trend. Their resistance and its implications, says Larry Hoff, are "*the* major considerations for the pharmaceutical industry's immediate future." Unquestionably, the pressure for "cost containment will persist," he forecasts.

One harbinger of this change was the expansion of the generic drug industry. Spinning out of that phenomenon, Hoff says, are the makings of a "two-tier industry with innovators in one group and a large number of generic manufacturers in the other segment competing fiercely on the sole basis of price." By the end of this decade the patents on most of the top 50 ethical drugs will have lapsed. Hence, he adds, they will be "multisource items — their exclusivity gone." With a patent limit of 17 years

on products that take seven to 10 years to bring to market, the innovative drug manufacturers have only a few years in which to try to recoup development costs. Meanwhile, generic producers, entering the market after some other firm created the products originally, are able to sell compounds at lower prices that do not include the costs of discovery and development.

In that case, who will keep on spending the nearly $100 million and the time it takes to develop a new compound? Upjohn, for one. It intends to continue being one of the innovators, according to Hoff. But, he adds, "I fear that as the price for new drug development rises, the number of companies that are willing to make such risk decisions may decrease."

Product marketers see other unsettling trends in distribution patterns. HMOs, multiplying fast, are banding together to buy pharmaceuticals by bid. More retail pharmacists go in for collective purchases. Consumer buying of nonprescription drugs at discount prices through mail-order houses is increasing. Each of these developments underlines the dilemma of a nation struggling to restrain the costs of tending to its sick and infirm citizens.

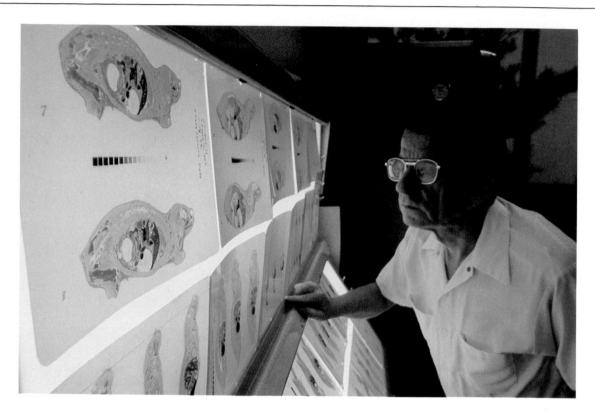

Meanwhile, the people of the nation and the world have benefited from extraordinary improvements in medicine and drug therapy, advances that surely rank among the outstanding accomplishments of the twentieth century. Time and again, cures have been discovered, perfected, and put into use. But disease can be perverse. Just as infantile paralysis succumbs to a vaccine, other conditions arise, awakening renewed alarm on all sides. In this year of Upjohn's centennial, many disorders still come under the heading "No Known Cure." At the same time, too many millions live on the threshold of starvation or at least severe malnutrition.

To stand up to the challenges on the road ahead, Upjohn cannot have a "business as usual" frame of mind. Vice Chairman Ted Cooper puts the issue squarely. "A rigid institution is an institution condemned to death," he says. "We need to remain flexible." Upjohn must also be ready to take responsible risks — such as in the young, exciting field of biotechnology. There *are* risks in it, but, adds Chairman Parfet, "I think it holds high promise."

As this complex work proceeds, Upjohn's senior management must be prepared to take on larger responsibilities in both the surrounding community and the world. Chairman Parfet makes this clear. "If industry leaders want a reasonable climate in which to operate and to make their case clearly," he believes, "then they are going to have to be more involved. I foresee that as something particularly applicable to Upjohn's top management. We will have to become even more involved than we have in the past."

But of all the challenges confronting Upjohn's leadership, none looms larger than having to come up with another Phenolax, another Medrol, another Motrin. Larry Hoff has a sanguine view of what three of the newer catalog items can mean to Upjohn's balance sheet. Xanax, Halcion, and the oral antidiabetes agent Micronase, he projects, "will be increasingly important in the immediate future of the Human Health Care business." However, what products come next? Hoff cites a Department of Commerce report asserting that the U.S. pharmaceutical industry can only remain competitive in the world through developing, producing, and marketing *new* drugs.

Yet new products have been difficult to come by in the stricter regulatory environment in the U.S. since the 1962 amendments to the drug law. One result has been that drug availability in the U.S. tends to lag behind other nations. The Government Accounting Office determined in 1975 that of 14 important new compounds, 13 went on sale in Europe years before they did in America. Dr. Louis Lasagna, professor of medicine and pharmacology at the University of Rochester School of Medicine, adds a specific example. "Calcium blockers were used to treat Europeans with heart disease," he has said, "for at least eight years before receiving approval in the U.S." The *New York Times* reported in February 1985 that the American pharmaceutical industry was "suffering from a dearth of new products, partially because of the high cost of developing and marketing." In 1982, 28 new compounds were introduced; in 1983, only 14.

Consider the stages in the drug pipeline. PR & D decides a compound warrants being called a "drug candidate" after as much as two years of animal testing. Upjohn files an Investigational New Drug (IND) application with the FDA. This is followed by two more years of Phase I and II studies of the compound's use in healthy humans and in patients. If the drug appears safe and effective, the company decides it has a "Product Candidate." Then comes Phase III, large-scale testing among patients. Based on data from that stage, Upjohn files a New Drug Application (NDA). On the average, two years of agency review follow. If the FDA is satisfied, it approves the drug for marketing.

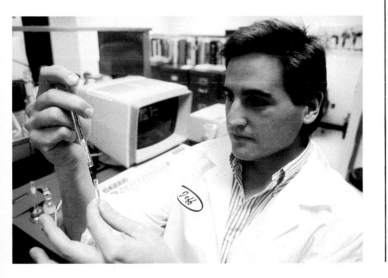

(left) The location to which a drug travels in a patient is crucial to the therapeutic effect that drug will have. A biologist in the company's Drug Metabolism Research unit studies an antianxiety drug to determine its presence in brain tissue, where it will be most effective.

(izquierda) El lugar a donde va una droga en el organismo de un paciente es crucial para el efecto terapéutico que tendrá dicha droga. Un biólogo en la unidad de Investigación sobre Metabolismo de la Droga, de la compañia, estudia una droga para combatir la ansiedad, a fin de determinar su presencia en el tejido cerebral, donde la misma será más efectiva.

(à gauche) L'effet thérapeutique d'un médicament dépend de sa propagation dans l'organisme d'un malade. Un biologiste de l'unité de recherche sur le métabolisme de la société Upjohn examine un médicament antidépresseur afin de déterminer sa présence dans les tissus du cerveau, où son efficacité sera optimale.

（左）医薬品が体内をどんな経路で通過してゆき、どんなふうに吸収されるかは、その薬剤の治療効果にとって非常に重要なポイントである。抗不安薬の脳組織内濃度を調べる薬物代謝研究部門の生物学者。

(right) Aerosol sprays, nasal sprays, skin patches, and controlled-release tablets are a few of the alternate drug delivery methods under study by investigators in Upjohn's Drug Delivery Systems Research unit.

(derecha) Atomizadores en aerosol, pulverizadores nasales, parches para la piel y tabletas de difusión controlada son algunos de los métodos alternos de aplicar la medicina, que estudian los investigadores de la undiad de Investigaciones sobre Sistemas de Aplicación de la Medicina, de la casa Upjohn.

(à droite) Atomiseurs, inhalateurs, plaques cutanées, et cachets à action contrôlée figurent parmi les divers conditionnements de médicaments étudiés actuellement par les chercheurs de l'Unité de recherche sur les systèmes de conditionnement des médicaments d'Upjohn.

（右）エアゾールスプレー、点鼻薬、スキンパッチ、徐放剤などが、アップジョン社ドラッグデリバリーシステム研究部門で研究中である。

FDA authority does not end at that juncture. It continues to keep an eye on a pharmaceutical in what is known as Phase IV — postmarketing surveillance — to see if any problems appear over time now that the product is in widespread use. (The company, too, through its Medical Affairs Division, monitors the product's performance in the real world.) Meanwhile, Upjohn tries to come up with new indications for the drug. As an example, when Solu-Medrol sterile powder was introduced in 1959, it had 14 indications. By 1984, there were more than 60.

Other challenges that Upjohn and the pharmaceutical industry must face include:

Product liability suits have been another torment for the maker of pharmaceuticals. It has become harder and harder for firms to get insurance for protection against the uppermost level of legal actions ($250 million and up). America in the 1980s is more litigious than at any time in history, and all industries live in the shadow of potentially damaging legal actions.

Off-shore competition shows every sign of mounting. The world's largest pharmaceutical manufacturers are based in Europe. And Japanese drug-makers have been making strong advances, partly, according to the *New York Times*, because Japanese industry "has been nurtured over the past decade by protectionist measures to keep European and American companies at bay." While Upjohn has long been a factor in world markets, it has lately taken steps to expand its presence in Japan, both through marketing and on-site R & D.

Financing the growth of a multinational company has become increasingly more complicated. Whereas the $36 million cost of the construction of Building 41 in 1951 was met entirely from earnings and reserves, greater costs of later construction and improvements have required the company to seek outside capital. Charles H. Ludlow, who joined Upjohn in 1950 and succeeded Gordon Knapp on his retirement in 1964 as vice president and treasurer, recalls Upjohn's attitude in the 1950s toward borrowing or external financing. "That was a completely foreign idea. To think that we might have to go out and borrow was almost sinful."

During his tenure as treasurer, Ludlow saw the company's philosophy change, and he was a principal figure in Upjohn's initial entry into foreign and domestic money markets in the 1970s. When Ludlow retired in

1984, he was succeeded by William U. Parfet, a great-grandson of the founder and son of chairman Ted Parfet. Bill Parfet has continued Upjohn's implementation of financing policies that secure for the company needed capital under the most favorable conditions.

Another move strengthening the company's long-range planning occurred in November 1986 with the election of Donald R. Parfet to the position of corporate vice president for administration. Don, also a great-grandson of W. E. Upjohn and son of chairman Ted Parfet, is responsible for the divisions of Employee Relations, Public Relations, and Corporate Planning and Development.

Public issues by the dozen swirl around the maker of pharmaceuticals in the 1980s. Upjohn monitors and addresses issues that could directly affect how the company does business through a corporate public affairs committee, chaired by Chairman Ted Parfet. Issues of primary concern to the committee include such ongoing questions as experimentation with animals, marketing pharmaceuticals in Third World countries, water supply, doing business in South Africa, and the company's controversial drug Depo-Provera.

Neat, clean answers to the questions these issues evoke are seldom forthcoming. No one in Upjohn management would claim that. For that matter, no one feels that any of the sobering realities facing drug manufacturers today will easily be put to rest. But they have not dampened Upjohn management's optimism. The company is spending as much as $75 million on additional research facilities in downtown Kalamazoo; upwards of $50 million to build a research facility in Japan that will be the largest PR & D site outside of Kalamazoo; $23 million to build a manufacturing facility for topical minoxidil solution, the as-yet-to-be-approved treatment for hair loss; $11 million to scale up a tissue-culture operation in Building 233; and $7 million for a new animal research building.

CHART FOR RESEARCH AND DEVELOPMENT

For at least four years, word had been spreading about an intriguing drug under investigation at The Upjohn Company. Then, in the spring of 1984, the media pounced on the story. A *New York Daily News* column was typical. Headlined "Upjohn's happy, hairy future," it told of how the company's medication for high blood pressure, Loniten, had produced an unexpected side effect — it

(left) Irregular beating of the heart — arrhythmia — is one of the many areas of investigation in Upjohn's Cardiovascular Diseases Research unit. Here, a researcher evaluates the rhythmic behavior of heart tissue.

(izquierda) Los latidos irregulares del corazón — arritmia — son una de las muchas áreas de investigación en la Unidad de Investigaciones de Enfermedades Cardiovasculares de Upjohn. Aquí un investigador evalúa el comportamiento rítmico del tejido del corazón.

(à gauche) Battement irrégulier du coeur, l'arythmie est une des affections faisant l'objet d'études à la division Upjohn de recherches sur les maladies cardiovasculaires. Sur cette photo, un chercheur évalue le comportement rythmique du coeur.

（左）心臓の不規則な鼓動、不整脈は、アップジョン社の循環器系病研究部門の研究分野の一つである。ここでは研究員が、心臓組織の規則的な動きを数値的に測定している。

(right) This central nervous system researcher observes the neural impulses of an animal's injured spinal cord on an oscilloscope to determine the effect of therapeutic agents on the injury.

(derecha) Este investigador del sistema nervioso central observa los impulsos nerviosos de la médula espinal lesionada de un animal, en un osciloscopio para determinar el efecto de los agentes terapéuticos en la lesión.

(à droite) Un spécialiste du système nerveux central (ci-contre) observe les pulsations dans la moelle épinière d'un animal blessé, sur l'écran d'un oscilloscope afin de déterminer l'effet des agents thérapeutiques sur la blessure.

（右）傷に対する治療剤の効果を調べるため、動物の損傷脊髄の神経インパルスを、オシロスコープで観察する中枢神経系研究部門の研究者。

(left) Upjohn animal health researchers are looking for more therapeutic products for disease, better growth-producing agents, reproductive products that will improve breeding efficiency, and antiparasiticides — developments which may be enhanced by genetic engineering projects now in place.

(izquierda) Los investigadores de Upjohn especialistas en salud animal buscan más productos terapéuticos para el tratamiento de diversas enfermedades, mejores agentes que promuevan el crecimiento, productos reproductivos que ayuden a mejorar la eficiencia en la crianza, y agentes antiparasiticidas —desarrollos que pueden beneficiarse por los projectos de ingenería genética en curso.

(à gauche) Des spécialistes Upjohn en santé animale. Objectif: découvrir de nouveaux produits pour le traitement des maladies, améliorer les agents de croissance dans la production, fabriquer des produits pouvant améliorer la capacité de reproduction, et mettre au point des anti-parasitaires-autant de progrès qui seront stimulés par les projets de génie génétique en cours d'exécution.

（左）アップジョン社の動物薬研究員は、より優れた治療効果をもつ製剤の開発、成長促進剤の改良、繁殖率を高める生殖用製剤や駆虫剤の開発に努力を傾け続けている。これらの開発には現在進行中の遺伝子工学プロジェクトが大きく寄与することになるだろう。

(right) Upjohn plant scientists want to create hybrids that are more disease- and insect-resistant. Many of these hybrids are the result of time-consuming hand-pollination. In the future, it is expected that much of the improvement in seeds will come through biotechnology.

(derecha) Los científicos de la planta de Upjohn desean producir híbridos que sean más resistentes tanto a las enfermedades como a los insectos. Muchos de estos híbridos son el resultado de una polinización manual, que lleva mucho tiempo en realizarse. En el futuro se espera que muchos de los adelantos en cuanto a semillas se refiere, se darán a través de la biotecnología.

(à droite) Des hommes de science des laboratoires Upjohn veulent créer des hybrides qui sont plus résistants aux maladies et aux insectes. La plupart de ces hybrides sont le résultat de la pollinisation manuelle. A l'avenir, l'amélioration des semences sera facilitée par la biotechnologie.

（右）アップジョン社の植物科学者たちは、病虫害に対して、より強い抵抗力を持つハイブリッドを生み出そうとしている。現在あるハイブリッドの多くは、時間のかかる人工受粉によってできたものであるが、将来、バイオテクノロジーが品種改良の主力となるであろう。

grew hair — and of how Upjohn had set about converting Loniten's active ingredient, minoxidil, into a topical treatment for male pattern baldness.

By mid-1984, the *New York Times* acknowledged the obvious. Wall Street, wrote reporter John Crudele, "is unanimous in believing the product will be important for Upjohn." Investors rushed to the phone, and, in short order, Upjohn stock, which stood at $45 a share in July 1984, found a new home above $100 a share. The company filed a New Drug Application for topical minoxidil solution in December 1985. Upjohn stock continued to rise. The board of directors called for a two-for-one stock split. When it split on May 1, 1986, Upjohn stock was $174 per share.

Topical minoxidil solution scarcely stands alone, however, and the strength of the stock reflected that as well. PR & D is bringing forward other strong prospects, as Dr. Mark Novitch affirmed not long after joining Upjohn on March 1, 1985. Former acting commissioner of the FDA, Dr. Novitch was named corporate vice president responsible for PR & D, Regulatory Affairs, Control, and Medical Affairs. In his view, "Upjohn research right now offers as much promise as at any time

in our history. In each of our therapeutic units, and in Medical Affairs, work is going on that can — and will — yield new products of immense importance." Some of these, says Dr. Novitch, could be expected in the near term. Others were "several years away: new analgesics, new antidepressants, new cardiovascular agents, new antibiotics, new gastrointestinal drugs."

Meanwhile, in the labs of PR & D, scientists are looking toward an even more distant future, and the company is backing them up. PR & D is currently receiving funds at levels as a percent of sales that are considerably higher than the 9.1 percent share in the prior five-year span.

For a long time, this commitment to PR & D has been used to attract "state-of-the-art" people to the firm. As a result, comments Ted Cooper, Upjohn "can accommodate a technological evolution or revolution because we have a superb infrastructure for successful drug development and effective research management." The top managers' most important task is to provide the scientists with "a program and an environment that fosters realization of creative potential," Dr. Cooper adds.

Still, there *are* constraints. Financial commitments may have reached admirable proportions, but the dollars cannot cover equally every single subtarget. Priorities have to be set, and they have been. Upjohn put aside dermatology research several years ago (it will probably re-enter this sphere, spurred by the valuable scientific findings in the work on minoxidil). In March 1985, the company decided to shut down further research on human reproductive physiology. Dr. Cooper provides this perspective: "We had gotten into a wide diversity of approaches. But you have to choose. We're trying to introduce the discipline that says we can't do everything. Let's concentrate on this."

In the course of 1985, Upjohn's scientists focused their emphases on seven principal disease groups. Decisions on priorities stemmed from three questions voiced by Dr. Cooper: What are the world's unmet medical needs? Where are the scientific opportunities? And how, if at all, do the answers to those questions match with Upjohn's strengths and experience? PR & D reviewed the responses and came up with these areas of activity:

Central Nervous System: Quite simply, the needs are great, the scientific opportunities many. Upjohn has

written a considerable success story with Xanax and Halcion and has established a critical mass of basic research on worldwide problems such as panic disorder. Other areas of need are Alzheimer's disease, memory modulation, aging of the central nervous system, analgesia, behavior problems, and dependencies.

Cardiovascular: This, says Dr. Cooper, "always is high on everybody's priority list." So far, Upjohn has not had enviable successes in this field. But recent leads offer hope. As for the potential, "it is an area of big public health problems," notes Dr. Cooper, "that are going to increase around the world as many areas pass through the phase that we have gone through, with changes in diet and standards of living."

Infectious Diseases: Upjohn, experienced and successful producer of antibiotics, will concern itself with all manner of microbes. The next generation of products, differing from the antibiotics, will probably involve "immune modulators" — substances to arm an individual's system of resistance against an infection.

Hypersensitivity Diseases: Upjohn's scientists continue to pursue compounds to treat arthritis. Their objective is to go beyond countering the symptoms and to seek ways of interfering with the progression of the disease. They will try to control the process through an immunologic approach. Meanwhile, other professionals in this group are working on compounds for treating asthma.

Diabetes and Gastrointestinal Diseases: The labs of this activity area have several targets. Some investigators are searching for compounds to control blood sugar in Type II maturity-onset diabetes. Their efforts are being aided by access to a special breed of hamsters in which diabetes develops spontaneously, thus enabling the researchers to study the condition in a highly controlled situation. This PR & D group is also concentrating on ulcers. Its work is directed at shutting off an ulcer's acid secretions in one or two doses.

Cancer Virus: Here, research aims to follow a rational approach in dealing specifically with the effects of compounds on solid tumors. The professionals want to know what routes to follow in seeking to confine the DNA in tumor cells, thus keeping the tumor from enlarging. Also, the scientists are looking for mechanisms to stop a tumor's essential blood vessels from developing. Elsewhere in the cancer group, a search has been going on for agents to change the human immunologic system. One drug prospect, by stimulating production of interferon in the body, may prove effective in treating genital herpes, a viral disease.

Atherosclerosis and Thrombosis Diseases: In this PR & D cluster, one line of research is tracking drug prospects that might be effective in reducing cholesterol by modulating the metabolism of lipids, a principal component of cells and a material factor in leading to atherosclerosis. In conjunction with a foreign research institute, the group also is hoping to produce compounds that will readily dissolve blood clots (*see* page 220).

Reviewing Upjohn's many options, Dr. Cooper talks with veiled intensity about the prospects ahead for Kalamazoo's 100-year-old pharmaceutical house. "Our ignorance about human health, despite all the well-publicized breakthroughs, is *great*," he observes. "Medical needs abound, and pain and suffering continue." Even so, he adds, scientists believe that "a new era of understanding has begun." Fortunately, Upjohn is well positioned to take a leading role in this era. It has size and resources. Therefore, it also has the staying power to see a commitment through. That commitment — to complete the transition from a chemistry-centered operation to a more sophisticated one built on biotechnology — represents the next milestone for Upjohn.

Upjohn's Biotechnology Thrust

Other implements and procedures have taken form in the past three decades in the highly promising field of biotechnology. After some preliminary effort as early as 1976, Upjohn has made a heavy commitment to this new scientific discipline as a remarkable ally in the campaign to find innovative pharmaceutical agents. The company did it in a way that Fred Heyl and his 1933 Upjohn fellows would have considered "very much Upjohn." Instead of buying an existing bioengineering company as other large pharmaceutical manufacturers have done, it located a top scientist-administrator to run its own venture, assigned him a budget, constructed a facility, and told him to hire the best people in the field.

In addition to clinical testing, elaborate record-keeping systems help assure product safety and efficacy. These women in Pharmaceutical Regulatory Affairs help monitor the ongoing safety records of Upjohn pharmaceuticals and help document new indications for their use.

Además de la prueba clínica, un elaborado sistema de registro ayuda a garantizar la seguridad y eficacia del producto. Estas mujeres ayudan en asuntos de control de calidad farmacéutica, a vigilar los registros en curso sobre seguridad de los productos farmacéuticos Upjohn, y ayudan a documentar nuevas indicaciones para su uso.

En plus des essais cliniques, un système d'archivage complexe permet de maintenir la sécurité et d'assurer l'efficacité des produits Upjohn. Ces femmes de la section des affaires de réglementation pharmaceutique font le suivi des archives pour la sécurité des produits Upjohn, et contribuent à établir une documentation appropriée pour leur usage.

臨床試験ばかりでなく、入念な記録管理システムも製品の安全性と有効性を保証するものである。薬事部門の女子社員たちは、アップジョン社の医薬品の安全性記録をモニターし、また追加適応症のための文書づくりも応援する。

Upjohn's choice as director, Dr. Ralph E. Christoffersen, had been a PR & D consultant to Upjohn for a decade. His specialty was large molecules. (Unlike the bench of his predecessors, his main lab instrument is an IBM 30-33 computer.) Hired in 1983, "Chris" Christoffersen, like Heyl before him, had the goal of attracting top academic talent to help lead Upjohn into novel areas of research. Specifically, he was to assemble a 150-person biotechnology unit — up to 50 of them Ph.D.'s. On his organizational chart, "Biotech" has three research sections: molecular biology, cell biology, and biopolymer chemistry. Gradually, talented scientists from within PR & D and newcomers, largely from academia, have joined their talents in this adventuresome unit.

Biotech's professionals have a two-part job. On the one hand, they look ahead. Some of them seek to isolate and purify genes that make particular proteins. Others may be trying to learn about the exact interactions occurring inside a cell. How does a cell membrane allow a molecule to get in or out? How do cells communicate with each other? What happens when a cell sets to work healing itself after an injury? The people of Biotech study the life of a cell, looking for an infinity of answers.

Biotech's second assignment is to support its associates elsewhere in PR & D. They build bridges between themselves and units within research and development. Through collaboration, through service projects, through the transfer of technology, they have to make sure that the discoveries they make and the concepts they develop are made known and are applicable in the development of products. Biotech works at the scientific frontier, but its scouts must remember that they are also bridge-builders.

Happily, topflight job candidates usually react favorably on visiting Research Tower in downtown Kalamazoo. One scientist, fresh from working with a Nobel laureate, turned down various tenured posts in academia because he felt that the scientific environment for research at Upjohn was better. Another, a full professor in biochemistry, concluded that his chances of doing research would be better at Upjohn than at his university, one of the nation's most distinguished. The "driving factor," says Dr. Christoffersen, is "where can they best keep up with the state of the art and do creative scientific research."

Reaching for New Ideas

Over time, Upjohn has continued to build a team of fine scientists. However, cautions Dr. Ted Cooper, "these researchers can't do everything." Hence, he forecasts, Upjohn "will seek other sources of good ideas besides our own good people. We will seek them from other companies. We will seek them from academia." Accordingly, the company will undertake what the vice chairman calls "special collaborative ventures" to create products that address unmet needs of contemporary medicine.

One such venture began formally on September 1, 1985, when PR & D reached an agreement with the Gaubius Institute, of Leiden, the Netherlands. In this project, scientists from Biotech and Gaubius will join together on pursuing agents to help dissolve blood clots. They will be attempting to make analogs of tissue plasminogen activators (TPAs) that will liberate the material capable of dissolving a clot. Biotech's specialists will be synthesizing the specific gene involved, then planting it in a cell with "instructions" to create the TPA analog. At Gaubius, researchers will focus on the TPA molecule to determine how and when it changes. For Upjohn, researchers in the atherosclerosis and thrombosis disease group will link together the various facets of the project, while fermentation researchers will stand ready to begin a suitable production scaleup as the work advances.

This is just one of an array of collaborations now in the works. It is one thing for Upjohn to find these opportunities and work out suitable arrangements. But the company needs to do something more, as Ted Cooper sees it. He believes Upjohn must streamline the development process and "get our products to the market as efficiently as before, but in less time and at a reasonable or lower cost." Dr. Cooper's ambitious aim is to slice as much as two years from development schedules.

At the same time, company scientists and physicians must continue their efforts to develop new indications for existing pharmaceuticals. The antibaldness properties of minoxidil, originally an antihypertension compound, may turn out to be the most dramatic example of such work. More typical, however, is to find an approach that will give the company renewed life on an expiring patent. Larry Hoff uses the example of the antibiotic clindamycin, on which Upjohn holds the patent. "If we can come along with a clindamycin ointment and do the clinical work to prove that it's safe and efficacious," he explains, "we could get three-year marketing exclusivity under an abbreviated NDA before anybody else could make it. That is what is going to be so tricky and important: extending the life cycle of our products."

Improving Drug Delivery

With the pressure of his thumb, Dr. W. E. proved that his friable pill would easily crumble. Thus Upjohn demonstrated in its earliest years that its pills would quickly yield all their medicinal value to the patient.

Ever since, Upjohn has sought to improve drug delivery, a search that, if anything, is gaining in importance. This is happening, in part, because fewer new compounds are being discovered in the industry, while R & D costs are escalating. The alternative approaches possible through new drug delivery systems may lead PR & D to new drug candidates.

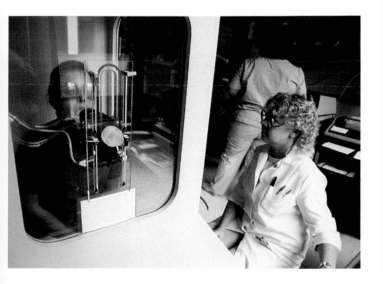

(left) Upjohn Medical Division personnel in Japan keep abreast of the latest medical developments. The Medical Division is also concerned with finding new product uses and formulations, and with questions of safety and continued efficacy for Upjohn products.

(izquierda) El personal de la División Médica de Upjohn en Japón se mantiene a la par de los descubrimientos médicos más recientes. La División Médica también está relacionada con el descubrimiento de nuevos usos de productos, fórmulas, y con aspectos de seguridad así como el mantenimiento de la eficacia de los productos de Upjohn.

(à gauche) Le personnel de la division médicale Upjohn au Japon suit de près les derniers progrès de la médecine moderne. La division médicale s'intéresse aussi à la recherche de nouvelles formules et à l'utilisation de nouveaux produits, de même qu'aux questions de sécurité et d'efficacité accrue des produits Upjohn.

（左）日本におけるアップジョン社の学術部スタッフは最先端の医学情報をキャッチしている。医薬品の新しい使途の発見や剤型、またアップジョン製品の安全性や、効能に関する追跡も、このスタッフの仕事である。

(right) Assuring the smooth transition of information from the laboratory to the clinical setting is among the goals of Upjohn's Clinical Investigation Units. Clinical investigators study human diseases and therapy, evaluate new medications, and provide educational opportunities to the medical community.

(derecha) El asegurar la continuidad de información del laboratorio a la clínica es una de las metas de las Unidades de Investigación Clínica de Upjohn. Los investigadores clínicos estudian las enfermedades humanas y la terapia, evalúan nuevos medicamentos y proporcionan oportunidades educativas a la comunidad médica.

(à droite) Assurer le transfert harmonieux de l'information, du laboratoire à la clinique, est une des tâches des unités de recherche clinique d'Upjohn. Les recherches cliniques se chargent d'étudier l'évolution des maladies et des thérapeutiques; elles évaluent les nouveaux médicaments, et fournissent de précieuses informations à la communauté médicale.

（右）研究室から臨床の場に、情報をスムーズに、そして確実に送ることが、アップジョン社の臨床試験部門の目的のひとつである。この部門の研究者たちは病気や治療法について研究し、新薬の評価をし、また医学界に教育材料としての情報提供も行なっている。

(left) The Fine Chemicals Division is expanding its fermentation research efforts to include the cloning and manipulation of genes. The result may be products that provide valuable inroads against the common cold and perhaps even cancer.

(izquierda) La División Química está multiplicando sus esfuerzos de investigación en fermentación para controlar la reproducción asexual y la manipulación de genes. Los resultados pueden ser productos que proporcionen valiosas fórmulas contra la gripe común e inclusive contra el cáncer.

(à gauche) La division chimie fine a intensifié ses travaux de recherche sur la fermentation pour y inclure la clonogénie et la manipulation des gènes. Le résultat de ces travaux conduira peut-être à la fabrication de produits qui feront progresser le traitement de la grippe et la lutte contre le cancer.

（左）ファイン・ケミカル部門では、醸酵の研究活動をクローニングや遺伝子操作にまで広げている。この成果としてごく普通の風邪の治療薬が生まれたり、あるいはがんに対して打撃を与えるような、貴重な医薬品が生まれたりするかもしれない。

(right) Fermentation output for Upjohn antibiotic and steroidal products at the Puerto Rico facility has risen dramatically since that center's opening in 1974. One key reason for this is the increase in sophisticated computer control systems.

(derecha) La producción de fermentación para productos Upjohn como antibióticos y esteroidales en la instalación de Puerto Rico ha aumentado drásticamente desde que el centro se inauguró en 1974. Una razón básica de ésto es el aumento en los sistemas sofisticados de control por computadora.

(à droite) Le niveau de fermentation des produits antibiotiques et stéroïdes à l'usine de Porto Rico a augmenté considérablement depuis l'ouverture de ce centre en 1974. Ceci s'explique principalement par l'introduction de systèmes de contrôle par ordinateurs ultra-modernes.

（右）アップジョン社のプエルトリコ工場における抗生物質製剤、ステロイド剤用の醸酵生産物は、1974年の開所以来、飛躍的に増加している。この増加の大きな理由の一つは、高度なコンピュータ制御システムである。

Drug delivery specialists concentrate on getting a compound to an exact site in the body with the greatest possible precision and efficiency. They also want to control the rate at which a drug is released into the body.

For certain disease conditions, aerosol sprays may be the most effective way to distribute medication to the lung. Or improved nasal sprays could get a compound into the bloodstream before it could be degraded by stomach and liver processes. Other methods include transdermal "patches," which diffuse an antidote gradually through the skin; parenteral methods that distribute drugs in ways other than through the intestine — perhaps by intramuscular injection; and controlled-release tablets and suppositories which release their active ingredients at precisely calculated rates. Another new technique will use a microemulsion containing a drug in a strictly controlled particle size which limits the areas in the body to which the drug will travel. Polymer-coated microparticles may also be useful for distributing potent compounds at a deliberately slow rate.

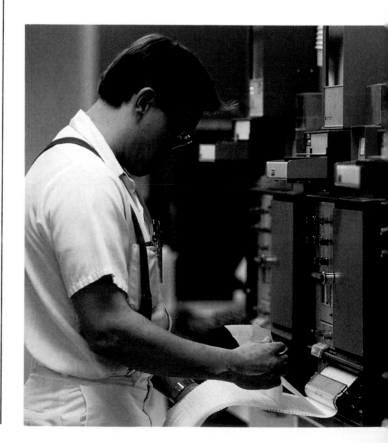

TO MAKE BETTER PRODUCTS

In Building 41, Line 9 in Sterile Products Preparation is the future face of pharmaceutical production. Every minute it operates, the line turns out 500 bottles, better than twice the achievable filling rate of two years ago. And fill weights are verified automatically, without stopping the line. There was a day when operators had to remove vials and weigh them by hand, but not anymore.

The heart of the new setup is a microprocessor. It keeps a constant eye on the sterilization tunnel, and it rides herd on the robotic checkweigher. The new microprocessor helps cut time, improve product quality, and increase lot sizes. And the bottom line has the numbers that any corporation enjoys: a savings of at least $850,000 a year.

When Building 41 officially opened its doors in 1951, it was widely admired as a plant with the very latest technology. No one else was making pharmaceuticals quite like that, basically on one level, with raw materials going in one side and leaving at the other as finished goods. In that era four decades ago, the planners of 41 were farsighted.

But ideas and processes changed, and with that, 41 has changed, too. The need for modification and modernization came home to roost in 1970 when the FDA made an industry-wide inspection tour. Another drug house had some problems with bacteria invading a faulty seal on sterile preparations. That started the whole industry thinking about sterile products. A sudden revolution ensued, and it is still going on.

Building 41's entire Sterile Products Production area was completely renovated. Huge rolling tanks of electropolished steel now carry bulk drug from the compounding area to the filling line, an Upjohn innovation that set the standard for the industry. Today, integrated production lines automatically wash and sterilize vials, put them through automatic filling and plugging stages, machine-cap them, and seal them. The vials are sent to Sterile Inspection, then to Sterile Packaging for automated labeling and cartoning. New employee gowning procedures, including use of fully enclosed "bunny suits" at critical points, further protect the product. NASA-developed air filters and "positive flow" airstreams protect and maintain a clean environment around the filling line.

The greater sophistication has meant not only better sterility but increased productivity. Today, 140 operators can produce the same volume that it took 230 persons to produce 20 years ago. As it stands, 41's Sterile Products operation ranks among the top three or four in the U.S. and still is moving ahead.

Change has reached other major areas of 41, too. For Dry Products Packaging, the oral antidiabetes agent Orinase in compressed tablet form turned into a big item. At first, after tablets filled a bottle, the cotton was stuffed into it by hand, a step inconsistent with large-volume output targets. So automation was applied — for cleaning and washing bottles, for cottoning and capping. In Fluids Packaging, dedicated facilities automatically bottle the cough medicine Cheracol and the antidiarrheal compound Kaopectate. Other operations have been upgraded, too. Once, Gelfoam, the product to control surgical bleeding, was stirred and cooked by hand and prepared in kitchen-like mixers. This year Production has finished automating almost every step of the process.

The pace of new developments does not let up. Production is adapting to a trend away from capsules, fluids, and powders to tablets and sterile products formulated from highly potent ingredients. As a result, more and more production lines have to be as tightly controlled as they are now in Sterile Products. Along with this development comes a much sharper focus on water, which can contribute more to rejection of product than anything else. Pharmaceutical Production has responded to this hazard by installing a "hot loop" system — its pipes continuously circulate purified water heated to 65°C all the way around 41. The closed hot-loop system is constantly sterilizing itself, eliminating the need for costly steam-sterilizing methods.

Upjohn didn't stop there, deciding to get better acquainted with robotics and how they could ease, improve, and speed pharmaceutical manufacture. One of the early steps led in 1984 to formation of a new unit, Automation Planning. Another step was to form a Strategic Planning Steering Committee and make it responsible for working up a 20-year charter of priorities. That committee has been asking itself such questions as: What is the future operating environment going to look like? Where do we want to be in 20 years?

Once this planning process has moved into high gear, Production will consider further investments in automation.

The Drive to Simplify

There's such a thing as being hypnotized by the technology of automation. To be realistic about it, automation must be just one part of a solution, not an end in itself. It is intended to make complex things simple, not simple things complex.

In that light, future production automation projects at Upjohn will have to meet three criteria. They must fit into the context of the worldwide Upjohn. They must be integrated; that is, the proposed machines must fit into systems which mesh with other systems. And they must display flexibility. Looking ahead, the company will call in outside consultants and design firms to help make conversions and introduce innovations. But, as has always been the case, the Kalamazoo concern will be thoroughly involved in making or adapting equipment for production use.

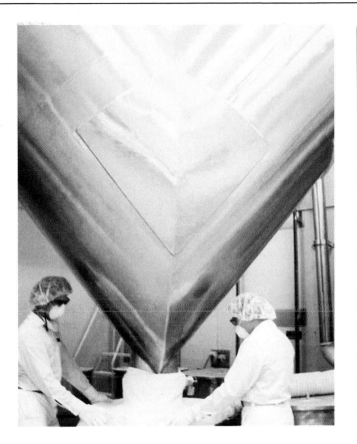

(left) At the Upjohn of Canada pharmaceutical manufacturing facility located in Don Mills, Ontario, antibiotic and steroidal products are brewed in tanks such as these.

(izquierda) En las instalaciones farmacéuticas de Upjohn en Canadá, ubicadas en Don Mills, Ontario, productos como antibióticos y esteroides son fabricados en tanques como éste.

(à gauche) Au centre de fabrication de produits pharmaceutiques de la société Upjohn du Canada, situé à Don Mills (Ontario), antibiotiques et stéroïdes sont préparés dans des citernes comme celles-ci.

（左）カナダのアップジョン社はオンタリオ州ドン・ミルスにあり、ここの医薬品製造工場では、抗生物質やステロイド製剤をタンクで醗酵させている。

(right) Drug mixing at Upjohn Manufacturing Company, Upjohn's pharmaceutical manufacturing facility in Arecibo-Barceloneta, Puerto Rico.

(derecha) La mezcladora de medicamentos en la compañía manufacturera de Upjohn, instalada en Arecibo-Barceloneta, Puerto Rico.

(à droite) Mélange de produits pharmaceutiques à l'usine Upjohn d'Arecibo-Barceloneta (Porto Rico).

（右）プエルトリコにあるアップジョン社の医薬品製造施設。薬品の混合が行なわれている。

The future is rich with possibilities, in large part because the microprocessor has come along to enhance a systems approach. A camera can now pass along a row of product containers and the microprocessor can make decisions about what the camera sees. "Intelligent" fillers and labelers, computer-driven, will control what happens on the line. Machines will "talk" to each other and to a central computer. "Smart" devices will spot problems, correct them, or call for help before a batch is ruined.

Along with automating Gelfoam production, Upjohn has a pilot automation program in place in Sterile Inspection. Three types of automation have been installed on one line of Sterile Inspection, a highly labor-intensive unit. A robot arm lifts and turns vials during cosmetic inspection, thus relieving operators of repetitive wrist actions which can lead to tendonitis. A Japanese-made visual analyzer studies vials for tiny particulates, and at the end of the line, another electronic apparatus counts the bottles to reconcile lots. The overall advantage is that automation eliminates the use of employees' hands but retains their eyes, which are the best means for making cosmetic inspection of vials. A further advantage of undertaking a pilot like this is that it will train operators for scaled-up automation later on. People will be trained, gain experience, and be ready for the next move.

Such changes will mean reducing the number of some old-style production jobs. However, management believes that training programs will prepare employees for the challenging new jobs of the future.

Elsewhere in Upjohn's production operations, other eyes are on the future. Fine Chemicals-Kalamazoo, well aware of the developments in biotechnology, is keeping in step, for example, by putting a lot of its effort into the new area of peptides. This involves manipulating and cloning genes, then having them react with microbes to make insulin and other products that may make valuable inroads against the common cold and perhaps even cancer. There, forecasts Fine Chemicals Vice President Chong Y. Yoon, lies "the revolution of the 1980s and 1990s." Fine Chemicals also has been expanding its fermentation research so that it can run with the leaders in this field.

Meanwhile, with the Puurs facility in Belgium operating at the forefront of modern pharmaceutical manufacturing (*see* pages 127-28), Upjohn's plant in Puerto Rico has also fixed its sights on the years to come. Both facilities incorporate many of the production-process innovations seen in 41.

PURSUIT OF THE EVER-WIDER MARKET SHARE

The cornerstone of Upjohn pharmaceutical marketing is and will remain the sales representative. Personal contact must be maintained between the company and the physicians, pharmacists, and hospitals it serves. Yet, behind the first-line sales representative is an organization that — through gathering and analysis of data, assessment of the competition, and planning — develops the strategies that determine the course of the rep's work throughout the year.

The complexities of drug discovery and product marketing demand systematic thinking, way up front. Over the past quarter-century, Upjohn has turned that science into familiar routine, and the process has shown that in this centennial year the road to Upjohn's goals is a steep one indeed.

For background, President Larry Hoff notes that the world pharmaceutical market in 1983 amounted to $72 billion. Upjohn forecasters figure it will grow eight to 8.5 percent a year and thus hit $270 billion in the year 2000. In 1985, Upjohn made roughly 1.5 percent of all worldwide sales. Its aim is to get to 2 percent by 1990. "If we do that," says Hoff, "we feel we will be assured of a spot in the top 10 drug companies in the world. That is our minimum goal." The corporation ranked between 13th and 15th in the world in 1985. To earn a place in the top 10, it will have to better the general market growth by 3.5 percent a year. "That will be difficult," concedes Hoff, "but that is our challenge."

Marketing's planning for the domestic market usually takes the better part of a year. Forecasting for the next five years, the analysts begin the job in January. By April, a plan is fairly well shaped, including an updating for the current year. After working out the kinks, Corporate Vice President Harold Chappelear and his associates take the plan to Corporate Senior Vice President for Worldwide Human Health Businesses Dan Witcher and then to the Office of the Chairman around mid-July. This projection will be incorporated in October into the company's overall five-year plan and budget drafting, and then the planners of Marketing prepare to go back to the drawing board to begin the process again, projecting another five-year period.

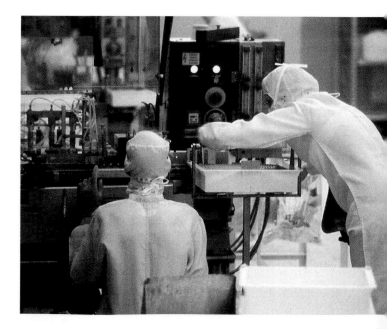

Planners make a practice of fixing on certain assumptions about the state of the world in the five — or 10 — years ahead. In the early 1980s, they operated from these assumptions: no major war, no serious interference in trade flows, no big currency upheavals worldwide, some slowdown in inflation, no major financial collapses, and, among other points, an expectation that the demand for health services will be "very income elastic"; that is, the richer a country is, the more it spends on health care. Through 1990, the forecasters projected, high-income countries would account for at least two-thirds of world health care expenditures. As a further consideration, two population groups would increase rapidly: children under five, mostly in developing regions, and adults over 65, concentrated largely in developed areas and requiring two to three times the average amount of health care.

(left) Sterile product filling line at Upjohn's United Kingdom manufacturing facility — Upjohn Limited — located in Crawley, Sussex, England.

(izquierda) La línea llenadora de productos estériles Upjohn en las instalaciones manufactureras ubicadas en el Reino Unido — Upjohn Limited — ubicado en Crawley, Sussex, Inglaterra.

(à gauche) Ligne d'assemblage de produits stériles au centre de fabrication des produits Upjohn au Royaume-Uni, situé à Crawley, Sussex (Grande-Bretagne).

（左）イギリスのクローリイにある英国アップジョン社工場の滅菌製剤充填作業ライン。

(right) Tablet production at Laboratorios Upjohn C.A., Upjohn's pharmaceutical manufacturing facility in Valencia, Venezuela. Other South American manufacturing plants are located in Guatemala and Colombia. A packaging, control, and distribution center is based in Santiago, Chile.

(derecha) La producción de tabletas en los Laboratorios Upjohn C.A. en su planta farmacéutica en Valencia, Venezuela. Otras plantas en Centro y Sudamérica se localizan en Guatemala y Colombia. También se encuentra un centro de empaque, control y distribucion en Santiago de Chile.

(à droite) Production de comprimés aux Laboratoires Upjohn S.A., centre de fabrication des produits pharmaceutiques Upjohn à Valencia (Vénézuéla). Les autres centres Upjohn de l'Amérique latine se trouvent au Guatémala et en Colombie. Le centre de conditionnement, de contrôle et de distribution des produits Upjohn se trouve à Santiago (Chili).

（右）ベネズエラのバレンシアにあるアップジョン社の医薬品製造工場。錠剤が作られている。南アメリカではベネズエラのほかに、グアテマラ、コロンビアに製造工場がある。チリのサンチアゴには、包装・品質管理・配送センターがある。

(left) Future production automation projects will include "intelligent" computer-driven fillers and labelers, machines that "talk" to each other, and "smart" devices that spot problems and call for help. All these projects will free line operators, such as this Upjohn of Canada worker, to monitor and observe.

(izquierda) Los futuros programas de producción automatizada incluirán dispositivos para llenar los frascos y colocar etiquetas, que sean "inteligentes" y accionados por computadoras, máquinas que "hablen" entre si, y dispositivos "vivos" que detecten los problemas y pidan ayuda. Todos estos programas liberarán de la línea a los operarios, tal como este operario de Upjohn en Canadá, para vigilar y observar.

(à gauche) Ordinateurs "intelligents" pour l'étiquetage et la mise en bouteille, des machines qui "parlent" entre elles, et des appareils "astucieux" capables de déceler les problèmes et de solliciter de l'aide figurent parmi les futurs projets d'automatisation de la production. Tous ces projets vont libérer les opérateurs, comme cet ouvrier de la société Upjohn du Canada, qui peut désormais observer et faire le dépistage d'éventuels défauts.

（左）未来のオートメーションの製造機械には、"聡明な" コンピュータ制御装置つき充填機やラベル貼り機が出来るだろう。機械同士で "話し合い" をし、故障を発見して助けを求める "賢い" 機械が出来るだろう。このような機械が出来れば、生産ラインで働くすべての人々はこのカナダ・アップジョン社の社員のように、モニター・監視係の仕事に変わってゆくだろう。

(right) Sterile Products Inspection line in Building 41, Portage, Michigan.

(derecha) Inspección en la Línea de productos estériles en el Edificio 41, Portage, Michigan.

(à droite) Chaîne d'inspection des produits stériles au Bâtiment 41, Portage, Michigan.

（右）無菌製品の検査ライン。ミシガン州ポーテージ、第41棟。

Marketing's planners survey the whole inventory of Upjohn products — those already in the marketplace, like Xanax and Halcion, those for which FDA approval might be expected in a year or so, and new formulations and new uses of existing compounds. They then face the formidable task of determining how their products fit into the external-element scenario they have developed.

All of this must remain flexible — to take advantage of a sudden internal breakthrough or setback, or to respond to a shift in the external environment. Except for the century-old, locked-in commitments to quality and team effort, virtually everything at Upjohn is subject to change. In one area in particular, the situation is likely to shift right before one's eyes. This is the nature of the action today in Consumer Products and where it appears to be headed.

Consumer Products handles the line known in shorthand as "OTC," for over-the-counter. The time was when OTC items were Upjohn's biggest stock-in-trade, adding up to sales of $43 million in 1958, about one-third of net sales. Then Upjohn accelerated its switch to an emphasis on prescription pharmaceuticals.

By 1971, however, declining OTC sales and earnings meant that Upjohn had to either stay in the consumer products business or get out. Ted Parfet, Bob Boudeman, Larry Hoff, and Bill Hubbard studied the business and came to the decision that it was potentially very profitable. They created Consumer Products, and through the balance of the decade, sales grew gradually. Then Cortaid, a topical hydrocortisone ointment, was added to the product list, and sales nearly doubled.

The example of Cortaid pointed the way. With it, Upjohn converted a prescription item into a compound the consumer could buy over the counter. In 1980 and 1981 alone, users of this OTC medication saved millions in doctors' bills. In 1986, Upjohn introduced Haltran, a nonprescription form of ibuprofen designed to relieve menstrual cramps, a similar indication found for Motrin at a higher dosage and by prescription only. The next prospects could be Orinase, the oral antidiabetes agent, or topical erythromycin, an antibiotic for use in acne. These and other products currently available only by prescription will be part of what the Stanford Research Institute estimates will be a $50 billion market in the U.S. by the year 2000.

The Mix of Sales Reps

Competitors respect Upjohn for the quality of its salespeople. And Marketing is properly proud of their many achievements in the field. But Upjohn, not given to complacency, holds the view that it should not take *anything* for granted — including the mix of marketing representatives and how it might be altered to suit changed conditions.

Marketing knows its recruits need to have a solid schooling in science or pharmacy. But it may be that in the wholly new health care-delivery environment, other talents would help, too. Perhaps other Upjohn sales reps will have backgrounds in law or personnel in the future.

Meanwhile, the existing structure of Medical Science Liaisons (MSLs) will, if anything, be strengthened in the months ahead. Upjohn has found that the ties between MSL and physician represent a unique exchange. The MSL will still serve as a link between scientific endeavor in Upjohn's PR & D and Medical Affairs units, as well as with science in the world of the teaching and practicing doctor (*see* page 146).

The MSL program is such a winner that Upjohn has launched several other types of specialists. In 1978, Medical Specialty Representatives (MSRs) were created; they now number more than 80. In 1983, Marketing added Surgical Specialty Representatives (SSRs), of whom there are now 11. Then, in mid-1985, yet another specialist came into being: PSLs, or Pharmacy Science Liaisons. The first group will work closely with pharmacists to make sure they have the most current information on products. This innovation responds to a present fact of life in health care: the growing independence of the pharmacist, increasingly empowered by state law to fill prescriptions on the basis of cost rather than a physician's specific brand order. Upjohn's concept is that if the customer, that is, the pharmacist, has all the information needed, chances are he will make a better decision.

Some of these specialists will be handing out timely issues of Upjohn's *Scope* publications. These have been issued for more than 45 years. Among the choices is the *Scope Monograph* series, designed as textbooks for medical students and providing fundamentals of such subjects as infectious diseases and immunology. The documents are written for the most part by people who are pioneers in their fields and are working at the frontiers of knowledge. Well over 90 percent of U.S. medical schools use *Scope Monographs* to supplement their teaching activities. Annually, more than 200,000 of these texts are distributed free to U.S. medical schools, while another 50,000 go to medical colleges abroad. Other educational materials include *Current concepts* booklets, written by national authorities, which reflect the latest information on topics such as pain or panic disorders, and slide sets on single topics — interarticular fluid examination, for example — showing the prescribed lab techniques.

Marketing at Upjohn today has a dynamic quality. Some new pressure or possibility materializes, and the company goes to work designing a way to compensate or capitalize. Marketing's men and women have learned that's how to stay ahead in a climate where *nothing* seems to be static any longer and where information and energy are the distinguishing qualities in developing a product's full commercial potential.

THE UPJOHN LABEL: SEASONED WORLD TRAVELER

The Upjohn label has traveled more and more aggressively through the world since those embarrassing months in 1922 when Mylax, the overseas version of the laxative Phenolax, failed miserably in the English market.

(left) Packaging line at Japan Upjohn Limited (J.U.L.), the company's pharmaceutical packaging facility in Takasaki, Japan. Japan will soon be home to a new research facility — Upjohn Pharmaceuticals Limited — to be located in Tokyo.

(izquierda) La línea de empaque en las instalaciones de la Japan Upjohn Limited (J.U.L.) en su planta farmacéutica en Takasaki, Japón. Japón será próximamente la nuevas sede de instalaciones de investigación — Upjohn Pharmaceuticals Limited — localizada en Tokio.

(à gauche) Opération d'assemblage chez Japan Upjohn Limited (J.U.L.), le centre de conditionnement des produits pharmaceutiques des laboratoires Upjohn à Takasaki (Japon). Tokyo sera bientôt le siège d'un nouveau centre de recherches des laboratoires Upjohn hors des Etats-Unis.

（左）日本の高崎にある、アップジョン社の医薬品包装工場の包装工程。日本では間もなく、アップジョン社の新しい研究施設が東京の近郊、筑波研究学園都市に建設される予定である。

(right) Many Upjohn line operators, such as these women at the Alcala de Henares, Spain, facility, engage in "hands on" work. Even though Upjohn production lines are becoming increasingly automated, certain processes still require the personal touch.

(derecha) Muchas operarias de la línea de producción de Upjohn, como estas mujeres de Alcalá de Henares, España, se ocupan en trabajo manual. Aún cuando las líneas de producción de Upjohn se automatizan más y más, ciertos procesos aún exigen el toque personal.

(à droite) Beaucoup d'opérateurs de la société Upjohn, comme ces femmes d'Alcala de Henares (Espagne), mettent "la main à la pâte". Malgré l'automatisation des lignes de production Upjohn, certains procédés de fabrication demandent une touche personnelle.

（右）スペイン・アルカラ工場の女子社員たち。流れ作業を行なうラインでは、スペインの場合のように多くが手作業である。アップジョン社の生産ラインはどんどん自動化されてきているが、特定の工程は、まだ人の手を借りなければならない。

Upjohn International, Inc., set sail in earnest during the 1950s, and the charts now point to future travels that will be more intensive, if not to more distant places, than ever before.

Like Upjohn's other divisions, International has ambitious goals for the months and years ahead. Its reference point is this: in 1984, Upjohn's foreign pharmaceutical operations achieved a one percent share of the market outside the U.S. By 1990, the aim is to reach 1.2 percent. Translating that into dollars, International intends to hit sales around the $1 billion mark by 1990.

All in all, doing pharmaceutical business overseas presents a range of eye-opening complications. The manufacturer faces a distinct variety of cultural preferences for different forms of drugs — for oral medications in the United Kingdom, for injectables in Latin America and the Orient, for suppositories in Italy and France, for effervescents in Europe, Japan, and some of Latin America. And the drug producer may also have to provide medications in very small amounts. A patient may go to the pharmacy and buy one day's treatment —

simply because he cannot afford to pay for a month's supply at once. Upjohn International has learned to deal with other unique differences as well:

The languages of foreign commerce come in multiples. At Upjohn's Puurs, Belgium, plant, for example, personnel must be ready to converse in Flemish, English, French, and German. To cope with this reality abroad, Upjohn International headquarters in Kalamazoo has access to a six-member translation section and two bilingual secretaries. Many executives also retain language strengths from earlier assignments in foreign lands.

The world economic environment bedevils International almost daily. The division performed quite well through the recent recession, but ironically, because of external economic factors, earnings suffered.

One of these factors pitted a strong U.S. dollar against foreign currencies. Sales in a given country might have equaled or surpassed the prior year's, but when the receipts in weak local currencies were converted to strong dollars, Upjohn's earnings turned out to be lower.

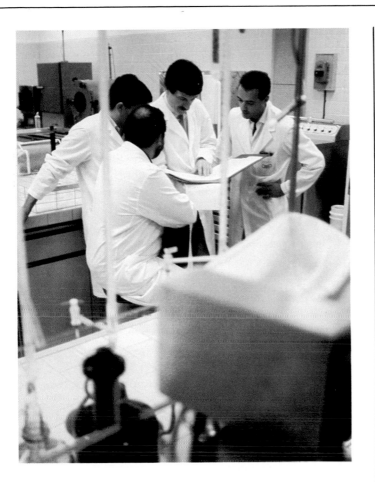

One response of governments to a second factor, inflation, has been to force drug price rollbacks. An extreme example has been Japan. Between 1981 and 1984, the government ordered a pharmaceutical price reduction averaging 40.1 percent. To counter these forces, International must trim other parts of its operation until the situation improves.

Product registration tends to differ from country to country, and International has to deal with all the variations on this standard theme. In Belgium, the staff at Puurs coordinates registrations in 30 nations. Fortunately, most foreign registrations do not take as long as the FDA practice in America, except in Japan, Venezuela, and the Scandinavian nations. The Scandinavians may have the highest standards in the world, and registration may be as lengthy on some products as it is in the U.S. Further, Sweden has added some wrinkles of its own, such as requiring that a product be tested in three animal species in that country.

(left) Packaging line at Upjohn's pharmaceutical and chemical manufacturing facility in Val de Reuil, France — Laboratoires Upjohn. France is also home to Asgrow France S.A., in Av Felix Louat, and Laboratoires Upjohn S.A.R.L., in Paris.

(izquierda) Instalaciones de la línea de empaquetado en la compañía manufacturera farmacéutica y química de Upjohn en Le Val de Reuil, Francia. (Laboratorios Upjohn). En Francia está también la compañía Asgrow France, S.A., en Av. Felix Louat y los Laboratorios Upjohn S.A. R.L., en Paris.

(à gauche) Opération d'emballage au centre de fabrication de produits chimiques et pharmaceutiques Upjohn au Val de Reuil (France). En France se trouvent également Asgrow France S.A., à Senlis, et le siège des Laboratoires Upjohn, à Paris.

（左）フランスにあるアップジョン社の医薬品および化学薬品製造工場の包装工程。フランスにはアズグロー・フランス社とLaboratoires Upjohn S. A. R. L. もある。

(right) Wherever Upjohn has a manufacturing operation, it also has a Pharmaceutical Control unit to ensure product safety and quality. Control personnel such as these chemists at Upjohn's Caponago, Italy, manufacturing facility monitor all phases of the production process.

(derecha) Upjohn tiene procesos de fabricación en muchos lugares incluyendo una unidad de Control farmacéutico que supervisa la seguridad y la calidad de los productos. El personal de control, así como estos químicos, operan maquinaria en Caponago, Italia, y vigilan todas las fases del proceso de producción.

(à droite) Partout où s'établit la société Upjohn, elle possède une unité de contrôle pharmaceutique pour assurer la qualité et la sécurité des produits Upjohn. Le personnel de contrôle, dont ces chimistes du centre de production Upjohn à Caponago (Italie), suit toutes les phases du processus de production.

（右）アップジョン社が製造を行っている国にはすべて、医薬品の品質管理部門があり、ここで製品の安全性と品質が確認される。品質管理担当者、たとえばイタリアのカパナゴのアップジョン社製造工場で働くこの化学者たちは、品質管理分析者として、製造の全工程をモニターする。

(left) A machinist works on equipment at Upjohn's pharmaceutical manufacturing subsidiary, Upjohn S.A., in Puurs, Belgium. The Puurs plant is the largest Upjohn production facility outside the U.S., producing nearly 100 health-care and agricultural formulations for shipment to 130 countries worldwide.

(izquierda) Un maquinista trabaja con el equipo de la fábrica subsidiaria de productos farmacéuticos Upjohn, S.A., en Puurs, Bélgica. La planta de Puurs es la mayor planta de producción de Upjohn fuera de Estados Unidos, y fabrica cerca de 100 fórmulas farmacéuticas para el cuidado de la salud y para la agricultura con destino a 130 países.

(à gauche) Un machiniste au travail à l'usine de fabrication de produits pharmaceutiques, Upjohn S.A., à Puurs, en Belgique. La filiale de Puurs est le plus important centre de production de la société Upjohn hors des Etats-Unis. Elle produit une centaine de préparations pharmaceutiques sur les chaînes automatisées ultra-rapides. Les produits agricoles et sanitaires manufacturés à Puurs sont expédiés à 130 pays dans le monde entier.

（左）ベルギーのプールスにある医薬品製造子会社アップジョン、Ｓ．Ａ．で備品を扱う機械技師。米国外で最大の製造施設であるプールス工場では、約100 種の医薬品を世界130ケ国へ向けて出荷している。

(right) Distribution warehouse at Upjohn S.A. de C.V., the company's pharmaceutical manufacturing facility in Mexico City, Mexico. Upjohn also maintains a chemical manufacturing plant in Cuernavaca and an Asgrow Seed Company facility in Matamoros.

(derecha) Almacén de distribución de Upjohn S.A. de C.V., las instalaciones manufactureras farmacéuticas de la compañia en la ciudad de México. Upjohn mantiene también una planta manufacturera química en Cuernavaca e instalaciones de la compañia Asgrow de semillas, en Matamoros.

(à droite) Entrepôt et centre de distribution Upjohn S.A. de C.V., à l'usine de fabrication de produits pharmaceutiques à Mexico (Mexique). Upjohn possède également un centre de fabrication de produits chimiques à Cuernavaca et un centre de production Asgrow à Matamoros, au Mexique.

（右）メキシコシティーにあるアップジョン社医薬品製造工場の配送倉庫。メキシコにはこの他アップジョン社の施設として、化学薬品製造工場とアズグロー種苗会社がある。

Commission payments have long been one of the facts of life in foreign commerce. And stories are legendary about the place of the *mordida*, or tip, in Latin American business. (In fact, L. N. Upjohn's and Donald Gilmore's distaste for such practices led them to slow the company's entry into the booming postwar international marketplace.) In May 1976, however, the company acknowledged that questionable payments totaling $2.7 million had been made to government administrators and others in 22 countries between 1971 and 1975. Management ordered the practice stopped. Chairman Parfet explained that, "while those payments may have seemed necessary in the competitive climate of countries whose trade customs differ markedly from those in the U.S., it is beyond question that they are a demeaning cost of business. Now . . . these practices must cease."

Foreign nations are as concerned about health care costs as is the U.S., and health cost containment is another fact of life in many countries. As a result, International often is hard put to get price increases to keep up with inflation. In Japan, a foreign drug manufacturer can only look forward to government-imposed price *decreases*. Faced with such pressure, the smaller and medium-size companies may well be forced out of business. "If you want to survive in the Japanese market," says International's President Vescovi, "you have to produce new products. The only way to do that is to have an active R & D program. If you really want to get products to the market more quickly, you have to put an R & D lab in Japan." This is what Upjohn has decided to do, announcing in mid-1985 that it will replace its existing lab with a larger, more sophisticated one.

In Europe and Japan, the political environment does not often jeopardize an American drug house's operations. But the Middle East is a dangerous environment today for commerce, and political instability in Central and Latin American nations can play havoc with business. Elsewhere, a government may insist that Upjohn build a plant within its national borders, if it wishes to market its products there. Some African countries are having a great deal of difficulty generating enough hard currency to buy the materials they need. Pharmaceuticals are not as badly affected as other goods, but they can feel the pinch.

Selvi Vescovi takes a realistic view of what's ahead. "I think the challenges in the next few years are going to be greater than they were five or 10 years ago, but we haven't just been wringing our hands," he says. International has built up its organization, expanding marketing and sales to a point at which Upjohn is now competitive with companies that have been there for a much longer period of time.

Planning for International's Future

Whereas everyday life in Europe and Japan is similar to that in the U.S., it is radically different in Third World countries. The health structure is different. So are drug requirements. For example, few people in a developing country would take an antianxiety medication or a sleeping pill. Instead, they need antibiotics, analgesics, perhaps nutritional supplements. Health administrations in developing countries are being pushed to opt for abandoning sophistication in favor of essential, basic health care, accessible to a much wider group of people. Therefore, Upjohn is weighing some fundamental questions. In what nations or regions should it compete? How can it compete in those nations? What are the basic manufacturers selling? Which of those basic compounds should Upjohn make? What segment of the market can it compete in most effectively?

Understanding the market is of key importance, and one way to improve understanding is through communications. A new structure for improving the vital communications links between Kalamazoo and sales outposts thousands of miles away is promising. Regional marketing managers — there were eight in 1985 — report to Kalamazoo from their offices in the field. Two are stationed in Europe, one in Latin America, and so it goes. Four to six times a year, these managers meet in Kalamazoo, where they spend up to two weeks. They learn about plans in the works, voice their reactions, then return to their respective areas to brief key individuals. Comment from those local discussions loops back to headquarters in Kalamazoo. "I want continuity of effort," says Vescovi. "Before we really embark on a project, I want all of the parts of this octopus to be working together."

So far, this communications device has shown enough promise to suggest that the nuclear group should be enlarged. And while it only applies now to sales and marketing activities, Vescovi believes that there may be "some other disciplines" in which the concept should be tried.

International is also engaged these days in carefully reallocating resources. "For the next year or so," explains Vescovi, "we will be taking our resources — manpower, research funds, promotional dollars, capital — and assigning them on the basis of potential." His aim is to get to a point at which more than 85 percent of the incremental resources or new investments are being spent in the dozen or so most important subsidiaries. Those subs have been identified in the strategic plan, and the available resources have been reallocated to them. Expenditures will be controlled by that formula until a major product is to be introduced. At that juncture, the division will divert sizable funds into the launch.

This strategy of resource reallocation took effect in 1984. And it paid off. International's share of the worldwide market hit one percent for the first time. "That doesn't sound like a lot," adds Vescovi, "but in terms of the size of the international market, I think we are doing quite well."

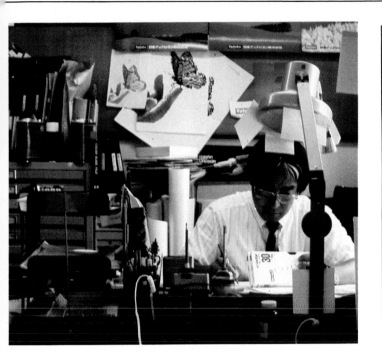

To make sure things continue that way, International has introduced another innovation: Operation Focus. Each of the key subsidiaries was asked to tell the division what it would like to do to improve sales and earnings. Double the local sales force? Double promotional expenses? Put on a prestigious symposium? The subs were to tell headquarters, in Vescovi's words, "If you give me $1,000, or $100,000, for my program, then I will give you so much in sales and earnings." Some 68 projects were nominated, some covering three- and four-year periods. Several called for speeding up the hiring of salespeople, others for more promotional expenditures. What particularly pleased Vescovi was that "it generated a lot of enthusiasm in the field and in the home office." At last report, proposals were still coming in from the subs.

A man who will have a special interest in those proposals is Ley S. Smith, who in May 1986 was appointed corporate vice president of international pharmaceutical subsidiaries and executive vice president of Upjohn International, Inc. Smith, Vescovi, and their associates in International live and work in a complicated world, but they're making it very clear that they are determined to get the better of it.

HELPING IMPROVE NATURE'S HANDIWORK

Upjohn's agricultural business's bright future can be glimpsed at almost any stop throughout the division — at Ames, Iowa, where Upjohn plant researchers plan to harness genetic engineering to eliminate the offensive odor in soybeans, a key to widening soybean markets in the U.S.; or at Upjohn Farms, where investigators are developing an antibiotic to treat shipping fever, a cause of almost 50 percent morbidity in cattle. Or make a call on Experimental Plant Genetics in Kalamazoo, where new Asgrow plant hybrids flourish from no more than bits of cell tissue; or visit Reproduction and Growth Physiology, part of the PR & D in Kalamazoo, where work is under way with a hormone that has real potential for bettering cows' milk production.

In 1985, the Ag Division had total sales of $415 million, and it employed 2,600 men and women. David Phillipson, vice president and general manager, is quietly confident that by 1987, sales will approach the half-billion-dollar mark. By the early 1990s, the division expects to have sales of $800 million, and it will have hired more than 400 new people. Regular applications of marketing elbow grease can ensure outcomes like these — as long as R & D actively supports them with new, or better, or bigger products. The division puts about nine percent of its budget into research. In the area of animal health product development, Ag Division scientists were assigned in 1984 to PR & D in downtown Kalamazoo in order to tie them in more closely with human pharmaceutical research. The researchers have lunch together, go to coffee together, think together. When something of agricultural interest comes out of basic PR & D study, then Ag's development specialists at the farm take it over.

Animal health researchers will be looking for more therapeutic products for disease, better growth-promoting agents, reproductive products that will improve breeding efficiency, and antiparasitacides.

Biotechnology gives Upjohn chances to do things with microorganisms that couldn't be done before. On the horizon, Ag scientists are looking at growth hormones and antigenic proteins of certain diseases that may become vaccines that are safer, cheaper, and better than whole culture vaccines, and also are patentable. There is interest, as well, in products made by genetically engineering compounds in fermentation vats, a process not too different from the way antibiotics and steroids are made. One of these is a new bovine growth hormone that may provide a product that will increase a cow's milk output with less feed.

(left) Sales recruits need to have a solid schooling in science or pharmacy. But it may be that in the wholly new health-care delivery environment, other talents would help, too. Perhaps future Upjohn sales reps will have backgrounds in law or personnel as well.

(izquierda) Los nuevos Agentes de Ventas necesitan tener una sólida enseñanza en ciencias o farmacología. Puede ocurrir, que en el campo completamente nuevo de provisión de servicios del cuidado de la salud otros talentos más sean de ayuda. Tal vez los futuros agentes de ventas de Upjohn tendrán que tener conocimientos legales y de manejo de personal.

(à gauche) Les nouvelles recrues ont besoin d'une formation solide en science ou pharmacie. Mais peut-être aussi dans une discipline nouvelle: des soins de santé pour l'écologie. Les futurs vendeurs Upjohn auront peut-être une formation en droit ou en gestion du personnel.

（左）販売員として採用される新人たちは、科学あるいは薬学の素養が要求される。しかし、ヘルス・ケアの状況が一変するときには、それ以外の知識も役立つことになるだろう。おそらく将来は法律畑や人事畑出身の医薬販売員も、アップジョンに登場することになるだろう。

(right) More than 1,200 teaching hospitals are on the rounds of 165 Upjohn hospital sales representatives. This representative pauses with a physician in front of Duke University Hospital in Durham, North Carolina.

(derecha) Más de 1.200 hospitales universitários son visitados por los 165 representantes de ventas de Upjohn. Este representante hace una pausa con un médico frente al Hospital de la Universidad de Duke en Durham, Carolina del Norte.

(à droite) Plus de 1.200 hôpitaux d'enseignement font partie des tournées de 165 délégués médicaux d'Upjohn. Ce délégué discute avec un médecin devant l'hôpital de l'université Duke à Durham en Caroline du Nord.

（右）アメリカでは、1,200 以上の教育基幹病院が、アップジョン社の病院担当の販売員165 人の訪問先である。ノースカロライナ州ダーラムのデューク大学病院前で、医師と立ち話をする販売員。

CHAPTER EIGHT

THE VOICES OF UPJOHN

Again and again, the passage of Upjohn through its first 100 years has revealed a hard-shelled fact of its life: from the beginning, *people* have been the company's main asset, the bullion in its bank.

In the beginning, four partners and 12 employees clustered together in a compact South Burdick Street building to roll and spray Dr. W. E. Upjohn's friable pills into shape. With more earnestness than sanitary method, they produced 186 medications for the first catalog. Research? That was a long way down the road. And as for salesmanship, the field men had little more than glib talk and a winning way to help push the products.

A century later, faded anecdotes are all that's left of the long-gone South Burdick Street space. Now, more than 21,000 men and women do Upjohn's work, nearly 8,000 of them in the Kalamazoo area. PR & D constructs molecules, deciphers genetic maps, and alters the inner machinery of the cell to change its mission.

Production operators in space suits maneuver highly potent substances in rooms sealed by air locks. And sales representatives visit special technical libraries to keep pace with the high-velocity science of modern pharmaceuticals.

Here in 1986, the world differs so much from that spring of 1886, when Dr. W. E. shifted his new enterprise into gear, that today the founder would be lost in his city and his company. The face of drug manufacture has changed dramatically, except in this respect: the people of Upjohn are as capable as they ever were. They are just as dedicated as that handful who filled the first bottles of pills a hundred years ago.

For so many of today's employees, Upjohn represents a piece of the past, a vivid and productive present, and a promising future. It is a good part of their life. They talk about their jobs with ease and candor. And because they are central to what Upjohn will be in months and years ahead, they are worth listening to. So the history of the company's second hundred years begins here with the voices of a small group of employees who work at very different jobs.

Three of the individuals have just over a quarter-century apiece at Upjohn. They are Jackie Talbert, line worker in Penicillin Processing, Building 156; salesman John Hall, who covers the Duke University Medical Center and the Veterans Administration Hospital in Durham, North Carolina; and chemist Jackson B. Hester, Jr., Ph.D., member of the Cardiovascular Diseases Research group in Building 209. Patent Attorney Sidney B. Williams has put in 19 years with Upjohn, while

electrician Don Jewett, who works in and around Building 41, joined the company 15 years ago. Wayne Fowler, Ph.D., a research plant scientist, came to Upjohn in 1974 and now conducts experiments at the Pacific Coast Breeding Station of the Ag Division's Asgrow unit in San Juan Bautista, California. At Upjohn's production plant in Puerto Rico, Luis R. Acevedo, with the company for six years, is group manager in the nonsteroidal anti-inflammatory drug facility. In Building 88, Compensation Representative Sheri Hudachek came to the firm in 1984.

By and large, they voice positive feelings about coming to work for Upjohn. "The minute you walked in," recalls Don Jewett, "it was the idea that you were here to help something, somebody. You were part of a whole, as opposed to one person trying to do something. I have been more than happy ever since." Sheri Hudachek has found a unique "opportunity for growth," one she doubts would have been available in other companies. At

Upjohn, Sid Williams has been able to mesh his prior training in chemical engineering and the practice of patent law.

On the Penicillin Processing line, Jackie Talbert and her friends like the fact that even when their supervisor is not around, "We know what to do and we go ahead and do it. He doesn't have to come back all the time to check on us. I think we do a pretty good job." In PR & D in downtown Kalamazoo, Dr. Jackson Hester has appreciated "a very good attitude" on management's part that "unless assignments are made, we can pretty much pursue research on our own." Dr. Wayne Fowler has "really enjoyed" his time with the Ag Division's Asgrow unit. "I like the idea of working in the free enterprise system," he says. "You have a lot of opportunity to do things you couldn't do in a university setting. I like dealing with people's immediate needs."

The city of Kalamazoo and neighboring communities have been a further asset, in Dr. Hester's view. "We are located in a good place," he says. "We keep very good people." Esteemed scientists, among others, enjoy and benefit from that. To be sure, not every job candidate has warmed to living in Michigan. The Patent Law unit has met that problem, Sid Williams explains, by bringing candidate and spouse to the city, then selling them on its people and its qualities.

For Williams, one distinct plus has been innovative work. "In a number of cases," he recalls, "we have established important precedents in the practice of pharmaceutical patent law." As the man who created the Xanax molecule, Jackson Hester knows that anyone interested in research wants to do challenging, meaningful work. And at Upjohn, he states, "We are doing good research. That has been one of the big drawing cards." Attorney Sid Williams has noticed that

the pharmaceutical industry today is "extremely exciting for everyone, particularly in the scientific area where people are developing new products all the time."

The acid test for a seasoned employee, of course, is whether he would want his children to work for Upjohn. To sales rep John Hall, that would depend on their preferences and training. But assuming they leaned toward the health care field, "I would certainly want them to work for Upjohn." Don Jewett would tell his children to "go for it" if Upjohn had something they wanted. He would explain to them that undeveloped skills can be brought to the surface at Upjohn, hence "you will have a chance to benefit both the company and yourself." Sid Williams would recommend the company to his two teenagers, "if for no other reason than that it has been good to me. I would say, 'Give it some consideration, because it is a good place to work.'"

Upjohn and the Years Ahead

Looking forward, these employees see much for Upjohn to do. Diseases remain to be understood and conquered. "I think it's necessary for us to stay in there and find answers to these," says John Hall. "But we've helped solve seemingly insurmountable problems before. I see no reason why we're not going to solve these other problems. It's going to take a commitment to research and a dedication to human needs. I feel confident we'll be able to do it."

Because Upjohn has expanded into a world marketplace, Jackson Hester believes it should address at least two important areas of international need. One is fertility control (the company, as Dr. Hester well knows, shelved this research in March 1985). The other urgent opportunity is for work on parasitology. "These are among the world's problems," says Dr. Hester. "These are two places that need improvement." Broadly, he thinks the

firm should take more active interest in Third World health deficits. "I don't think we are facing those at all," he observes. In that same category of need, Sid Williams observes that Upjohn may wind up being "outmoded" by the Japanese in their approach to the lesser developed nations. "The Japanese have more patience," he has found. "They will take 40 percent return on their investment, but will wait ten years for it. We should be like them."

What advice would these men and women offer top management? The strongest thread running through their recommendations has to do with a concern for people.

"In this age of machinery and computers," says John Hall, "I hope management doesn't forget the reason for existing, and that's people. We are definitely a people-oriented company. We could lose some of that by becoming too automated." Adds Jackie Talbert, "I hope that Upjohn doesn't change and get too big. I hope it can always stay a big family." She remembers the years when upper-level managers would tour the production line and "walk right up to us. That meant a lot." Sheri Hudachek agrees, saying, "I would like to see more of that."

In this same vein, Sid Williams would want Upjohn to be a "leader" in its minority employment practices. His advice would be to permit "no barriers [against] anyone getting a job or anyone moving up in the system of management." Don Jewett would hope for actions that help individuals "feel important."

Sheri Hudachek believes more effort should go into recruiting women and minority candidates for jobs. "Finding them is not easy," she concedes. "But they are there. We have to sell them on the company, the community, and the job." Mrs. Hudachek also advocates more training for positions in management, supervision, and production — "all areas where we can start employing more women, too," she adds.

"Keep the company strong and profitable." This is the recommendation of plant scientist Wayne Fowler. "In R & D, we have no income," he explains. "We only spend money. We would like to have much more to spend. But before we spend anything, we have to know there'll be something coming in next year."

Unavoidable Change

Jackie Talbert puts her finger on the dilemma. If she could have her way, Upjohn would continue being one big family. "But things have to change," she adds. "This is life. It goes on."

Don Jewett has seen the process of change over his 15 years with the company. "Everybody thinks of Upjohn as a family," he says in a wise assessment. "But all families grow and then spread out. And then those families start new ones. I think this is about where we're heading. We

are no longer a family, we are a community. It can't be a family anymore. The next best thing is to make it a community where all these individual families can interact and work with each other."

There are those who have been disturbed by the advent of automation. "They have talked about it," Jackie Talbert acknowledges. "Of course we are worried about it. I just hope that I am always here." Yet, Mrs. Talbert also knows that the company "would always find another department for you." Adds Sheri Hudachek, "This is one of the few companies I'm familiar with which has a reputation for always trying to find a position for someone to keep him employed. I think it's wonderful."

Change notwithstanding, Upjohn will be there in the future. John Hall offers the perspective of someone who has been with the drug-maker since 1960. "Being a strong research company as we are," he says, "and with a strong sales organization, I think that as long as there are people

who are sick and need pharmaceuticals, Upjohn will be in the business — and we're going to be up there at the top." Hall has made his own commitment to the enterprise. "I've cast my lot with Upjohn," he asserts, "and I plan to stay with it."

Sheri Hudachek, looking on the bright side of change, provides another kind of perspective. "Our jobs have been continually changing," she believes. "That will never stop. Wherever Upjohn people work around the world, there is always going to be something different to do. There will always be challenges for all of us to face. That makes the future for any of us in this company truly exciting."

About the Author

A Century of Caring is the tenth book written by New Jersey native Robert D. B. Carlisle. Five of those volumes have traced the beginnings of institutions. He has also written two book-length narrative poems.

Mr. Carlisle began his career as a newspaperman. He was Detroit Bureau Chief for *Newsweek*, wrote copy for the three major TV networks, was a producer for public TV station WNET in New York City, and was in charge of educational projects for the Corporation for Public Broadcasting. He has been a free-lance communications consultant and writer since 1973.

Mr. Carlisle served in both World War II and the Korean War. He is a graduate of Princeton University and holds a Master's degree from Montclair State College. He is married and lives in Montclair, New Jersey.

Index